# 128 MACHINE LANGUAGE FOR BEGINNERS



Richard Mansfield



COMPUTE!™ Publications,Inc. abc
Part of ABC Consumer Magazines, Inc.
One of the ABC Publishing Companies
Greensboro, North Carolina

Appendix C, "Commodore 128 Memory Map," was originally published in *COMPUTE!'s 128 Programmer's Guide*, copyright 1985, COMPUTE! Publications, Inc.



Printed in the United States of America

10 9 8 7 6 5 4 3 2 1

ISBN 0-87455-033-5



COMPUTE! Publications, Inc., Post Office Box 5406, Greensboro, NC 27403, (919) 275-9809, is part of ABC Consumer Magazines, Inc., one of the ABC Publishing Companies, and is not associated with any manufacturer of personal computers.

# Contents

# Preface

Few personal computers—indeed few computers of any kind—have been as thoughtfully designed or as attractive to people who enjoy programming as the Commodore 128. It has several environments, optimized disk access, 16 memory configurations, and dozens of special codes, escape sequences, and screen controls. It's a generously equipped toolbox for people who like to customize their computers and their software. And it offers the programmer a set of tools which are hitherto unmatched in variety and power in a consumer computer.

It represents the best of a breed: the eight-bit machine. These computers are built on chips which work with one byte at a time—the 8502 chip in the 128 and the 6502 chip upon which most of the first consumer computers were built. They are a technology in its twilight, but the 128 has significant strengths and could well survive for years as a model of what personal computers can be.

The 68000 chip is emerging—Commodore's Amiga, Atari's ST, and Apple's Macintosh all use it—and no one can turn back the clock. This new 68000 is bigger, faster, and much more flexible than eight-bit chips. It can manipulate four bytes at a time and directly access massive amounts of memory. It doesn't need to switch banks, and it races along at eight times the speed of the older chips. It's the end of an age.

Nevertheless, excellence can and often does appear at the end of an age. Bach, probably the finest musician ever, summarized and synergized the music of his time. He embodied the best of what was then known. As it turned out, his summaries and synergism have proven timeless and durable. There has been more dramatic music since, equal music perhaps, but no better music. The Commodore 128 is a complex, full, and rich summation of the best that is possible with an eight-bit machine architecture. It is a classic programmer's computer. You can spend years exploring its abilities.

However, the heart of a computer is only accessible via machine language. Several years ago I decided to learn to program in machine language, the computer's own language. I understood BASIC fairly well and I realized that it was simply not possible to accomplish all that I wanted to do with my computer using BASIC alone. BASIC is sometimes just too slow.

I faced the daunting (and exhilarating) prospect of learning to go below the surface of my computer, of finding out how to talk directly to a computer in *its* language, not the imitation English of BASIC. As I was to discover, something amazing lies beneath BASIC.

Few events in learning to use a personal computer have had more impact on me than the moment that I could instantly fill the TV screen with any picture I wanted because of a machine language program I had written. I was amazed at its speed, but more than that, I realized that anytime large amounts of information were needed onscreen in the future—it could be done via machine language. I had, in effect, created a new BASIC "command" which could be added to any of my programs. This command—using a SYS instruction to send the computer to my custom-designed machine language routine—allowed me to have previously impossible control over the computer.

BASIC might be compared to a reliable, comfortable car. It will get you where you want to go. Machine language is like a sleek racing car—you get there with lots of time to spare. When programming involves large amounts of data, music, graphics, or games, speed can become the single most important factor.

After becoming accustomed to machine language, I decided to write an arcade game entirely without benefit of BASIC. It was to be in machine language from start to finish. I predicted that it would take about 20 to 30 hours. It was a space invaders game with mother ships, rows of aliens, sound ... the works. It took closer to 80 hours, but I am probably more proud of that program than of any other I've written.

After I'd finished it, I realized that the next games would be easier and could be programmed more quickly. The modules handling scoring, sound, screen framing, delay, and player/enemy shapes were all written. I only had to write new sound effects, change details about the scoring, create new shapes. The essential routines were, for the most part, already written for a variety of new arcade-type games. When creating machine language programs, you build up a collection of reusable subroutines. For example, once you find out how to make sounds on your 128, you change the details, but not the underlying procedures, for any new songs.

The great majority of books about machine language assume a considerable familiarity with both the details of microprocessor chips and with programming technique. This book assumes only a working knowledge of BASIC. It was designed to speak directly to the amateur programmer, the part-time computerist. It should help you make the transition from BASIC to machine language with relative ease.

You'll quickly discover that machine language is your key to the excellence and power waiting within Commodore's 128.

# Why Machine Language?

Sooner or later, many programmers find that they want to learn machine language. BASIC is a fine general-purpose tool, but it has its limitations. Machine language (often called *assembly language*) performs much faster. BASIC is fairly easy to learn, but most beginners do not realize that machine language can also be easy. And, just as learning Italian goes faster if you already know Spanish, if a programmer already knows BASIC, much of this knowledge will make learning machine language easier. There are many similarities.

This book is designed to teach machine language on the Commodore 128 to those who have a working knowledge of BASIC. For example, Chapter 9 is a dictionary of BASIC commands. Following each BASIC command is a machine language routine which accomplishes the same task. In this way, if you know what you want to do in BASIC, you can find out how to do it in machine language.

To make it easier to write programs in machine language (called ML from here on), most programmers use a special program called an *assembler*. This is where the term *assembly language* comes from. ML and assembly language programs are both essentially the same thing. Using an assembler to create ML programs is far easier than being forced to look up and then POKE each byte into RAM memory. That's the way it used to be done, when there was too little memory in computers to hold *languages* (like BASIC or assemblers) at the same time as *programs* created by those languages. The old-style hand-programming was very laborious.

There is an assembler at the end of this book called LADS, for Label Assembly Development System. It will let you type in ML instructions (like INC 2) and will translate them into the right numbers and POKE them for you wherever in memory you decide you want your ML program to be located. LADS will help you in a variety of other ways as well. It was designed to offer you a fast, convenient, and effective ML programming environment, a way of writing programs which is both natural and familiar.

ML *instructions* are like BASIC commands; you build an ML program by using the ML *instruction set*. A complete, descriptive table of all the 8502 ML instructions can be found in Appendix A. Whenever you see a three-letter abbreviation (like INC) in this book that you don't recognize, it's an ML instruction and you can look it up in Appendix A, where you'll find its purposes, modes, and syntax fully described.

It's a little premature, but if you're curious, INC 2 will increase the number in your computer's second memory cell (the second byte of RAM memory) by one. If 15 is the number currently in cell 2, it will become a 16 after INC 2. Think of it as "increment address two." Like BASIC, ML has a series of commands which you use to communicate with the computer when you write a program. ML commands are always three-letter abbreviations, like INC, and LADS will help you write your ML programs using these commands and numbers that you generally add to the commands as additional information, like INC 2.

Throughout the book you'll be learning how to handle a variety of ML instructions, and LADS will be of great help. You might want to familiarize yourself with it. Knowing what it does (and using it to enter the examples in this book), you will gradually build your understanding of ML, hexadecimal numbers, and the extraordinary range of new possibilities open to the computerist who knows ML. Knowing ML, being able to talk directly to your machine, changes things so much that it's like getting a whole new computer, a much more powerful computer.

## Seeing It Work

Chapters 2–8 each examine a major aspect of ML where it differs from the way BASIC works. In each chapter, examples and exercises lead the programmer to a greater understanding of the methods of ML programming. By the end of the book, you should be able to write, in ML, most of the programs and subroutines you will want or need.

Let's examine some advantages of ML, starting with the main one—ML runs extremely fast.

Here are two programs which accomplish the same thing. The first is in ML, and the second is in BASIC. They get results at very different speeds indeed as you'll see:

**Machine Language**

**169 1 160 0 153 0 4 153 0 5**
**250 153 0 6 153 0 7 200 208 241 96**

**BASIC**
**5 FOR I = 1 TO 1000: PRINT "A";: NEXT I**

These two programs both print the letter *A* on the screen 1000 times. The ML version takes up 21 bytes of RAM (Random Access Memory). The BASIC version takes up 45 bytes and takes about 30 times as long to finish the job. If you want to see how quickly the ML works, you can POKE those numbers somewhere into RAM and run the ML program with a SYS command to the little program. (For this and other example programs in this book which directly store characters to the screen RAM, please switch to 40-column mode when trying the example.)

In both BASIC and ML, many instructions are followed by an *argument*. We mentioned the instruction INC 2. In that example, the number 2 is the argument. In BASIC, the SYS instruction must be given an argument which tells it where to SYS, where the ML program it's going to run is located in RAM. The SYS instruction will turn control of the computer over to the address given as its argument. There would be an ML program waiting there.

Just remember that an argument is the second item in a pair and that an argument modifies (makes more specific) a given instruction. In the pairs INC 2, SYS 2816, and Send a Letter, the *2, 2816,* and *Letter* are the arguments. The INC, SYS, and Send are the instructions.

To make it easy to see the speed of our 1000 *A*'s example ML program, we'll just load it into memory without yet knowing much about it. We'll use a BASIC loader program that simply POKEs all the numbers of the ML program into memory; then you SYS 2816 from BASIC to activate the ML program.

This little ML program is just numbers so far (and that's all the computer needs anyway). But for us humans it would be worthwhile being able to see what the program looks like as instructions. There's a way. A *disassembly* is like a BASIC LIST. You can give the starting address of an ML program to a *disassembler,* and it will translate the numbers it finds in the computer's memory into a readable series of ML instructions. The built-in monitor on the 128 contains a disassembler that you can use to examine and study ML programs. Note that you have to give a start address whenever you write (with an assembler), list (with a disassembler), or run (with SYS) an ML program. That's because, unlike BASIC programs, ML programs can be located anywhere in RAM memory.

Here's what our little example ML program looks like when it has been translated by a disassembler:

```
., 0B00 A9 01     LDA #$01
., 0B02 A0 00     LDY #$00
., 0B04 99 00 04 STA $0400,Y
., 0B07 99 00 05 STA $0500,Y
., 0B0A 99 00 06 STA $0600,Y
., 0B0D 99 00 07 STA $0700,Y
., 0B10 C8        INY
., 0B11 D0 F1     BNE $0B04
., 0B13 60        RTS
```

The following BASIC program (called a *loader*) will POKE the ML instructions (and their arguments) into memory for you:

```
10 FOR I = 2816 TO 2835:READ A:POKE I,A:NEXT I
20 PRINT"SYS 2816 TO ACTIVATE"
30 DATA 169,1,160,0,153,0,4,153,0,5
40 DATA 153,0,6,153,0,7,200,208,241,96
```

After running this program, switch to 40-column mode and type SYS 2816 as instructed. The screen will instantly fill.

BASIC stands for Beginner's All-purpose Symbolic Instruction Code. Because it is all-purpose, it cannot be the perfect code for any specific job. The fact that ML speaks directly to the machine, in the machine's language, makes it far the more efficient language. This is because however cleverly a BASIC program is written, it will nevertheless always require extra running time to finish a job. This same problem slows down every other computer language as well: Logo, Forth, Pascal, C, whatever. None of them is the machine's language and, thus, none can run at maximum speed.

To see why this is, think of the common PRINT instruction in BASIC. A PRINT statement drags BASIC into a series of operations which ML avoids. BASIC must ask and answer a series of questions. Where is the text located that is to be printed? Is it a variable? Where is the variable located? What's its length? Where on the screen is the text to be placed?

ML is far more efficient. As we will discover, ML does not need to hunt for a string variable. And 40-column screen addresses do not require a complicated series of searches in an ML program. Each of these tasks, and others, slows BASIC down because it must serve so many general purposes. The screen fills slowly because BASIC has to make so many more decisions about every action it attempts than does ML.

### Inserting ML for Speed

A second benefit which you derive from learning ML is that your understanding of computing will be much greater. On the abstract level, you will be far more aware of just how computers work. On the practical level, you will be able to choose between BASIC or ML, whichever is best for the purpose at hand. This choice between two languages permits far more flexibility and allows a number of tasks to be programmed which are clumsy or even impossible in BASIC. Quite a few of your favorite BASIC programs would benefit from a small ML routine, "inserted" into BASIC with a SYS, to replace a heavily used, but slow, loop or subroutine. Large sorting tasks, smooth animation, and many arcade games and other kinds of programs *must* involve ML. And most programs can benefit from ML patches. It's no accident that nearly all commercial computer programs are written in machine language.

### BASIC vs. Machine Language

Because of the great efficiency and speed of ML, it's not surprising that *BASIC itself is written in ML*. It's made up of many ML subprograms stored in your 128's Read Only Memory (ROM). BASIC is a collection of special words such as STOP and RUN, each of which stands for a cluster of ML instructions. One such cluster sits in ROM (unchanging memory) just waiting for you to type LIST. If you do type in that word, the computer turns control over to the ML routine which accomplishes a program listing. The BASIC programmer understands and uses these BASIC words to build a program. You hand instructions over to the computer and then rely on the convenience of referring to all those prepackaged ML routines by their BASIC names. The computer *always* works with ML instructions. That's why you cannot honestly say that you truly understand computing until you understand the computer's language: machine language.

Another reason to learn ML is that custom programming is then possible. Computers come with a disk operating system (DOS) and BASIC (or other higher-level languages). After awhile, you will likely find that you are limited by the rules or the commands available in these languages. You will want to add to them, to customize them. An understanding of ML is necessary if you want to add new words to BASIC, to modify a word processor (which was written in ML), to personalize your computer—to make it behave precisely as you want it to. This book will give you the knowledge and the tools to fully understand and to speak directly to your 128.

### BASIC's Strong Points

Of course, BASIC has its advantages and in some cases is to be preferred over ML. BASIC is usually simpler to *debug* (to get all the problems ironed out so that it works as it should). In Chapter 3 we'll examine some ML debugging techniques which work quite well, but BASIC is the easier of the two languages to correct. For one thing, BASIC often just comes out and tells you your programming mistakes by printing error messages on the screen. Nevertheless, if you use the LADS assembler from this book, it too will print error messages and identify the offending line number.

Contrary to popular opinion, ML is not always a memory-saving process. ML can use up about as much memory as BASIC does when accomplishing the same task. Short programs can be somewhat more compact in ML, but longer programs generally use up bytes fast in both languages. However, worrying about using up computer memory is quickly becoming less and less important.

Soon programmers will probably have more memory space available than they will ever need. The 128 is particularly RAM rich. In any event, a talent for conserving bytes, like skill at trapping wild game, will likely become a victim of technology. It will always be a skill, but it seems as if it will not be an everyday necessity.

So, which language is best? They are both best—but for different purposes. Many programmers, after learning ML, find that they continue to construct some of their programs in BASIC or some other language, but add ML modules where speed is important. An all-ML program will, however, generally be more efficient, more flexible, and far faster than any alternative. Remember, it's no accident that the great majority of professional and commercial programs are written in pure ML.

But perhaps the best reason of all for learning ML is that it is fascinating and fun.

# Chapter 1

# How to Use This Book

# How to Use This Book

Throughout this book there are short example programs in machine language for you to type in and experiment with. They vary in length, but most are quite brief and are intended to illustrate an ML concept or technique. The best way to learn something new is often to just jump in and do it. Machine language programming is no different. Machine language programs are written using a program called an *assembler*, just as BASIC programs are written using a program inside the computer called Microsoft BASIC.

This book includes a powerful assembler, LADS, in Appendix F. In addition to being versatile, LADS offers the beginner a number of conveniences such as error messages and a familiar working environment. And the more sophisticated features of the assembler are there for you when you're ready to use them.

### The First Step: Assembling

It is probably a good idea to first type LADS into your computer (typing instructions are in Appendix F). Once you've got a working version, you're ready to use the assembler with the practice examples throughout the book. (If you prefer, you can order a disk which contains LADS and other programs from this book. See the coupon in the back of this book for details.)

Frequently, the examples in the book are designed to do something to the screen. The reason for this is that you can then tell at once if things are working as planned. If you are trying to send the message TEST STRING to the screen and it comes out TEST STRI or TEST STRING@, you can go back and quickly reassemble with LADS until you get it right. More important, you'll discover what you did wrong.

Many programs manipulate data within a database or make calculations with some numbers somewhere in RAM, but the action takes place offscreen. When learning ML, however, it's often helpful to put your data manipulations right up in front of your eyes on the screen so that you can see precisely how things are going. When everything is working correctly, you can redirect the data to some less visible place elsewhere in RAM.

However, the 80-column screen cannot be directly POKEd. So, while LADS works with 40 or 80 columns, you may want to test some of the examples using the 40-column mode. Any examples which access $0400 or 1024 (for example, STA $0400) will be visible only on the 40-column screen. You can assemble the source code in 80-column mode, but when you run the object code, it will not be visible except in the 40-column mode. Other examples use JSR $FFD2 or JSR PRINT, and these examples will run as is on either screen.

### A Sample Program

The following little ML program will show you how to go about entering and testing the practice examples in this book. At this point, of course, you won't yet recognize the ML instructions involved. This sample program is intended only to serve as a guide to working with the examples you will come upon later in the text.

After you've typed in and made a few backup copies of LADS, you can use it to create runnable ML programs. Detailed instructions on using all of the LADS features are found in Appendix B, but for now, we just want to know how to enter a short, easy program.

The LADS environment is very like BASIC. In fact, you write your programs as if you were writing a BASIC program, except you use ML commands rather than BASIC commands. You use line numbers and, if you wish, colons to separate statements. The first line, however, must tell LADS where you want your ML program located in memory (since ML can be placed anywhere in RAM). A safe place to locate your shorter ML programs is address 2816 (we'll learn why later), so:

```
10 *= 2816
20 .S
30 .O
31 LDA #0:STA $FFD0; SWITCH TO BANK 15
40 LDA #65
50 JSR $FFD2
60 RTS
```

Try this. Turn on your computer. If you have a 1571 disk drive with a bootable LADS disk inside, LADS will have already been loaded into your 128 when you turned it on.

If you've also typed in the LADS loader (see Appendix F), it will load LADS in and also set up a small template so you won't have to type *= or .S or .O each time you start a program. If you prefer not to have this template, delete the POKE loop in line 50 of the loader.

You might also want to type

**AUTO10**

so that the 128 makes automatic line numbers as you type. Entering an ML program for LADS is indistinguishable from entering a BASIC program as far as the 128 is concerned.

So, type in the program above, in BASIC mode, just as if it were a BASIC program. If you didn't have LADS autoload itself, type BLOAD"LADS". Be sure to use BLOAD so LADS will load in where it's supposed to be in RAM, not at the start of BASIC memory. Then type SYS 10000 which will activate LADS, and you'll see your program changed into an ML program. This transformation is called an *assembly*. You've just *assembled* this little program.

By the way, the LADS loader program sets up the F1 key to SYS 10000, so you could just hit F1 instead of typing SYS 10000 if you've booted the LADS disk. You can hit F1 from anywhere on the screen; you need not be on a blank line. It will clear the screen as does LADS when it begins assembling.

LADS will print out the results on the screen while it works (the .S in line 20 tells LADS to provide a screen listing to show you what's happening during assembly), and it will store the resulting finished machine language program in RAM memory starting at address 2816. The .O in line 30 tells LADS to store the program into RAM memory.

If you made any typing errors and LADS couldn't assemble this program, LADS will ring the bell and print the line number where the error is located. It will also give you an error message. (To fix such things, just LIST and change the offending line as you would to modify a BASIC program.) You might want to see what happens if you change line 40 to a misspelling:

**40 LDR #65**

Or if you forget to give the number:

**40 LDR**

In any case, once you've loaded LADS into memory, you won't need to load it again if you want to assemble other programs later. This program is supposed to print the letter *A* on your screen. To test the program, simply type SYS 2816. The

.O caused the results of the assembly to be stored in RAM where you can test them.

The little ML program will do its job, you'll see the letter *A* appear, and then the computer will return control back to the normal BASIC environment. If you want to try making an adjustment, change the number 65 in line 40 to some other number to print a different character. Type LIST, and you'll see that your original program is still there in memory (2816 is outside the ordinary BASIC programming locations, so neither our little ML program nor LADS disturbed our code written in the BASIC environment). Just change it the way you would change a BASIC program by writing over the 1 and pressing RETURN. Then, hit the F1 key or type SYS 10000 to re-assemble the new version and test it again with SYS 2816.

This is the general method you'll want to use for creating ML programs. There is another, more elaborate way to handle very large ML programs, to automatically save the results to disk, and a number of other LADS features we'll come to later. For now, you know pretty much everything you need to know to use LADS with the brief examples in this book. (If you want to experiment with all LADS's features right away, see Appendix B, "How to Use LADS.")

The main thing to learn here is how to type in programs and assemble them using LADS. Primarily, you should remember three things:

1. LADS always has to know where you want to store your ML program, so the first line of any program you give LADS must have *= 2816 and nothing else on that line. We're going to give various start addresses for the example programs in this book because this will help you learn where to put ML and learn more about memory usage. But, if an example doesn't have *= 2816 as the first line, you can safely put it in. Many examples are given in the form they would look if you disassembled them from the monitor, as we'll discover in Chapter 3. However, you're always safe putting your test routines at 2816.

   If you should forget to include a starting address, LADS will alert you to the fact by printing an error message onscreen and halting. Some of the examples give *= $B00 as the starting address, but that's just another way of writing 2816. They mean the same thing, but $B00 is hex and we'll learn about hex in the next chapter.

2. You don't need to tell LADS where your ML program ends. Like BASIC, LADS can tell when it's come upon the last line number in a program. You can just type in a program without indicating where it ends, just as you do when writing a BASIC program. LADS will see the end and calculate the proper addresses in RAM to store your entire program.
3. You should be in BASIC mode—you should see READY.—when you start to type in programs that you want LADS to assemble. The environment will be quite familiar if you've done any BASIC programming (with a few exceptions such as using ; instead of REM as illustrated in line 31 of the example above). Generally, though, everything's the same as BASIC. You can use AUTO 10 to set up automatic line numbering, replace lines by typing their number, insert lines, and everything else you would do when working with a normal BASIC program. Of course what you write are ML commands. These commands are *not* the same commands as BASIC's, but that's the subject of rest of this book.

Chapter 2

# The Fundamentals

# The Fundamentals

The difficulty of learning ML has sometimes been exaggerated. There are some new rules to learn and some new habits to acquire. But most ML programmers would probably agree that ML is not inherently more difficult to understand than BASIC. More of a challenge to debug in some cases, but it's not worlds beyond BASIC in complexity. In fact, in the 1970s, many of the first home computerists learned ML before they learned BASIC. This is because an average version of the BASIC language used in microcomputers takes up around 12,000 bytes of memory, and the early personal computers (KIM, AIM, etc.) were severely restricted—they had only a small amount of available memory. These early machines were unable to offer BASIC; it took up more space than they had, so everyone programmed in ML.

Interestingly, some of these pioneers reportedly found BASIC to be just as difficult to grasp as ML. In both cases, the problem seems to be that the rules of a new language simply are "obscure" until you know them. In general, though, learning either language probably requires roughly the same amount of effort.

The first thing to learn about ML is that it reflects the construction of computers. ML programmers often use a number system (hexadecimal, or hex for short) which is not based on ten.

We count by tens because it is a familiar (though arbitrary) grouping for us. Humans have ten fingers. If we had eleven fingers, the odds are that we would be counting by elevens.

### What's a Natural Number?

Computers count in groups of twos. It is a fact of electronics that the easiest way to store and manipulate information is by on/off states. A light bulb is either on or off. This is a two-group; it's *binary,* and so the powers of two become the natural groupings for electronic counters: 2, 4, 8, 16, 32, 64, 128, 256. Finger counters (us) have been using tens so long that we have come to think of ten as *natural,* like thunder in April.

Tens isn't natural at all. What's more, twos is a more efficient way to count.

To see how the powers of two relate to computers, we can run a short BASIC program which will give us some of these powers. *Powers* of a number is the number multiplied by itself.

Two to the power of two (2^2) means 2 times 2 (in other words, 4). Two to the power of three (2^3) means 2 times 2 times 2 (8).

```
10 FOR I = 0 TO 16
20 PRINT 2 ^ I
30 NEXT I
```

ML programming *can* be done entirely in the familiar decimal number system. For beginners, that's probably a wise thing to do. The LADS assembler in this book allows you to use either decimal or hex, as you wish. However, you'll probably see hex used in magazine articles and books, and hex does format on the screen or paper more neatly than decimal numbers. Another advantage of hex is that it relates visually to the binary numbers that the computer is using. The arguments for some advanced ML commands like ROL and EOR are more easily visualized with hex than with decimal.

Why not just always program in the familiar decimal numbers (as we do in BASIC)? Because hex is based on groups of 16 digits, not decimal's groups of 10. And 16 is one of the powers of two. Thus, 16 is a convenient grouping (or *base*) for ML because it organizes numbers the way the computer looks at numbers. For example, at the most elementary level all computers work with *bits*. A bit is the smallest piece of information possible: Something is either on or off, yes or no, plus or minus, true or false. This two-state condition (binary) can be remembered by a computer's smallest single memory cell. This single cell is called a bit. The computer can turn each bit *on* or *off* as if it were a light bulb, or a flag raised or lowered.

It's interesting that the word *bit* is frequently explained as a shortening of the phrase BInary digiT. In fact, the word *bit* goes back several centuries. There was a coin which was soft enough to be cut with a knife into eight pieces. Hence, *pieces of eight*. A single piece of this coin was called a bit and, as with computer memories, it meant that you couldn't slice it any further. We still use the word *bit* today as in the phrase *two bits*, meaning 25 cents.

Whatever it's called, the bit is a small, essential aspect of computing. Imagine that we wanted to remember the result of a subtraction. When two numbers are subtracted, they are actually being compared with each other. The result of the subtraction tells us which number is the larger or if they are equal. ML has an instruction, like a command in BASIC, which compares two numbers by subtraction. It is called CMP (for *compare*). This instruction sets *flags* in the CPU (Central Processing Unit) of the computer, and one of the flags always shows whether or not the result of the most recent action taken by the computer was a zero. We'll go into this again later. What we need to realize now is simply that each flag—like the flag on a mailbox—has two possible conditions: up or down. In other words, this information (that there's a zero result or a nonzero result) is *binary* and can be stored within a single bit. Each of the seven flags within the 8502 chip is a bit. Together, the flags are all held within a single byte. That byte is called the status register.

## Byte Assignments

Our computers group bits into units of eight, called *bytes*. This relationship between bits and bytes is easy to remember if you think of a bit as one of the "pieces of eight." Eight is a power of two also (two to the third power). Eight is a convenient number of bits to work with as a group since we can count from 0 to 255 using only eight bits. We'll see how this is done in a minute.

A byte—able to "hold" 256 different numbers—gives us enough room to assign all 26 letters of the alphabet (and the uppercase letters, punctuation marks, and so on) so that each character we might want to print will have its own particular number. The letter *A* (uppercase) has been assigned the number 65 (in the standard ASCII code that computers use to communicate). The letter *B* is 66, and so on. Most microcomputers, however, do not adhere strictly to the ASCII code, except when they are communicating with other computers, for example, through telephone links. The 128 uses the code in Appendix G for its internal operations. It's pretty close to standard ASCII.

The ASCII code, an assignment of numbers to letters and symbols, forms a convention by which computers worldwide can communicate with each other. Text can be sent via modems and telephone lines, and it will arrive meaning the same thing to an alien computer. It's important to visualize each byte, then, as being eight bits ganged together and that a byte is able to represent 256 different things. As you might have suspected, 256 is another power of two (two to the power of eight).

So these groupings of eight, these bytes, are a major aspect of computing; but we also want to simplify our counting from 0 to 255. We want the numbers to line up in a column on screen or on paper. Obviously, *decimal* numbers are erratic: The number 5 takes up one space, the number 230 takes up three spaces. Hex numbers between 0 and 255 will always, predictably, take up two spaces (here's 0–255 expressed in the hexadecimal format: $00–$FF).

In addition to being easier to format in printouts, hex is also somewhat easier to visualize in terms of the *binary* number system—the on/off, single-bit way that the computer manipulates numbers:

| Decimal | | Hex | Binary |
|---|---|---|---|
| 1 | | 01 | 00000001 |
| 2 | | 02 | 00000010 |
| 3 | | 03 | 00000011 (1+2) |
| 4 | | 04 | 00000100 |
| 5 | | 05 | 00000101 (4+1) |
| 6 | | 06 | 00000110 (4+2) |
| 7 | | 07 | 00000111 (4+2+1) |
| 8 | | 08 | 00001000 |
| 9 | | 09 | 00001001 (8+1) |
| 10 | (Note new digits) → | 0A | 00001010 (8+2) |
| 11 | | 0B | 00001011 (8+2+1) |
| 12 | | 0C | 00001100 (8+4) |
| 13 | | 0D | 00001101 (8+4+1) |
| 14 | | 0E | 00001110 (8+4+2) |
| 15 | | 0F | 00001111 (8+4+2+1) |
| 16 | (Note new column → | 10 | 00010000 |
| 17 | in the hex) | 11 | 00010001 (16+1) |

See how hex $10 (hex numbers are usually preceded by a dollar sign to show that they are not decimal) *looks like* binary? If you split a hex number into two parts, 1 and 0, and the equivalent binary number into two parts, 0001 and 0000, you can see the relationship.

### The Rationale for Hex Numbers

Many ML programmers like to use hexadecimal numbers because they are a superior visual symbol of the manipulations inside the computer; hex is simply more like binary because hex is a power of two and decimal (base ten) is not a power of two. It's really up to you whether or when you add hex to your bag of tricks. (In the early days of programming, another base—base eight—called *octal* was very popular. It's still used today when programming some large computers.) You will see that you can choose to use hex or decimal when writing ML with the LADS assembler in this book. And you can use them interchangeably, even on the same line of program code. You can write LDA $0A or LDA 10, whichever you prefer.

Here's what it looks like when you count up from zero in both systems:

**Decimal**

0 1 2 3 4 5 6 7 8 9

And now you start over by moving to a new column with the number 10.

**Hex**

00 01 02 03 04 05 06 07 08 09 0A 0B 0C 0D 0E 0F

And then you start over with $10, $11, and so on.

See how we ran out of digits when trying to count up to 16 in hex? Hex substitutes the first few letters of the alphabet to count past 09.

The first thing to notice is that instead of the familiar decimal symbol 10, hex uses the letter *A* because this is where we run out of symbols and must start over again with a 1 and a 0. Zero always reappears at the start of each new grouping in any number system: 0, 10, 20, and so on. The same thing happens with the groupings in hex: 0, 10, 20, 30, ... The difference is that, in hex, the 1 in the "10's" column is actually what we would call a 16 (in our normal decimal way of counting).

*The second column is now a 16's column;* 11 (hex) means 17 (decimal), and 21 means 33 (2 times 16 plus 1). Learning hex is probably the single biggest hurdle to overcome when getting to know ML.

Don't be discouraged if it's not immediately clear what's going on. (It probably never will be totally clear—hex is, after all, unnatural.) And remember that hex is an *option,* not a requirement, when programming in ML.

It's just that much ML printed in magazines and books uses hex. That's why you at least need to be able to recognize what it means. Nobody really knows it that well. Most ML programmers use one of the calculators sold by Sharp, TI, or Hewlett-Packard that perform hex/decimal conversions. Also, you can give a decimal number to the 128 in monitor mode and it will print the hex, octal, and binary versions of the same number. Just precede the number with a plus sign (+). For example, to see versions of 100, type +100 and press RETURN. You can translate a hex number into decimal by preceding it with a dollar sign ($) and pressing RETURN. If you happen to be in BASIC mode, writing some LADS source code, you can use ?HEX$(15) to get the hex of 15 or ?DEC("0F") to get the decimal of $0F. Ultimately, though, hex is one of those things, like telephone books and dictionaries, that you have to know how to use, but you don't have to memorize.

It's possible that someday hex will go the way of octal, and we'll stick to the easy, obvious decimal mode entirely (except for excursions into binary numbers from time to time). If you want more understanding, you might want to practice the exercises at the end of this chapter. As you work with hex, it will gradually seem less and less alien.

To figure out a hex number, multiply the second column by 16, and add the other number to it. So, $2A would be 2 times 16 plus 10 (recall that A stands for 10).

Hex does seem impossibly confusing when you come upon it for the first time. It will never become second nature, but it should be at least generally understood. You need not memorize hex beyond learning to count from 1 to 16; this teaches you the symbols. Be able to count from 00 up to 0F. (By convention, even the smallest hex number is listed as two digits as in 03 or 0B. The other distinguishing characteristic is the dollar sign that is usually placed in front of the digits: $05 or $0E.)

It's enough to know what hex numbers look like and be able to find them when you need them.

### The First 255

Another thing that makes all this easier is that if you *do* need to work with hex, most ML programming involves working with hex numbers only between 0 and 255. This is because a single byte (eight bits) can hold no number larger than 255. Manipulating numbers larger than 255 is of no real importance in ML programming until you are ready to work with more advanced ML programs. This comes later in the book. For example, all 8502 ML instructions are coded into one byte, all the flags are held in one byte, and many addressing modes use one byte.

To learn all we need to know about hex for now, we can try some problems and look at some ML code to see how hex is used in the majority of ML work. But first, let's take an imaginary flight over computer memory. Let's get a visual sense of what bits and bytes and the inner workings of the computer's RAM look like.

## The City of Bytes

Imagine a city with a single long row of houses. It's night. Each house has a peculiar Christmas display: On the roof is a row of eight lights. The houses represent bytes; each light is a single bit (Figure 2-1).

If we fly over the City of Bytes, at first we see only darkness. Each byte contains nothing (zero), so all eight of its bulbs are off. (On the horizon we can see a glow, however, because the computer has memory up there, called ROM memory, which is very active and contains built-in programs.) But we are down in RAM, our free user-memory, and there are no programs in RAM yet, so every house is dark. Let's observe what happens to an individual byte when different numbers are stored there; we can randomly choose byte 1504. We hover over that house to see what information is "contained" in the light display:

Like everywhere else in the City of Bytes, this byte is dark. Each bulb is off. Observing this, we know that the byte here is "holding," or representing, a zero. If someone at the computer types in POKE 1504,1, suddenly the rightmost light bulb goes on and the byte holds a one instead of a zero:

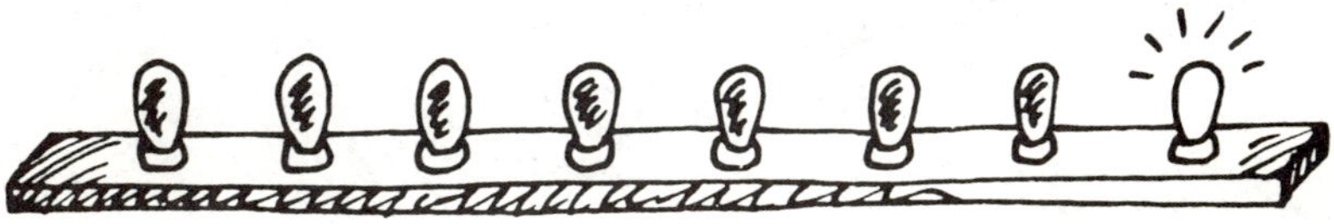

Figure 2-1. Night in the City of Bytes

This rightmost bulb is the one's column (so far, this is exactly the way things would work in our usual way of counting by tens, our familiar *decimal* system). But the next bulb is in the two's column, so POKE 1504, 2 would be:

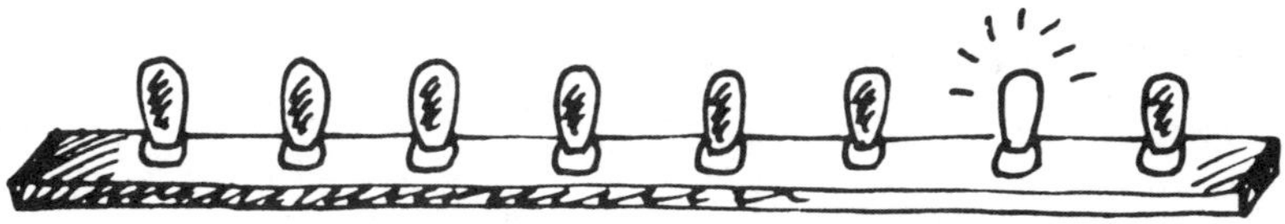

And three would be one and two:

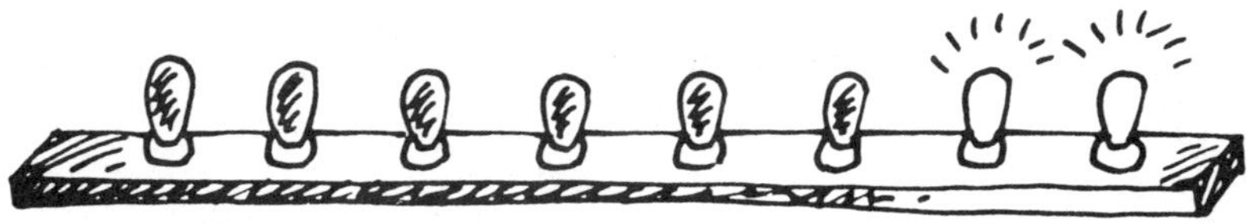

In this way—by checking which bits are turned on and then adding them together—the computer can look at a byte and know what number is there. Each light bulb, each *bit*, is in its own special position in the row of eight and has a value twice the value of the one just before it:

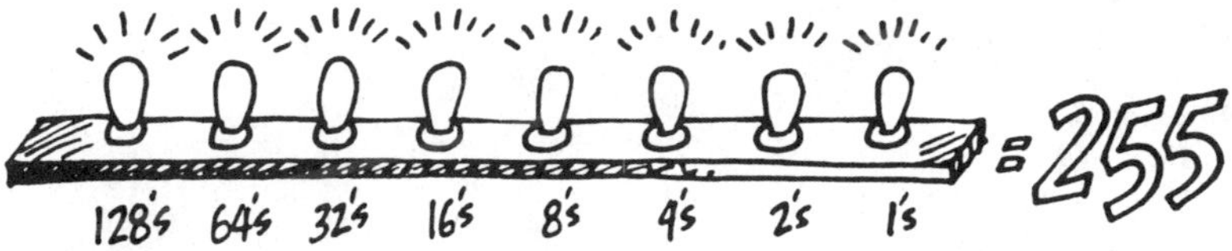


Eight bits together make a byte. A byte can hold a number from 0 through 255 decimal. We can think of bytes, though, in any number system we wish—in hex, decimal, or binary. Because the computer uses binary, it's useful to be able to visualize it. Hex has its uses in ML programming. And decimal is familiar. But a number is still a number, no matter what we call it. After all, five pennies are always five pennies, whether we symbolize them by 5 (decimal) or $05 (hex) or 00000101 (binary) or just call them a nickel.

### A Binary Quiz

BASIC doesn't understand numbers expressed in hex or binary. Binary, for humans, is very *visual*. It forms patterns out of zeros and ones and lets you see an x-ray of the interior of a byte. The following program will let you quiz yourself on these patterns.

Here is a game which will show you a byte as it looks in binary. You then try to give the number in decimal:

**Program 2-1. Binary Quiz**

```
10 REM BINARY QUIZ
20 C1 = 49:C0 = 48
30 X = INT(256 * RND (1)):D = X:P = 128
40 PRINT"{CLR}"
50 FOR I = 1 TO 8
60 IF INT(D / P) = 1 THEN PRINT CHR$(C1);:D = D -
   {SPACE}P:GOTO 80
70 PRINT CHR$(C0);
80 P = P / 2:NEXT I:PRINT
90 PRINT"WHAT IS THIS IN DECIMAL?":PRINT
100 INPUT Q:IF Q = X THEN PRINT"CORRECT":GOTO 120
110 PRINT"SORRY, IT WAS"X
120 FOR T = 1 TO 1000:NEXT T
130 GOTO 30
```

This next program will print out an entire table of binary numbers from 0 through 255.

**Program 2-2. Binary Table**

```
100 REM COMPLETE BINARY TABLE
120 FOR X = 0 TO 255:PRINTX;
130 Z = X:L = 7
140 FOR Q = 0 TO 7:T = INT (X / 2)
150 K$(L) = CHR$(48 + (X - T * 2))
160 L = L - 1:X = T:NEXT Q
170 X = Z
180 PRINT TAB(10);
190 FOR I = 0 TO 7:PRINT K$(I);:NEXT I
200 PRINT
210 NEXT X
```

## Examples and Practice

Here are several ordinary decimal numbers. Try to work out the hex equivalent:

1. 10 ______
2. 15 ______
3. 5 ______
4. 16 ______
5. 17 ______
6. 32 ______
7. 128 ______
8. 129 ______
9. 255 ______
10. 254 ______

We are not making an issue of learning hex or binary. If you used your monitor to get the answers, fine. As you work with ML, you will familiarize yourself with some of the common hex numbers. And remember, you can program in ML without needing to worry about hex numbers. For now, we only want to be able to recognize what hex is. The LADS assembler or the 128's built-in monitor will do the translations for you any time you need them.

One other reason that we're not stressing hex too much is that ML is generally not programmed without the help of an assembler. LADS will handle your input automatically. It allows you to choose whether you prefer to program in hex or decimal. With LADS, just use the $ symbol when you intend a number to be interpreted as hex. Otherwise, LADS will assume you mean decimal.

This short BASIC program is good for practicing hex and also shows you how a two-byte hex number relates to a one-byte hex number. It will take decimal in and give back the correct hex.

**Program 2-3. Hex Practice**

```
10 PRINT"{CLR}"
20 INPUT"ENTER A DECIMAL NUMBER";X
30 IF X> 255 THEN 20:REM NO NUMBERS BIGGER THAN 25
   5 ALLOWED
40 PRINT "$";RIGHT$(HEX$(X),2)
50 PRINT:GOTO 20
```

For larger hex numbers (up to two bytes, $FFFF equals 65535), we can just make a simple change to Program 2-3. Change line 30 to IF X > 65535 THEN 20, and change line 40 to PRINT "$";HEX$(X). This will give us four-place hex numbers. These larger hex numbers are used in ML mainly for addresses, since the 8502 can directly address 65536 bytes (bytes with addresses from 0 through 65535). This is the reason that many microcomputers max out at 64K. There are special ways to get around this, but an eight-bit microprocessor like the 8502 is generally limited in the total amount of RAM memory it can access directly.

The number 65535 is interesting because it represents the limit of our computers' memories. The 128 has additional ROM and RAM in *banks* which we'll discuss later. The 128 can directly address only 64K at any one time, but it can quickly switch banks in and out so that it appears to address more than 65535 bytes at once. But 64K is the upper limit of direct addressing without bank switching because the 8502 chip is designed to be able to *address* (put bytes in or take them out of memory cells) only up to $FFFF (65535).

### Ganging Two Bytes Together to Form an Address

The 8502 often addresses by attaching two bytes together and looking at them as if they formed a unit. It's like the way that putting eight bits together forms the unit we call a *byte*. The largest number that two bytes can represent is $FFFF (65535), and the most that *one* byte can represent is $FF (255). Three-byte addressing is not possible for the 8502 chip. *Machine language* means programming instructions which are understood directly by the 8502 chip itself. There are other CPU (Central Processing Unit) chips, but the 8502 is the 128's CPU that's covered in this book.

### Reading a Machine Language Program

Before getting into an in-depth look at the *monitor*, that bridge between you and your machine's language—we should first learn how to read ML program listings. You've probably seen them often enough in magazines.

These commented, labeled, but very strange-looking programs are called *source code* (see Program 2-7 for an example). Source code is what you write when you want to create an ML program. It can be translated by an *assembler program* (like LADS) into an ML program. When you have an assembler program attack your source code, it looks at the keywords (the instructions and their arguments, and their addresses) and then POKEs a series of numbers into the computer. This series of numbers is called the *object code* and is the runnable ML program. You can CALL object code and it will do whatever you've designed it to do.

Source code usually contains a great deal of information in the form of comments which are of interest to the programmer, but which the computer ignores. It's rather like the way a BASIC program has REMarks to which the computer pays no attention.

The computer needs only a list of numbers which it can execute in order. That's what an ML program is. But for most people, lists of numbers are only slightly more understandable than Morse code. The solution is to let us use words which are then translated into numbers for the computer. The primary job of an assembler is to recognize an ML instruction. These instructions are called *mnemonics*, which means "memory aids." They are like BASIC words except that they are always three letters long and are somewhat less like standard English.

If you type the mnemonic instruction JMP, the assembler POKEs a 76 into RAM memory. It's easier for us to remember something like JMP than the number 76. Seeing a 76, however, the computer immediately knows that it's supposed to perform a JMP. The number 76 is an *operation code*, or *opcode*, to the computer.

We write the mnemonic instruction JMP, an assembler translates this into the number 76, and the computer recognizes 76 as the command JUMP. These three-letter words we use in ML programming were designed to sound like what they do. JMP does a JUMP (like a GOTO in BASIC). Deluxe assemblers like LADS also let you use labels instead of numbers. These labels can refer to individual memory locations, special values like the score in a game, or entire subroutines. (See the instructions for LADS in Appendix B for more information about using labels.)

## Four Ways to List a Program

Labeled, commented source code listings are the most elaborate kind of ML program representation. There are also three other kinds of ML listings you might come across. Let's see how these four styles of representing an ML program would look by using a simple example program that just adds 2 + 5 and stores the result in RAM memory location 848. The first two styles are simply ways for you to type a program into the computer. The last two styles show you what to type in, but also illustrate what is going on in the ML program. First, let's look at the most elementary kind of ML found in books and magazines: the BASIC loader.

### Program 2-4. BASIC Loader

```
10 FOR ADDRESS = 2816 TO 2824
20 READ BYTE
30 POKE ADDRESS, BYTE
40 NEXT ADDRESS
50 DATA 24,169,2,105,5,141,80,3,96
```

This is a series of decimal numbers in DATA statements which are POKEd into memory beginning at decimal address 2816 (or, expressed as hex, $B00). This is a BASIC program. When you run this program, these numbers are stashed into RAM, and they form a little ML routine which clears the carry (so there won't be any holdover from previous addition—you always clear the carry before any addition in ML), then puts the number 2 into the *accumulator*—a special location in the computer that we'll get to later—and then adds 5. The result of the addition is then copied from the accumulator into decimal address 848. If you try this program out, you can SYS 2816 to execute the ML program and then PRINT PEEK (848) and you'll see the answer: 7. BASIC loaders are convenient for magazines to publish because the user doesn't need to know anything at all about ML to enter and use the ML programs. The BASIC loader POKEs the ML program into memory, and then the only thing the user has to do is SYS to the right address and the ML transfers control back to BASIC when its job is done. Many ML programs end with an RTS (ReTurn from Subroutine) instruction which causes the computer to revert to BASIC mode after the ML program has finished.

Getting even closer to the machine level is the second way you might see ML printed in books or magazines: the hex dump. The 128 has a special *monitor* program in ROM which lets you list memory addresses and their contents as hex numbers.

More than that, with the monitor you can type in new numbers and change the program. That's what a hex dump listing is for. You copy its numbers into your computer's RAM by using your computer's monitor. (The monitor is so important to ML programming that we'll spend all of Chapter 3 exploring what it can do for us.)

A hex dump, like a BASIC loader, tells you nothing about the functions or strategies employed within an ML program.

Program 2-5 is the hex dump version of the same 2 + 5 addition program.

The third type of listing is called a *disassembly*. It's the opposite of an assembly: A program called a *disassembler* takes machine language (the series of numbers, the opcodes in the computer's memory) and translates it into the words, the mnemonics, which humans can read and understand. The instruction (the mnemonic) you use when you want to put something into the accumulator is called LDA, and you store what's in the accumulator by using an STA. We'll get to them later.

In this version of our addition routine, Program 2-6, it's a bit clearer what's going on and how the program works. Notice that on the far left we have the memory addresses (in hex), then hex numbers representing the actual bytes of the program and, on the right, the translation into ML instructions. ADC means ADd with Carry and RTS means ReTurn from Subroutine. A disassembly is to ML what LIST is to BASIC. Your monitor has a disassembler built-in which will produce these listings.

## The Deluxe Version

Finally, we come to that full, luxurious, commented, labeled, deluxe source code we spoke of earlier. Program 2-7 includes the hex dump and the disassembly, but it also has labels and comments and line numbers added to further clarify the purposes of things and to make it easier for programmers to enter and edit their programs. This kind of listing can be produced with the LADS assembler by invoking the .S or .P features to create a full listing on screen or printer during the assembly process.

Note that in Program 2-7 all the numbers (except the line numbers on the far left) are in hex. LADS makes this optional. To make them decimal, use the .NH option and your listing will be entirely in decimal.

On the far left are the line numbers for the convenience of the programmer when writing the source code (the program you write to feed into the assembler). The line numbers can be used the way BASIC line numbers are used: deleted, inserted, and so on. Next are the memory addresses where each individual instruction in this routine is located in RAM. Then come the hex numbers of the instructions. (So far, it resembles the traditional hex dump.) Next are the disassembled translations of the hex, but note that you can replace numbers with labels as we'll see in Program 2-8. Last are the comments. They are the same as REM statements in BASIC.

Program 2-8 is functionally the same as 2-7, but we've defined some labels and used them instead of numbers. That can be a good way to remember the purpose of various things, just the way variable names in BASIC assist the programmer.

## Program 2-5. Hex Dump

```
.: 0B00 18 A9 02 69 05 8D 50 03 60 AA AA AA AA AA AA AA.).i..P.`*******
```

## Program 2-6. Disassembly

```
., 0B00 18          CLC
., 0B01 A9 02       LDA #$02
., 0B03 69 05       ADC #$05
., 0B05 8D 50 03    STA $0350
., 0B08 60          RTS
.
```

```
                                 ┌──── Source Code ─────┐
Line   Memory  Object            Disassembly            Comments
Number Address Code

 100 0B00 18                     CLC              CLEAR THE CARRY FLAG
 110 0B01 A9 02                  LDA #$02         LOAD A WITH 2
 120 0B03 69 05                  ADC #$05         ADD 5
 130 0B05 8D 50 03               STA $0350        STORE AT DECIMAL LOCATION 848
 140 0B08 60                     RTS              RETURN
2-8
= $B00
```

**Program 2-8. Labeled Assembly**

```
40 ØBØØ                         TWO = 2              DEFINE LABEL TWO AS 2
50 ØBØØ                         ADDER = 5            DEFINE "ADDER" AS A 5
60 ØBØØ                         STORAGE = 848        DEFINE STORAGE ADDRESS
70
80 ØBØØ 18                      CLC                  CLEAR THE CARRY FLAG
90 ØBØ1 A9 Ø2                   LDA #TWO             LOAD A WITH 2
100 ØBØ3 69 Ø5                  ADC #ADDER           ADD 5
110 ØBØ5 8D 5Ø Ø3               STA STORAGE          STORE AT DECIMAL LOCATION 848
120 ØBØ8 6Ø                     RTS                  RETURN
ADDITION
 = $BØØ
```

**Program 2-9. The Source Code by Itself**

```
10 *= $BØØ
20 .P
30 .S
40 TWO = 2;               DEFINE LABEL TWO AS 2
50 ADDER = 5;             DEFINE "ADDER" AS A 5
60 STORAGE = 848;         DEFINE STORAGE ADDRESS
70 ;
80 CLC;                   CLEAR THE CARRY FLAG
90 LDA #TWO;              LOAD A WITH 2
100 ADC #ADDER;           ADD 5
110 STA STORAGE;          STORE AT DECIMAL LOCATION 848
120 RTS;                  RETURN
130 .END ADDITION
140 ; LINE 130 ONLY NECESSARY IF YOU ARE USING .D
```

Where Programs 2-7 and 2-8 show you what LADS prints out during an assembly if you request a listing, Program 2-9 illustrates just the *source code* part, what you would type into your 128 prior to assembly. Source code is the program you write; it's what's fed to the assembler to produce object code (the runnable ML program.) The object code has not yet been generated from this source code. The code has not been *assembled* yet. You can save or load source code in the same way that you can save or load programs via BASIC. Once Program 2-9 is typed in, you could SYS 10000 (if you'd previously loaded LADS into memory), and LADS would translate the instructions and print them on the screen and/or POKE them into memory if so instructed.

Those few differences between Programs 2-8 and 2-9 are conveniences for the programmer. The *= symbol tells the assembler where you want the ML program located in memory. The .P turns on the printer, and .S turns on listing to screen during assembly. The semicolons announce that a remark follows and the assembler should ignore the rest of the line, just like REM in BASIC.

A simple assembler, like the one found in the 128's monitor, operates differently. It translates, prints, and POKEs as soon as you hit RETURN on each line of code. You can save and load the object, but not source code, with this simple assembler.

Before we get into the heart of ML programming, a study of the opcodes and ways of moving information around (called *addressing*), we should look at that major ML programming aid: the monitor. It deserves its own chapter.

**Answers to quiz**

| | |
|---|---|
| 1. 0A | 6. 20 |
| 2. 0F | 7. 80 |
| 3. 05 | 8. 81 |
| 4. 10 | 9. FF |
| 5. 11 | 10. FE |

# Chapter 3

# The Monitor

# The Monitor

A monitor is a program which allows you to work directly with your computer's memory. When you "go below" BASIC into the monitor mode, BASIC is no longer active. If you type RUN, it will not execute anything. BASIC commands are not recognized. The computer waits, as usual, for you to type in some instructions. There are only a few instructions to give to a monitor. When you're working with it, you're pretty close to talking directly to the machine in machine language.

The 128 has a monitor in ROM. This means that you do not need to load the monitor program into the computer; it's always available to you. You can use hex, decimal, or binary numbers with the monitor. Signify hex as usual with $ before the number and use % before binary numbers. However, you don't need to use the $ when giving an address for disassembly or assembly, or a range of addresses for hunting, and so forth. Hex is assumed in these cases as the default condition.

Also, you can specify any memory bank by giving its number before the actual address number. For example, M 3000 will show you what's in address 3000 (hex) and beyond of bank 0 (always the default bank). To see memory in bank 1 you would type M 13000.

Debugging is the main purpose of a monitor. You use it to check your ML code to find errors. Some computer manufacturers, Apple, for instance, even call their monitor a debugger.

You enter the 128 monitor by hitting the F8 key (SHIFT-F7). You will see the registers displayed and the cursor below the display. Here are the monitor instructions:

### 1. Assemble

**A** (*address*) (*mnemonic*) (*argument*) will assemble a line of source code.

Example: **2000 LDA #$15**

will assemble that at address 02000. Remember that anytime you want to access memory banks other than bank 0, you can type the bank number before the actual memory address. If you want to assemble to bank 1, address 2000, you would type 12000 LDA #$15.

If you make a mistake, a question mark (?) will appear on the line. As always, you can cursor up and correct your mistake; RETURN always enters each line. Also, like autonumbering, the next address for assembly will automatically appear on the line below, so you need specify the address only when you first start assembling.

You can also use the period (.) to signify assembly. The monitor prints periods at the start of each line.

This mini-assembler cannot use labels and has other drawbacks. However, it's a fine tool for testing small ideas, a few lines long, and for making little adjustments to a larger program while debugging.

### 2. Compare memory

**C** (*start of block*) (*end of block*) (*start of second block*)

To see whether two sections of memory are identical or which bytes differ, you type C followed by the start and end address of the first block (which lets the assembler also calculate the length of the blocks being compared) and then give the address of the start of the second block.

Example: **C 1000 1020 4000**

This will print the addresses of any bytes which do not match when the blocks of memory between 1000-1020 and 4000-4020 are compared. This facility can be useful if you want to see where two versions of the same routine differ. If, for example, version 5 of the game you're writing always works, but version 6 turns the screen black, you can load the two versions into memory, targeting one of them to a different location in memory (see a special feature of Load described below), and then compare them to see where they differ. Alternatively, you could use a BASIC-Aid type program to compare their source codes. When possible, that's the preferred method.

### 3. Disassemble

**D** (*start address*) (*optional end address*)

This allows you to see the ML equivalent of a program listing in BASIC. Raw object code in memory will be printed to the screen in a readable, rough source code form, as it appears when you type in source code using A (Assemble) described above. There still won't be labels, but you can interpret what a piece of code does.

D, like M described below, can simply be given a start address, in which case it disassembles about 20 bytes and stops. Alternatively, you can give both a start and an end address, whereupon it will scroll through the range of memory requested. You can always slow down the scrolling by holding down the Commodore key, freeze the scroll with CONTROL-S, or end the scroll with RUN/STOP.

Disassembly is perhaps the single most useful command in the monitor. You will sometimes be trying out a program you've written, and, bing (the monitor makes a noise when you enter it this way), you'll find yourself staring at the register display. This means that your program failed, but luckily the computer didn't harden into immobility (the worst kind of bug to fix). Instead, you gained some valuable information: You can look at the PC (Program Counter) and see where you fell into monitor mode (disassemble a few bytes before the PC address and you'll find the 00 (BRK) that sent you into the monitor). Not only that, but sometimes the values in the accumulator or Y or X registers will be a clue about what went awry.

In tough situations, where a bug is enigmatic, you'll find yourself following a path through your program, disassembling until you find a JSR or JMP, then disassembling the subroutine indicated by the JSR, trying to see where your program goes off the rails. One obvious case would be if the disassembler reported that it couldn't make sense of your code (it will print ??? when it cannot disassemble something). This probably means that you typed in your source code incorrectly ($#B0 with the # in the wrong place, for example) which confused the assembler.

When debugging larger programs, you'll be deliberately inserting BRK at key points in the code to force the computer into the monitor so that you can examine the registers or key variables (maybe your zero page pointers) in your program. Here D helps you discover which of perhaps several breakpoints you've landed on.

You can also make direct modifications to the code. You can't change the hex numbers, the object code, but you can cursor over and change the source code. For example, .B00 A9 00 LDA #$00 can be altered by moving to the #$00 and changing it to, say, #$05 and hitting RETURN. Because the period at the start of the line is the same as the A (Assemble) command, you'll have activated the mini-assembler.

If you do want to change the object bytes, you can put a greater-than symbol (>) at the start of the line and then change the 00 to 05, but you must get rid of the LDA #$00 which follows on that line. The > (memory change) command cannot make sense of LDA #$00. The fastest way to eliminate the end of the line is ESC then Q, one of the 128's convenient escape code tricks. Note that you press ESC, but do not hold it down while pressing Q.

The reason we bother with this Disassemble/Memory change method is that sometimes you'll want to insert NOPs directly into your program to eliminate something temporarily and test the program without it. Let's say that you have a change screen color subroutine at $3500 and you suspect it might be what's crashing your program.

```
LDA #$04
JSR $3500
LDY #$03
```

might be a segment of your program. You could disassemble this, insert EA EA EA over the 20 00 35 which represented your jump to that suspect subroutine, and then rerun your program. EA is the code for NOP, NO oPeration. It does nothing, so you've temporarily removed that entire subroutine from the program you're testing (if this is the only JSR to that subroutine). Alternatively, you could place a 60 (RTS, ReTurn from Subroutine) at $3500 to remove it from all attempts to call it throughout your program.

These and other debugging tricks will occur to you as you test and work with your programs. The Disassemble function will prove invaluable.

It's also instructive to use the disassembler to follow the logic of the BASIC in your 128. Try looking at bank 15 wherein BASIC, I/O, and the Kernal reside between $4000—$FFFF. Just D F4000. To continue, type D RETURN repeatedly. Around F41C0 you'll start to see lots of ??? which means it's likely to be a table of some sort. Switch to M F41C0 to see the meaning of this section. See if you can locate the BASIC keywords.

Because it's such a valuable tool, let's briefly review the elements of disassembly. A disassembly will contain three *fields* (a field is a "zone" of information). The first field will contain the address of an instruction (in hex). The address field is somewhat comparable to BASIC's line numbers. It defines the order in which instructions will normally be carried out.

The second field shows the hex numbers for the instruction, and the third field is where a disassembly differs from a "memory" or "hex" dump (see Memory below). This third field translates the hex numbers of the second field back into a mnemonic and its argument.

Here's an example of a disassembly:

```
2000   A9 41      LDA #$41
2002   8D 23 32   STA $3223
2005   A4 99      LDY $99
```

Recall that a dollar sign shows that a number is in hexadecimal. The pound sign (#) means "immediate" addressing (put the *number itself* into the A register at 2000 above). Confusing these two symbols is a major source of errors for beginning ML programmers.

You should pay careful attention to the distinction between LDA #$41 and LDA $41. The second instruction (without the pound sign) means to load A with whatever number is found in *address* $41 hex.

LDA #$41 means put the *actual number 41 itself* into the accumulator.

If you are debugging a routine, check to see that you've got these two types of numbers straight, that you've loaded from addresses where you meant to (and, vice versa, that you've loaded *immediately* where you intended).

### 4. Fill

**F** (*start address*) (*end address*) (*value*)

This fills the zone between start address and end address with the byte value which follows. It's most useful when trying to see what areas of memory are unsafe to use, particularly when you are modifying a commercial program like a word processor and are unsure where it might be storing variables. Load the word processor, F 0B00 0BFF 00 (filling the cassette buffer with zeros), and put the word processor through its paces. Then, enter the monitor and examine the "snow," the zeros you sprayed there, to see if any of them changed, if the word processor left any tracks. This is a quick way to find out if your use of this buffer will conflict with the word processor's need for the same space.

### 5. Go

**G** (*address*)

You can run an ML program from within the monitor with the G instruction. The program must end with a BRK if you expect to return to the monitor when the program ends. Try this: Type A B00 LDA #$15 and then hit RETURN. Then type TAY (and press RETURN), then BRK (and RETURN twice). You've created a little program that puts $15 into the accumulator, transfers it to the Y register, and stops. Type R to see the condition of the accumulator and the Y register. Then type G B00 and see what happened to the accumulator and Y registers.

Note that you can Go to Mars if you give G the wrong address. If you've written something lengthy, you might want to first save it with S (described below) to be on the safe side. Also, remember that the ML *must* end with a BRK; otherwise, you may be kicked out of the monitor back into BASIC or the program may crash altogether. For routines that normally end with RTS, simply change the RTS to BRK to use the G instruction (remember to change the BRK back to an RTS after you've tested the routine). Or, if you don't need the register display that G provides when the program ends you can use the J instruction instead (see below).

### 6. Hunt

**H** (*start address*) (*end address*) (*pattern*)

This can be useful when you're exploring a commercial program or BASIC or even want to find a particular location in your own program. It will search between the start and end addresses for a match to the pattern you give it. The pattern can be a series of hex numbers or a character string. Let's try locating BASIC's table of keywords:

**H F4000 FFFFF 'PRIN**

and wait a few seconds while the monitor reports where it finds matches. (We left off the *T* in PRINT because BASIC stores its keywords with the final letter "shifted" by adding 128 to it. This is how it knows the end, the length of each keyword.) Then, use M (described below) to see the memory and look at whatever you find.

Be sure to use a single quotation mark to set off a character string.

Here's another use for H. Assume that you know that a certain pattern of bytes is going to appear in BASIC and you want to find them. Let's look for all locations where BASIC switches in ROM bank 15. To get the pattern, type:

```
A B00 LDA #0
      STA $FF00
```

and you can then see what pattern of bytes to look for. So now hunt:

```
H F4000 FFFFF A9 00 8D 00 FF
```

and then you can disassemble to learn more about what's going on in your ROM.

## 7. Jump

J *(address)*

This instruction is similar to G, but if the ML program being executed ends with RTS it doesn't break back into the monitor with a display of registers. Instead, it just quietly returns to the monitor with no special display—just the usual blinking cursor. You might want to use J if you are testing a routine which affects the screen, such as printing a message. You'd get cleaner results with J than G in this case.

Remember that ML programs you run with the J instruction should end with RTS if you want to avoid the register display. If the ML ends with BRK, the effect will be the same as if you had used the G instruction.

## 8. Load

L (*"filename"*) (*,8 for disk or ,1 for tape*) (*,optional load address*)

If you've worked with ML on a computer which has no monitor, you'll welcome the convenience of this and Save, its companion function. With L you can retrieve any file from tape or disk (it's like BASIC's BLOAD command), and, even more helpful, you can load an ML program to an address which is different from the one whereat it normally resides, different from the address from which you originally saved it. This is a good way to test versions of a program (see Compare above).

If you write a program in bank 1 and save it, it will load back into bank 0 unless you specify bank 1 in the optional load address field. Notice, too, that commas are necessary with this command to separate the argument fields. Load and

Save are odd this way; you must type L "FILENAME",8 rather than L "FILENAME" 8.

### 9. Memory

**M** (*optional start address*) (*optional end address*)

Among the most useful of all monitor commands, this memory display shows you a visual display of your memory. It's sometimes called a *hex dump* because you will see the value in each memory cell displayed as a two-character hex digit. To the right, you'll see the same bytes displayed as characters when possible. Unprintable characters are signified by a period (.). You can change any of the bytes (except the address) as long as the > symbol appears at the first position in the line. You can thus quickly check your tables and variables to see if they're behaving properly or modify them for testing purposes.

If you provide no argument, M will show you the zone of memory most recently accessed. If you give a start address, that's the memory you'll see. As before, if you use a number like B00, you'll see bank 0. If you want to specify another bank, type its number first: 10B00 would show you B00 in bank 1.

### 10. Registers

**R**

This will show you the current status of your registers. It looks like this:

```
     PC   SR AC XR YR SP
; 00B09 30  00  05  FF  F9
```

The PC is the program counter, the place in memory where you last were when the monitor was invoked. Perhaps you had a BRK instruction which forced your program to halt so you could test it. If you have a BRK at 0B07, the PC will show 0B09 as above. It's always two bytes past where you actually break for some reason. Just remember that this is what happens. You can locate the BRK with Disassemble described above.

The SR is the status register (the byte that holds the flags). It's not useful in this form because it's too hard to figure out what flags are up or down to achieve, as above, for example, a total byte value of $30. The AC is the accumulator;

the X and Y registers follow. The SP is the stack pointer. Forget about it, too.

You can cursor over and directly change the values in the AC, XR, or YR, which can be useful sometimes during testing.

Note that the monitor always supplies that first digit signifying bank number, but for you it's optional. Most of the time you'll be in the default bank 0.

### 11. Save

**S** (*"filename"*) (*,8 for disk or ,1 for tape*) (*,start address*) (*,end address plus one*)

S saves a section of memory to disk or tape, like BSAVE. The commas are necessary to separate the fields as shown. You could save screen RAM if you wanted or anything else, but the most common use for this is to save ML programs. The bank conventions and other rules described under Load above apply to Save as well.

Notice, however, a special oddity here: The end address must be *one byte beyond the actual end of your program*. Again, nobody who knows why, tells, but you've got to remember this mysterious fact or you'll lop off your RTS or BRK or whatever is the highest byte in your program.

```
00B00 A9 00        LDA #$00
00B02 8D 00  FF    STA $FF00
00B05 60           RTS
00B06 00           BRK
```

If you want to save this and include the RTS, you must S "FILENAME",8,0B00,0B06, and if you wanted to include that BRK, you'd need to specify 0B07 as the end address.

Remember, too, that if you save from within bank 1 or somewhere other than bank 0, that information is not transferred to the disk with the program. You must specify which bank you are saving from if it's not 0, but when you go to load your program back in, it will load into bank 0 unless you specify the bank in the optional address field at the end.

### 12. Transfer

**T** (*start address of source*) (*end address of source*) (*start address of target*)

This isn't too useful since you can load to any target. It *does not* make your programs relocatable. It simply, dumbly moves the zone of bytes between start and end address of source and sets them down unchanged at the target. So, if you've got a direct JMP to some address within your ML program, JMP $B09 for example, the new version after the transfer will still JMP $B09 to a subroutine which is no longer at that location. Also, references to tables like error messages will be similarly erroneous. It's difficult to think of a real use for this function, but it's there if you ever come up with one.

**13. Verify**

**V** (*"filename"*) (*,8 for disk or ,1 for tape*) (*,optional alternate start address*)

This reports any errors caused by Save or it could be a way of comparing two program versions for identity. In practice, because the Commodore mass storage systems are so highly intelligent and reliable, you may find you'll never need to verify I/O.

**14. X (Exit to BASIC)**

**X**

Takes you out of the monitor.

**15. @ (communicate with disk drive)**

**@** (*unit number*), (*command string*)

You can see the directory from the monitor by @,$ or see the disk status (as with ?DS$ in BASIC) by @ with no command string at all. You can also initialize a disk with @,I, but you should be in BASIC for things like that anyway.

**16. $, +, &, %**

These symbols are put directly before a number to indicate whether it is hex (the default, so you don't need $), decimal, octal (forget this; you'll probably never meet anyone who uses octal, base 8, numbers), and binary.

Thus, if you want to assemble LDA #2 you can do it three useful ways: decimal (LDA #+2), hex (LDA #$02), or binary which shows you how the bits look in the byte (LDA #%00000010). Whichever form you use, the 128 will convert the input to hex when you enter the line. No matter which way you enter the example instruction, it will change to LDA #$02 after you press RETURN.

Another use for these symbols is to type in a number at the start of a line in the monitor and let it translate the number into the four number bases. If you want to know what decimal 1024 is in hex, type:

**+1024**

then press RETURN and you'll see:

**$0400**
**+1024**
**&2000**
**%10000000000**

Conversely, you can see what a hex number would be in decimal by typing:

**$400**

or take a look at binary. This can be useful, particularly when looking at someone else's program or working with a map of ROM such as the one in Appendix C.

## Using the Monitor

You will make mistakes. Monitors are for checking and fixing ML programs. ML is an exacting programming process, and causing bugs is as unavoidable as mistyping when writing a letter. It will happen, be sure, and the only thing for it is to go back and try to locate and fix the slip-up. It is said that every Persian rug is made with a deliberate mistake somewhere in its pattern. The purpose of this is to show that only Allah is perfect. This isn't our motivation when causing bugs in an ML program, but we'll cause them nonetheless. The best you can do is try to get rid of them when they appear.

Probably the most effective tactic, especially when you are just starting out with ML, is to write very short subroutines. Because they are short, you can more easily check and examine them to make sure that they are functioning the way they should. Let's assume that you want to write an ML subroutine to ask a question on the screen. (This is often called a *prompt* since it prompts the user to do something.)

The message can be PRESS ANY KEY. First, we'll have to store the message in RAM somewhere. Let's put it at hex $2000.

*ASCII*
**2000 80 P**
**2001 82 R**
**2002 69 E**
**2003 83 S**
**2004 83 S**
**2005 32**
**2006 65 A**
**2007 78 N**
**2008 89 Y**
**2009 32**
**200A 75 K**
**200B 69 E**
**200C 89 Y**
**200D 00**

(The final zero is a special signal to the computer called the *delimiter* which shows that the message is concluded.)

We'll put our "print-it-out" subroutine at address $1F00, a RAM zone where BASIC programs usually reside. So, we've got the data at address $2000 and the subroutine that uses the data located at $1F00. All this is entirely arbitrary. The ML programmer can put things wherever in RAM he or she wishes as long as the location doesn't conflict with other needs of the computer as would be the case in zero page. Remember, you can safely put your ML between $0B00–$0BFF or $1C00–$FF00 in bank 0 and anywhere between $0400–$FF00 in bank 1 (or between $1C00–$4000 in bank 15).

We haven't gotten into actual programming yet, but this example is a good place to see if you can spot an error in ML programming. This subroutine will not work as printed. There are two errors in this program. See if you can spot them:

```
1F00  LDY  #$00      Set up the Y register to count events.
1F02  LDA  $2000,Y   Get the first character from the data.
1F05  CMP  $00       Is it the delimiter?
1F07  BNE  $1F0A     If not, continue on.
1F09  RTS            It was zero, so quit and return to whatever
                     JSRed, or called, this subroutine.
1F0A  STA  $0400,Y   The 128's text display area in 40-column
                     mode.
1F0D  INY            Raise the counter by one.
1F0E  JMP  $1F00     Always JMP back to address $1F00.
```

Since we haven't yet gone into addressing or opcodes much, this is like learning to swim by the throw-them-in-the-water method. Nevertheless, see if you can make out how these instructions interact. Here's some help: a BASIC version of the same routine, containing the same errors.

```
10 DATA P,R,E,S,S, ,A,N,Y, ,K,E,Y
20 Y = 0
30 READ X: IF X <> PEEK(0) THEN 50
40 RETURN
50 POKE 1024 + Y,X
60 Y = Y + 1
70 GOTO 20
```

This subroutine won't work. In the ML version, you'll find two of the most common bugs in ML programming. Unfortunately, they are not obvious bugs. An obvious bug would be mistyping LDS when you meant LDA. Any assembler would alert you to this error by printing an error message to let you know that no such instruction as LDS exists in 8502 ML.

No, the bugs in this program are errors in logic, in the flow or sense of the thing. If you disassemble it, it will also look just fine to the disassembler program, and no error messages will be printed out by the disassembler either.

But, the routine will not work the way you want it to. Before reading on, see if you can spot the two errors. Also, see if you can follow the events as the ML routine runs through its loop, picking up the characters in the message and supposedly depositing them onscreen. Where does the computer go after the first pass through the code? When and how does it know that it's finished with its job?

## Two Common Errors

A very common bug, perhaps the most common ML bug, is caused by accidentally using *zero page addressing* when you mean to use *immediate addressing*. We mentioned this distinction before, but it is the cause of so much puzzlement to the beginning ML programmer that we're going to pound away at it several times in this book. Zero page addressing looks very similar to immediate addressing. Zero page means that you are dealing with one of the cells, or bytes, in the first 256 addresses in RAM memory in the computer. The lowest locations possible.

A *page* of memory is 256 bytes. Page 1 is from addresses 256 through 511 and is special. It's called the *stack*, and the computer has a special use for it. We'll get to it later, but don't try storing anything in page 1 unless you're fond of havoc. Addresses 512–767 comprise page 3 which is the input buffer (where a line is stored when you type it in) for BASIC. The 128 text screen memory starts at address $0400 (1024 in decimal), and this is the start of page 5. And so on, in 256-byte blocks, on up memory to the very top, page 255.

In contrast to zero page addressing is immediate addressing. Immediate addressing means that the number you're dealing with is right within the ML code (not somewhere else in memory). It means that you knew what number you were dealing with and put it right into your program when you wrote the program. Immediate addressing means that the number directly follows an instruction; it's the argument, the operand, of an instruction. LDY #0 is immediate addressing. It puts the number 0 into the Y register (see line 1F00 in the example routine above).

LDY 0 is *not* immediate addressing, and you very well might not get a zero into the Y register. LDY 0 is zero page addressing. LDY 34 is also zero page addressing. Using any address lower than 256 would mean zero page addressing. LDY 34 might put anything, any number, into the Y register because *whatever number is in address 34* will be placed into the Y register. The key is that # symbol, the number symbol. If you mean to load the number 34 into the Y register, use LDY #34. Think of it as LoaD Y with number 34.

If you mean to fetch whatever is currently in address 34, use LDY 34. If you mean *hex* address 34, use LDY $34. It's easy and very common to mix up these two modes—immediate loading which uses # and zero page which has no symbol except, perhaps, the $ to identify a hex number. So, look for this error first when debugging a faulty program. Check to see that all your zero page addressing is supposed to fetch from RAM and that all your immediate mode numbers are supposed to come from within the ML code itself, *immediately* following the instruction.

In our example ML program, LDY #0 is correct—we do want to set the Y register to zero so that it can help us put the characters in the proper places on the screen (STA $0400,Y stores each character at address 0400, the screen, *plus* the current value of Y). For this purpose, we want the immediate, the *actual*, number zero.

Take a close look, however, at the instruction at location $1F05. Here we are trying to see if we've picked out that zero in the message that tells us the message is finished. We want to CoMPare to the *number* zero. But, we left off the # symbol that tells the computer to use the number zero. Instead, we're going to cause a comparison against whatever unpredictable value might be in location zero, address zero. To fix this bug, the instruction should be changed to read CMP #0 so that it will be immediate mode, not zero page mode. (If this confuses you, take a look at line 30 in the BASIC version to see the same flaw in a familiar context. If it still confuses you, don't worry, we'll be going over all this in much greater detail in Chapters 4 and 6.)

### It Never Quits

The second bug in this example routine is also a very common one. The subroutine, as written, can never quit; it will endlessly loop. Loop structures are usually preceded by a short setup of some kind. You have to initialize counters before the loop can begin because you have to tell it where to start and how many times to loop. In BASIC, FOR I = 1 TO 10 tells the computer to cycle ten times.

In ML, we set the Y register to zero and let it act as our counter. In this particular routine, we don't use Y to tell us when to stop (that's the job of the delimiter, the embedded zero at the end of the message itself). Instead, Y serves two other purposes. It kills two birds with one stone. It is the offset (the pointer to the current position in a list or series) to load the message in the data and is also the offset to position the letters of the message on the screen. Without Y going up one (INY) each time through this loop, we would always print the first letter of the message and always print it in the first position on the screen.

What's the problem? It's that JMP instruction at $1F0E. We should be jumping back to address $1F02, but the JMP tells us to jump back to $1F00. As things stand, the Y register will always be reset to zero, there will never be a chance to read through the message and pick up that 0 which ends things, and we cannot therefore ever exit this loop. We will endlessly cycle, printing *P* over and over again. Y will never go up past zero because each loop puts a zero back into Y. Look at the relationship between lines 70 and 20 in the BASIC example.

## Tracking Them Down and Nabbing Them

The monitor will let you locate these and other errors. You can replace an instruction with a zero (the BReaK command) which will stop your ML program midrun and let you see the condition of your variables and what's going on in the registers at the *breakpoint*.

If this doesn't help, you can get more specific by single stepping through your program in order to discover, for example, that you are using CMP 0 when you meant CMP #0. Unfortunately, the monitor built into this otherwise excellent programmer's computer does not contain one of the best debugging tools: single-step tracing. With this, you see the results of each instruction in turn as the computer executes your code one step at a time. That can be a real shortcut to locating errant programming. Monitor add-ons for all the previous Commodore computers have included single-step functions and, doubtless, one will be published in *COMPUTE!* magazine or *COMPUTE!'s Gazette* soon. But, as of this writing, no such tool is yet available.

It would also be easy, by stepping, to notice that your Y register is being reset to zero every time through the loop. For single stepping, it's good to first make a printout of the suspect area of your program so that you can follow along during the single stepping. If the Y register keeps turning back into zero, that clues you that this register isn't cooperating; it's not counting up each time through the loop the way you intended it to. These and other errors, if not always immediately obvious, are at least discoverable from within the monitor.

Also, the disassembler function of the monitor will permit you to study the program and look, deliberately, for the correct use of #00 and $00. Since that mixup between immediate and zero page addressing is so common an error, always check for it first.

## Programming Tools

The single most significant quality of monitors which contributes to easing the ML programmer's job is that monitors, like BASIC, are *interactive*. This means that you can make changes and test them right away, right then. In BASIC, you can find an error in line 120, make the correction, and run a test immediately. You can insert a STOP in BASIC or a BRK in ML and look at your variables and registers.

It's not always that easy to locate and fix bugs in ML: There are few error messages which point out faulty program logic, so finding the location of a logic bug can be difficult.

But a monitor does allow interactivity: You make changes and test them on the spot. This is one of the drawbacks of complex assemblers, especially those which have several steps between the writing of the source code and the final assembly of executable object code (ML which can be executed). LADS, however, was designed to maximize interactivity, and you should find that its speed of assembly, its open architecture (you can easily modify it, adding your own error messages and bug traps), and its BASIC-like environment will all contribute to quick program adjustments and quick testing.

Unfortunately, other sophisticated assemblers often require several steps between writing an ML program and being able to test it. These assemblers can require linkers, relocatable loaders, mapping, global/local variable definition, macros, separate and clumsy source code editors, and other "features" which contribute little to the actual assembly of a program or to the comfort of the programmer. If you don't already know the function of these "enhancements," count it a blessing. They greatly retard program development except in professional, programming-by-committee situations. These functions make it easier to rearrange ML subroutines, put them anywhere in memory without modification, and so forth. They make ML greatly modular (composed of very small, self-sufficient modules or subroutines), but they also make it far less interactive. You cannot easily make a change and see the effects at once.

One obvious reason for this kind of assembler, for it having value at all, is that you want to *discourage* interactivity when five people are writing separate sections of the same program. In that environment, all programmers must play by the same rules and things like macros and relocatability have value. For the individual programmer, however, restrictions like these can prove, in the long run, more of a hindrance than a help. Industrial-strength linker/assemblers are, for the individual programmer, rather like installing pay toilet stalls in your bathroom. For most people, it's not merely unnecessary, it's downright inconvenient.

However, using the monitor's mini-assembler, or LADS from this book, you are right near the monitor level, and fixes can be easily and quickly tested. In other words, the assemblers which are best for individual programmers trade efficiency for group-programming communication requirements. Personal assemblers, like personal computers, should reflect the needs of the programmer, not the needs of industrial, programming teams. Personal assemblers should involve little, if any, preplanning, less forethought, less abstract analysis, and no rules for communicating between one programmer and another. If something goes awry, you can just try something else until it all works. Not only does this help you learn, it's also significantly the fastest way to program.

### Plan Ahead or Plunge In?

Some people find such trial-and-error programming uncomfortable, disgraceful even. Industrial assemblers (and some assemblers currently sold for personal use) discourage interactivity, requiring flowcharts, even expecting the programmer to write out a program ahead of time on paper and debug it before even sitting down at the computer.

In one sense, these large assemblers are a holdover from the early years of computing, when computer time was extremely expensive.

There was a clear advantage to coming to the terminal as prepared as possible. Interactivity was costly. But, like the increasingly outdated advice urging programmers to worry about saving computer memory space, it seems that strategies designed to conserve computer time are also anachronistic. You can spend all the time you want on your personal computer.

Complex assemblers tend to downgrade the importance of a monitor, to reduce its function in the programming process. Some programmers who've worked on large IBM mainframe computers for 20 years do not know what the word *monitor* means in the sense we are using it.

To them, monitors are CRT screens. The machine language tools used for years by mainframe programmers often have what we call a monitor, but it will be seriously restrictive. It can, for example, have no provision for saving an ML program to disk or tape from within the monitor.

Whether or not you prefer the interactive style of personal programming, its greater reliance on the monitor and on trial-and-error programming, is your decision. If you're used to group programming, you might find it difficult to abandon the preplanning, the flowcharts, and all the rest. The choice is ultimately a matter of personal style.

## Time Is Cheap

Some programmers are uncomfortable unless they have a fairly complete plan before they even get to the computer keyboard. Others are quickly bored by elaborate flowcharting, "dry computing" on paper, and can't wait to get on the computer and see-what-happens-if.

Perhaps a good analogy can be found in the various ways that people make telephone calls. When long-distance calls were extremely expensive, most people made lists of what they wanted to say and carefully planned the call before dialing. They would also watch the clock during the call. (Some still do this today.) As the costs of phoning came down, many people found that spontaneous conversation was more satisfying. It's up to you.

Computer time, though, is now extremely cheap. If your computer uses 100 watts and your electric company charges 5 cents per kilowatt-hour, never turning your machine off would only cost about 12 cents a day.

# Chapter 4

# Addressing

# Addressing

The 8502 processor is an electronic brain. It performs a variety of manipulations with numbers to allow us to write words, draw pictures, control outside machines such as recorders and disk drives, calculate, and do many other things. It was designed to be logical and fast, to work accurately and efficiently.

If you could peer down into the CPU (Central Processing Unit), the heart of the processor, you would see numbers being delivered and received from memory locations all over the computer. Sometimes the numbers arrive and are sent out, unchanged, to some other address. Other times they are compared, added, or otherwise modified, before being sent back to RAM or to a peripheral.

Writing an ML program can be compared with planning the activities of this message center. This can be illustrated by thinking of computer memory as a City of Bytes with the CPU acting as the main post office (Figure 4-1). The CPU uses four tools to do its job: three registers, a program counter, a stack pointer, and seven little one-bit flags.

The monitor, if you type R (for registers), will display the present status of these tools. It looks something like this:

```
  PC   SR AC XR YR SP
;FB000 30 01 00 FF F8
```

A, X, and Y are the registers, SR is the processor status flags (each bit in this byte is a flag), PC is the program counter (the address of the last instruction executed *plus two* before we entered monitor mode), and SP is the stack pointer. You can more or less let the computer handle the stack pointer. It keeps track of numbers, usually return-from-subroutine addresses, which are kept together in a list called the stack.

The computer will automatically manipulate the stack pointer. It will also handle the program counter (PC) which keeps track of where you are located at any given time within the computer. For example, each ML instruction can be either one, two, or three bytes long. TYA has no argument and is the instruction to transfer a number from the Y register to the accumulator. Since it has no argument, the PC can locate the next instruction to be carried out by adding one to itself. If the

**Figure 4-1. Postal Executives at Work on an Instruction: 21254 STA $3300,Y**

PC held $4000, it would hold $4001 after execution of a TYA. Whenever you insert a BRK instruction, you cause the program to halt at that point and enter monitor mode. The PC shows you where, in your program, you halted.

LDA #$01 is a two-byte instruction. It takes up two bytes in memory, so the next instruction to be executed after LDA #$01 will be two bytes beyond it. In this case, the PC will raise itself from $4000 to $4002. But we can just let it work merrily away without worrying about it other than to note the location when setting several BRKs in a program to debug it.

### The Accumulator: The Busiest Register

SR, A, X, and Y, however, are our business. They are all eight bits, or one byte, in size. They are not located in memory proper. You can't PEEK them since they have no address like the rest of memory. They are zones of the CPU. The A register, most often called the *accumulator*, is the busiest place in the computer. The great bulk of the mail comes to rest here, if only briefly, before being sent to another destination.

Any logical transformations (EOR, AND, ORA) or arithmetic operations leave their results in the accumulator. Most of the bytes streaming through the computer come through the accumulator. You can compare one byte against another using the accumulator. And nearly everything that happens which involves the accumulator will have an effect on the *status register* (SR, the flags). We won't need to actually work directly with the status register, but the information it holds will be significant because several important instructions, like Branch if EQual (BEQ) test to see if a flag is up or down when deciding where to send the program for the next task. BEQ looks at the SR and checks whether or not the Z flag (zero was the result of the most recent event) is up.

The X and Y registers are similar to each other in that one of their main purposes is to assist the accumulator. They are used as addressing indexes. There are some methods of addressing that we'll get to in a minute which add an index value to another number. For example, if the X register is currently holding a five, LDA $4000,X will load the byte in address $4005 into A. In other words, the real address when you're using indexed addressing is the number *plus* the index value. If X has a six, then we load from $4006. Why not just LDA $4006? The reason is that it's far easier to raise or lower an index inside a loop structure than it would be to write in each specific address literally.

A second major use of X and Y is in counting and looping. We'll go into this more in the chapter on the instruction set. We'll also have some things to learn later about SR, the status register, which holds some flags showing current conditions. Among other things, the SR can tell a program or the CPU if there has been a zero, a carry, or a negative number as the result of some operation. Although it's not important to be able to work directly with the status register, knowing about carry and zero flags is especially significant in ML. The branching instructions will check these flags for you, but you should be aware of what some of the flags signify.

But we can leave learning about the instructions until we get to Chapter 6. For now, the task at hand is to explore the various "classes" of mail delivery, the 8502 addressing modes.

The computer must have a logical way to pick up and send information. Rather like a postal service in a dream—everything should be picked up and delivered rapidly, and nothing should be lost, damaged, or delivered to the wrong address.

The 8502 accomplishes its important function of getting and sending bytes (GET and PRINT would be examples of the same activity in BASIC) by using several *addressing modes*. There are 13 different ways that a byte might be "mailed" either to or from the central processor.

When programming, in addition to picking an instruction (of the 56 available to you) to accomplish the job you are working on, you must also make one other decision. You must decide how you want to *address* the instruction—how, in other words, you want the mail sent or delivered. There is some room for maneuvering, however. It will rarely matter if you should choose a slower delivery method than you could have. Nevertheless, it is worth knowing about the various addressing modes; most of them are designed to be helpful during some particular programming activity.

### Absolute and Zero

Let's picture a postman's dream city, a city so well planned from a postal-delivery point of view that no byte is ever lost, damaged, or sent to the wrong address. It's the City of Bytes we first toured in Chapter 2. It has 65536 houses all lined up

Figure 4-2. The First Few Addresses on a Street with 65536 Houses

on one side of a street (a long street). Each house is clearly labeled with its number, starting with house 0 and ending with house 65535. When you want to get a byte from or send a byte to a house (each house holds one byte), you must "address" the package (See Figure 4-2).

Let's look at the most elementary mode of addressing. It's quite popular and could be thought of as "first class." Called *absolute* addressing, it can send a number to or receive one from any house in the city. It's what we normally think of first when the idea of *addressing* something comes up. You just put the number on the package and send it off. No indexing or special instructions. If it says 2500, then it means house 2500.

**1000 STA $2500**

or

**1000 LDA $2500**

These two, STore A and LoaD A, STA and LDA, are the instructions which get a byte from or send it to the accumulator. The *address,* though, is those numbers following the instruction. The item following an instruction is sometimes called the instruction's *argument.* You could have written the above addresses several ways. Writing $2500, however, tells the computer to carry out the instruction with respect to address $2500, to store or load the byte from that location. This kind of addressing uses just a simple $ (to show that this is a hex, not decimal, number) and a four-digit number. You can send the byte in the accumulator to anywhere in normal 64K memory by this method (or retrieve it from anywhere). Remember, too, that if you send a byte from the accumulator, it also remains in the accumulator. It's more a copying than a literal sending. Getting and sending to the 128's alternative RAM banks is another matter; it will be covered below.

## Heavy Traffic in Zero Page

A second addressing mode, called *zero page,* we've touched on before. If you are sending a byte down to anywhere between addresses 0 and 255 ($0000 and $00FF), the *zero page,* you can just leave off the first two numbers: 1000 STA $07. (Remember that the 1000 is the address, the location, of the *instruction,* not the argument, or target, of the instruction.)

Zero page addressing, using only two hex digits or decimal numbers lower than 256, is pretty fast mail service: The mail carrier has to worry about choosing between only 256 instead of 65536 possible houses. And, also, the computer is specially wired to service these special addresses. Think of them being close to the post office. Things get picked up and delivered rapidly in zero page. That's precisely why your BASIC and operating systems tend to use it so often.

Although zero page addressing works only with the first 256 locations in your computer, it gets more than its share of the mail. The 128's BASIC language, its operating system, and disk operating systems use up most of zero page to hold flags and other temporary information they need. Why? Because zero page addressing is the fastest of all the addressing modes. It's nearly instantaneous. Since the 128 has appropriated these first 256 houses for its own use, there's not much room left over down there for you to store your own ML pointers or flags, not to mention entire subroutines. You will, however, want to squeeze in some address *pointers,* which we'll get to in a minute. After all, your programs, too, will sometimes want the fastest possible service.

These two addressing modes, absolute and zero page, are very common ones. In your programming, however, you probably won't get to use zero page as much as you might want to. You will notice on a map of the 128 that zero page is heavily trafficked. You could cause a problem by storing things in zero page where the 128 expects to use it for its own purposes. You can find a map of the 128 in Appendix C. Maps not only tell you what space must be avoided, but also where to access the many built-in BASIC routines in your computer. More about this later.

There are, however, safe areas for you to use down there in those exclusive locations in lower RAM memory. The buffer for the cassette recorder ($B00) or for BASIC activities like floating-point arithmetic are safe when you're not using a tape drive or BASIC. So, if you put your pointers and flags into these addresses, things will be fine. In any case, zero page is a popular, busy neighborhood. Don't put any of your actual ML programs there. Your main use of zero page will be to hold pointers for an especially useful addressing mode called *indirect Y* that we're going to look at in detail. But you've always got to make sure that you aren't interfering with the 128's own requirements for space in zero page. If BASIC is active, you can only be sure of the safety of addresses $FA–$FE.

However, if your ML routine isn't accessing I/O routines at the time, you can use cassette-specific zero page areas. If it's not using floating point, you can use the accumulators. Sometimes, it's easiest just to try using some addresses in zero page and see if your program runs correctly.

While we're on the subject of places to avoid, keep out of page 1 (decimal addresses 256–511), too. That's for the *stack*, about which more later. We'll get to the safe places in RAM that you can use for your ML programs and their flags, variables, tables, and so on. It's always okay to use ordinary higher RAM as long as you keep BASIC programs from putting their variables on top of the ML and keep the ML from writing over BASIC (if you want them to coexist during a program run). And, using the special addressing techniques and bank switching we'll discuss below, you can access the entire 64K of bank 1 which is all blank RAM.

The safest place of all for short ML routines is between addresses 2816 ($B00) and 3071 ($BFF) since the 128 leaves these RAM locations essentially undisturbed unless the cassette drive is active. So, when you want to practice with the examples in this book, it's always okay to give the LADS assembler a start address instruction of *= $B00 or its decimal equivalent *= 2816.

## Immediate

Another very common addressing mode is called *immediate* addressing—it deals directly with a number. Instead of sending away for the number, we can just shove it directly into the accumulator by putting the number right in the same place where the other addressing modes would have an address. Let's illustrate this:

| | |
|---|---|
| **B00 LDA $2500** | Absolute mode, loading from address 2500 |
| **B00 LDA #$9** | Immediate mode, put number 9 into the accumulator |

The first example will load the accumulator with whatever number is found in address $2500. In the second example, we simply wanted to put a $9 into the accumulator. We know that we want the number $9. So, instead of sending off for the $9, we just type in a $9 where we normally would put a memory address. And we tack on the # symbol to show that the $9 is the number we're after. Without that #, the computer would load the accumulator with whatever it finds at *address* $9 (as in LDA $9). Without the #, it would be zero page addressing, not immediate addressing.

In any case, immediate addressing is very commonly used, since you often know already what number you are after and do not need to send away for it at all. One example would be printing out a carriage return on the screen. You already know that the code for a carriage return is 13, so you just load it into the accumulator with LDA #13. This is similar to BASIC where you define a variable (10 VARIABLE = 9). In this case, we have a variable being given a known value. LDA #9 is the same idea. (When using the mini-assembler in 128's built-in monitor, remember that it assumes numbers are hex unless otherwise indicated. For the LADS assembler from this book, LDA #10 means "put the value 10 into the accumulator," but the same instruction to the mini-assembler will put the decimal value 16 (hex $10) in the accumulator. To use decimal numbers you must always add a + sign: LDA #+10.)

To repeat, immediate addressing is used when you know what number you're dealing with; you're not sending off for it. It's put right into the ML program code *as a number, not as an address.* To illustrate immediate and absolute addressing working together, imagine that you wanted to copy the number 15 ($0F) into address $4000 (see Program 4-1).

### Implied

Here's an easy one. You don't use *any* address or argument with this one. You just type the instruction; it sits alone, needs no argument.

This is probably the easiest addressing mode to grasp. It's called *implied,* since the mnemonic, the instruction itself, implies what is being sent where: TXA means Transfer the X register's contents to the Accumulator. Implied addressing means that you do not type anything following the instruction. The instruction defines what's being done without your having to give it any argument.

TYA and others are similar short-haul moves from one register to another. Included in this implied group are the SEC, CLC, SED, CLD instructions as well. They merely clear or set the flags in the status register, thereby letting you and the computer keep track of whether or not the most recent arithmetic resulted in a zero, whether or not a carry occurred, and so forth.

**Program 4-1. Putting an Immediate 15 into Absolute Address $4000**

```
10 *= $BØØ
20 ;         ML PROGRAM STARTS AT $BØØ (*= MEANS "START AT")
30 ;
40 LDA #15;           LOAD A WITH THE NUMBER (NOT THE ADDRESS)
50 STA $4ØØØ;         STORE IT IN ADDRESS $4ØØØ
```

Also "implied" are such instructions as RTS (ReTurn from Subroutine), BRK (BReaK, which is the ML equivalent of BASIC's STOP command), PLP, PHP, PLA, PHA (which "push" or "pull" the processor status register or accumulator onto or off the stack).

Increasing by one (incrementing) the X or Y register's number (INX, INY) or decreasing it (DEX, DEY) are also "implied." What all of these implied addressing modes have in common is the fact that you do not need to actually give any address. By comparison, an LDA $2500 (the absolute mode) must have that $2500 address to know where to pick up the package. TXA already says, in the instruction itself, that the address, the destination, is the accumulator. Likewise, you do not put an address after RTS since the computer always memorizes its jump-off address when it does a JSR. NOP (NO oPeration) is, of course, implied mode, too.

### Relative

One particular addressing mode, the *relative* mode, used to be a real headache for programmers. Not so long ago, in the days when ML programming was done "by hand," this was a frequent source of errors. Hand computing—entering each byte by flipping eight switches up or down and then pressing an ENTER key—meant that the programmer had to first write a program on paper, translate the mnemonics into their number equivalents, and then "key" the whole thing into the machine with that set of switches.

It was a big advance when hexadecimal numbers permitted entering $0F instead of eight switches: 00001111. This reduced errors and fatigue.

An even greater advance was having enough free memory so that an assembler program could be in the computer while the ML program was being written. An assembler not only takes care of translating LDA $2500 into its three (eight-switch) numbers—10101101 (the code for the instruction LDA) and 00000000 00100101 (the number $2500)—but an assembler also does relative addressing. So, for the same reason that you can program in ML without knowing how to deal with binary numbers, you can also forget about relative addressing. The assembler will do it for you. All you need to remember about it is that you can't go very far away from the current instruction when using relative addressing and LADS will warn you if you try.

Relative addressing is used with eight instructions only: BCC, BCS, BEQ, BMI, BNE, BPL, BVC, BVS. They are all branching instructions. They force the control of the program to *branch* (jump) when the overflow flag is set (or cleared); when the carry flag is set (or cleared); or if the most recent arithmetic resulted in equal, less than, not equal, or more than.

Branch if EQual (BEQ) would look like this in BASIC: IF X = 0 THEN GOTO. It forces the computer to branch somewhere else in a program if something is equal to zero.

All these B instructions can branch only as far as 128 addresses forward or 127 backward from where the instruction is located. If you were delivering the mail in the City of Bytes, you would probably dislike relative addresses; it would mean extra work. You would be going peacefully from house to house up the road and then, suddenly, one of the letters has a giant *B* on it and a number like −5 or +47. You've then got to stop your orderly progress up the road and take this letter 5 houses back from the current house or 47 houses forward.

Remember that these branches, these jumps, can be a distance of only 128 bytes from their own addresses, but they can go in either direction. Thus, if a BNE instruction above is located in RAM at address $3500, you cannot specify $5600 as its target. That would be much too big a branch. However, if you do exceed the limit of branching, LADS will print "Branch Out Of Range" and give you the line number where the error was so that you can easily correct it.

When using the B instructions to branch relatively, you specify *where* the branch should go by giving an address within the boundaries of 128 bytes in either direction. Here's an example:

```
1000  LDX  #$00
1002  INX
1003  BNE  $1002
1005  BRK
```

(The X register in this example will count up by ones until it hits 255 decimal. At that point, it resets itself to zero. When it does become zero, that will fail to trigger the Branch if Not Equal to zero instruction, and we will "fall through" the branch to the BRK at $1005.)

This is how you create an ML FOR-NEXT loop. You are branching *relative* to address 1003, which means that the assembler will calculate what address to place into the computer that will get you to address $1002. You might wonder what's wrong with the computer just accepting the number $1002 as the address to which you want to branch. Absolute addressing *does* give the computer the actual address, but the branching instructions all need addresses which are offsets of the starting address. After assembling the example above, the assembler puts the following into the computer:

```
1000 A2 00
1002 E8
1003 D0 FD
1005 00
```

The odd thing about this piece of code is the FD which LADS will assemble into address $1004. How does $FD tell the computer to branch back to $1002? $FD is 253 decimal. Now it begins to be clear why relative addressing used to be so messy to program. If you are curious, numbers larger than 127, when used as arguments for the B instructions, tell the computer to go *back down* to lower addresses. What's worse, the larger the number, the *less* far down it goes. In this case, the computer counts the address $1005 as zero and counts backward thus:

```
1005 =   0 = $00
1004 = 255 = $FF
1003 = 254 = $FE
1002 = 253 = $FD
```

Not a very pretty counting method. It's easy for the computer to deal with this, but to us it's awkward and strange. Fortunately, all that we LADS assembler users need do is to assign a label to the address we're branching to and use the label as the address (as if it were an *absolute* address). The assembler will do the hard part. So, relative branching becomes quite easy when using LADS because you label addresses and, thus, don't need to know the particular address to give as the argument of the B instructions (or JSR or JMP either). (However, if you're using the simple assembler in the 128's monitor, you *will* need to specify an address; there are no labels permitted in the monitor.)

The strange counting method illustrated by relative addressing is the way that the computer handles negative numbers. It thinks of the leftmost bit in a byte as the sign bit.

Whether the bit is on or off signifies a positive or negative number. For the beginning ML programmer, however, it's just as well to forget all about negative numbers. You won't find that you'll need to use them since practically everything you'll want to do can be done with positive integers.

Before leaving our discussion of branching, let's look at one special problem that you *will* need to deal with if you use the simple assembler in the monitor. When you are using one of the branch instructions, you sometimes branch forward. Let's say that you want to have a different kind of FOR-NEXT loop:

```
1000  LDX  #$0
1002  INX
1003  BEQ  $100A
1005  JMP  $1002
1008  BRK
1009  BRK
100A  BRK
```

When jumping forward, you often do not yet know the precise address you want to branch to. In the example above, we really wanted to go to $1008 when the loop was finished (when X was equal to zero), but we just entered an approximate address ($100A) and made a note of the place where this guess appeared ($1004). Then, using the direct memory changing function in the monitor, we can change location $1004 to the correct offset when we know what it should be.

Forward counting is easy. When we learned that we wanted to go to $1008, we would change the number $5 in address $1004 to $3.

Remember that you start counting from zero from the address immediately following the branch instruction. For example, a jump to $1008 would be three because you count $1005=0, $1006=1, $1007=2, $1008=3. All this confusion disappears after writing a few programs and practicing with estimated branch addresses. Luckily, the assembler does all the backward branches. That's lucky because they are much harder to calculate.

## Unknown Forward Branches

If you are using LADS, all branches are given *names* rather than addresses. These names are called *labels,* and they are automatically calculated for you by the assembler. You would write the above example with LADS in this way:

```
            LDX  #0
COUNTUP     INX
            BEQ  MORETHINGS ;or any other label you want
                              to give it
            JMP  COUNTUP    ;jumps also have labels as
                              their targets
MORETHINGS BRK
```

With LADS and other advanced assemblers, you'll generally want to use labels instead of actual addresses. This makes things pretty easy on the programmer. LADS does much of the busywork for you, particularly if you make good use of its pseudo-ops. By the way, pseudo-ops are essentially instructions directly to the assembler, such as "please insert the following as pure ASCII text," but which are not normal 6502 instructions that get translated into ML object code. Instead, a pseudo-op is a request to the assembler program to perform some extra service for the programmer. We'll go into them in detail later.

## Absolute,X and Absolute,Y

Another important mode provides you with an easy way to access lists or tables. This method looks like absolute addressing, but you attach an X or a Y to the address. The X and Y stand for the X and Y registers, which are being used in this technique as *offsets*. That is, if the X register contains the number 3, then whatever address you type in will have 3 added to it. If X holds a 3 and you type LDA $1000,X, you will LoaD Accumulator with the value (number) which is in memory cell $1003. *The register value is added to the absolute address.*

Another addressing method called *zero page,X* works the same way: LDA $05,X. (Load from cell 5 plus whatever's in the X register.) These indexed addressing modes let you easily transfer or search through messages, lists, or tables. Error messages can be sent to the screen using such a method. Assume that you set it up so that the words SYNTAX ERROR are held in some part of memory because you sometimes need to send them to the screen from your program. You might have a whole *table* of such messages. But we'll say that the words SYNTAX ERROR are stored at address $3000. Your screen memory address is 1024 ($0400 hex); here's how you would send the message:

| | | | | |
|---|---|---|---|---|
| **1000** | **LDX** | **#$00** | | Set the counter register to zero. |
| **1002** | **LOOP** | **LDA** | **$3000,X** | Get a letter at 3000 + X. |
| **1005** | **BEQ** | **QUIT** | | If the letter is a zero, we've reached the end of the message, so we branch to the end of this routine. |
| **1007** | **STA** | | **$0400,X** | Send the letter to 0400 + X. |
| **100A** | **INX** | | | Increment the counter so that the next letter in the message as well as the next screen position are pointed to. |
| **100B** | **JMP** | **LOOP** | | Jump to the load instruction to fetch the next character. |
| **1010** | **QUIT** | **BRK** | | Task completed, message transferred. |

This sort of indexed looping is an extremely common ML programming device. It can be used to create delays (FOR T = 1 TO 5000: NEXT T), to transfer any chunk of memory to another place, to check the status of memory (to see, for example, if a particular word appeared somewhere on the screen), and to perform many other tasks. It is a fundamental, all-purpose machine language technique.

Here's a fast way to fill your screen or any other area of memory. This is a full source code for the demonstration screen-fill example we tried in Chapter 1. See if you can follow how this indexed addressing works. What bytes are filled in and when? At ML speeds, it isn't necessary to fill them in order—nobody would see an irregular filling pattern because, like magic, it all happens too fast for the eye to see (see Program 4-2).

### Program 4-2. Filling the Screen with the letter *A*

```
10 *= $B00
20 .O
30 .S
40 A = $01;                   SCREEN CODE FOR "A"
50 ;
60 LDY #0;                    SET COUNTER TO ZERO
70 LDA #A
80 STA $0400,Y
90 STA $0500,Y
100 STA $0600,Y
110 STA $0700,Y
120 INY;                      RAISE COUNTER BY 1
130 BNE LOOP;                 IF Y IS NOT YET ZERO, KEEP GOING
140 RTS
```

Compare this with the program on page *xii* to see the effects of using a different screen starting address and how source code is a more elaborate version of what you get when you run the monitor's disassembler to get an ML program listing.

## Indirect Y

This addressing mode is a real workhorse; you'll use it often. Several of the examples in this book refer to it and explain it in context. The argument you use with this mode isn't so much an *address in itself* as a method of *creating* an address. It looks like this:

```
4000 STA ($80),Y
```

Seems innocent enough. That Y works like the other kinds of index modes we've discussed before. Whatever is in the Y register is added to the final address.

But watch out for those parentheses. They mean that $80 is *not* the real address here. We're not going to put the byte in the accumulator into address $80 plus the value of Y. Instead, addresses $80 and $81 are themselves *holding* the address we are sending our byte to. We are not sending to $0080; hence, the name for this mode is *indirect* Y.

Where does the byte in the accumulator end up? It depends what address you've stored in bytes $80 and $81. If $80 and $81 have these numbers in them:

```
$0080 01
$0081 20
```

and Y is holding a 5, then the byte in A will end up in address $2006. How did we get $2006?

First, you've got to mentally swap the numbers in $80 and $81. The 8502 requires that *address pointers* be listed in backward order: The pointer is holding $2001, not $0120. Then, you've got to add the value in the Y register, 5, and you get $2006.

This is a valuable tool, even if it's perplexing at first. You should familiarize yourself with it. It lets you get easy access to many memory locations very quickly by just changing the Y register (using INY or DEY) or by directly changing the address pointer itself (using INC or DEC, instructions that raise or lower a byte in RAM memory by one). You can make radical shifts with this pointer-changing technique. You can shift up a whole page (256 bytes) by simply INC $81: That will change your target address from $2001 to $2101. To go down four pages, subtract four from address $81. Combine this with the indexing that the Y register is doing for you, and you've got greater efficiency, greater reach to all the RAM you want to manipulate.

Right now you're paying the only price you'll ever pay for this valuable tool: It's possibly the most perplexing thing when you're learning ML. You've got to try it a few times, scratch your head, and get the concept.

Let's clear away some of the fog. How were those bytes at $80 and $81 selected to be the ones holding our indirect address? The programmer decides where *address pointers* are stashed (they must be in zero page). You figure out where the safe places are in zero page, and you use them for your pointers. That's the main use that you'll have for zero page. Remember that the creators of the 128 set aside zero page bytes $FA through $FE for our use. The 128 leaves them alone, so there's room for two of your indirect Y pointers in that safe area.

How did the numbers $20 and $01 get into the pointer in the example above? The programmer put them there. As part of the initial activities of an ML program, you stick byte-pairs (these address pointers) into zero page. If you're using a simple assembler, you'll need to keep a record of the pointers on paper. If you're using LADS, you give the pointers labels like this:

**SCREENPOINTER = $80**

And you can also have a label for the actual screen address:

**SCREEN = $0400**

Then, to set up a pointer, you use some pseudo-ops in LADS which break a two-byte address like $0400 into halves for storage in pointers:

```
LDA #<SCREEN;          loads the low byte
STA SCREENPOINTER
LDA #>SCREEN;          loads the high byte
STA SCREENPOINTER+1;   stores into address SCREENPOINTER
                       plus 1 ($81)
```

When an address is set up in a pointer, it's split in half. The address $0400 was split in the example above. When programming in ML, it's useful to distinguish between the two halves by saying that one of the bytes is the LSB (least significant byte) and the other is the MSB (most significant byte). In our example, the $00 is the LSB, and the $04 is the MSB. That's not because one number is smaller than the other; rather, it's because they are in different positions in the two-byte address. The position on the left is of far more significance than the position on the right in $0400. It's the same for decimal numbers: 5015 when chopped in half means that the left half stands for fifty 100's and the right half only stands for fifteen 1's. Clearly the right position is the *less significant*.

Note that every time you add one to the MSB of a double-byte hex number in ML, you are adding one page, 256. This is how you can INC or DEC the MSB of your pointer and move quickly through the "pages" of memory. And, remember, you store pointers in reverse order when you are setting up a pointer, LSB, MSB:

```
0080 00
0081 04;  a pointer to the screen memory of the 128
```

## Indirect X

This addressing mode is rarely used. It makes it possible to set up a *group* of pointers, a cluster of them, in zero page. It's like indirect Y, except the X register value is not added to the address pointer to form the ultimate address target. Rather, X points to the *pointer* you desire to use. Nothing is added to the address held in the pointer. It looks like this:

```
5000 STA ($90,X)
```

To see it in action, let's assume that you've already set up a cluster of pointers in zero page. It's a table of pointers, not just one:

```
0090  $00;  Pointer 1
0091  $04;  points to $0400
0092  $05;  Pointer 2
0093  $70;  points to $7005
0094  $EA;  Pointer 3
0095  $81;  points to $81EA
```

If X holds a 2 when we STA ($90,X), then the byte in the accumulator will be sent to address $7005. If X holds a 4, the byte will go to $81EA.

All things considered, this addressing mode has little to recommend it. If you set up the same table, you could access these pointers just as easily and have the flexibility of that Y index into the bargain. Who knows why the designers of the 8502 chip included this mode?

### Accumulator Mode

ASL, LSR, ROL, and ROR shift the *bits* in the byte held in the accumulator. We'll touch on this shifting in Chapter 6 when we discuss the instruction set. This mode doesn't really have much to do with addressing as such, but it's always listed as a separate mode.

### Zero Page,Y

This mode can be used with only two instructions: LDX and STX. Otherwise, it operates just like zero page,X discussed above.

### What to Remember

There you have them, 13 addressing modes to choose from. However, there are only six that you should focus on. Try practicing with them until you understand their uses: immediate, absolute (plus absolute,X and ,Y), zero page, and indirect Y. The rest are either unimportant when you're programming because they are automatic (like the *implied* mode) or are not really worth bothering with. Now that we've surveyed the ways you can move numbers around, it's time to see how to do arithmetic in ML.

# Chapter 5

# Arithmetic

# Arithmetic

There'll be many things that you'll want to do in ML, but complicated math is not one of them. Mathematics beyond simple addition, subtraction, multiplication, and division will not be covered in this book. For games and most other ML for personal computing, you won't need to use complex math. In this chapter we'll cover what you are likely to use. BASIC is well-suited to sophisticated mathematical programming and is far easier to work with for such tasks. If you're planning a program that's going to involve trigonometry or quadratic equations, use BASIC.

But before we look at ML arithmetic, let's briefly review an important concept: how the computer tells the difference between addresses, numbers as such, and instructions. It is valuable to be able to visualize what the computer is going to do as it comes upon each byte in your ML routine.

Even when a computer appears to be working with words, letters of the alphabet, graphics symbols, and the like, *it is still working with numbers*. A computer works *only* with numbers. The ASCII code is a convention by which a computer understands that when the context is alphabetic, the number 65 means the letter *A*. At first this is confusing. How does it know when 65 is *A* and when it is just 65? And there's a third possibility: The 65 could represent the cell 65 in the computer's memory, the sixty-fifth address.

It is worth remembering that, like us, the computer means different things at different times when it uses a symbol (like 65). We can mean a street address by it, a temperature, or a code. We could agree that whenever we used the symbol 65, we were ready to leave the party. We would look meaningfully at our companion and say, "Everyone expects to retire at *sixty-five*." Then hope they get the hint and remember the code.

The point is that symbols aren't anything in themselves. They *stand* for other things, and what they stand for must be agreed upon in advance. There must be rules. A code is an agreement in advance that one thing symbolizes another.

## The Computer's Rules

Inside your machine, at the most basic level, there is a stream of input. The stream flows continually past a "gate" like a river through a canal. For 99 percent of the time, the 128 sees a continuous stream of 88's.

When you first turn it on, the computer just sits there.

What's it doing? It will be updating its clock, and it's holding things coherent on the TV screen—but it mainly waits in an endless loop for you to press a key on your keyboard to let it know what it's supposed to do.

There is a memory cell inside your 128 which the computer constantly checks. This byte in the 128 is located at $D4. While no key is pressed, $D4 holds the number 88. When a key is hit on the keyboard, however, a different number appears in $D4, a number unique to the key pressed called its *keyboard matrix code.* This isn't the same as the ASCII code that you use to print to the screen. However, you can use this matrix code to make branches and decisions just as well as any other code. For example, anything other than 88 in $D4 signals that someone is typing something on the keyboard. If the RETURN key is pressed, a 1 will appear in location $D4. Finally, after centuries (the computer's sense of time differs from ours) here is something to work with. Something has come up to the gate at last.

But assume that someone hits the RETURN key, and a 1 appears in location $D4. You notice the effect at once—everything on the screen moves up one line, because 1 (in the keyboard matrix code) stands for a carriage return. How did the 128 know that you were not intending to type the *number* 1 when it saw 1 in the keyboard sampling cell? Simple. The number 1, and any other keyboard input, is always read from $D4 as a keyboard matrix code number. Besides, there's a difference between the number 1 and the ASCII or matrix codes for the *character* 1.

Let's look at this a slightly different way. Say that someone typed in the number 141 on they keyboard. The matrix code for each of those three *characters* 1, 4, and 1 would appear, in turn, in cell $D4 for as long as each key was being pressed. But, in the matrix code or ASCII, the digits from 0 through 9 are the only number symbols. There is no single symbol for the three characters 1 4 1. So, when you type in a 1 followed immediately by a 4 and then another 1, the computer's input-from-keyboard routine notices that you have not pressed one of the "instant action" keys (such as the ESC, TAB, or cursor-control keys). Rather, you typed 1 and 4 and another 1—the keyboard sampling cell, the "which key pressed" location in zero page at $D4, received the matrix code for 1, and then for 4, and finally another 1. And, in between each of these codes, it received 88 showing that the human, operating at slow human speeds, was not pressing any keys for a time.

The point is that hitting the key labeled 1 followed by the key labeled 4 followed by another 1 is not storing those numbers into that sampling cell at $D4. Instead, these keypresses are stored as *characters*. On the ML level, numbers are distinct from characters. A character like 3 has an ASCII and matrix code value which differs from its numeric value. In other words, typing 1 4 1 will not result in the computer seeing a 1, a 4, and a 1. Type in this little BASIC program to see what's happening in $D4:

```
10 PRINT PEEK(212);:GOTO 10
```

and then type on the keyboard. Each key has a different matrix value. What happens when you SHIFT or ESC a key?

Incidentally, 128's ASCII code representations (as distinct from the matrix code) of the digits are easy to remember in hex: 0 is $30, 1 is $31, ... up to $39 for 9. In decimal, the digits would be 48 through 57. The matrix code follows no particular pattern.

The point of all this is that the computer decides the "meaning" of the numbers which flow into and through it by each number's *context*. If it is in "alphabetic" mode, the computer will see the number 65 as *A*; or if it has just received an *A*, it might see a subsequent number 65 as an address to store the *A*. It all depends on the events that surround a given number. We can illustrate this with a simple example:

```
2000  LDA #$C1   $A9 (169)  $C1 (193)
2002  STA $C1    $85 (133)  $C1 (193)
```

This short ML program (the numbers in parentheses are the decimal values) shows how the computer can "expect" different meanings from the number 193 ($C1 hex). When it receives an *instruction* to perform an action, it is then prepared to act *upon* a number. The instruction comes first and, since it is the first thing the computer sees when it starts a job, it *knows that the number $A9 (169) is not a number.*

It has to be one of the ML instructions from its set of instructions (see Appendix A).

### Instructions and Their Arguments

The computer would no more think of this first 169 as the *number* 169 than you would seal an envelope before the letter was inside. If you are sending out a pile of Christmas cards, you perform instruction-argument just the way the computer does: You (1) fill the envelope (instruction) (2) with a card (argument, or operand). You don't get the envelopes confused with the cards and try to stuff an envelope into a card.

All actions do something *to* something. A computer's action is called an instruction (or, in its numeric form as part of an ML program inside the computer's memory, it's called an *opcode* for *operation code*). The target of the action is called its *argument,* or *operand.* In our program above, the computer must LoaD Accumulator with 193. The # symbol means *immediate;* the target is right there in the next memory cell following the LDA instruction, so it isn't supposed to be fetched from a distant memory cell. That 193, however, is not another instruction; it's the number 193.

Then, after this action has been completed, after the accumulator contains the number 193, the next number (the 133 which means STore Accumulator in zero page, the first 256 cells) *must be* an instruction, the start of another complete action. And, once again, the computer knows that the instruction 133 must be followed by an address of a cell in memory to store to. So, in the example, we've got a total of four numbers: 169, 193, 133, and 193. If you PEEKed at this little ML routine, you'd find these numbers in this order. But when this ML program is run, is executed by the 8502, it will see 169 as an instruction, 193 as a number, 133 as another instruction, and the 193 following that instruction as an address in memory. Instructions, numbers, addresses—they are all mixed in together, but the chip can figure out which is which based upon their context. It knows that LDA # will be followed by a single-byte *number* because that's what LDA in the immediate addressing mode demands. The computer would no more expect an address to come after LDA # than you would expect someone to say "1700 Taylor Street" when you asked what time it was.

Think of the computer as completing each action and then looking for another instruction. It moves through your list of instructions logically. Recall from the last chapter that the target can be "implied" in the sense that INX simply increases the X register by one. The one is "implied" by the instruction itself, so there is no target argument in these cases. The next cell in this case *must* also contain an instruction for a new instruction-argument cycle.

Some instructions call for a single-byte argument. LDA #193 is of this type. You cannot LoaD Accumulator with anything greater than 255. The accumulator is only one byte large, so anything that can be loaded into it can also be only a single byte large. (Recall that 255, $FF, is the largest number that can be represented by a single byte.)

STA $C1 also has a one-byte argument because the target address for the STore Accumulator is, in this case, in zero page.

Storing to zero page or loading from it will need only a one-byte argument—the address. Zero page addressing is a special case, but an assembler program will take care of it for you. It will pick the correct opcode for this addressing mode when you type LDA $C1. Typing in LDA $00C1 would create ML code that performs the same operation, though it would use three bytes instead of two to do it.

But how does the chip know that a given instruction is self-contained like the INY, implied addressing mode? Or another instruction uses up two bytes like zero page addressing (STA $15 uses one byte for the STA command and one byte for the $15)? Or the biggest addressing modes, like STA $1500, absolute addressing, take three bytes before they can look for the next instruction in a program?

Inside the chip is a *program counter* (PC). It has a list of all the ML instructions. And it knows how many bytes—one, two, or three—that each instruction takes up. During an ML program's execution, the program counter acts like a finger that keeps track of where the computer is located at any given time in its trip up the series of ML instructions that comprise your program. Each instruction takes up one, two, or three bytes, depending on what type of addressing is going on. The program counter looks at its list and moves up the appropriate number of bytes to show where the next instruction will be.

## Context Defines Meaning

TXA uses only one byte, so the program counter moves ahead one byte and stops and waits until the value in the X register is moved over into the accumulator. TXA is supposed to transfer into the accumulator whatever number is in the X register. Then the computer asks the PC, "Where are we?" and the PC is pointing to the address of the next instruction. The PC never points to an argument. It skips over them because it knows how many bytes each addressing mode uses up in a program.

Say that the next instruction after TXA is LDA $15. This is a two-byte-long, zero page addressing mode. The PC looks on its list and moves up two bytes. The longest possible instruction would use three bytes, such as LDA $5000 (absolute addressing). The PC counts up three and points. Your assembler would translate LDA $15 into $A5 and POKE it. It would translate LDA $1500 into $AD and POKE that. Since the opcodes that get POKEd are different, even though the LDA mnemonics are identical, the computer can know how many bytes a given instruction will use up. That's how it knows where the next instruction must be in your program.

Having reviewed the way that your computer makes *contextual* sense out of the mass of seemingly similar numbers of which an ML program is composed, we can now move on to see how elementary arithmetic is performed in ML.

## Addition

Arithmetic is performed in the accumulator. The accumulator holds the first number, the target address holds the second number (but is not affected by the activities), and the result is left in the accumulator. So,

**LDA #$40** Remember, the # means immediate, the $ means hex.
**ADC #$01**

will result in the number $41 being left in the accumulator. We could then STA that number wherever we wanted. Simple enough.

The ADC means ADd with Carry. If an addition results in a number higher than 256 (if we added, say, 250 + 7), then there would have to be a way to show that the number left behind in the accumulator isn't the correct result—that what's in the accumulator isn't the total, it's the *carry*.

After adding 250 + 7, you would find a 1 in the accumulator, and the *carry flag* would be up.

That means that you must add 256 to whatever is in the accumulator to find the real answer: 257.

To make sure that things never get confused, *always CLC (CLear the Carry flag) before you do any addition.* CLC will push the carry flag down (in case it was up from some previous event in your program). Then, if you find that it is up after the addition (ADC), you'll know that you need to add 256 to whatever is in the accumulator. You'll know that the accumulator is holding the carry, not the total result.

One other point about the status register: There is another flag, the *decimal* flag. If you ever set this flag up (with the SED, SEt Decimal instruction), all addition and subtraction is performed in a *decimal mode* in which the carry flag is set whenever an addition exceeds 99. In this book, we are not going into the decimal mode at all. Decimal mode has little value in ML programming. It's another one of those things that sounds good, but doesn't do much in practice.

## Adding Numbers Larger Than 255

We have already discussed the idea of setting aside some memory cells as a table for data. To do this, we simply make a note to ourselves that, say, addresses $D6 and $D7 are declared a zone for our personal use as a storage area. Using a typical example, let's think of this two-byte zone as the place that holds the address of a "moving finger" going through a list of names we've stored in RAM. As long as the zone is not in ROM or used by our program elsewhere or used by the computer (see the memory map in Appendix C or use the safe areas like $FA–$FE we discussed earlier), it's fine to declare an area a data zone. It is a good idea (especially with longer programs) to make notes on a piece of paper to show where you intend to have your subroutines, your main loop, your initialization, and your miscellaneous data—names, messages for the screen, input from the keyboard, and so on. This is one of those things that BASIC does for you automatically, but which you must do for yourself in ML. However, you can set up data zones with the LADS assembler by using the .BYTE, =, or *= pseudo-ops. It's generally a good idea to put message tables, and so forth, at the very end of your program.

When BASIC creates a string variable, it sets aside an area to store variables. This is what DIM does. In ML, you set aside your own areas by simply finding a clear memory space and not writing a part of your program into it (or by staking out some memory with .BYTE or *= in LADS). Part of your data zone can be special registers you declare to hold the results of addition or subtraction.

But back to our example: You might make a note to yourself that after finding these zero page locations safe to use, $D6 and $D7 will hold the current position within a list of names in your database. This is a *pointer,* and we can look at all the bytes within our database by adjusting this pointer in $D6 and $D7. In this way we can efficiently search through the database.

Since the "moving finger" searching through the database is constantly in motion, this pointer will be changing all the time as it looks for your target information. Notice that you need *two* bytes for this pointer. That is because one byte could hold only a number from 0 through 255. Two bytes together, though, can hold a number up to 65535 (all the possible addresses in the 128 without bank switching).

To define the pointer location, you could do this in LADS:

**FINGER = $D6**

If you needed another two-byte pointer to hold another address, you could write this:

**OTHER = $EB**

and so on, using safe areas, for as many pointers as you needed.

Since your 128 can address only a total of 65536 memory cells with any single instruction, two-byte registers like these can address *any* addressable cell in your current bank. So if your "moving finger" is supposed to look up the name "Mitchell, Nancy" in the database, you'll want to start off by looking for the letter *M.* In setting up your list of names, you decided that each entry, each record, would be given 40 bytes of space. Thus, you are going to be adding 40 to the FINGER if the first character in the first record isn't an *M.* Let's say that the list of records starts in memory at address $8000.

Before accessing the list, we punch in the target address:

**LDA #0:STA $D6:LDA #$80:STA $D7**

Or you could accomplish the same thing with the LADS assembler by using labels and the #> and #< pseudo-ops which extract the MSB and LSB of a label's address:

**LDA #<DATA:STA FINGER:LDA #>DATA:STA FINGER+1.**

The FINGER address register now looks like this in the monitor: $00D6 00 80 (remember that the higher, most significant byte, comes *after* the LSB, the least significant byte). To move to the next name in the list, we want FINGER to be $00D6 28 80. (The 28 is hex for 40.) In other words, we're going to move the finger up one record in the database list. To do this, we need to add $28 (40 decimal) to the pointer, the FINGER.

Remember the indirect Y addressing mode which lets us use an address in zero page as a *pointer* to another address in memory? The number in the Y register is added to whatever address sits in $D6 and $D7, so we don't STA to $D6 or $D7, but rather to the address that they *contain:* STA ($D6),Y.

How to add $28 to the FINGER pointer? First of all, CLC (CLear the Carry) to be sure that flag is down. This example is written for the mini-assembler in the monitor:

```
1000  CLC        $1000 is the location of our "add 40 to FINGER"
                 subroutine.
1001  LDA  $D6   We fetch the LSB of FINGER.
1003  ADC  #$28  Add 40.
1006  STA  $D6   Put the new result into FINGER.
1008  LDA  $D7   Get the MSB of FINGER.
100A  ADC  #$00  Add with carry to the MSB of FINGER.
1010  STA  $D7   Update FINGER'S MSB.
```

That's it. Any carry will automatically set the carry flag up during the ADC action on the LSB and will be added into the result when we ADC to the MSB. It's all quite similar to the way that we add numbers, putting a carry onto the next column when we get more than a ten in the first column. And this carrying is why we always CLC (clear the carry flag; put it down) just before additions. If the carry is set, we could get the wrong answer if our problem did not result in a carry. Did the addition above cause a carry? (Remember, we started with a value of $8000 in FINGER.)

Note that we need not check for any carries during the MSB+MSB addition. Any carries resulting in a database address greater than $FFFF (65535) would be impossible on our machines.

The 8502 is permitted to address $FFFF tops, under normal conditions. However, it is possible to add numbers larger than 65535 by simply using more than two bytes and continuing to add *with carry* across a multibyte chain.

The example above would be somewhat easier with LADS because you would substitute label names (FINGER and DATA, in this case) for the numbers. Also, you could define another label to hold the size of a record (RECORD = 40), and then line 1003 would read ADC #RECORD.

### Subtraction

As you might expect, subtracting single-byte numbers is a snap:

```
LDA  #$41
SBC  #$01
```

results in a $40 being left in the accumulator. As before, though, it's important to make it a habit to deal with the carry flag before each calculation. When subtracting, however, you *set* the carry flag: SEC. Why is unimportant. *Just always SEC before any subtractions,* and your answers will be correct. Here's double subtracting that will move the FINGER back down one record in the data list:

```
$1020 SEC          $1020 is where we arbitrarily decided to locate
                   our "take 40 from FINGER" subroutine.
 1021 LDA  $D6     Get the LSB of FINGER.
 1023 SBC  #$28    LSB of the size of a single record.
 1026 STA  $D6     Put the new result into FINGER.
 1028 LDA  $D7     Get FINGER's MSB.
 102A SBC  #$00    Subtract the MSB of the size of a single record.
 102D STA  $D7     Update FINGER's MSB.
```

### Multiplication and Division

Multiplying could be done by repeated adding. To multiply 5 × 4, you could just add 4 + 4 + 4 + 4 + 4. One way would be to set up two registers like the ones we've used before. Both registers (or storage zones) could contain a 4, and then you could loop through an add-these-two-registers subroutine five times. For practical purposes, however, multiplying and dividing are more easily accomplished in BASIC. They are simply not worth the trouble of setting up in ML, especially if you need to involve decimal-point fractions (floating-point arithmetic). Perhaps surprisingly, for games and most personal computing tasks where ML routines and programs are created, there is little use either for negative numbers or arithmetic beyond simple addition and subtraction. When we get into division and multiplication, we've gone beyond the simple arithmetic that you'll need—unless you're writing an accounting program or a spreadsheet program.

If you find that you do need complicated mathematical structures, create the program in BASIC, adding ML where super speeds are desirable. Such hybrid programs are efficient and, in their way, elegant.

One final note: An easy way to divide the number in the accumulator by two is to LSR. Try it. Similarly, you can multiply by two with ASL. We'll define LSR and ASL in the next chapter. If you're interested in using these techniques, take a look at the "Library of Subroutines" (Appendix E).

### Double Comparison

One rather tricky technique is used fairly often in ML and should be learned. It is tricky because two of the B branching instructions *seem* to be worth using in this context, but are best avoided for this kind of comparing. If you're trying to keep track of the location of a record within a database, this will be a two-byte address. If you need to compare those two bytes against another two-byte address, you'll need a "double-compare" subroutine. You might, for example, want to check whether or not one record is located higher in the database than another.

Double-compare is also useful in any other ML where you need to manipulate numbers larger than can be held in one byte (where the single CMP instruction would be able to compare them for you).

The problem is the BPL instruction (Branch on PLus) and its companion, BMI (Branch on MInus). *Don't use them* for comparisons. In any comparisons, whether single- or double-byte, use BEQ to test if two numbers are equal, BNE for not equal, BCS for equal or higher, and BCC for lower. You can remember BCS because its *S* is *higher* and BCC because its *C* is *lower* in the alphabet. Program 5-1 shows one easy way to perform a double-compare.

**Program 5-1. Double-Compare**

```
10 *= $B00
20 .S
30 .O
40 START SEC
50 LDA TESTED;       COMPARE THE LOW BYTES
60 SBC SECOND
70 STA TEMP
80 LDA TESTED+1;     COMPARE THE HIGH BYTES
90 SBC SECOND+1
100 ORA TEMP
110 BEQ EQUAL;       TESTED = SECOND
120 BCC LOWER;       TESTED < SECOND
130 BCS HIGHER;      TESTED > SECOND
140 ;
150 ;------------ LANDING PLACES -----------
160 LOWER BRK
170 EQUAL BRK
180 HIGHER BRK
400 ;------------ STORAGE AREA -------------
500 TEMP .BYTE 0
600 SECOND .BYTE 0 0
700 TESTED .BYTE 0 0
710 .END 5-1
```

This is LADS at work. Recall that with assemblers like LADS, you can use line numbers and labels, add numbers to labels (see the TESTED + 1 in line 80), add comments, and all the rest.

To try out this double comparison, type in the source code in Program 5-1. Then assemble it with LADS. Now go into the monitor with F8, and type D $B00 to see the results of your assembly. Notice the eight zeros at the end of the little program. You can then try putting different numbers into TESTED and SECOND and reassemble (or just insert them in the monitor using the > monitor memory change command).

Notice that the numbers being compared are not really interchangeable. One is the "tested" number, and the other is the number it is being tested against, the one we're calling SECOND in our label scheme here. As you can see, you've got to keep it straight in your mind which number is being tested, or the results won't make much sense.

When you've set up two double-byte numbers in the registers (TESTED and SECOND), you can run this routine from within the monitor by typing G B00. All that will happen is that you will land on a BRK instruction and halt further activity. Where you land tells you the results of the comparison. If the numbers are equal, you land at EQUAL's address. If the tested number is less than the second number, you'll end up in the location of LOWER, and so forth. (The monitor will give a PC number which is *two bytes above* the actual BRK instruction, so take that into account.)

You could test using only a BNE if all you needed to know is whether or not the two numbers are equal. You could leave out some of these branch tests if you're not interested in them. Play around with this until you've understood the ideas involved.

In a real program, you would be branching to addresses in your ML program which *do something* if the numbers under comparison are equal or one is greater or whatever. This example sends the computer to LOWER, EQUAL, or HIGHER, where it comes to an abrupt halt just to let you see the effects of a double-compare subroutine, but in a real program EQUAL would be the start of a subroutine which accomplished something based on the discovery of equality. Above all, remember that you should use BCC and BCS (*not* BPL or BMI) when comparing in ML.

Some might wonder why we use CMP to test the low bytes and then switch to SBC to test the high bytes. It's just a convenience. CoMPare is a subtraction of one number from another. The only difference between CMP and SBC, really, is that subtraction replaces the number in the accumulator with the result. LDA #5:SBC #2 will leave 3 in the accumulator. Using LDA #5:CMP #2 leaves the 5 in the accumulator, and all that happens is that flags are affected. Both SBC and CMP have an effect on the zero, negative, and carry flags. In our double-compare we don't care if there is a result left in the accumulator or not. So, we can use either SBC or CMP. The reason for starting off with CMP, however, is that we don't have to SEC (set the carry flag) as we always need to do before an SBC.

# Chapter 6

# The Instruction Set

# The Instruction Set

There are 56 instructions (commands) available in 8502 machine language. Most versions of BASIC have about 50 commands. Some BASIC instructions are rarely used by the majority of programmers, for example, END, SGN, TAN, USR. Some, such as LET, contribute nothing to a program and seem to have remained in the language for nostalgic reasons. Others, like TAN, have uses that are highly specialized.

There are surplus commands in computer languages just as there are surplus words in English. People don't often say *culpability*. They usually just say *guilt*. The message gets across without using the entire dictionary. The simple, common words can do the job.

Machine language is the same as any other language in this respect. There are around 20 heavily used instructions. The 36 remaining ones are used far less often. You can switch into the 128's monitor with F8 and look at part of your computer's ROM. To look at BASIC ROM, once in the monitor, type D F4000 and press RETURN. To see more, press D and RETURN. You can now read the machine language routines which comprise BASIC. You'll find interesting things all the way from $4000 up to $FFFF in bank 15. You'll also quickly discover that the accumulator is heavily trafficked (LDA and STA appear frequently in the disassembly), but you will have to hunt to find BVC, CLV, ROR, RTI, or SED.

ML, like BASIC, offers you many ways to accomplish the same job. Some programming solutions, of course, are better than others, but the main thing is to get the job done. An influence still lingers from the early days of computing when memory space was rare and expensive. This influence—that you should try to write programs using up as little memory as possible—can be safely ignored. Efficient memory use will often be at the bottom of your list of objectives when programming ML. It could hardly matter whether you use 25 instead of 15 bytes to print a message to the screen when your computer has space for programming which exceeds 130,000 bytes.

Rather than memorize each ML instruction individually, we will concentrate on the workhorses. Bizarre or arcane instructions will get only passing mention. Unless you are planning to use ML programs to interface to strange peripherals or need to do complex mathematical calculations and such, you will be able to write excellent machine language programs for nearly any application with the instructions we'll focus on in this book.

For each instruction group, we will describe three things before getting down to the details about programming with them: (1) what the instructions accomplish, (2) the addressing modes you can use with them, and (3) what they do, if anything, to the flags in the status register. A condensed, reference version of this information is also found in Appendix A.

### The Six Instruction Groups

The best way to approach the instruction set might be to break it down into the following six categories which group the instructions according to their functions:

1. Transporters
2. Arithmetic Group
3. Decision Makers
4. Loop Group
5. Subroutine and Jump Group
6. Debuggers

We will deal with each group in order, pointing out similarities to BASIC and describing the major uses for each.

As always, the best way to learn is by doing. Move bytes around. Use each instruction, typing a BRK as the final instruction to see the effects. If you LDA #65, look in the A register to see what happened. Then, STA $12 and check to see what was copied into address $12. If you send the byte in the accumulator (STA), what is left behind in the accumulator? Is it better to think of bytes being *copied* rather than being *sent*?

Play with each instruction to get a feel for it. Discover the effects, qualities, and limitations of these ML commands.

# 1. The Transporters: LDA, LDX, LDY STA, STX, STY TAX, TAY TXA, TYA

These instructions move a byte from one place in memory to another. To be more precise, they *copy* whatever value is in a source location into a target location. The source location still contains the byte, but after a "transporter" instruction, a copy of the byte is also in the target location. This *does* replace whatever used to be in the target.

All of them affect the N and Z flags, except STA, STX, and STY which do nothing to any flag.

There are a variety of addressing modes available to different instructions in this group. Check the chart in Appendix A for specifics.

Remember that the computer does things *one at a time*. Unlike the human brain which can carry out a thousand different instructions simultaneously (walk, talk, and smile, all at once), the computer goes from one tiny job to the next. It works through a series of instructions, raising the program counter (PC) each time it handles an instruction.

If you do a TYA, the PC goes up by one to the next address, and the computer looks at that next instruction. STA $80 is a two-byte-long instruction; it's zero page addressing, so PC=PC+2. STA $8600 is a three-byte-long absolute addressing mode, and PC=PC+3 automatically.

Recall that there's nothing larger than a three-byte increment of the PC. However, in each case, the PC is cranked up the right amount to make it point to the address for the next instruction. Things would quickly get out of control if the PC pointed to some argument (some address) thinking it was an instruction. It would be incorrect (and soon disastrous) if the PC pointed to the $15 in LDA $15.

If you type SYS 15000 from BASIC, the program counter is loaded with 15000, and the computer transfers control to the ML instructions which are (we hope) sitting at address 15000 (decimal) on up. It will then look at byte 15000 (decimal), expecting it to be an instruction. Since the computer does all this very fast, it can seem to be keeping score, bouncing the ball, moving the paddle, and everything else—simultaneously. It's not, though. It's flashing from one task to another and doing it so fast that it creates the illusion of simultaneity much the way that 24 still pictures per second look like motion in movies.

### The Programmer's Time Warp

Movies are, of course, lots of still pictures flipping by in rapid succession. Computer programs are composed of lots of individual instructions performed in rapid succession.

Grasping this sequential, step-by-step activity makes our programming job easier: We can think of large programs as single steps, coordinated into meaningful, harmonious actions. Now the computer will put a blank over the ball at the ball's current address, then adjust the ball address to move it slightly downward on the screen, then print the ball character to the new address. The main single-step action is moving information, as single-byte numbers, from here to there, in memory. We are always creating, updating, modifying, moving, and destroying single-byte variables. The moving is generally done from one double-byte address to another. But it all looks smooth to the player during a game.

Programming in ML can pull you into an eerie time warp. You might spend several hours constructing a program which executes in seconds. You are putting together instructions which will later be read and acted upon by coordinated electrons, moving at electron speeds. It's as if you spent an afternoon slowly and carefully drawing up pathways and patterns which would later be a single bolt of lightning.

### Registers

In ML there are three primary places where variables rest briefly on their way to memory cells: the X, the Y, and the A registers. And the A register (the accumulator) is the most frequently used; X and Y are used for looping and indexing. Each of these registers can grab a byte from anywhere in memory or can grab the byte from the address right after its own opcode (immediate mode addressing):

| | |
|---|---|
| **LDY $8000** | Puts the number at hex address 8000 into Y, without destroying it at $8000. |
| **LDY #65** | Puts the *decimal number* 65 into Y. (Remember, with the 128's built-in monitor, you'd need to add a + sign in front of the 65 to have the mini-assembler consider the 65 a decimal value: LDA #+65.) |
| **LDA** and **LDX** | Work the same. |

Be sure you understand what is happening here. LDY $1500 does not copy the byte in the Y register into address $1500. It's just the opposite. The number (or *value*, as it's sometimes called) in $1500 is copied into the Y register. This is *LoaD Y*.

To copy a byte from X, Y, or A, use STX, STY, or STA. For these "store-bytes" instructions, however, there is no immediate addressing mode. No STA #$15. It would make no sense to have STA #$15. That would be disruptive, for it *would modify the ML program itself. It would put the number 15 into the next cell beyond the STA instruction within the ML program itself.*

Another type of transporter moves bytes *between* registers—TAX, TAY, TXA, TYA. See the effect of writing the following. Look at the registers after executing this:

```
1000  LDA #$65
1002  TAY
1003  TAX
```

The number $65 is placed into the accumulator, then transferred to the Y register, then sent from the accumulator to X. All the while, however, the A register (the accumulator) is *not* being emptied. Sending bytes is not a transfer in the usual sense of the term *sending*. It is more as if a photocopy were made of the number, and then the *copy* was sent. The original stays behind after the copy is sent.

LDA #$15 followed by TAY would leave the $15 in the accumulator, sending a copy of $15 into the Y register.

Notice that you cannot directly move a byte from the X to the Y register or vice versa. There is no TXY or TYX.

### Flags Up and Down

Another effect of moving bytes around is that it sometimes throws a flag up or down in the status register. LDA (or LDX or LDY) will affect the N and Z, negative and zero, flags.

We will ignore the N flag. It changes when you used "signed numbers," a special technique to allow for negative numbers. For our purposes, the N flag will fly up and down all the time, and we won't care. We won't pay any attention to it; we won't test to see where it is. If you're curious, signed numbers are manipulated by allowing the seven bits on the right to hold the number, the leftmost bit to stand for positive or negative. We normally use a byte to hold values from 0 through 255. If we were working with "signed" numbers, anything higher than 127 would be considered a negative number since the leftmost bit would be "on"—and an LDA #255 would be thought of as −1.

This is another example of how the same thing (the number 255 in this case) can signify several different conditions, depending on the context in which it is being interpreted.

The Z flag, on the other hand, is quite important; we can't ignore this flag. It shows whether or not some action during a program run resulted in a zero. The branching instructions and looping depend on this flag, and we'll deal with the important zero-result effects below with the BNE and INX instructions, and so on.

No flags are affected by the STA, STX, or STY instruction.

### The Stack Can Take Care of Itself

There are some instructions which move bytes to and from the stack. These are for advanced ML programmers. PHA and PLA copy a byte from A to the stack and vice versa. PHP and PLP move the status register to and from the stack. TSX and TXS move the stack pointer to or from the X register. Forget them. Unless you know precisely what you are doing, you can cause havoc with your program by fooling with the stack. The main job for the stack is to hold the return addresses pushed into it when you JSR (Jump to SubRoutine). Then, when you come back from a subroutine (RTS), the computer pulls the addresses off the stack to find out where to go back to.

For most ML programming, avoid stack manipulation until you are an advanced programmer. If you manipulate the stack without great care, you'll cause an RTS to the wrong return address, and the computer will travel far, far beyond your control. If you are lucky, it sometimes lands on a BRK instruction and you fall into the monitor mode. The odds are that you would get lucky roughly once every 256 times. Don't count on it. Since BRK is rare in your BASIC ROM, the chances are pretty low.

You could fill large amounts of RAM with "snow" by putting zeros everywhere. This greatly improves the odds that a crash *will* hit a BRK. But why bother? Play it safe when you're writing a program.

As an aside, there is another use for snow, a blanket of "zero page snow." Recall that you can safely use some locations in zero page (addresses 0–255), but that your computer and many commercial programs compete for space in zero page because it's such a fast place to access. If you are planning to modify, say, a commercial word processor and need to make sure that it's not using a particular area of zero page for its own purposes, fill zero page with 00 (snow), put the word processor through its paces, and then take a look at the tracks, the nonzeros, in the snow.

## 2. The Arithmetic Group: ADC, SBC, SEC, CLC

Here are the commands which add, subtract, and set or clear the carry flag. ADC and SBC trigger the N, Z, C, and V (overflow) flags. CLC and SEC, needless to say, affect the C flag, and their only addressing mode is implied.

ADC and SBC can be used in eight addressing modes: immediate, absolute, zero page, (indirect,X), (indirect),Y, zero page,X, and absolute,X and ,Y.

Arithmetic was covered in the previous chapter. To review, the carry flag must be cleared with CLC before any addition. Before any subtraction, it must be set with SEC. The decimal mode should be cleared at the start of any program (the initialization) with CLD. You can multiply by two with ASL and divide by two with LSR. You can divide by four with LSR LSR or by eight with LSR LSR LSR. You could multiply a number by eight with ASL ASL ASL. What would this do to a number: ASL ASL ASL ASL? To multiply by numbers which aren't powers of two, use addition plus multiplication. To multiply by ten, for example, copy the original number temporarily to a vacant byte somewhere in memory. Then ASL ASL ASL to multiply it by eight. Multiply the original number by two with a single ASL. Then add them together.

If you're wondering about the V flag, it is rarely used for anything. You can forget about the branch which depends on it, BVC, too. Only five instructions affect it, and it relates to twos complement arithmetic which we've not touched on in this book. Like decimal mode or negative numbers, you will be able to construct your ML programs very effectively if you remain in complete ignorance of this mode. We have largely avoided discussion of most of the flags in the status register: B, D, I, N, and V. This avoidance has also removed several branch instructions from our consideration: BMI, BPL, BVC, and BVS. These flags and instructions are not usually found in ML programs, and their use is confined to specialized mathematical or interfacing applications. They will not be of use or interest to the majority of ML programmers. The only use for BPL or BMI which might interest you is that they can quickly detect whether a character is *shifted* above 128 in value. In the lower/uppercase character set, small *a* is 65, but capital *A* is 193. If you were going through a list of names and the way you had arranged to separate them was by shifting the first letter in each name, you could quickly LDA TARGET:BMI SHIFTED to detect that you had reached the end of a particular target name. Otherwise, forget BPL and BMI.

The two flags of interest to most ML programmers are the carry flag and the zero flag. That is why, in the following section, we will examine only the four branch instructions which test the C and Z flags. They are likely to be the only branching instructions that you'll ever find occasion to use.

## 3. The Decision Makers: BCC, BCS, BEQ, BNE, CMP

The four "branchers" here—they all begin with a *B*—have only one addressing mode. In fact, it's an interesting mode unique to the B instructions and created especially for them: *relative* addressing. They do not address a memory location as an *absolute* thing; rather, they address a location which is just a certain distance from their position in the ML code. Put another way, the argument of a B instruction is an offset which is *relative* to the position of the instruction itself. You never have to worry about relative instructions if you relocate an ML program, if you locate the ML program in some other place in RAM memory. The B instructions will work just as well no matter where your ML program is moved.

That's because their argument just says "add 5 to the present address" or "subtract 27" or whatever argument you give them. You *do* give the branchers actual addresses as you would in absolute addressing: BEQ $3560. However, your assembler will translate that $3560 into a different, somewhat strange, number that is used in relative addressing. (If you are using an advanced assembler like LADS, you will give label names as the argument of the branchers instead of actual numeric addresses.)

*The branchers cannot branch further back than 127 or further forward than 128 bytes.*

None of the brancher instructions have any effect whatsoever on any flags; instead, they are the instructions which *look at* the flags. They are the only instructions which base their activity on the condition of the status register and its flags. They're why the flags exist at all.

CMP is an exception. Many times it is the instruction that comes just before the branchers and sets flags for them to look at and make decisions about. Lots of instructions—LDA is one—will set or clear (put down) flags—but sometimes you need to use CMP to find out what's going on with the flags. CMP affects the N, Z, and C flags. CMP has many addressing modes available to it: immediate, absolute, zero page, (indirect,X), (indirect),Y, zero page,X, and absolute,X and ,Y.

You might, for example, LDA NAME:CMP SECONDNAME to see if both names start with the same letter (you would BEQ) or if they don't (BNE) or if the first is higher than the second (BCS) or lower (BCC). In all these cases, you branch based on what the CMP did to the flags. Let's take a closer look at what branching does for us and how to make the best use of it.

### The Foundations of Computer Power

This decision-maker group and the following group (loops) are the basis of our computers' enormous strength. The decision makers allow the computer to decide between two or more possible courses of action. This decision is based on comparisons. *If* the ball hits a wall, *then* reverse its direction. In BASIC, we use IF-THEN and ON-GOTO structures to make decisions and to make appropriate responses to conditions as they arise during a program run.

Recall that the 128 uses *memory-mapped video* in its 40-column mode, which means that you can treat the screen like an area of RAM memory. You can PEEK and POKE into it to create animation, text, or other visual events. In ML, you PEEK by LDA SCREEN and examine what you've PEEKed with CMP. You POKE via STA SCREEN.

CMP does comparisons. It tests the value at an address against what is in the accumulator. Less common are CPX and CPY.

Assume that we have just added 40 to a register we set aside to hold the current address-location of FINGER which points to records in our database. We want to POKE in a new record, but we need to locate a vacant record. We don't want to cover over a record that's in use.

In practical terms, you might have deleted several records within your database and, each time one is deleted, you just stick a zero into the first byte of the record's 40-byte space to show that it's empty. Thus, we can bounce along the records, looking at the first byte of each, to find an available empty record.

Recall that the very useful indirect Y addressing mode allows us to use an address in zero page as a *pointer* to another address in memory. The number in the Y register is added to whatever address sits in $D6,$D7; so we don't LDA from $D6 or $D7, but rather from the address that they *contain*, plus Y's value.

To see what's in the first byte of a record, we can do the following:

**LDY #$0** We want to fetch from the first byte, so we don't want to add anything to it. Y is set to zero.

**LDA ($D6),Y** Fetch whatever is sitting there. To review indirect,Y addressing once more, say that the address we are fetching from here is $1077. Address $D6 would hold the least significant byte, LSB ($77), and address $D7 would hold the MSB ($10). Notice that the argument of an indirect,Y instruction only mentions the lower address of the two-byte pointer, the $D6. The computer knows that it has to combine $D6 and $D7 to get the full address—and it does this automatically.

At this point, we might come upon a $CD or some other number which we would know indicated that this record was not deleted. Now that this questionable number sits in the accumulator, we will CMP it against a $0 which signals a deleted record. We could compare it with other numbers, too, numbers which we—in setting up the database—had decided would mean "old record" or "duplicated record" or some other housekeeping information which would help us in managing the data. It doesn't matter. The main thing is to compare it and find out the condition of this particular record:

| | | | |
|---|---|---|---|
| **2000** | **CMP** | **#$0** | Is it a zero? |
| **2002** | **BNE** | **$200A** | Branch if Not Equal (if not zero) to address $200A, which contains the first of a series of comparisons to see if it's an "old" or "duplicated" record, or the like. On the other hand, if the comparison *worked,* if it was a zero, so we didn't Branch Not Equal, then the next thing that happens is the instruction in address $2004. We "fall through" the BNE to an instruction which jumps to the subroutine, JSR, which moves the new record into the vacant record space, thus jumping past the series of comparisons for old, duplicated, and so forth. |
| **2004** | **JSR** | **$3000** | Insert new record subroutine. |
| **2007** | **JMP** | **$2020** | Jump over the rest of the comparisons. |
| **200A** | **CMP** | **#$1** | Is it an old record? |
| **200C** | **BNE** | **$2014** | If not, continue to next comparison. |
| **200E** | **JSR** | **$3050** | Perform the "old records" subroutine and... |
| **2011** | **JMP** | **$2020** | jump over the rest, as before in $2007. |
| **2014** | **CMP** | **#$2** | Is it a duplicated record? ... and so forth with as many comparisons as needed. |

This structure is to ML what ON-GOTO or ON-GOSUB is to BASIC. It allows you to take multiple actions based on a single LDA. Doing the CMP only once would be like IF-THEN.

## Other Branching Instructions

In addition to the BNE we just looked at, there are BCC, BCS, BEQ, BMI, BPL, BVC, and BVS. Learn BCC, BCS, BEQ, and BNE and you can safely ignore the others.

All of them are branching, if-then, instructions. They work in the same way that BNE does. You would write BEQ followed by the address you want to go to. If the result of the comparison is "yes, equal-to-zero is true," then the ML program will jump (branch) to the address which is the argument of the BEQ instruction. "True" here means that something EQuals zero. One example that would send up the Z flag (thereby triggering a branch with BEQ) is LDA #$00. The action of loading a zero into the accumulator sets the Z flag up.

You are allowed to branch either forward or backward from the address that holds the B instruction. However, you cannot branch any further than 128 bytes in either direction. If you want to go further, you must JMP (JuMP) or JSR (Jump to

SubRoutine). For all practical purposes, you will usually be branching to instructions located within 30 bytes of your B instruction in either direction. You will be taking care of most things right near where the CoMPare, or other flag-flipping event, takes place.

If you need to use an elaborate, big subroutine which cannot reside within 128 bytes of a branch, simply JSR to it at the target address of your branch:

| | | | |
|---|---|---|---|
| **2000** | **LDA** | **$65** | |
| **2002** | **CMP** | **$85** | Is what was in address 65 equal to what was in address 85? |
| **2004** | **BNE** | **$2009** | If Not Equal, branch over the next three bytes which perform some elaborate job. |
| **2006** | **JSR** | **$4000** | At $4000 sits the elaborate subroutine to take care of cases where addresses $65 and $85 turn out to be equal. |
| **2009** | | | Continue with the program here. |

If you are branching backward, you've already written that part of your program, so you know the address to type in after a BNE or one of the other branches. But, if you are branching forward—to an address in part of the program not yet written—how do you know what to give as the address to branch to? In two-pass assemblers like LADS, you can just use a word like BRANCHTARGET, and the assembler will pass twice through your program when it assembles it. The first pass simply notes that your BNE is supposed to branch to BRANCHTARGET, but it doesn't yet know where that is.

When it finally finds the actual address of BRANCHTARGET, it makes a note of the correct address in a special *label table*. Then, it makes a second pass through the program and fills in (as the next byte after your BNE or whatever) the correct address of BRANCHTARGET.

All of this is automatic, and the labels make the program you write (called the *source code*) look almost like English. In fact, assemblers like LADS include so many special features that they approach *higher-level* languages like BASIC:

| | | |
|---|---|---|
| **2000** | **TESTBYTE = $80** | These initial definitions of labels... |
| **2000** | **NEWBYTE = $FC** | are sometimes called *equates*. |
| **2000** | **LDA #TESTBYTE** | |
| **2002** | **CMP NEWBYTE** | |
| **2004** | **BNE BRANCHTARGET** | |

**2006 JSR SUBROUTINE**
**BRANCHTARGET 2009** ...etc.

Instead of using lots of numbers (as you do when using the built-in mini-assembler in the monitor) for the target/argument of each instruction, LADS allows you to *define* (equate) the meanings of words like *testbyte* and then use the word instead of the number. And LADS does simplify the problem of forward branching since you just give (as above) address $2009 a name, BRANCHTARGET, and the word at address $2005 is later replaced with $2009 when the assembler does its passes.

Program 6-1 shows how the example above looks as source code to be fed into LADS.

Actually, we should point out in passing that a $2009 will not be the number which finally appears at address $2005 to replace BRANCHTARGET. (Take a look at Program 6-1.) As we mentioned, all branches are relative, an offset from the address of the branch. The number which will finally replace BRANCHTARGET at $2005 is, as you can see, a 3. This is similar to the way that the value of the Y register is *added* to an address in zero page during indirect Y addressing: The number given as an argument of a branch instruction is *added* to the address of the next instruction. So, $2006 + $3 = $2009. If this seems confusing, forget about it. LADS, or even the mini-assembler in the monitor, will take care of all this for you. All you need to do is give $2009 as the argument to the mini-assembler, or a label name to LADS, and they will compute the three for you.

## Forward Branch Solutions

There is one responsibility that you do have, though, if you are using the monitor's mini-assembler. When you are writing 2004 BNE $2009, how do you know to write in $2009? You can't yet know to exactly which address up ahead you want to branch. There are two ways to deal with this. Perhaps easiest is just to put in BNE $2004 (have it branch to itself). This will result in an $FE being temporarily left as the target of your BNE. Then, you can make a note on paper to later change the byte at $2005 to point to the correct address, $2009. You've got to remember to "resolve" that $FE, to POKE in the correct offset to the target address, or you will leave a little bomb in your program—an endless loop.

**Program 6-1. Labeled Assembly**

```
30 2000                         TESTBYTE = $80
40 2000                         NEWBYTE = $FC
50
60 2000 A9 80       START       LDA #TESTBYTE     IMMEDIATE ADDRESSING
70 2002 C5 FC                   CMP NEWBYTE             ZERO PAGE ADDRESSING
80 2004 D0 03                   BNE BRANCHTARGET        RELATIVE ADDRESSING
90 2006 20 0C 20                JSR SUBROUTINE          ABSOLUTE ADDRESSING
100 2009 AD 00 04   BRANCHTARGET LDA $400  YOU CAN FREELY MIX LABELS
110                        AND SUBROUTINES. ALSO, COMMENTS
120 WILL BE IGNORED.
130 PUT THEM ANYWHERE
140 BUT PUT THE SEMICOLON RIGHT
150 AFTER ANY INSTRUCTIONS (SPACES CAN BE ADDED
160 BEYOND THE SEMICOLON FOR A MORE ATTRACTIVE
170 FORMAT.  SEE EXAMPLE LINES ABOVE)
180
190
200 200C A5 21      SUBROUTINE LDA 33
210 ETC. ETC.
```

The other, even simpler, way to deal with forward branch addresses will come after you are familiar with which instructions use one, two, or three bytes. The BNE–JSR–TARGET construction is common and will always be three above the next address, an *offset* of three. If your branch instruction is at $2004, you just add two to get the next address ($2006), then count off three: $2006,7,8 and write BNE 2009.

Other, more complex branches such as ON-GOTO constructions will also become easy to count off when you're familiar with the instruction byte lengths. In any case, it's simple enough to make a note of any unsolved branches and correct them before running the program.

Of course, LADS is the easiest assembler to use for forward branching: It allows you to branch to any address by just giving the label name of that address.

Recall our previous warning about not using the infamous BPL and BMI instructions? BPL (Branch on PLus) and BMI (Branch on MInus) sound good, but should be avoided. To test for less-than or more-than situations, use BCC and BCS respectively. (Actually, the BCS test is "true" for greater-than-or-equal-to, not just greater-than.) Remember that BCC is alphabetically *less-than* BCS—an easy way to remember which to use. The reasons for this are exotic. We don't need to go into them. Just be warned that BPL and BMI which sound so logical and useful are not. They can fail you, and neither one lives up to its name. Stick with the always trustworthy BCC, BCS.

Also remember that BNE and the other three main B group branching instructions often don't need to have a CMP come in front of them to affect a flag that can be tested by a following B instruction. Many actions of many opcodes will automatically affect flags. For example, LDA $80 will affect the Z flag so that you can tell (using BNE or BEQ) if the number in address $80 was or wasn't zero. LDA $80 followed by BNE would branch away if there were anything besides a zero in address $80. If in doubt about which flags are affected by which instructions, check Appendix A. You'll soon get to know the common ones. If you are really in doubt, go ahead and stick in a CMP. It can't do any harm.

## 4. The Loop Group: DEX, DEY, INX, INY, INC, DEC

INX and INY raise the X and Y register values *by one* each time they are used. If Y is a 17 and you INY, Y becomes an 18. Likewise, DEX and DEY decrease the values in these registers by one. There is no such increment or decrement instruction for the accumulator.

Similarly, INC and DEC will raise or lower a memory address by one. You can give arguments to these instructions in four addressing modes: absolute, zero page, zero page,X, and absolute,X. These instructions affect the N and Z flags.

The loop group are generally used to set up FOR-NEXT structures. The X register is used most often as a counter to allow a certain number of events to take place. In the structure FOR I = 1 TO 10:NEXT I, the value of the variable I goes up by one each time the loop cycles around. The same effect is created by:

```
2000  LDX  #$0A   Decimal 10
2002  DEX         "DEcrement" or "DEcrease X" by one
2003  BNE  $2002  Branch if Not Equal (to zero) back up to ad-
                  dress $2002
```

Notice that DEX is tested by BNE (which sees if the Z flag, the zero flag, is up). DEX sets the Z flag up when X finally gets down to zero after ten cycles of this loop. The only other flag affected by this loop group is the N (negative) flag for signed arithmetic.

Why didn't we use INX, INcrease X by one? This would parallel exactly the FOR I = 1 TO 10, but it would be clumsy since our starting count which is #10 above would have to be #245. This is because X will not become a zero *going up* until it hits 255. So, for clarity and simplicity, it is customary to set the count of X and then DEX it downward to zero. The following program will accomplish the same thing as the one above and allow us to INX, but it too is somewhat clumsy:

```
2000  LDX  #$0
2002  INX
2003  CPX  #$0A
2005  BNE  $2002
```

Here, we had to use zero to start the loop because, right off the bat, the number in X is INXed to one by the instruction at $2002. In any case, it is a good idea simply to memorize the simple loop structure in the first example. It is easy and obvious and works very well.

## Big Loops

How would you create a loop which has to be larger than 256 cycles? When we wanted to add large numbers, numbers too big to be held in a single byte, we simply used two-byte units instead of single-byte units to hold our information. Likewise, to do large loops, you can count down using two bytes rather than one. In fact, this is quite similar to the idea of nested loops (loops within loops) in BASIC.

```
2000  LDX  #$0A    Start of first loop.
2002  LDY  #$0     Start of second loop.
2004  DEY
2005  BNE  $2004   If Y isn't yet zero, loop back to DEcrease Y
                   again—this is the inner loop.
2007  DEX          Reduce the outer loop by one.
2008  BNE  $2002   If X isn't yet zero, go through the entire DEY
                   loop again.
200A               Continue with the rest of the program....
```

One thing to watch out for: Be sure that a loop BNEs back up to *one address after* the start of its loop. The start of the loop sets a number into a register and, if you keep looping up to it, you'll always be putting the same number into it. The DEcrement (decrease by one) instruction would then never bring it down to zero to end the looping. You'll have created an endless loop. This is another one of those common bugs. So if your program hangs up, check to see if you're looping back into an initialization section.

The example above could be used for a timing loop in a way that's similar to the method that BASIC creates delays with FOR T = 1 TO 2000: NEXT T. Also, sometimes you *do* want to create a pseudo-endless loop (the BEGIN–UNTIL in structured programming). A useful pseudo-endless loop in BASIC waits until the user hits any key: 10 GET K$: IF K$ = "" THEN 10.

The simplest way to accomplish this in ML is to look on the map of your computer to find which byte holds the *last key pressed* number. On the 128, it's $D4. In any event, when a key is pressed, it deposits its special numeric value into this cell. If no key is pressed, $D4 contains the number 88. However, there's a built-in ROM routine at $FFE4 which will return the ASCII value of a keypress. It's often easier to use than polling $D4 because $D4 gives character values in the *keyboard matrix code* which differ from ASCII. (To find out more about your keyboard input options, see INPUT and GET in Chapter 9.) Here's $FFE4 in action:

```
4000  JSR  $FFE4
4003  BEQ  $4000
```

Unless a key is being pressed on the keyboard, a JSR to $FFE4 results in a zero result (setting the Z flag), and so when we test the Z flag with BEQ, we'll keep looping back to address 4000 in the example above until someone presses a key. When a key *is* finally pressed, the BEQ test will then fail and we'll fall through to whatever instruction you have put at address $4005 right below the BEQ. *At this point, the accumulator will hold the ASCII value of the key that was pressed.*

## Dealing with Strings

You've probably been wondering how ML handles strings.

It's pretty straightforward. There are essentially two ways: known-length and zero-delimit. If you know how many characters there are in a message, you can store this number at the very start of the text: 5ERROR. (The number 5 will fit into one byte.) If this message is stored in your "message zone"—some arbitrary area of free memory set aside by you at the beginning to hold all of your messages—you would make a note of the particular address of the "ERROR" message. Say it's stored at address $0FE6 (4070).

To print out the message, you pluck off the length and then repeatedly JSR to $FFD2, the 128's character output routine in ROM. But remember that any time you want to access the built-in ROM routines, you must have switched in bank 15 by LDA #0:STA $FF00.

Alternatively, you could simply set up your own zero page pointers to the screen and use the STA *(NN)*,Y addressing mode (the *NN* means "any number").

Screen memory starts at $0400 (1024). You can set up a "cursor management" system for yourself. To simplify, we'll send our message to the beginning of the 128's screen and just use the simple absolute,Y addressing mode:

| | | |
|---|---|---|
| **2000** | **LDX $0FE6** | Remember, we put the length of the message as the first byte of the message, so we load our counter with the length. |
| **2003** | **LDY #$0** | Y will be our message offset. |
| **2005** | **LDA $0FE7,Y** | Gets the character at the address plus Y. Y is zero the first time through the loop, so the "e" from here lands in the accumulator. It also stays in $0FE7 (4071). It's just being copied into the accumulator. |
| **2008** | **STA $0400,Y** | We can make Y do double-duty as the message and the screen-printout offset. Y is still zero, so the "e" goes to $0400 the first time through the loop. |
| **200B** | **INY** | Prepare to add one to the message-storage location and to the screen-print location. |
| **200C** | **DEX** | Lower the counter. |
| **200D** | **BNE $2005** | If X isn't used up yet, go back and get-and-print the next character, the "r." |

One thing you should remember when printing to the screen: there are two different codes you can use. If you STA $0400 as we do in the example immediately above, you are using the screen POKE code, the same code that would apply were you to POKE that value from BASIC. The other code (very similar to standard ASCII) applies when you load the character value into the accumulator and then JSR $FFD2.

When you turn on the 128, its default mode is uppercase/ graphics. You can change it to uppercase/ lowercase by printing CHR$(14)—in ML, LDA #14:JSR $FFD2—and back to graphics by printing CHR$(12). Alternately, you can switch between modes by pressing the SHIFT and Commodore keys simultaneously. If, when you are testing the examples below, you are getting graphics rather than letters of the alphabet, you should switch to the uppercase/lowercase screen mode as described. Using the $FFD2 printing routine, however, will work as expected in any mode.

## If the Length Is Not Known

There is yet another way to print to the screen—probably the most common and the easiest, and it doesn't require that you know the length of the string. You just put a special character (usually zero) at the end of each message to show its limit. This is called a *delimiter*. A zero works well because, in ASCII, the value zero has no character or function (such as a carriage return) coded to it. Consequently, any time the computer loads a zero into the accumulator (which will flip up the Z flag), it will then know that it is at the end of your message. At $0FE6, we might have a couple of error messages: "Ball out of range0Time nearly up!0". (These zeros are not ASCII zeros, remember. ASCII zero, the zero *character* that can be printed, has a value of 48.)

To print the time warning message to the top of the screen:

| | | | |
|---|---|---|---|
| **2000** | **LDY** | **#$0** | |
| **2002** | **LDA** | **$0FF8,Y** | Get the "T." |
| **2005** | **BEQ** | **$2005** | The LDA just above will flip the zero flag up if it loads a zero, so we *forward branch* out of our message-printing loop. |
| **2007** | **STA** | **$0400,Y** | We're using the Y as a double-duty offset again. |
| **200A** | **INY** | | |
| **200B** | **JMP** | **$2002** | In this loop, we always jump back. Our exit from the loop is not here, at the end. Rather, it is the Branch if EQual which is within the loop. This is similar to the BEGIN–UNTIL structure in structured programming. |
| **200E** | | | Continue with another part of the program. |

Now that we know the address which follows the loop ($200E), we can store that address into the "false forward branch" we left in address $2006. What number do we store into $2006? Just subtract $2007 from $200E, which is 7.

Of these two ways of handling strings, the zero-delimit method is the most popular and probably the easiest to use. It's even easier if you use LADS. With LADS, you don't need to remember the address of the stored string, you just give each string a label. Also, you don't need to translate the message into ASCII, just use the .BYTE pseudo-op in LADS. Here's how you would write the source code for LADS using the zero-delimit technique example above:

| | |
|---|---|
| **100 SCREEN = 1024** | This variable is defined at the start of the program, not with the body of the ML. The numbers on the left are *not* addresses;. they are line numbers that you use when writing the source code. The assembler handles memory addresses for you. |

```
     .
     .
     .
500 LDY #0
510 MESSAGE LDA TIMEOUT,Y       Get the "T."
520 BEQ MORE
530 STA SCREEN,Y
540 INY
550 JMP MESSAGE
560 MORE      Continue with another part of the program.
     .
     .
     .
1000 TIMEOUT .BYTE "TIME
    NEARLY UP!": .BYTE 0   Message stored with a true zero at
                           the end. This is stored at the very
                           end of the ML program, not in with
                           the instructions themselves.
```

All the ways of handling messages discussed above are effective, but you must keep a list on paper of the starting addresses of each message if you are using the monitor assembler so that you can remember from where to pick off the letters of the message. In ML, you have the responsibility for some of the tasks that BASIC (at an expense of speed) does for you. If you're using LADS, however, you can simply define the location of the message with a label.

Also, when using these techniques, no message can be larger than 255 characters because the offset and counter registers (X and Y) can count only that high before starting over at zero again. To print two strings back-to-back gives a longer, but still less than 255-byte-long, message:

```
2000  LDY  #$0
2002  LDX  #$2       In this example, we use X as a counter which
                     represents the number of messages we are
                     printing.
2004  LDA  $4000,Y   Get the "B" from "Ball out of...."
2007  BEQ  $2011     Go to increment Y, reduce (and check) the
                     value of X.
2009  STA  $0400,Y   We're using the Y as a double-duty offset
                     again.
200D  INY
200E  JMP  $2004
2011  INY            We need to raise Y since we skipped that step
                     when we branched out of the loop.
```

| | |
|---|---|
| **2012 DEX** | At the end of the first message, X will be a one; at the end of the second message, it will be zero. |
| **2013 BNE $2004** | If X isn't down to zero yet, reenter the loop to print out the second message. |

This example, too, could not deliver a message longer than 255 characters. To fill your screen with instructions instantly (say, at the start of a game), you can use the following mass-move. We'll assume that the instructions go from $5000 to $6024 in memory and that you want to transfer them to the screen (at $0400):

```
2000  LDY  #$0
2002  LDA  $5000,Y
2005  STA  $0400,Y
2008  LDA  $5100,Y
200B  STA  $0500,Y
200E  LDA  $5200,Y
2011  STA  $0600,Y
2014  LDA  $5300,Y
2017  STA  $0700,Y
201A  INY
```

| | |
|---|---|
| **201B BNE $2002** | If Y hasn't counted *up to* 0—which comes just above 255—go back and load-store the next character in each quarter of the large message. |

This technique is fast and easy anytime you want to mass-move one area of memory to another. It makes a copy and does not disturb the original memory. To mass-clear a memory zone (to clear the screen, for example), you can use a similar loop, but instead of loading the accumulator each time with a different character, you load it at the start with 32, the 128's code for the character that prints a space:

```
2000  LDA  #32
2002  LDY  #0
2004  STA  $0400,Y
2007  STA  $0500,Y
200A  STA  $0600,Y
200D  STA  $0700,Y
2011  INY
2012  BNE  $2004
```

Of course a simpler way to clear the screen would be to JSR to the PRINT routine in BASIC ROM after having loaded the clear-screen character into the accumulator: LDA #$93:JSR $FFD2. In Chapter 7 we will explore the techniques of using

BASIC as a group of examples to learn from and also as a collection of ready-made ML subroutines. Now, though, we can look at how subroutines are handled in ML.

## 5. The Subroutine and Jump Group: JMP, JSR, RTS

JMP has only one useful addressing mode: absolute. You give it a firm, two-byte argument and it goes there. The computer puts the argument into the program counter, and control is transferred to this new address where an instruction located there is acted upon. (There is a second addressing mode, JMP indirect, which has a bug and is best left unused.)

JSR can use only absolute addressing.

RTS's addressing mode is implied. The address is on the stack, put there during the JSR.

JSR (Jump to SubRoutine) is the same as GOSUB in BASIC, but instead of giving a line number, you give an address in memory where the subroutine sits (or, with LADS, you give a label name). BASIC's SYS is a kind of JSR, too. It acts like GOSUB, except the destination is an ML routine rather than a BASIC subroutine.

RTS (ReTurn from Subroutine) is the same as RETURN in BASIC, but instead of returning to the next BASIC command, you return to the address following the JSR instruction (it's a three-byte-long instruction containing JSR and the two-byte target address). JMP (JuMP) is GOTO. Again, you JMP to an address or label name, not a line number. As in BASIC, there is no RETURN from a JMP.

### Some Further Cautions About the Stack

The stack is like a pile of coins. The last one you put on top of the pile is the first one you'll pull off later. The main reason that the 8502 chip sets aside an entire page of memory for the stack is that it has to know where to go back to after GOSUBs and JSRs.

A JSR instruction "pushes" the address held in the program counter plus two onto the stack and, later, the next RTS "pulls" the top two numbers off the stack, increments the result, and uses this number as its argument (target address) for the return. Some programmers, as we noted before, like to play with the stack and use it as a temporary register to PHA

(PusH Accumulator onto stack). This sort of thing is best avoided until you are an advanced ML programmer. Stack manipulations often result in a very confusing program. Handling the stack is one of the few things that the computer does *for you* in ML. Let it.

The main function of the stack (as far as we're concerned) is to hold return addresses. It's done automatically for us by "pushes" with the JSR and, later, "pulls" (sometimes called *pops*) with the RTS instruction. If we don't bother the stack, it will serve us well. There are thousands upon thousands of cells where you could temporarily leave the accumulator—or any other value—without fouling up the orderly arrangement of your return addresses.

Subroutines are extremely important to ML programming.

ML programs are designed around them, as we'll see. There are times when you'll be several subroutines deep (one will call another which calls another); this is not as confusing as it sounds. Your main player-input routine might call a print-message subroutine which itself calls a wait-until-key-is-pressed subroutine. If any of these routines PHA (PusH the Accumulator onto the stack), they then disturb the addresses on the stack. If the extra number on top of the stack isn't PLAed off (PulL Accumulator), the next RTS will pull off the number that was PHAed along with half the correct address. It will then merrily return to what it thinks is the correct address: It might land somewhere in the RAM, it might go to an address somewhere in the outer reaches of your operating system—but it certainly won't go where it should.

Some programmers like to change a GOSUB into a GOTO (in the middle of the action of a program) by PLA PLA. Pulling the two top stack values off with PLA PLA has the effect of eliminating the most recently stored RTS address. It does leave a clean stack, but why bother to JSR in the first place if you later want to change it to a GOTO? Why not use JMP in the first place. (There is some use for this technique, but it's for advanced ML programming where you want to speed up a program by returning directly to some routine elsewhere in the calling subprogram. LADS uses this method in places.)

There are cases, too, when the stack has been used to hold the current condition of the flags (the status register byte).

This is pushed/pulled from the stack with PHP and PLP. You probably never will, but if you should need to "remember" the condition of the status flags, why not just PHP PLA STA $NN (*NN* means the address is your choice)? Set aside a byte somewhere that can hold the flags (they are always changing inside the status register during a program run) for later and keep the stack clean. Leave stack acrobatics to Forth programmers. The stack, except for advanced ML, should be inviolate.

Forth, an interesting language, requires frequent stack manipulations. But in the Forth environment, the reasons for this and its protocol make excellent sense. In ML, though, stack manipulations are a sticky business.

## Saving the Current Environment

There are two exceptions to our leave-the-stack-alone rule. Sometimes (especially when you are "borrowing" a routine from BASIC by JSRing into the ROM) you will want to take up with your own program from where it left off. In other words, you want to preserve what's in the registers.

However, when you JSR into one of these ready-made subroutines, you often don't know what sorts of things the subroutine will do to your accumulator or X and Y registers. To illustrate, let's say you are going to open a disk file and you've written the necessary subroutine and labeled it OPEN. You will JSR to OPEN and it will have to JSR, in turn, several times into the ROM to accomplish the job of opening a disk file. However, you need to retain the status of the registers because your program is going to need them. You sometimes cannot afford to have unpredictable things happen to your X, Y, A, and status registers. If you know you don't need to preserve the state of the accumulator or the X or Y register, then JSR blithely away. The JSR into ROM will probably change the registers, but you don't care.

However, sometimes you are using, let's say, Y to hold the offset of a line of information or a screen line. You can't allow it to suffer from some unknown event in a ROM subroutine. In such cases, you can use the following "save the state of things" routine:

```
2000 PHP          Push the status register onto the stack.
2001 PHA
2002 TXA
```

| | | |
|---|---|---|
| **2003 PHA** | | |
| **2004 TYA** | | |
| **2005 PHA** | | |
| **2006 JSR** | **OPEN** | To the various ROM calls necessary to open a file that you've written as a subroutine called "OPEN." When the subroutine is finished, it will end with an RTS. This RTS will remove the return address ($2009) from the stack, and you'll then have access to a mirror image of the things you had pushed onto the stack. They are pulled out in reverse order, as you can see below. This is because the first pull from the stack will get the *most recently pushed* number. If you make a little stack of coins, the *first* one you pull off will be the *last* one you put onto the stack. |
| **2009 PLA** | | Now we reverse the order to get them back. |
| **200A TAY** | | |
| **200B PLA** | | |
| **200C TAX** | | |
| **200D PLA** | | This one stays in A. |
| **200E PLP** | | The status register. |

This example demonstrates how to save the registers, JSR to a subroutine where unpredictable things will happen to the registers, and then restore the registers to their previous state. It preserves everything, including the flags (PHP, push processor status register) as it was before you JSRed. Use this technique when you're unsure. Nearly *every* ROM routine mentioned in this book will alter one or more of the registers. The only truly safe one is JSR $FFD2, the output-a-character routine. You can use this one with impunity.

Saving the current state of things before visiting an uncharted, unpredictable subroutine is probably the only valid excuse for playing with the stack as a beginner in ML. The routine above is constructed to leave the stack intact. Everything that was pushed on has been pulled back off.

If you dare, you can also use the stack as a temporary storage place when you need to save something briefly. You could save the accumulator (while JSRing to the GET routine in BASIC) by PHA:JSR $FFE4:PLA. That would temporarily push the accumulator onto the stack, hold it there beneath the two-byte return address pushed onto the stack by the JSR, and then pull it off again after the RTS had fetched the return address (leaving your accumulator on top of the stack). This pushing is sometimes considered a dangerous practice because, if you forget to match every push with a subsequent pull, the stack will overflow and you might not realize why. Use this trick at your own risk. For simple register saves, it's pretty easy to define register "holding bytes" using LADS and then stuff things there whenever you need temporary storage:

```
10 GET = $FFE4
100 STY Y:STA A:LOOP JSR GET:BEQ LOOP:LDA A:LDY Y
```

While, somewhere after the end of your program proper, down with the messages and other things that are data, not program, you have:

```
5000 A .BYTE 0
5010 Y .BYTE 0
5020 X .BYTE 0
```

## The Significance of Subroutines

Possibly the best way to approach ML program writing—especially a large program—is to think of it as a collection of subroutines. Each of these subroutines should be small. It should be listed on a piece of paper followed by a note on what it needs as input and what it gives back as *parameters*. "Parameter passing" simply means that a subroutine needs to know things from the main program (parameters) which are handed to it (passed) in some way. Alternatively, if you are using LADS, you can insert comments about parameters into the body of the source code of the program using the semicolon (;) remark pseudo-op.

The current position of the record in a database is a parameter which has its own "register" (we would have set aside a register for it at the start when we were assigning memory space either on paper for simple assemblers or by using the *equate* pseudo-op for LADS). So, the "look at the next record in the database" subroutine is a double-adder which adds 40 or whatever to the "current position register." This value always sits in the register to be used anytime any subroutine needs this information. In other words, the register (we called it FINGER in a previous example) is always pointing to our current position within the database. This is why such registers are called *pointers*.

The "look at the next register" subroutine *sends* the current-position parameter by *passing* it to the current-position register.

This is one example of a way that parameters are passed. Another example might be when you are telling a delay loop how long to delay. Ideally, your delay subroutine will be multipurpose. That is, it can delay for anywhere from 1/2 second to 60 seconds or something. This means that the subroutine itself isn't locked into a particular length of delay.

The main program will "pass" the amount of delay to the subroutine.

```
3000  LDY  #$0
3002  INY
3003  BNE  $3002
3005  DEX
3006  BNE  $3000
3008  RTS
```

Notice that X never is initialized (set up) here with any particular value. This is because the value of X is passed to this subroutine from the main program. If you want a short delay, you would:

```
2000  LDX  #$5
2002  JSR  $3000
```

And for a delay which is twice as long as that:

```
2000  LDX  #$0A  10 decimal
2002  JSR  $3000
```

In some ways, the less a subroutine does, the better. If it's not entirely self-sufficient, and the shorter and simpler it is, the more versatile it will be. For example, our delay above could function to time responses, to hold sounds for specific durations, and so on. When you make remarks about a general-purpose routine, write something like this: 3000 ; DELAY LOOP (expects duration in X; returns zero in X).

The longest duration delay would be set up with LDX #0. This is because the first thing that happens to X in the delay subroutine is DEX. If you DEX a zero, you get 255. If you need longer delays than the maximum value of X, simply:

```
2000  LDX  #$0
2002  JSR  $3000
2005  JSR  $3000   Notice that we don't need to set X to zero this
                   second time. It returns from the subroutine with
                   a zeroed X.
```

You could even make a loop out of the JSRs above for extremely long delays. The point to notice here is that it helps to document each subroutine in your library: what parameters it expects; what registers, flags, and so on, it changes; and what it leaves behind as a result. This documentation—on a single sheet of paper or within LADS source—helps you remember each routine's address and lets you know what effects and preconditions are involved.

## JMP

Like BASIC's GOTO, JMP is easy to understand. It goes to an address: JMP $5000 leaps from wherever it is to start carrying out the instructions which start at $5000. It doesn't affect any flags. It doesn't do anything to the stack. It's clean and simple. Yet some advocates of structured programming suggest avoiding JMP (and GOTO). Their reasoning is that JMP is a shortcut and a poor programming habit.

For one thing, they argue, using GOTO makes programs confusing. If you drew lines to show a program's "flow" (the order in which instructions are carried out), a program with lots of GOTOs would look like boiled spaghetti. Many programmers feel, however, that JMP has its uses. Clearly, you should not overdo it and lean heavily on JMP. In fact, you might see if there isn't a better way to accomplish something if you find yourself using it all the time and your programs are becoming impossibly awkward. But JMP is convenient, often necessary, in ML.

## An 8502 Chip Bug

On the other hand, there is another, rather peculiar JMP addressing mode which is hardly, if ever, used in ML: JMP ($5000). This is an *indirect* jump which works like the indirect addressing we've seen before. Remember that with the indirect,Y addressing mode, LDA ($81),Y, the number in Y is added to the *address* found in $81 and $82. This address is the *real* place we are LDAing from, sometimes called the *effective address*. If $81 holds a 00, $82 holds a $40, and Y holds a 2, the address we LDA from is going to be $4002. Similarly (but without adding Y), the effective address found at the two bytes within the parentheses becomes the place we JMP to in JMP ($5000).

There are no necessary uses for this instruction. Best avoid it the same way you avoid playing around with the stack until you're an ML expert. If you find it in your computer's BASIC code, it will probably be involved in an "indirect jump table," a series of registers which are dynamic. That is, they can be changed as the program progresses. Such a technique is very close to a self-altering program and would have few applications in ML. But worse than than, there is a bug in the 8502 chip itself which causes the indirect JMP instruction to malfunction under certain circumstances. Just put JMP ($*NNNN)* into the same category as BPL and BMI. Avoid them.

If you decide that for some reason you must use indirect JMP, be sure to avoid the edge of pages, such as JMP ($*NN*FF). Whenever the low byte is right on the edge of a page ($FF is on the edge, it's ready to reset to $00), an indirect JMP will correctly use the low byte (LSB) from the pointer at $*NN*FF, but it will not pick up the high byte (MSB) from $*NN*FF+1 as it should. Instead, it gets the high byte from $*NN*00.

Here's how this error would work if you had set up a pointer to address $5043 with the pointer located at $40FF:

```
$40FF  43
$4100  50
```

Your intention would be to JMP to $5043 by bouncing off this pointer. You would write JMP ($40FF) and expect that the next instruction the computer would follow would be the instruction located at $5043. Unfortunately, your pointer would malfunction in this example. You would land at $0043 (if address $4000 held a zero). The indirect JMP would get its MSB from $4000.

This bug does not apply to any other addressing modes, just JMP (indirect). So, unless you want to take a chance with an addressing mode that's strictly for advanced programmers, contains a bug, and has no compelling uses, avoid JMP (indirect).

## 6. Debuggers: BRK and NOP

BRK and NOP have no arguments and are therefore members of that class of instructions which use only the implied addressing mode. They also affect no flags in any way with which we would be concerned. BRK does affect the I and B flags, but since it is a rare situation which would require testing those flags, we can ignore this flag activity altogether.

After you've assembled your program and it doesn't work as expected (few do), you start *debugging*. Some studies have shown that debugging takes up more than 50 percent of programming time. Such surveys can be misleading, however, because "making improvements and adding options" frequently take place after a program is allegedly finished and would be thereby categorized as part of the debugging process.

Another factor is that these surveys reflect the sometimes inefficient programming styles adopted by professional or academic programming teams. Some assemblers and compilers used by professionals are extraordinarily cumbersome, requiring heroic efforts with linkers, maps, variable definition, and so forth, before a piece of program can be tested. LADS, by contrast, is virtually instantaneous. It will make the process of debugging very efficient.

In ML, debugging is facilitated by setting *breakpoints* with BRK and then seeing what's happening in the registers or memory. If you insert a BRK, it has the effect of halting the program and throwing you into the monitor where you can examine, say, the Y register to see if it contains what you would expect it to at this point in the program. It's similar to BASIC's STOP instruction:

```
2000  LDA #$15
2002  TAY
2003  BRK
```

At this point, you could use the monitor to examine any areas of memory just as you would examine variables after having your BASIC program STOP.

## Debugging Methods

In practice, you debug whenever your program runs merrily along and then does something unexpected. It might crash and lock you out. You look for a likely place where you think it is failing and just insert a BRK right over some other instruction.

Remember that when you're in the monitor mode, you can directly change bytes, you can insert $00 (BRK) where you want.

In the example above, imagine that we put the BRK over a STY $8000. Make a note of the instruction you covered over with the BRK so that you can restore it later. After checking the registers and memory, you might find something wrong, some variable or register isn't behaving as it should or you somehow never even arrive at the break (some branch or JMP is being incorrectly activated). Now you have narrowed things down. Now you can locate and fix the error.

Sometimes it helps to have a printed listing of the suspect area in a program. You can turn your printer on and off with the .P and .NP options in LADS, printing out only the suspect zone of the program and use that to help you locate errors while working with the monitor. Alternatively, you can check the program with the built-in disassembler.

If nothing seems wrong at this point, restore the original STY over the BRK, and put BRK in somewhere further on. By this process, you can isolate the cause of the oddity in your program. Setting breakpoints (like putting STOP into BASIC programs) is an effective way to run part of a program and then examine the variables.

Like BRK ($00), the hex number of NOP ($EA) is worth memorizing. If you're working within your monitor, you will need to use hex numbers, and these two are particularly worth knowing.

NOP means NO oPeration. The computer slides over NOPs without taking any action other than increasing the program counter. There are two ways in which NOP can be effectively used.

First, it can be an eraser. If you suspect that JSR $8000 is causing all the trouble, try running your program with everything else the same, but with JSR $8000 erased. Simply put three $EAs over the instruction and argument. (Make a note, though, of what was under the $EAs so that you can restore it.) Then, the program will run without this instruction, without going to that subroutine at $8000, and you can watch the effects.

Second, it is sometimes useful to use $EA to hold open some space temporarily. If you don't know something (an address, a graphics value) during assembly, $EA can mark that this space needs to be filled in later before the program is run. As an instruction, it will let the program slide by. $EA could become your "fill this in" alert within programs in the way that we use self-branching (leaving a zero) to show that we need to put in a forward branch's address when using a mini-assembler.

### Less Common Instructions

The following instructions are not often necessary for beginning applications, but we can briefly touch on their main uses. There are several logical instructions which can manipulate or test individual bits within each byte. This is most often necessary when interfacing. If you need to test what's coming in from a disk drive, or translate on a bit-by-bit level for I/O (input/output), you might work with the logical group.

In general, I/O is handled for you by your machine's operating system and is well beyond beginning ML programming. I/O is perhaps the most difficult, or at least the most complicated, aspect of ML programming. When putting things on the screen, programming is fairly straightforward, but handling the data stream into and out of a disk is pretty involved. Timing must be precise, and the preconditions which need to be established are complex.

For example, if you need to *mask* a byte by changing some of its bits to zero, you can use the AND instruction. After an AND, *both* numbers must have contained a one in any particular bit position for it to result in a one in the answer. This lets you set up a mask: 00001111 will zero any bits within the left four positions. So, 00001111 and 11001100 result in 00001100.

The unmasked bits remained unchanged, but the four high bits were all masked and, thus, zeroed.

There is a minor use for AND when you want to change a character to a reverse (black on white) or change it back to normal. The reversed letter *A*, for example, has a value of $C1 which looks like this in binary (all the bits within the byte showing): 11000001. Notice that the left two bits are "on." To change this to a normal *A* character, we need to turn the leftmost bit off so that we end up with 01000001, which is $41. You can turn off the leftmost bit by 11000001 AND 01111111, which will leave 01000001. When this is expressed in hex numbers, you take the reversed *A* ($C1) and AND it with 01111111 ($7F) to get the normal $41. Likewise, reversed *B* ($C2) AND $7F results in a normal *B* ($42).

Going the other way, you can change a normal *A* into a reversed *A* by $41 ORA $80 (10000000). The ORA instruction is the same as AND, except it lets you mask to *set* bits (make them a one). Thus, 11110000 ORA 11001100 results in 11111100. The accumulator will hold the results when these instructions are used.

EOR (Exclusive OR) permits you to toggle bits. *Toggle* means to switch back and forth between two states, like toggling a light switch on and off. If a bit is 1, it will go to 0. If it's 0, it will flip to 1. EOR is sometimes useful in games. If you are heading in one direction, for example, and you want to go back when bouncing a ball off a wall, you could toggle. Let's say that you use a register to show direction: When the ball's going up, the byte contains the number 1 (00000001), but down is 0 (00000000). To toggle this least significant bit, you would EOR with 00000001. This would flip 1 to 0, and 0 to 1. This action results in the *complement* of a number. Thus, 11111111 EOR 11001100 results in 00110011.

To know the effects of these logical operators, we can look them up in *truth tables* which give the results of all possible combinations of zeros and ones:

| AND | OR | EOR |
|---|---|---|
| 0 AND 0 = 0 | 0 OR 0 = 0 | 0 EOR 0 = 0 |
| 0 AND 1 = 0 | 0 OR 1 = 1 | 0 EOR 1 = 1 |
| 1 AND 0 = 0 | 1 OR 0 = 1 | 1 EOR 0 = 1 |
| 1 AND 1 = 1 | 1 OR 1 = 1 | 1 EOR 1 = 0 |

Another instruction, BIT, also tests (it does an AND), but, like the BNE, and so forth, branch instructions, it does not affect the number in the accumulator—its sole purpose is to set flags in the status register. The N flag is set (has a one) if bit 7 has a one (and vice versa). The V flag responds similarly to whatever value is in the sixth bit of the tested byte. The Z flag shows whether or not the result of the AND resulted in a zero. Instructions, like BIT, which do not affect the numbers being tested are called *nondestructive.*

We discussed LSR and ASL in the chapter on arithmetic: They can conveniently divide and multiply by two. ROL and ROR *rotate* the bits left or right in a byte, but, unlike with the Logical Shift Right or Arithmetic Shift Left, no bits are lost off one end during the shift. ROL will leave the seventh (most significant) bit in the carry flag, leave the carry flag in the zeroth bit (least significant bit), and move every other bit one space to the left:

**ROL 11001100** With the carry flag set, results in:
**10011001** Carry is still set; it got the leftmost one.

If you disassemble your computer's BASIC, you may well look in vain for an example of ROL, but it and ROR are available in the 8502 instruction set if you should ever find a use for them.

Should you go into advanced ML arithmetic, ROL and ROR can be used for multiplication and division routines.

Please see Appendix A for more details on some of these obscure instructions if you're interested.

Three other instructions remain to be discussed: SEI (SEt Interrupt), RTI (ReTurn from Interrupt), and CLI (CLear Interrupt). These operations are also beyond the scope of a book on beginning ML programming, but we'll briefly note their effects. Your computer gets busy as soon as the power goes on. Things are always happening: Timing registers are being updated; the keyboard, the video, and the peripheral connectors are being refreshed or examined for signals. To *interrupt* all this activity, you can SEI, perform some task, and then CLI to let things pick up where they left off.

SEI sets the interrupt flag. Following this, all *maskable* interruptions (things which can be blocked from interrupting when the interrupt status flag is up) are no longer possible.

There are also *nonmaskable* interrupts which, as you might guess, will jump in anytime, ignoring the status register.

The RTI instruction (ReTurn from Interrupt) restores the program counter and status register (takes them from the stack), but the X and Y registers, and so on, might have been changed during the interrupt. Recall that our discussion of the BRK instruction involved the above actions. The key difference is that BRK stores the program counter plus two on the stack and sets the B flag on the status register. CLI puts the interrupt flag down and lets all interrupts take place.

If these last instructions are confusing to you, it doesn't matter. They are essentially hardware and interface related.

You can do nearly everything you will want to do in ML without them. How often have you used WAIT in BASIC?

## A Newer Chip

The venerable 6502 chip, which has been the brains of most of the popular home computers for years, has been replaced in the 128 by the 8502. From a programmer's point of view, there's no difference between the two.

Commodore owns the manufacturer of the 6502 and its newer cousins. When the 64 was built, they decided to make a few changes to the 6502 and called it the 6510. Similarly, a few more changes resulted in the 8502 inside the 128. These chips are physically different—they are not pin-compatible. This means you cannot pull a 6502 out of a socket and plug an 8502 in its place, because the operating signals appear on different pins. (If you're interested, the data bus is pins 30–37 on a 6510, but pins 26–33 on a 6502. The 6510 is a 6502 with an on-chip six-bit I/O port addressed at locations 0000 and 0001. The 8502 is an enhanced 6510, capable of operating at 2 megahertz and with a seven-bit I/O port.)

For programmers, though, the significant thing is that none of the physical differences reflect any modifications to the *instruction set*, the commands we've been learning in this chapter. From a programmer's perspective, *the three processors used in the Commodore machines are identical.*

In any event, we've covered all the instructions now. It's time to explore some important shortcuts. Life would be far tougher for ML programmers if they had to write, for example, the entire complex of instructions necessary to communicate with the disk drive. Fortunately, we can turn jobs like that over to the ML routines already written, already inside BASIC. That's the subject of the next chapter.

# Chapter 7

# Borrowing from BASIC

# Borrowing from BASIC

BASIC is a collection of ML subroutines. It is a large web of hundreds of short ML programs. Why not use some of them by JSRing to them? At times, this is in fact the best solution to a problem.

How would this differ from BASIC itself? Doesn't BASIC just create a series of JSRs when it runs? Wouldn't using BASIC's ML routines in this way be just as slow as BASIC is?

In practice, you will not be borrowing from BASIC for everything you try to do. One reason is that such JSRing makes your program far less *portable,* less easily run on other computers or other models of your computer. When you JSR to an address within your ROM set to save yourself the trouble of reinventing the wheel, you are, unfortunately, making your program applicable only to machines which are the same model as yours.

While Commodore has been better than many computer companies at keeping important ROM addresses like $FFD2 in the same place in new models, there are no guarantees that this will always be the case.

However, if you want your program to work on many different computer brands, you'll need to limit the degree to which you make it ROM-specific. Stick to the few essential ones (see the equates at the beginning of the LADS program for the few ROM routines that it needed to use).

If you try to get too tricky—using your BASIC's or operating system's ROM to the maximum—your programs will be pretty hard to translate to other Commodore computer models, not to mention other computer brands. For example, the subroutine to allocate space for a string in memory is found at $D3D2 in the earliest Commodore PET model. A later version of PET BASIC (Upgrade) used $D3CE, and the current models use $C61D. Although Microsoft BASIC is nearly universally used in personal computers (Atari is the exception), each computer's version differs in both the order and the addresses of key subroutines.

### Jump Tables and Other Menus

To help overcome this lack of portability, some computer manufacturers set aside a group of frequently used subroutines and create a "jump table," or, as Commodore calls it, a Kernal, for them. The idea is that future, upgraded BASIC versions will still retain this table. It would look something like this:

| | | | | |
|---|---|---|---|---|
| **FFCF** | **4C** | **15** | **F2** | INPUT one byte |
| **FFD2** | **4C** | **66** | **F2** | OUTPUT one byte |
| **FFD5** | **4C** | **01** | **F4** | LOAD something |
| **FFD8** | **4C** | **DD** | **F6** | SAVE something |

This example is part of the Commodore Kernal and is intended to apply to all future versions of BASIC on Commodore machines.

One interesting thing about this table of jumps is that there is a trick to the way this sort of table works, and you might want to use it yourself sometime. Notice that each member of the table begins with 4C. That's the JMP instruction and, if you land on it, the computer bounces right off to the address which follows.

Now, at that address following the 4C, there is going to be a subroutine (so it will end in RTS). So, when we JSR to one of the JMPs inside this table, to, say, FFD2, we're going to land on a JMP and rebound, just bounce right off the JMP table to the correct subroutine. When that subroutine finally finishes its work and ends in RTS, we will be returned to our starting place. That's how a JMP table works and it can be a useful technique.

By the way, the PRINT subroutine is a fundamental one in any computer because it offers you so much value. For one thing, it keeps track of the cursor position which is incremented each time you access PRINT. It works semiautomatically, and you don't have to keep track of where you are on the screen. The PRINT-the-character routine in the 128 is $FFD2 (65490 decimal). This is a very important address; you should memorize it.

For convenience, you might want to make a standard "header" for all your ML source programs that you use with LADS. It would consist of a series of "equates" which define frequently used internal subroutines by giving them labels:

```
30 PRINT = $FFD2; PRINTS CHARACTER IN
   ACCUMULATOR
40 SCREEN = $0400; LOCATION OF TEXT SCREEN
```

Then, when you're writing an ML source program using LADS and want to print some character, you just JSR PRINT. ML can thus be very similar to BASIC in that when you are going to use a known subroutine, a subroutine that you've given a label at the beginning of your program in the manner illustrated above, you just type a word like SCREEN that means something to your program and also means something memorable to you. You might want to use the routines defined in the Defs subprogram of LADS as a useful starter set of ROM routines.

The same PRINT routine will work for a printer or a disk or a tape—anything that the computer sees as an output device. However, unless you open a file to one of the other devices, the computer defaults to (assumes) the screen as the output device, and $FFD2 prints there. To see how to set up different output targets, see the Open1 source code of LADS in Appendix D. It will show you the way to load or save a program.

So, if you look into any ML program and discover a series of JMPs (4C *xx xx* 4C *xx xx*), you've found a jump table. Using a jump table should help make your programs compatible with later versions of BASIC which might be released.

## What's Fastest?

Since, when a BASIC program runs, it is JSRing around inside itself, how, then, is a JSR into BASIC code any faster than a BASIC program? The answer is that a program written entirely in ML, aside from the fact that it borrows only sparingly from BASIC prewritten routines, differs from BASIC in an important way.

A finished ML program is like *compiled* code; that is, it is ready to execute without any overhead. BASIC, for each command or instruction, must be interpreted *as it runs*. This is why BASIC is called an *interpreter*. Each instruction must be looked up in a table to find its address in ROM. And many other aspects of a BASIC instruction need to be interpreted. All this takes time. Your ML code will contain the direct addresses for its JSRs. When that ML program runs, the instructions don't need elaborate interpretation, time-consuming cross-checking, table lookups, or any other delay. The JSR just leaps into the right area of BASIC ROM without further ado.

There are special programs called *compilers* which can take a BASIC program and transform (compile) it into ML-like code which can then be executed like ML, without having to interpret each command during the program's run. The JSRs are within the compiled program, just as in ML. Compiled programs will run perhaps 20 to 40 times faster than the BASIC program they grew out of. (Generally, there is a small price to pay in that the compiled version is almost always larger than its BASIC equivalent.)

Compilers are interesting; they act almost like automatic ML writers. You write it in BASIC, and they translate it into an ML-like program. Even greater improvements in speed can be achieved if a program uses no floating point (decimal points) in the arithmetic. Also, there are "optimized" compilers which take longer during the translation phase to compile the finished program, but which try to create the fastest, most efficient compiled program design possible. No compiler is excessively slow, however. A good optimizing compiler can translate an 8K BASIC program in two or three minutes. Well, why not just compile BASIC programs and forget about ML altogether? The main reason is that ML is always far faster than even optimized compilations. You just can't beat the efficiency of hand-crafted communications which speak directly to the chip in its own language.

## GET and PRINT

Two of the most common activities of a computer program are getting characters from the keyboard and printing them to the screen. To illustrate how to use BASIC from within an ML program, we'll show how both of these tasks can be accomplished from within ML.

Try this program and hit a key on the keyboard. Notice that the code number for whatever character you typed on the keyboard appears in the accumulator.

The 128's BASIC's GET:

```
10 *= $B00
20 .S
30 .O
40 LOOP JSR $FFE4; get a key from the keyboard
50 BEQ LOOP; if no key pressed, try again
60 BRK; now check what's in the accumulator
```

This routine will wait until the user types in a character, but will not show a cursor on the screen. Nor will it print an "echo," an image of the character on the screen.

To print any character to the screen:

| | | |
|---|---|---|
| **2000** | **LDA #$41** | Put the character's ASCII value into the accumulator. |
| **2002** | **JSR $FFD2** | Print it. |

If you combine these routines into a "GET and PRINT," you can leave out the LDA #$41, because JSR $FFE4 will have left the value of whatever key you typed in the accumulator, and JSR $FFD2 will print whatever is in the accumulator to the next available location onscreen. Here's the completed GET and PRINT routine:

```
10 *= $B00
20 .S
30 .O
40 LOOP JSR $FFE4; get a key from the keyboard
50 BEQ LOOP; if no key pressed, try again
60 JSR $FFD2; print it
```

However, if you intend to use or analyze what's being typed into the computer, you must also store each character somewhere in RAM:

```
10 *= $B00
20 .S
30 .O
35 LDY #0:STY STOREY; set up pointer to string buffer
40 LOOP JSR $FFE4; get a key from the keyboard
50 BEQ LOOP; if no key pressed, try again
60 JSR $FFD2; print it
70 LDY STOREY:STA BUFFER,Y:INY:STY STOREY; save
   character and Y
80 JMP LOOP; get another character

500 BUFFER .BYTE 0 0 0 0 0 0 0 0 0 0 0 0 0 0 0 0 0 0 0 0 0 0 0 0 0 0 0
510 STOREY .BYTE 0; safe place to keep the value of Y
```

$FFD2 doesn't change the value of X or Y when we JSR to it. When it RTSs back to our ML program, X and Y are the same as when we JSRed to $FFD2. Most BASIC ROM routines, however, aren't that considerate. Usually, they'll use X and Y and RTS back to your ML with those registers changed unpredictably. So, it's sometimes necessary to preserve the values in X or Y, prior to JSRing into ROM, if you're using X or Y for looping or other purposes. We've done that in the example above by setting aside a byte to hold Y (line 510) and by fetching, updating, and saving Y when necessary (line 70).

Notice that this example is an endless loop: It has no way to exit its loop. You would need to add a CMP #13 if you wanted to exit when the typist hit the RETURN key. You would CMP #13:BEQ END to branch to a label called END which you put somewhere beyond this loop, beyond that JMP LOOP instruction in line 80. You could insert your check for carriage return at line 55. Or, because we've set aside a buffer with only 23 bytes to hold the characters (line 500), you might want to check the value of Y and CPY #23:BEQ END to prevent further input when the buffer had been filled.

In any event, the ML routine within BASIC ROM which keeps track of the current cursor position and will help you print things to the screen is often needed in ML programming. $FFD2 will handle this for you.

You will discover that there are many freeze-dried ML modules sitting in BASIC. These routines were written by the professionals who built BASIC itself, and their methods can seem intimidating at first. However, disassembling some of these routines and picking them apart is a good way to discover new techniques, new efficiencies, and to see how the best ML programs are constructed.

Here's another example to look at. It illustrates how to print out a string, the length of which is known in advance. Although this is less common than the zero-delimiter method of printing strings (BEQ is triggered by a zero at the end of the string), you'll still see this printout method in some software:

```
10 *= $2000
30 LENGTH = 10
40 PRINT = $FFD2
50 ;
60 START LDY #0
70 CLOSE LDA STRING,Y
80 JSR PRINT
90 INY
100 CPY #LENGTH
110 BNE CLOSE
120 RTS
130 ;
140 STRING .BYTE "SUPERDUPER

READY.
```

Studying your computer's BASIC is worth the effort, and it's something you can do for yourself. You won't understand everything (some shortcuts are taken which are obscure in the extreme). Nevertheless, if you've got some time, take a look at a particular routine and see if you can see the logic in it, its purpose and structure. And, as you can see by the example above, you have great freedom to construct the customized INPUT routine that suits your ML program perfectly, that reflects precisely what you want to allow or disallow the user to INPUT, and that formats to the screen or saves in a buffer in the exact way that's most efficient for your purposes.

# Chapter 8

# Building a Program

# Building a Program

Using what we've learned so far and adding a couple of new techniques, let's build a useful program. This example will demonstrate many of the techniques we've discussed and will also show some of the thought processes involved in writing ML.

Among the computer's more impressive talents is searching. It can run through a mass of information and find something very quickly. We can write an ML routine which looks through any area of memory to find matches with anything else. Based on an idea by Michael Erperstorfer published in *COMPUTE!* magazine, this ML program will report the line number of all the matches it finds. You'll also find this a useful utility to keep on your LADS disk. If you need to find a particular subroutine in a long source code file, this "Searcher" program can save considerable time and effort.

## Safe Havens

Before we go through some typical ML program-building methods, let's review the "where do I put it?" question. ML can't be just dropped anywhere in RAM. When you give the starting address to LADS at the beginning of your source code with the *= symbol, you can't just put in any address that pops into mind.

There are other things going on in the computer in addition to your hard-won ML program. RAM is used in many ways. There is always the possibility that you want to have a BASIC program coresident with your ML program. If so, you'll need to figure out where to put the ML so that it won't cover up, or be covered up by, the BASIC. Too, BASIC needs to use part of RAM to store some of its variables. During execution, these variables might be written (POKEd) into your vulnerable ML if you located it in a vulnerable zone. That would fatally corrupt your ML.

Also, the operating system, the disk operating system, cassette or disk loads, printers—they all use parts of RAM for their housekeeping activities. There are other things going on besides your ML. And you obviously can't put your ML program into ROM addresses. That's impossible. Nothing can be

POKEd into those frozen ROM addresses; they're *read only memory*, no writing allowed.

This is one good use for a map of the 128. It will tell you where you can safely store your programs and variables without interfering with space used by the computer itself. For example, assume that you're writing a program which will need to access the disk drive. To complicate things, you want to use about six two-byte spaces in zero page (the lowest 256 bytes in memory) for your own program. ROM routines also make heavy use of zero page, but you can't use bytes they'll be using since the ROM routines would then interfere with your data and mess up your pointers. The solution is to look at the map (see Appendix C).

To solve the above problem, you'd notice that addresses 250–254 are safe. But we need more than this. Looking at the map of the 128, you can see that addresses 99–111 are used for floating-point operations and thus can be expected to be safe, too. We'll be accessing the disk drive but the floating-point routines won't be involved in this program. That solves our problem.

On the 128, the tape-drive zero page usage is not conveniently contiguous, but you can still find two-byte pairs which are safe. Also, if you're not using other ROM routines in your program, look for their zero page areas. For example, the floating-point accumulators can often be used if you're not accessing math routines in ROM.

You'll also be able to stash things (though not for zero page access) safely in various other places in RAM where your ML program won't be in the way. If you're not using sprites, you can put your program or variables between addresses 3584 and 4095. Also free for ML use is the foreign language and function key area between 4864 and 7167 or the section reserved for a BASIC program even when bank 15 is operative (7168–16384).

The 128 is a very RAM-rich machine, though, so you'll also be able to use most of banks 0 and 1 even if you do require ROM routines. Just switch them in and out as necessary, or invoke the special long-distance LDA, STA, CMP, JSR, and JMP Kernal routines available in the 128.

## Misleading the Computer

If the ML is a short piece of program, you can stash it into the safe $B00–$BFF zone mentioned before, the cassette drive buffer area. Because this safe area is only 256 bytes long, and because so many ML routines will want to use that area, it can become crowded. Worse yet, it isn't 100 percent safe. The 128 uses the top part of this area sometimes. If you notice odd things happening, memory conflict is one of the first things to suspect. For example, you might be able to run an ML program at $B00 the first time, but subsequent SYSs to it will crash. If you've used a ROM routine, it might well have "borrowed" a few bytes from the $B00 zone. That would have the effect of damaging your ML.

An alternative, particularly worthwhile when you're using ML as an extension of BASIC and they are supposed to work together, is to deceive the computer into thinking that its RAM is smaller than it really is.

Your ML will be truly safe if your computer doesn't even suspect the existence of some set-aside RAM. It will leave the now-safe RAM alone because you've told it that it has less RAM than it really does. Nothing can overwrite your ML program after you've misled your computer's operating system about the size of its RAM memory. There are two bytes in zero page which tell the computer what its highest RAM address is for bank 1. You just change those bytes to point to a lower address. You can have your ML program do this as its first job. While this trick is effective on the 64, the 128's memory management system makes things more complicated.

Nevertheless, if you want to try, these crucial top-of-memory bytes are 57,58 ($39,$3A hex).

To repeat, pointers such as these are stored in LSB,MSB order. That is, the more significant byte (the one that's multiplied by 256) comes second (this is the reverse of normality). For example, $8000, divided between two bytes in this top-of-RAM pointer, would look like this:

**0039 00**
**003A 80**

As we mentioned earlier, this odd inversion of normal numeric representation is a peculiarity of the 8502 that you just have to get used to. You can take comfort in the fact that the

8502 and its family of chips have far fewer peculiarities and illogical rules than their main rivals, the Z80 family. You can be driven to distraction with chips where the language is frequently at odds with the way humans think. Destinations precede sources, and so on. It's maddening. Fortunately, the 68000 chip, the chip in the Amiga, is a sensible, programmer-friendly chip, too. If you go on to learn how to work with this new generation of chips, the 8502 family will seem both familiar and reasonable. But do beware of the pointer inversion: The LSB is stored in the lower byte in memory. It's a small price to pay for an otherwise well-designed microprocessor.

Anyway, you can lower the computer's opinion of the top-of-RAM-memory, thereby making a safe place for your ML in 64 mode, by changing only the MSB. If you need one page (256 bytes), POKE 58, PEEK (58)−1. For four pages, POKE 58, PEEK (58)−4, and so on. You don't need to fiddle around with the LSB of the pointer. Give yourself plenty of room. Note that for the POKEs to be effective, they must be followed by a BASIC CLR (CLeaR variables) command. The full statement would be something like POKE 58, PEEK(58)−4:CLR. Since the CLR erases all variable values, this should generally be the first statement in any program in which this technique is used.

This chapter also introduces an important consideration when assembling source code that's larger than 1K (1024 bytes). When your work begins to exceed this size, you should switch to disk-based assembly (see Appendix B for complete instructions). The reason is that LADS reserves all of bank 1 for object code and all of bank 0 for source code. LADS itself is in bank 15 (which uses the same RAM as bank 0) and, when you are assembling with RAMLADS—as we have for all the examples in the book thus far—small source code will create no memory conflicts.

However, source code for RAMLADS resides at 7168 and, as you type in more source code, it builds up from there. RAMLADS itself resides at 10000. This leaves 2832 bytes free. During assembly, LADS builds its label array down from 10000 and so, when your source code reaches a size somewhat larger than 1K, the labels and source will meet and you'll start getting error messages about undefined labels that you know you've defined, and so forth.

RAMLADS is best for trying out short, under 1K, source

code. When your program grows beyond this size, you need to switch to DISKLADS. With DISKLADS, source code or object code can be much larger since each source file is loaded from disk into bank 0 RAM above LADS, assembly takes place on the source code in memory, and the resulting object code is stored in bank 1 where it will be entirely safe. When all source files have been assembled, the object code will be saved to disk.

Because of all the comments, the source code of Searcher, the example program in this chapter, is 4K large. You can type it all in without worry, but you should make a habit of first DSAVEing source code prior to assembling in case you run into memory conflict or other problems during the assembly. It is necessary to invoke DISKLADS with Searcher. If you attempt to assemble it via RAMLADS, LIST will reveal that part of the source code has been overwritten by the label array.

## Building the Code

Now we return to the subject at hand—building an ML program. Most people find it easiest to mentally divide a task into several tasks, solve the individual small tasks, and then weave them all together into a complete program. That's how we'll attack the job of building a search program.

We will build our ML program in pieces and then tie them all together at the end. The first phase, as always, is the initialization. We set up the variables and fill in the pointers. Lines 90 and 100 define two, two-byte zero page pointers. L1L is going to point at the address of the BASIC line we are currently searching through; L2L points to the starting address of the line following it.

BASIC stores four important bytes just prior to the start of the code in each BASIC line. Take a look at Figure 8-1. The first two bytes contain the address of the next line in the BASIC program. Thus, when BASIC has finished evaluating and acting upon the current line, it will already know where to go to find the next line. This is called *linking*.

The second two bytes hold the line number. The end of a BASIC line is signaled by a zero. Zero does not stand for anything in the ASCII code or for any BASIC command. This is quite similar to the way we signal in ML programs that a text message is finished—by storing a zero at the end of the text. We discussed this earlier when we talked of *delimiting* an ASCII message.

If there are three zeros in a row, it tells BASIC that it has reached the end of the program in memory. Three zeros is a super delimiter.

But back to our examination of the ML program. In line 110 is a definition of the zero page location which holds a two-byte number that BASIC looks at when it is going to print a line number on the screen. We'll want to store line numbers in this location as we come upon them during the execution of our ML search. Each line number will temporarily sit waiting in case a match is found. If a match is found, the program will JSR to the BASIC ROM routine we're calling PLINE, as defined in line 140. This routine prints a line number on the screen, and it will need to have the "current line number" where it expects to find it.

Line 120 establishes that BASIC RAM starts at $1C00, and line 130 gives the address of the "print the character in the accumulator" ROM routine. Use *= $B00 to put the object code into the traditional "safe" RAM area to store short ML programs.

Refer to Program 8-1 to follow the logic of the construction of our search program. The search is initiated by typing in line 0, followed by the item we want to locate. It might be that we are interested in removing all REM statements from a program to shorten it. We would type 0REM and hit RETURN to enter this line into the BASIC program. Then we would start the search by a SYS to the starting address of the ML program: SYS 2816.

By entering the "sample" string or command into the BASIC program, we simplify our task in two ways. First, if the thing we're searching for is a string, it will be automatically stored as the ASCII code for that string, just as BASIC stores strings.

If it is a keyword like REM, it will be translated into the "tokenized," one-byte representation of the keyword, just as BASIC stores keywords.

The second problem this method solves is that our sample is located in a known area of RAM. By looking at Figure 8-1, you can tell that the sample's starting address will always be the start of BASIC plus five. In Program 8-1 that means $1C05 (see line 1090).

**Figure 8-1. A BASIC Program's Structure**

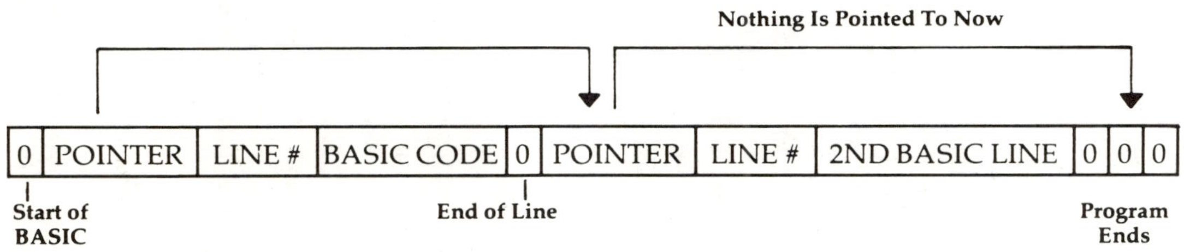


```
10 PRINT"HI"
20 END

1C00                          1C0B           1C11
00 0B 1C 0A 00 99 22 48 49 22 00 11 1C 14 00 80 00 00 00
         LINE    ? "   H  I  "        LINE  END
          10                           20
```

## Set Up the Pointers

Our first job, as always when we're going to be using ROM routines, is to switch in bank 15. We do this in lines 190–200.

Then we'll need to get the address of the next line in the BASIC program we are searching. And then we need to store it while we look through the current line. The way that BASIC lines are arranged, we come upon the link to the next line's address and the line number before we see any BASIC code itself. Therefore, the first order of business is to put the address of the next line into our L1L location for safekeeping. Lines 240–270 take the link found in start-of-BASIC RAM (plus one) and move it to the storage pointer L1L.

Next, lines 320–380 check to see if we have reached the end of the BASIC program. It would be the end if we had found two zeros in a row as the pointer to the next line's address. If it is the end, the RTS sends us back to BASIC mode.

The subroutine in lines 540–720 saves the pointer to the following line's address and also the current line number.

Note the double-byte addition in lines 670–720. We *always* CLC before any addition. If adding four to the LSB (line 680) results in a carry, we want to be sure that the MSB goes up by one during the ADd with Carry in line 710. At first glance, it seems to make no sense to add a zero in that line. What's the point? We're doing an addition *with carry*; in other words, if the carry flag has been set up by the addition of four to the LSB in line 680, then the MSB will have one added to it. That's the carry. The carry flag makes this happen.

## First Characters

When you're searching for something, say, your car in a parking lot, you look for something distinctive. You might search for the color blue, or perhaps a plastic flower that you've attached to the antenna. You certainly don't look at each entire car, at the hood, the wheels, the windows, the size, the color, etcetera, etcetera. You look for a single attribute; then, if the car is blue, you compare other attributes to see if it is indeed entirely the same as yours.

Likewise, it's better just to compare the first character in a word against each byte in the searched memory than to try to compare the entire sample word. If you are looking for the word MEM, you don't want to stop at each byte in memory and see if M-E-M starts there. Just look for *M*'s. When you come upon an *M, then* go through the full string comparison. If line 920 finds a first-character match, it transfers the program to the subroutine labeled SAME (line 1060) which will perform a thorough comparison.

On the other hand, if the routine starting at line 890 comes upon a zero (line 900), it knows that the BASIC line has ended (all BASIC lines end with zero, and zero is not used in any other way within a BASIC program). Our search program then goes down to STOPLINE (line 1240), which puts the "next line" address pointer into the "current line" pointer, and the whole process of reading a new BASIC line begins anew.

If, however, a perfect match *was* found (line 1100 found a zero at the end of the 0:REM line, showing that we had come to the end of the sample string), we go to PERFECT and it makes a JSR to print out the line number (line 1390). The PERFECT subroutine bounces back (RTS) to STOPLINE, which replaces the "current line" (L1L) pointer with the "next line" pointer (L2L).

Then we JMP back to READLINE, which, once again, pays very close attention to zeros to see if the whole BASIC program has ended with a pair of zeros. We have now returned to the start of the main loop of this ML program.

This all sounds more complicated than it is. If you've followed it so far, you can see that there is enormous flexibility in constructing ML programs. If you want to put the STOPLINE segment before the SAME subroutine—go ahead. Self-contained subroutines are not position-dependent.

It is quite common to see a structure like this:

```
Definitions
SCREEN = $0400
Initialization
LDA #15
STA $83
Main Loop

START  JSR 1
       JSR 2
       JSR 3
BEQ START  Until some index runs out
RTS        To BASIC
```

***Subroutines***
*1*
*2* Each ends with RTS back to the Main Loop
*3*
***DATA***
***Table 1***
***Table 2***
***Table 3***

These are the main subdivisions of machine language programs. If you use this structure, you will find that it simplifies locating the different parts of a program, and it also prevents nonprogram data (such as tables, messages, definitions) from getting mixed in with the program code proper. LADS is designed using this nearly universal format. Since all but the shortest programs will have defined variables, initialization, a main loop, a cluster of subroutines, and, finally, a collection of data tables, why not organize all your programs in this simple, straightforward, and sensible way?

Try typing in the source code in Program 8-1 and assembling it with LADS. (Refer to Appendix B for instructions on using LADS.) As mentioned earlier, because of the length of the source code, you'll need to save it on disk and use DISKLADS. After you've assembled the source code, you'll need to BLOAD the object file created during the assembly. Next, load the BASIC program you wish to search and add line number 0 containing the word or words you want to seach for. Then use SYS 2816 to activate the program; that's where it sits in RAM.

As your skills improve, you will likely begin to appreciate, and finally embrace, the extraordinary freedom that ML confers on the programmer.

At first, learning ML can seem fraught with apparently endless obscure tricks and rules. It can even seem menacing, beyond your understanding. It's this way with every new language because the words are still new, still odd.

Everyone passes through this (surprisingly brief) sense of dread. Once you know how to tell your computer, directly in its language, how to print something on the screen, you don't need to relearn this trick. Things fall into place. It won't take as long as it might now seem for you to begin to grasp the relatively few novelties of machine language programming. ML isn't the theory of relativity; it's no more difficult than BASIC.

It's just a new vocabulary for the same programming techniques you've been using with BASIC.

And this brief sensation, this brief confusion, is a very small price to pay for the flights you will soon be taking through your computer. Work at it. Try things. Learn how to find your errors. It's not circular—there will be steady advances in your understanding. One day soon, you'll be able to easily turbocharge your BASIC programs with ML, to write convenient, custom utilities like our search routine, and to do pretty much anything you could want to do with your machine.

**Program 8-1. Search Source Code**

```
10 *= $B00
20 .S
30 .D 8-1 SEARCHER
40 ;SEARCH THROUGH BASIC
50 ;128 MODE VERSION
60 ;-----------------------
70 ;      DEFINE VARIABLES BY GIVING THEM LABELS
80 ;
90 L1L = $FA;        ZERO PAGE
100 L2L = $FC
110 FOUND = $3B
120 BASIC = $1C00;       START OF BASIC
130 PRINT = $FFD2;      PRINT A CHARACTER
140 PLINE = $8E2E;      PRINT LINE #
150 ;-----------------------
160 ; SWITCH TO BANK 15 SO WE HAVE ACCESS
170 ; TO THE ROM ROUTINES.
180 ;
190 LDA #0
200 STA $FF00
210 ;-----------------------
220 ;     INITIALIZE POINTERS
230 ;
240 LDA BASIC+1;GET ADDRESS OF NEXT
250 STA L1L;BASIC LINE
260 LDA BASIC+2
270 STA L1L+1
280 ;-----------------------
290 ;      SUBROUTINE TO CHECK FOR 2 ZEROS
```

```
300 ;     IF WE DON'T FIND THEM, WE ARE
310 ;    NOT AT THE END OF THE PROGRAM
320 READLINE LDY #Ø
330 LDA (L1L),Y
340 BNE GOON;NOT END OF LINE
350 INY
360 LDA (L1L),Y;ØØ ØØ IS END OF PROG.
370 BNE GOON
380 END RTS;RETURN TO BASIC MODE
390 ;----------------------
400 ;      SUBROUTINE TO UPDATE POINTERS
410 ;      TO THE NEXT LINE AND STORE
420 ;     THE CURRENT LINE NUMBER IN
430 ;     CASE WE FIND A MATCH AND NEED
440 ;     TO PRINT THE LINE #.
450 ;     ALSO, WE ADD 4 TO THE CURRENT
460 ;     LINE POINTER SO THAT WE ARE
470 ;     PAST THE LINE # AND THE
480 ;     "POINTER-TO-NEXT-LINE"
490 ;     INFORMATION.  WE ARE THEN
500 ;     POINTING AT THE 1ST CHAR.
510 ;     IN THE CURRENT LINE AND CAN
520 ;     COMPARE IT TO THE SAMPLE.
530 ;
540 GOON LDY #Ø
550 LDA (L1L),Y;GET NEXT LINE
560 STA L2L;ADDRESS
570 INY;AND STORE IT IN L2L
580 LDA (L1L),Y
590 STA L2L+1
600 INY
```

```
610 LDA (L1L),Y;PUT LINE NUMBER
620 STA FOUND;IN STORAGE TOO
630 INY;IN CASE IT NEEDS
640 LDA (L1L),Y;TO BE
650 STA FOUND+1;PRINTED OUT LATER
660 LDA L1L
670 CLC; MOVE POINTER FORWARD
680 ADC #4;TO 1ST PART OF BASIC TEXT
690 STA L1L;(PAST LINE NUMBER AND
700 LDA L1L+1; ADDRESS OF NEXT LINE)
710 ADC #Ø
720 STA L1L+1
730 ;----------------------
740 ;SUBROUTINE TO CHECK FOR Ø
750 ; (IS LINE FINISHED) AND THEN
760 ; CHECK 1ST CHARACTER IN THE BASIC
770 ; LINE AGAINST THE 1ST CHARACTER
780 ; IN THE STRING AT LINE Ø. IF
790 ; THESE CHARACTERS MATCH, WE MOVE
800 ; TO A FULL STRING COMPARISON IN
810 ; THE SUBROUTINE BELOW CALLED "SAME"
820 ; BUT IF THE 1ST CHARS. DON'T MATCH
830 ; WE RAISE THE "Y" COUNTER AND
840 ; CHECK FOR A MATCH IN THE 2ND
850 ; CHARACTER OF THE CURRENT LINE'S
860 ; TEXT
870 ;
880 LDY #Ø
890 LOOP LDA (L1L),Y
900 BEQ STOPLINE;    ZERO MEANS LINE FINISHED
910 CMP BASIC+5;    SAME AS 1ST SAMPLE CHAR
```

```
920 BEQ SAME;        YES CHECK WHOLE STRING
930 INY;             NO CONTINUE SEARCH
940 JMP LOOP
950 ;-----------------------
960 ;SUBROUTINE TO LOOK AT EACH CHARACTER
970 ;IN BOTH THE SAMPLE (LINE Ø) AND THE TARGET
980 ;(CURRENT LINE) TO SEE IF THERE IS A PERFECT
990 ;MATCH.  Y KEEPS TRACK OF THE TARGET AND X
1000 ;KEEPS TRACK OF THE SAMPLE AT Ø.  IF WE FIND
1010 ;A MISMATCH BEFORE A LINE-END ZERO, WE FALL
1020 ;THROUGH TO LINE 1130 AND THEN JUMP BACK UP
1030 ;TO LINE 890 WHERE WE CONTINUE ON LOOKING
1040 ;FOR 1ST CHAR. MATCHES IN THE CURRENT LINE
1050 ;
1060 SAME LDX #Ø;    COMPARE SAMPLE TO TARGET
1070 COMPARE INX
1080 INY
1090 LDA BASIC+5,X
1100 BEQ PERFECT;  LINE ENDS SO PRINT
1110 CMP (L1L),Y
1120 BEQ COMPARE;  CONTINUE COMPARE
1130 JMP LOOP;     NO MATCH
1140 PERFECT JSR PRINTOUT
1150 ;-----------------------
1160 ;SUBROUTINE TO REPLACE "CURRENT LINE"
1170 ;POINTER WITH THE "NEXT LINE" POINTER THAT
1180 ;WE SAVED IN THE SUBROUTINE STARTING AT
1190 ;LINE 54Ø.
1200 ;THEN JUMP BACK TO THE START WHERE
1210 ;WE'LL CHECK FOR THE END-OF-PROGRAM DOUBLE ZERO.
1220 ;THIS IS THE LAST SUBROUTINE IN THE MAIN LOOP OF THE PROGRAM.
```

```
1230 ;
1240 STOPLINE LDA L2L;   TRANSFER NEXT LINE
1250 STA L1L;           ADDRESS POINTER TO
1260 LDA L2L+1;         CURRENT LINE POINTER
1270 STA L1L+1;         TO GET READY TO READ
1280 JMP READLINE;      THE NEXT LINE.
1290 ;-----------------------
1300 ;SUBROUTINE TO PRINT OUT A BASIC LINE NUMBER.
1310 ;THE ROM ROUTINE PLINE TAKES THE NUMBER
1320 ;IN $3B,3C AND THEN PRINTS.
1330 ;THE ROM ROUTINE WILL PRINT THE NUMBER AT THE
1340 ;NEXT CURSOR POSITION ON THE SCREEN. THEN WE
1350 ;PRINT A BLANK SPACE AND RETURN TO LINE 610
1360 ;TO CONTINUE ON WITH THE MAIN LOOP AND
1370 ;MAYBE FIND MORE MATCHES.
1380 ;
1390 PRINTOUT JSR PLINE
1400 LDA #$20;     PRINT A BLANK
1410 JSR PRINT;    SPACE BETWEEN NUMBERS
1420 RTS
1430 .END 8-1

READY.
```

# Chapter 9

# ML Equivalents of BASIC Commands

# ML Equivalents of BASIC Commands

What follows is a small dictionary, arranged alphabetically, of the major BASIC commands. If you need to accomplish something in ML—TAB, for example—look it up in this chapter to see one way of doing it in ML. Often, because ML is so much freer than BASIC, there will be several ways to go about a given task.

Of these choices, one might work faster, one might take up less memory, and one might be easier to program and understand. For this chapter, example routines were selected to favor those which are easier to program and understand.

At ML's extraordinary speeds, and with the large amounts of RAM memory available to today's computerists, it will be rare that you will need to opt for velocity or memory efficiency.

## CLR

In BASIC, this clears all variables. Its primary effect is to reset pointers. It is a somewhat abbreviated form of NEW since it does not "blank out" your program as NEW does.

CLR, in fact, is rarely used.

We might think of CLR, in ML, as the *initialization* phase of a program which erases (fills with zeros) the memory locations you've set aside to hold your ML flags, pointers, counters, and so on. You can see an example of this in the LADS source code in Eval between lines 30 and 70 (Appendix D).

Before an ML program runs, you will usually want to be sure that some of its variables are set to zero. If they are in different places in memory, you will need to zero them individually:

```
2000  LDA #$0
2002  STA $1990   Put zero into one of the "variables."
2005  STA $1994   Continue putting zero into each byte which
                  needs to be initialized.
```

On the other hand, if you've put all your variables together at the end, the job is easy: Just loop through the list, putting zero in each variable. BASIC sets up a group of its variables (pointers) in zero page, so you can use a loop to zero them out:

| | | |
|---|---|---|
| **2000** | **LDA #$0** | |
| **2002** | **LDY #$0F** | Y will be the counter. There are 15 bytes to zero out in this example. |
| **2004** | **STA $199,Y** | The highest of the 15 bytes. |
| **2007** | **DEY** | |
| **2008** | **BNE $2004** | Let Y count down to zero, BNEing until Y is zero, then the Branch if Not Equal will let the program fall through to the next instruction at $200A. |

## CONT

This BASIC command allows your program to pick up where it left off after a STOP command. You might want to look at STOP, below. In ML, you can't usually get a running program to stop with the RUN/STOP key. If you like, you could write a subroutine which checks to see if a particular key is being held down on the keyboard and, if it is, BRK:

| | | |
|---|---|---|
| **3000** | **JSR $FFE4;** | Routine to get the key currently pressed. |
| **3003** | **BEQ 3000;** | If nothing is currently pressed, keep looking. |
| **3005** | **CMP #13** | This is the RETURN key on your machine, but you'll want CMP here to the value that appears in the "currently pressed" byte for the key you select as your "stop" key. It could be any key. If you want to use A for your "stop" key, try CMP #$41. |
| **3007** | **BNE $300A** | If it's not your target key, jump to RTS. |
| **3009** | **BRK** | If it is the target, BRK... |
| **300A** | **RTS** | back to the routine which called this subroutine. |

However, the above routine *requires* that some key be pressed. It will keep branching back to 3000 until some key is pressed. This is the kind of input you would use when you printed a menu and wanted the program to pause until a selection was made.

There is, however, a location in zero page, the byte at $D4, which detects keypresses on the fly. You could LDA $D4:CMP #10:BEQ FOUNDA (FOUNDA is your routine that does something whenever the user presses the A). Notice that the code for the letter *A* has a value of ten here. Unlike a JSR $FFE4, the value returned from location $D4 is not regular ASCII. It's a different code, the "keyboard matrix code," and there's no use learning it or having a chart of it. Carriage return is 1, the letter *A* is 10; when no key is pressed, $D4 contains an 88. If you need to know sometime what value will be in $D4 for a particular keypress, just look at $D4 via BASIC with this simple program:

```
10 PRINT PEEK(212);:GOTO 10
```

and then press the key you're interested in.

Now back to CONT, the matter at hand. The 8502 places the program counter (plus two) on the stack after a BRK. A close analogy to BASIC is the placement of BRK within ML code to cause a halt to program execution. Then, after examining registers or variables or *buffers* (places that hold input or output before it's received or sent), you can restart your program by using the monitor G (go) command. G is the equivalent of CONT.

## DATA

In BASIC, DATA announces that the items following the word DATA are to be considered pieces of information (as opposed to being thought of as parts of the program). That is, the program will probably *use* this data, but the data elements are not BASIC commands.

In ML, such a zone of "nonprogram" is called a *table*. It is unique only in that the program counter never starts trying to run through a table to carry out instructions. This never happens because you never transfer program control, using JMP, JSR, or a branching instruction, to anything within a table. (This is similar to the way that BASIC slides right over DATA lines.) There are no meaningful instructions inside a table. To see what a table looks like and what it does, see the Tables subprogram in the LADS source code in Appendix D.

To keep things simple, tables of data are usually stored together either above or below the program. Usually, tables are stored above, at the very end of the ML program (see Figure 9-1).

Tables can hold messages that are to be printed to the screen, hold variables, hold flags (temporary indicators), and so on. If you disassemble your BASIC in ROM, you'll find the words STOP, RUN, LIST, and so forth, gathered together in a table. You can suspect a data table when your disassembler starts giving lots of ??? error messages. It cannot find groups of meaningful opcodes within tables.

**Figure 9-1. Typical ML Program Organization**

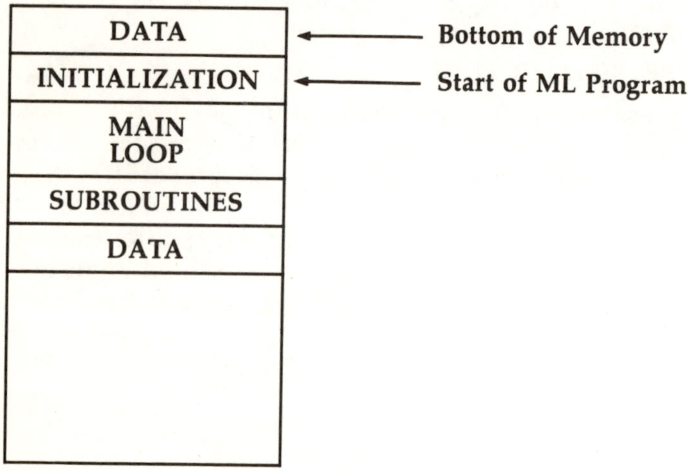


# DIM

With its automatic string handling, array management, and error messages, BASIC makes life easy for the programmer.

The price you pay for this hand holding is that it slows down the program when it's run. In ML, the DIMensioning of space in memory for variables is not explicitly handled by the computer. You must make a note that you are setting aside memory from $6000 to $6500, or whatever, to hold variables. It helps to make a simple map of this "dimensioned" memory so that you know where permanent strings, constants, variable strings, and variables, flags, and so on, are *within* the dimensioned zone. Because this set-aside memory will not contain meaningful ML instructions, it is generally placed at the end of the actual ML program. With LADS, you can make Tables the final file in your chain of files. That will automatically put the tables at the end of your program proper. To define data (string or numeric), you use the .BYTE instruction; .BYTE automatically makes space, like DIM.

A particular chunk of memory (where, and how much, is up to you) is reserved; that's all. You don't write any instructions in 8502 ML to set aside the memory; you just start using the .BYTE pseudo-op and it fills in your tables. That's why it's best to place tables at the end of your program. This way, they can be enlarged conveniently without affecting any other part of the program.

## END

There are several ways to make a graceful exit from ML programs. You can JMP to the "warm start" address ($4003). Or you can go to the "cold start" address ($4000).

If you went into the ML *from* BASIC with a SYS, you can return to BASIC with an RTS. Recall that every JSR matches up with its own RTS. Every time you use a JSR, it shoves its "return here" address onto the top of the stack. If the computer finds another JSR (before any RTS), it will shove another return address on top of the first one. So, after two JSRs, the stack contains two return addresses. When the first RTS is encountered, the top return address is lifted from the stack and put into the program counter so that the program returns control to the current instruction following the most recent JSR.

When the next RTS is encountered, it pulls *its* appropriate return (waiting for it on the stack), and so on. The effect of a SYS from BASIC is like a JSR from within ML. The return address to the correct spot *within BASIC* is put on the stack. In this way, if you are within ML and there is an RTS (without any preceding JSR), what's on the stack will be a return-to-BASIC address left there by SYS when you first went into ML.

Another way to END is to put a BRK in your ML code. This drops you into the machine's monitor. Normally, you use BRKs during program debugging. When the program is finished, though, you would not want this ungraceful exit any more than you would want to end a BASIC program with STOP.

In fact, many ML programs, if they stand alone and are not part of a larger BASIC program, never end at all. They are an endless loop. The main loop just keeps cycling over and over. A game will not end until you turn off the power. After each game, you see the score and are asked to press a key when you are ready for the next game. Arcade games which cost a quarter will ask for another quarter, but they don't end.

They go into "attract mode." The game graphics are left running onscreen to interest new customers.

An ML word processor will cycle through its main loop, waiting for keys to be pressed, words to be written, format or disk instructions to be given. Here, too, it is common to find that the word processor takes over the machine, and you cannot stop it without turning the computer off. Among other things, such an endless loop protects software from being pirated. Since it takes control of the machine, this makes it harder for someone to save it or examine it once it's in RAM? Some such programs are "autobooting" in that they start themselves running as soon as they are loaded into the computer.

BASIC, itself an ML program, also loops endlessly until you power down. When a program is running, all sorts of things are happening. BASIC is an *interpreter*, which means that it must look up each word (like INT) it comes across during a RUN (interpreting, or *translating*, its meaning into machine-understandable JSRs). Then, BASIC executes the correct sequence of ML actions from its collection of routines.

In contrast to BASIC RUNs, BASIC spends 99 percent of its time waiting for you to *program* with it. This waiting for you to press keys is its endless loop, a tight, small loop indeed.

It would look like our "which key is pressed?" routine:

```
2000 LOOP LDA $D4; THE "WHICH KEY IS BEING
     PRESSED" LOCATION
2002 CMP #88; IF 88, KEEP LOOPING
2004 BEQ LOOP
```

If there is an 88 in $D4, this means that no key has been pressed. So, we keep looping until the value in address $D4 is something other than 88. This setup is similar to INPUT in BASIC because not only does it wait until a key is pressed, but it also leaves a unique value of the key in the accumulator when it's finished.

## FOR-NEXT

Everyone has had to use delay loops in BASIC (FOR T = 1 TO 1000: NEXT T) which are also tight loops, sometimes called do-nothing loops because nothing happens between the FOR and the NEXT except the passage of time. For example, when you need to let the user read something on the screen, it's sometimes easier just to use a delay loop than to say, "When finished reading, press any key."

In any case, you'll need to use delay loops in ML just to *slow ML itself down*. In a game, the ball can fly across the screen. It can get so fast, in fact, that you can't see it. It just "appears" when it bounces off a wall. And, of course, you'll need to use loops in many other situations. Loops of all kinds are fundamental programming techniques.

In ML, you don't have that convenient little counter (T in the BASIC FOR-NEXT example above) which decides when to stop the loop. When T becomes 1000, go to the instructions beyond the word NEXT. Again, you must set up and check your *counter variable* by yourself.

If the loop is going to be smaller than 255 cycles, you can use the X register as the counter—Y is saved for the very useful *indirect indexed* addressing discussed in Chapter 4: LDA (96),Y. Anyway, by using X, you can count to 200 by:

```
2000  LDX  #200    (or $C8 hex)
2002  DEX
2003  BNE  $2002
```

For loops involving counters larger than 255, you'll need to use two bytes to count down, one going from 255 to 0 and then clicking (like a gear) the other (more significant) byte.

To count to 512:

```
2000  LDA  #$2
2002  STA  $6000   Put the 2 into address 6000, our MSB, most
                   significant byte, counter.
2004  LDX  #$0     Set X to 0 so that its first DEX will make it 255.
                   Further DEXs will count down again to 0, when
                   it will click the MSB down from 2 to 1 and then
                   finally to 0.
2006  DEX
2007  BNE  $2006
2009  DEC  $6000   Click the number in address 6000 down 1.
200B  BNE  $2006
```

Here we used the X register as the LSB (least significant byte) and address 6000 as the MSB. Why use address 6000? Why not? Use any RAM byte you want that won't interfere with other things going on in the computer. In practice, you'll want to set aside a byte in your Tables at the end of your ML program to be sure that it's not going to interfere with something. See DATA above for a discussion of Tables.

We could use addresses $FA *and* $FB to hold the MSB/LSB if we wanted. This is commonly useful because then address $FA (or some available, two-byte space in zero page) can be used for LDA ($FA),Y. You would print a message to the screen using the combination of a zero page counter and LDA (zero page address),Y.

## FOR-NEXT-STEP

Here you would just increase your counter (usually X or Y) more than once. To create FOR I = 100 TO 1 STEP −2 you could use:

```
2000  LDX  #100
2002  DEX
2003  DEX
2004  BNE  $2002
```

For larger numbers you create a counter which uses two bytes, working together, to keep count of the events. Following our example above for FOR-NEXT, we could translate FOR I = 512 TO 0 STEP −2:

```
200  2000  LDA  #$2
210  2002  STA  COUNTER   This is going to hold our MSB.
220  2004  LDX  #$0       X is holding our LSB.
230  2006  DEX
240  2007  DEX            Here we click X down a second time,
                          for −2.
250  2008  BNE  $2006
260  200A  DEC  COUNTER
270  200c  BNE  $2006

400  COUNTER .BYTE 0; A single byte set aside in our Tables
```

(In this example, we've shown how you would create LADS source code to set aside a COUNTER byte above the main code. However, the addresses of this code, 2000–200C, are not known when you write source code. They are created after you activate LADS. They're here just for illustrative purposes. *You don't type in addresses when writing source code for LADS.*)

To count up, use the CoMPare instruction. FOR I = 1 TO 50 STEP 3:

```
2000 LDX #$0
2002 INX
2003 INX
2004 INX
2005 CPX #$50
2007 BNE $2002
```

For larger STEP sizes, you can use a *nested loop* within the larger one. This would avoid a whole slew of INXs. To write the ML equivalent of FOR I = 1 TO 50 STEP 10:

```
2000 LDX #$0
2002 LDY #$0
2004 INY
2005 CPY #$0A
2007 BNE $2004
2009 CPX #$32
200B BNE $2002
```

## GET

Every computer must have that important "which key is being pressed?" address, where it holds the value of a character typed in from the keyboard. To GET, you create a very small loop which tests this address. See a complete description of this technique under CONT above.

## GOSUB

This is nearly identical to BASIC. Use JSR $*NNNN* and you will go to a subroutine at address *NNNN* instead of a line number as in BASIC. (*NNNN* just means that you can substitute any hex number for the *NNNN* that you want to. This is a form of math shorthand.) LADS allows you to give *labels,* names to JSR to, instead of addresses. A simple assembler like the one in the monitor does not allow labels. You are responsible (as with DATA tables, variables, and so on) for keeping a list of your subroutine addresses *and the parameters involved* if you're not using LADS.

*Parameters* are the number or numbers handed to a subroutine to give it information it needs. Quite often, BASIC subroutines work with the variables already established within the BASIC program. In ML, though, managing variables is up to you. Subroutines are useful because they can perform tasks repeatedly without needing to be written into the body of the program each time the task is to be carried out. Beyond this, they can be *generalized* so that a single subroutine can act in a variety of ways, depending upon the variable (the parameter) which is passed to it.

A delay loop to slow up a program could be general in the sense that the amount of delay is handed to the subroutine each time. The delay can, in this way, be of differing durations, depending on what it gets as a parameter from the main routine.

Let's say that we've decided to use address $40 to pass parameters to subroutines. We could pass a delay of five cycles of the loop by:

```
                  2000  LDA  #$5
The Main Program  2002  STA  $40
                  2004  JSR  $5000
                  .
                  .
                  .
                  .
                  5000  DEC  $40
                  5002  BEQ  $500C  If address $40 has counted
                                    all the way down from 5
                                    to 0, RTS back to the main
                                    program.
                  5004  LDY  #$0
                  5006  DEY
The Subroutine    5007  BNE  $5006
                  5009  JMP  $5000
                  500C  RTS
```

A delay which lasted twice as long as the above would merely require a single change to the calling routine: 2000 LDA #$0A.

## GOTO

In ML, it's JMP. JMP is like JSR, except the address you leap away from is not saved anywhere. You jump, but cannot use an RTS to find your way back.

There are two basic kinds of branching in computing. A *conditional* branch would be CMP #0:BEQ 5000. The condition of equality is tested by BEQ, Branch if EQual. BNE tests a condition of inequality, Branch if Not Equal. Likewise, BCC (Branch if Carry is Clear) and the rest of these branches are testing conditions within the program.

GOTO and JMP do not depend on any conditions within the program, so they are *unconditional* branches. The question arises when you use a GOTO: Why did you write a part of your program that you must *always* (unconditionally) jump over? GOTO and JMP are sometimes used to patch up a program, but used without restraint, they can make your program hard to understand later. On the other hand, JMP can many times be the best solution to a programming problem. In fact, it is hard to imagine ML programming without it.

One additional note about JMP: It makes a program nonrelocatable. If you later need to move your whole ML program to a different part of memory, all the JMPs (and JSRs) need to be checked to see if they are pointing to addresses which are no longer correct. (JMP or JSR into your BASIC ROMs will still be the same, but not those which are targeted to addresses *within* the ML program.)

```
2000  JMP  $2005
2003  LDY  #$3
2005  LDA  #$5
```

If you moved this little program up to $5000, everything would survive intact and work correctly except the JMP $2005. It would still say to jump to $2005, but it should say to jump to $5005, after the move. You have to go through with a disassembly and check for all these incorrect JMPs. To make your programs more "relocatable," you can use a special trick with unconditional branching which *will* move without needing to be fixed:

```
2000  LDY  #$0
2002  BEQ  $2005   Since we just loaded Y with a zero, this Branch
                   if EQual to zero instruction will always be true
                   and cause a pseudo-JMP.
2004  NOP
2005  LDA
      #$5
```

Your monitor includes a "moveit" routine, invoked with T (Transfer), which will take an ML program and relocate it somewhere else in memory for you. You can go into the monitor and type T 2000 2006 5000 (you give the monitor these numbers in hex). The third number is the target address. The first and second are the start and end of the program you want to move.

The best solution to relocatability, however, is LADS. With it, you never JMP to actual addresses; rather, you JMP or JSR or branch to labels. This way, relocating your program couldn't be simpler. You just change the start address with *= and reassemble. Everything is taken care of and the program reassembles to the new location flawlessly. With LADS, the example above is written like this:

```
100 JMP NEXTROUTINE
110 LDY #3
120 NEXTROUTINE LDA #5
```

(The numbers at the left are not addresses; they are line numbers for your convenience when writing the program, and they have no effect on the resulting ML code after assembly.)

## IF-THEN

This familiar and fundamental computing structure is accomplished in ML with the combination CMP-BNE or any other conditional branch: BEQ, BCC, and so forth. Sometimes, the IF half isn't even necessary. Here's how it would look:

```
2000  LDA $57     What's in address $57?
2002  CMP #$0F    Is it $0F, 15 decimal?
2004  BEQ $200D   IF it is, branch up to $200D.
2006  LDA #$0A    Or ELSE, put a $0A, 10 decimal, into address
                  $57.
2008  STA $57
200A  JMP $2011   And jump over the THEN part.
200D  LDA #$14    THEN, put a $14, 20 decimal, into address $57.
200F  STA $57
2011              Continue with the program....
```

Often, though, your flags are already set by an action, making the CMP unnecessary. For example, if you want to branch to $200D if the number in address $57 is zero, just LDA $57:BEQ $200D. This works because the act of loading the accumulator will affect the status register flags. You don't need to CMP #0 because the zero flag will be set if a zero was just loaded into the accumulator. It won't hurt anything to use a CMP, but you'll find many cases in ML programming where you can shorten and simplify your coding if you wish to. As you gain experience, you will see these patterns and learn what affects the status register flags.

## INPUT

This is a series of GETs, echoed to the screen as they are typed in, which end when the typist hits the RETURN key. The reason for the echo (the symbol for each key typed is reproduced on the screen) is that few people enjoy typing without seeing what they've typed. This also allows for error correction using cursor control keys or DELETE and INSERT keys.

To handle all of these actions, an INPUT routine must be fairly complicated. We don't want, for example, the DELETE to become a character within the string. We want it to act immediately on the string being entered during the INPUT, to erase a mistake.

Our INPUT routine must also be smart enough to know what to add to the string and what keys are intended only to modify it. Here is the basis for constructing your own ML INPUT. It simply receives a character from the keyboard, prints it to the screen, and ends when the RETURN key is pressed. We'll write this INPUT as a subroutine. That simply means that when the 13 (ASCII for carriage return) is encountered, we'll perform an RTS back to a point just following the main program address which JSRed to our INPUT routine. Let's do it in the LADS source code format, with line numbers instead of addresses:

```
10 *= $B00
20 .S
30 .O
40 LOOP JSR $FFE4:BEQ
LOOP;                    If we got a zero, no key had been
                         pressed
50 JSR $FFD2;            Print the character to the screen
60 CMP #13;              Is it a carriage return
70 BNE LOOP;             If not, return for more keypresses
80 RTS;                  Otherwise return to the calling
                         routine
```

If you try this out, you'll notice that even the cursor keys and delete, screen clear, and so forth, work correctly. This is because when you JSR $FFD2 (PRINT), it is just as if you printed any character from BASIC (with cursor control codes embedded in a string). This INPUT could be, however, much more complex. As it stands, it will hold the string on the screen only. To save the string, you would need to store it in some buffer of yours in addition to its appearance on the screen. However, if you're going to store the string into some safe location where you are keeping string variables, you'll need to refuse storage to such things as the delete character or your stored string will be corrupted (will include delete) if the user needs to correct a misspelling. Or you might want to prevent the user from hitting a key like carriage return. In that case, just CMP #13:BEQ LOOP so that nothing is echoed to the screen or stored in your string when the user trys to enter that particular key.

The great freedom you have with ML is that you can redefine anything you want. You can *softkey*: define a key's meaning via software; have any key perform any task you want. You might even decide to use the $ key to DELETE.

Along with this freedom goes the responsibility for organizing, writing, and debugging these routines.

## LET

Although this word is still available on most BASICs, it is a holdover from the early days of computing. It is supposed to remind you that statements like LET NAME = NAME + 4 is an *assignment* of a value to a variable, not an algebraic equation. The two numbers on either side of the equal sign, in BASIC, are not intended to be equal in the algebraic sense. Most people write NAME = NAME + 4 without using LET. The function of LET applies, though, to ML as well as to BASIC: We must assign values to variables.

In the 128, for example, where the RAM bank can change depending on how you configure the computer, there has to be a place where we can find out which bank is the current bank (it's address $FF00). Likewise, a program will sometimes require that you *assign* meanings to string variables, counters, and the like. This can be part of the initialization process, the tasks performed before the real program, your main routine, gets started. Or it can happen during the execution of the main loop. In either case, there has to be an ML way to establish, to *assign*, variables. This also means that you must have zones of memory set aside to hold these variables unless, like the bank-switching location, the computer has already defined a variable. Normally, you will store your variables as a group at the end of an ML program.

For strings, you can think of LET as the establishment of a location in memory. In our INPUT example above, we might have included an instruction which would have sent the characters from the keyboard to a table of strings as well as echoing them to the screen. If so, there would have to be a way of managing these strings. For a discussion on the two most common ways of dealing with strings in ML, see Chapter 6 under the subhead "Dealing with Strings."

In general, you will probably find that you program in ML using somewhat fewer variables than in BASIC. There are three reasons for this:

1. You will probably not write many programs in ML like databases where you manipulate hundreds of names, addresses, and so forth. It might be somewhat inefficient to create an entire database management program, an inventory program for example, in ML. Keeping track of the variables would require careful programming. (For an example database manager, see LADS's Equate and Array subprograms, Appendix D.)

   The value of ML is its speed of execution, but its drawback is that it requires more precise programming and, at least for beginners, can take more time to write. So, for an inventory program, you could write the bulk of the program in BASIC and simply attach ML routines for *sorting* and *searching* tasks within the program.
2. The variables in ML are often handled within a series of instructions (not held elsewhere as BASIC variables are). FOR I = 1 TO 10 : NEXT I becomes LDY #1:INY:CPY #10:BNE.

   Here, the BASIC variable is counted for you and stored outside the body of the program. The ML "variable," though, is counted by the program itself. ML has no *interpreter* which handles such things. If you want a loop, you must construct all of its components yourself.
3. In BASIC, it is tempting to assign values to variables at the start of the program and then to refer to them later by their variable names, as in 10 BALL = 79. Then, anytime you want to PRINT the BALL to the screen, you could say, PRINT CHR$(BALL). Alternatively, you might define it this way in BASIC: 10 BALL$ = "O". In either case, your program will later refer to the word BALL. In this example we are assuming that the number 207 will place a ball character on your screen (the letter *O*).

In ML we can use variable names precisely the same way if we are programming with an advanced assembler like LADS. However, with an elementary assembler like the one in the monitor, you will just LDA #207, STA (screen position) each time. Some people like to put the 207 into their zone of variables (that arbitrary area of memory set up at the end of a program to hold tables, counters, and important addresses). They can pull it out of that zone whenever it's needed. That is somewhat cumbersome, though, and slower. You would LDA 1015, STA (screen position), assuming you had put a 207 into this "ball" address, 1015, earlier.

Obviously, a value like BALL will always remain the same throughout a program. The ball will look like a ball in your game, whatever else happens. So, it's not a true variable; it does not *vary*. It is constant. A true variable *must* be located in your "zone of variables," your variable *table*.

It cannot be part of the body of your program itself (as in LDA #207) because it will change. You don't know when writing your program what the variable will be. So you can't use *immediate mode* addressing because it might not be a #207. You have to LDA 1015 from within your table of variables.

Elsewhere in the program you have one or more STA 1015 or INC 1015 or some other manipulation of this address which keeps updating this variable. In effect, ML makes you responsible for setting aside areas which are safe to hold variables if you are using the monitor assembler. What's more, you have to remember the addresses and update the variables in those addresses whenever necessary. This is why it is so useful to keep a piece of paper next to you when you are writing ML using the monitor. The paper lists the start and end addresses of the zone of variables, the table. You write down the specific address of each variable as you write your program. LADS, of course, makes variable zones and names automatic with the .BYTE pseudo-op. See LADS's Tables subprogram (Appendix D) to see how variables (and constants) can be handled efficiently.

## LIST

This is done via a *disassembler*. It will not have line numbers (though, again, advanced assembler packages like LADS do have line numbers). You will see the address of each instruction in memory. You can look over your work and plan debugging strategies, where to set BRKs into problem areas, and so on.

The most common way to list and check your work, however, is to read over the *source code*. This does not require a disassembler. You write LADS source code as if it were a BASIC program and, thus, can LIST it and modify it as if it were a BASIC program. There is a subtle difference between studying source code and studying object code (via disassembly). The former is most useful for making modifications and for locating the more obvious bugs. The latter is for patiently tracking down those last few stubborn bugs that no amount of reading over the source code will reveal.

## LOAD

The method of saving and loading an ML program varies from computer to computer. You have two options: loading from within the monitor or from BASIC. When you finish working on a program, or a piece of a program, on the mini-assembler, you will know the starting and ending addresses of your work. Using these, you can save to disk or tape using the S monitor command (described in Chapter 3). To load, the simplest way is just to L "FILENAME",1 (for tape) or ,8 (for disk). You can also load ML when you're in BASIC mode by BLOAD. With both the monitor's L and BASIC's BLOAD commands, you can reassign your ML routine to a different target address (see your manual). However, this will not adjust the JSRs, and so on, so you haven't really relocated the program, and it probably would not run at the new location. To truly relocate it, you need to change the start address *= and reassemble it with LADS. However, loading in a version of your ML program to a different location with the L command and then loading in another version in its normal location does allow you to compare them with the monitor's C command.

To see how to save and load from *within* your ML programs, to write ML which itself saves and loads files, please refer to the Open1 subprogram of LADS in Appendix D.

## NEW

In Microsoft BASIC, this has the effect of resetting some pointers which make the machine think that you are going to start over again. The next program line you type in will be put at the "start-of-a-BASIC-program" area of memory. Some computers, the Atari for example, even *wash* memory by filling it with zeros. There is no special command in ML for NEWing an area of memory, though the monitor has a "fill memory" option which will fill an area of memory as large as you want with whatever value you choose.

The reason that NEW is not found in ML is that you do not always write your programs in the same area of memory as you do in BASIC, building up from some predictable address. You might have a subroutine floating up in high memory, another way down low, your table of variables at the end, and your main program in the middle. Or you might not. We've been using $2000 as our starting address for many of the examples in this book and $5000 for subroutines, but this is entirely arbitrary.

To "NEW" in ML, just start assembling over the old program.

Alternatively, you could just turn the power off and then back on again. This would, however, have the disadvantage of wiping out LADS along with your program.

## ON-GOSUB

In BASIC, you are expecting to test values from among a group of numbers: 1, 2, 3, 4, 5, .... The value of X must fall within this narrow range: ON X GOSUB 100, 200, 300, ... (X must be 1 or 2 or 3 here). In other words, you could not conveniently test for widely separated values of X (18, 55, 220). There is also an improved form of ON-GOSUB where you can test for any values. If your computer were testing the temperature of your bath water:

```
CASE
     80 OF GOSUB HOT ENDOF
    100 OF GOSUB VERYHOT ENDOF
    120 OF GOSUB INTOLERABLE ENDOF
ENDCASE
```

ML permits you the greater freedom of the CASE structure. Using CMP, you can perform a *multiple branch* test:

```
2000  LDA $96      Get a value, perhaps input from the keyboard.
2002  CMP #$50     Decimal 80
2004  BNE $2009
2006  JSR $5000    Where you would print "hot," following our ex-
                   ample of CASE.
```

```
2009  CMP #$64   Decimal 100
200B  BNE $2011
200D  JSR $5020  Print "very hot"
2010  CMP #$78   Decimal 120
2012  BNE $2017
2014  JSR $5030  Print "intolerable"
```

This illustrates one way that bugs get into ML—by not cleanly entering and leaving subroutines. The potential problem here is triggering the CMPs more than once. Since you are JSRing and then will be RTSing back to *within* the multiple branch test above, you will have to be sure that the subroutines up at $5000 do not change the value of the accumulator. If the accumulator started out with a value of $50 and, somehow, the subroutine at $5000 left a $64 in the accumulator, you would print "hot" and then also print "very hot." One way around this would be to put a zero into the accumulator before returning from each of the subroutines (LDA #$0). This assumes that none of your tests, none of your cases, responds to a zero.

## ON-GOTO

This is more common in ML than the ON-GOSUB structure above. It eliminates the need to worry about what is in the accumulator when you return from the subroutines. Instead of RTSing back, you jump back, *following all the branch tests.*

```
2000  LDA $96
2002  CMP #$50
2004  BNE $2009
2006  JMP $5000  Print "hot"
2009  CMP #$64
200B  BNE $2010
200D  JMP $5020  Print "very hot"
2010  CMP #$78
2012  BNE $2017
2014  JMP $5030  Print "intolerable"
2017             All the subroutines JMP $2017 when they
                 finish.
```

Instead of RTS, each of the subroutines will JMP back to $2017, which lets the program continue without accidentally "triggering" one of the other tests with something left in the accumulator during the execution of one of the subroutines.

## PRINT

You *could* print out a message in the following way:

```
2000  LDY  #$0
2002  LDA  #72        The letter H
2004  STA  $0400,Y    An address on the screen
2007  INY
2008  LDA  #69        The letter E
200A  STA  $0400,Y
200D  INY
200E  LDA  #76        The letter L
2010  STA  $0400,Y
2013  INY
2014  LDA  #76        The letter L
2016  STA  $0400,Y
2019  INY
201A  LDA  #79        The letter O
201C  STA  $0400,Y
```

But this is clearly a clumsy, memory-hungry way to go about it. In fact, it would be absurd to print out a long message this way. The most common ML method involves putting message strings into a data table and ending each message with a zero. Zero is never a printing character in computers; to print the *number* zero, you use 176: LDA #$30, STA $0400. So, true zero (not the code for the character 0) can be used as a delimiter to let the printing routine know that you've finished the message. In a data table, we first put in the message "hello":

```
1000  $48  H
1001  $45  E
1002  $4C  L
1003  $4C  L
1004  $4F  O
1005  $00       The delimiter
1006  $48  H
1007  $49  I     Another message
1008  $0        Another delimiter
```

Such a message table can be as long as you need; it holds all your messages and they can be used again and again:

```
2000  LDY  #$0
2002  LDA  $1000,Y
2005  BEQ  $200F    If the zero flag is set, it must mean that we've
                    reached the delimiter, so we branch out of this
                    printing routine.
```

```
2007  STA  $0400,Y  Put it on the screen.
200A  INY
200B  JMP  $2002    Go back and get the next letter in the message.
200F                Continue with the program.
```

Had we wanted to print HI, the only change necessary would have been to put $1006 into the LDA at address $2003. To change the location on the screen that the message starts printing, we could just put some other address into $2008. The message table, then, is just a mass of words, separated by zeros, in RAM memory.

The process of printing messages is even simpler using the LADS label-based assembler and its .BYTE trick for storing numbers or words:

```
 10 SCREEN = $0400
100 LDY #0:MORE LDA MESSAGE,Y:BEQ FINISH
110 STA SCREEN,Y:INY:JMP MORE
```

with, at the end of your source code, the following line included somewhere in your table of variables, your data:

```
400 MESSAGE .BYTE "HELLO":.BYTE 0
410 MESSAGE1 .BYTE "HI":.BYTE 0
```

See the Tables section of LADS (Appendix D) for more examples of message storage.

The fastest way to print to the screen, especially if your program will be doing a lot of printing, is to create a subroutine which will print any of your messages. It can use some bytes in zero page (addresses 0–255) to hold the location of the message within your table of data.

To put an address into zero page, you will need to put it into two bytes. Addresses are too big to fit into one byte. With LADS, you can use the #< and #> pseudo-ops to extract the LSB and MSB of a label and thus store the address of your message into a zero page pointer:

```
 10 MSGADDRESS = 56
 20 SCREEN = $0400
100 LDA #<MESSAGE:STA MSGADDRESS; set up pointer
110 LDA #>MESSAGE:STA MSGADDRESS+1
120 JSR PRINTMSG; go to universal print subroutine
500 PRINTMSG LDY #0:LOOP LDA (MSGADDRESS),Y:BEQ
    END:STA SCREEN,Y
510 STA SCREEN,Y:INY:JMP LOOP
520 END RTS
```

This same trick can be done with the simple assembler in the monitor, but it is more cumbersome.

First, you split the hex number in two. The left two digits, $10, are the MSB (most significant byte) and the right digits, $00, make up the LSB (least significant byte). If you are going to put this target address into zero page at 56 (decimal):

```
2000  LDA  #$00     LSB
2002  STA  $56
2004  LDA  #$10     MSB
2006  STA  $57
2008  JSR  $5000    Printout subroutine

5000  LDY  #$0
5002  LDA  ($56)Y
5004  BEQ  $5013    If zero, return from subroutine...
5006  STA  $0400,Y  to screen.
5009  INY
500A  JMP  $5002
500D  RTS
```

One drawback to this PRINT subroutine we've constructed is that it will always print any messages to the same place on the screen. That $0400 is frozen into your subroutine. Solution? Use another zero page pair of bytes to hold the screen address. Then, your calling routine sets up the message address as above, but also goes on to specify a screen address as well.

The 128's screen starts at $0400 (1024 decimal), so you will want to put 0 and 4 into the LSB and MSB respectively for your screen pointer.

```
2000  LDA  #$00    LSB
2002  STA  $56     Set up message address
2004  LDA  #$10    MSB
2006  STA  $57
2008  LDA  #$0     LSB

200A  STA  $58     We'll just use the next two bytes in zero page
                   above our message address for the screen
                   address.
200C  LDA  #$4     MSB
200E  STA  $59
2010  JSR  $5000
5000  LDY  #$0
5002  LDA  ($56)Y
5004  BEQ  $500D   If zero, return from subroutine...
```

```
5006  STA  ($58),Y  to screen.
5009  INY
500A  JMP  $5002
500D  RTS
```

The easiest way to print messages to particular places on the screen, however, is to use the 128's built-in BASIC PRINT routine to send the characters, one by one, each to the next cursor position onscreen. The built-in routine updates and keeps track of the current cursor position for you. So, you can get around having to keep a screen pointer in zero page this way. In the example immediately above, just replace line 5006 with JSR $FFD2 (the 128's PRINT routine) and remove lines 2008–200E.

## READ

There is no reason for a *read*ing of data in ML. Variables are not placed into "DATA statements." They are entered into a table when you are programming. The purpose of READ, in BASIC, is to assign variable names to raw data, or to take a group of data and move it somewhere, or to manipulate it into an array of variables. These things are handled by you, not by the computer, in ML programming.

If you need to access a piece of information, *you* set up the addresses of the datum and the target address to which you are moving it. (See the PRINT routines above.) As always, in ML you are expected to keep track of the locations of your variables. If you are using the simple assembler in the monitor, you must keep a map of data locations, vectors, tables, and subroutine locations. This pad of paper is always next to you as you program in ML. It would seem that you would need many notes, but in practice an average program of, say, 1000 bytes could be mapped out and commented on, using only one sheet.

Alternatively, with more sophisticated assemblers like LADS, the labels themselves within the program will keep track of things for you, and embedded comments serve to remind you of the use and function of all data.

## REM

You do this on a pad of paper, too, when working with a simple assembler. If you want to comment or make notes about your program (and it can be a necessary, valuable explanation of what's going on), you can disassemble some ML code like a BASIC listing. If you have a printer, you can make notes on the printed disassembly. If you don't use a printer, make notes on your pad to explain the purpose of each subroutine, the parameters it expects to get, and the results or changes it effects.

The more sophisticated assemblers like LADS will permit comments within the source code. As you program, you can include REMarks by typing a semicolon, which is a signal to the assembler to ignore the REMarks when it is assembling your program. In these assemblers, you are working much closer to the way you work in BASIC. Your REMarks remain part of the source program, and can be listed out and studied.

## RETURN

RTS works the same way that RETURN does in BASIC: It takes you back to *just after* the JSR (GOSUB) that sent control of the program away from the main program and into a subroutine. JSR pushes, onto the stack, the address which immediately follows the JSR itself. That address, then, sits on the stack, waiting until the next RTS is encountered. When an RTS occurs, the address is pulled from the stack and placed into the *program counter*. This has the effect of transferring program control back to the instruction just after the JSR.

## RUN

There are several ways to start an ML program. If you are taking off into ML from BASIC, you just SYS to it by giving its address (in decimal) as the argument of the SYS. This acts just like JSR and will return control to BASIC, just as RETURN would, when there is an unmatched RTS in the ML program. By *unmatched,* we mean the first RTS which is not part of a JSR/RTS pair. SYS can take you into ML either in *immediate mode* (directly from the keyboard) or from within a BASIC program as one of the BASIC commands.

If you need to "pass" information from BASIC to ML, it is easiest to use integer numbers and just POKE them into some predetermined ML variable zone that you've set aside and noted on your notepad. Then just SYS to your ML routine, which will look into the set-aside, POKEd area when it needs the values from BASIC.

If you are not going between BASIC and ML, you can start (RUN) your ML program from within the built-in monitor. To enter the monitor, press F8. To run an ML program from within the monitor, type G 2000 (that's address 8192 in decimal; this presumes that you've either loaded in your ML program at that address or have just assembled one there).

The 128 expects to encounter a BRK instruction to end the run and return control to the monitor.

## SAVE

When you save a BASIC program, the computer automatically handles it. The starting address and the ending address of your program are calculated for you. In ML, you must know the start and end address. From the monitor, you type S, then the name of your program, then 8 for disk or 1 for tape, the starting address, and the ending address. All these items are separated by commas:

**S "FILENAME",8,2000,2010**

(Note that these addresses are in hex. The addresses are 8192 and 8208, in decimal, but you must use hex from the monitor unless you specify otherwise. See Chapter 3 for more information about the monitor.) For more information about BSAVE and BLOAD, the ML save and load routines in BASIC, please see your *User's Guide*.

Saving object code is automatic with LADS; if you use the .D NAME pseudo-op, LADS will automatically save your ML program after it has finished assembling it. To see how to save and load from *within* your ML programs—to write ML which itself saves and loads files—please refer to the Open1 subprogram of LADS in Appendix D.

## STOP

BRK (or an RTS with no preceding JSR) throws you back into the monitor mode after running an ML program. BRK is most often used for debugging programs because you can set "breakpoints" in the same way that you would use STOP to examine variables when debugging a BASIC program.

## SYS

This is BASIC's way of using a piece of ML code, an ML routine, as a subroutine. The only difference between SYS and GOSUB is that the computer is alerted to the fact that it needs to switch mental gears: The next series of instructions will be ML. In other words, the computer shouldn't try to interpret what it finds at the SYS address as more BASIC instructions. Later, when it comes upon an RTS instruction in the ML program which was not matched by a previous JSR instruction, it will then revert to the BASIC program and pick up where it left off, following the SYS instruction.

There are times when you want to write in ML and use it as a subroutine for a BASIC program. This can greatly speed up the execution of the BASIC program. To put an ML program in RAM where it will be safe from BASIC's dynamic variable storage (where it won't be overwritten by BASIC), you lower the "top-of-memory" pointer ($39,3A) to create some space in high RAM of which the computer is "unaware." This pointer contains the address (in the usual LSB,MSB format discussed earlier) beyond which BASIC is forbidden to intrude. If you're going to use only one page of memory (256 bytes), just DEC #3A which has the effect of making it point 256 bytes lower than it normally would. This pointer affects bank 1.

After resetting this pointer, you are free to load in your ML program into the now-safe RAM between where the pointer points and the true highest RAM byte in your computer.

Short ML routines can always be stored in the page between $B00 and $BFF without any special preliminaries.

## String Handling
## ASC

In BASIC, this will give you the number of the ASCII code which stands for the character you are testing. ?ASC("A") will result in a 65 being displayed. There is never any need for this in ML. If you are manipulating the character *A* in ML, you *are using ASCII already*. In other words, the letter *A is* 65 in ML programming. The Commodore ASCII code isn't standard ASCII; it stores character symbols in some nonstandard ways, so you will need to write a special program to be able to translate to standard ASCII if you are using a modem or some other peripheral which uses true ASCII. Appendix G lists both Commodore ASCII and true ASCII.

## CHR$

This is most useful in BASIC to let you use characters which cannot be represented within normal strings, will not show up on your screen, or cannot be typed from the keyboard.

For example, if you have a printer attached to your computer, you could send CHR$(13) to it, and it would perform a carriage return. The correct numbers which accomplish various things sometimes differ, though decimal 13—an ASCII code standard—is nearly universally recognized as carriage return, and the 128 uses this convention, too.

Or, you could send the combination CHR$(27) CHR$(8), and the printer would backspace.

There is no real use for CHR$ within ML. If you want to specify a carriage return, just LDA #13. In ML, you are not limited to the character values which can appear onscreen or within strings. Any value can be dealt with directly.

## LEFT$

As usual in ML, *you* are in charge of manipulating data. Here's one way to extract a certain "substring" from the left side of a string as in the BASIC statement LEFT$(X$,5):

```
2000  LDY  #$5
2002  LDX  #$0       Use X as the offset for buffer storage.
2004  LDA  $1000,Y   The location of X$.
2007  STA  $4000,X   The "buffer," or temporary storage area, for
                     the substring.
200A  INX
200B  DEY
200C  BNE  $2004
```

## LEN

In some cases, you will already know the length of a string in ML. One of the ways to store and manipulate strings is to know beforehand the length and address of a string. Then you could use the subroutine given for LEFT$, above. More commonly, though, you will store your strings with delimiters (zeros) at the end of each string. To find out the length of a certain string:

```
2000  LDY  #$0
2002  LDA  $1000,Y  The address of the string you are testing.
2003  BEQ  $2009    Remember, if you LDA a zero, the zero flag is
                    set. So you don't really need to use a CMP #0
                    here to test whether you've loaded the zero
                    delimiter.
2005  INY
2006  BNE  $2002    We are not using a JMP here because we as-
                    sume that all your strings are less than 256
                    characters long.
2008  BRK           If we still haven't found a zero after 256 INYs,
                    we avoid an endless loop by just BRKing out
                    of the subroutine.
2009  DEY           The LENgth of the string is now in the Y
                    register.
```

We had to DEY at the end because the final INY picked up the zero delimiter. So, the true count of the LENgth of the string is one less than Y shows, and we must DEY one time to make this adjustment.

## MID$

To extract a substring which starts at the fourth character from within the string and is five characters long—MID$(X$,4,5):

```
2000  LDY  #$5      The size of the substring we're after.
2002  LDX  #$0      X is the offset for storing the substring.
2004  LDA  $1003,Y  To start at the fourth character from within the
                    X$ located at $1000, simply add three to that
                    address. Instead of starting our LDA,Y at
                    $1000, skip to $1003. This is because the first
                    character is not in position 1. Rather, it is at
                    the zeroth position, at $1000.
2007  STA  $4000,X  The temporary buffer to hold the substring.
200A  INX
200B  DEY
200C  BNE  $2004
```

## RIGHT$

This, too, is complicated because normally we do not know the LENgth of a given string. To find RIGHT$(X$,5) if X$

starts at $1000, we should find the LEN first and then move the substring to our holding zone (buffer) at $4000:

```
2000  LDY  #$0
2002  LDX  #$0
2004  LDA  $1000,Y
2007  BEQ  $200D    The delimiting zero is found.
2009  INY
200A  JMP  $2004
200D  TYA           Put LEN into A so that we can subtract the
                    substring size from it.
200E  SEC           Always set carry before any subtraction.
200F  SBC  #$5      Subtract the size of the substring you want to
                    extract.
2011  TAY           Put the offset back into Y, now adjusted to
                    point to five characters from the end of X$.
2012  LDA  $1000,Y
2015  BEQ  $201E    We found the delimiter, so end.
2017  STA  $4000,X
201A  INX
201B  DEY
201C  BNE  $2012
201E  RTS
```

## TAB

This formatting instruction moves you to a specified column on a given line. TAB 10 moves you ten spaces from the left side of the screen.

In ML, you have more direct control over what happens: You would just add or subtract the amount you want to TAB over to. If you were printing to the screen and wanted ten spaces between A and B so it looked like this:

**A                    B**

you could write:

```
2000  LDA  #$41    A
2002  STA  $0400   Screen RAM address
2005  LDA  #$42    B
2007  STA  $040A   You've added ten to the target address.
```

Alternatively, you could add ten to the Y offset (this is LADS format):

```
 10 SCREEN = $0400
100 LDY #0:LDA #"A:STA SCREEN,Y:LDY #10:LDA #"B:STA
   SCREEN,Y
```

An even simpler LADS method uses the + pseudo-op to add whatever amount you wish to a label:

```
 10 SCREEN = $0400
100 LDA #"A:STA SCREEN:STA SCREEN+10
```

As an example, we are writing to the screen here, but in practice, you would print to the screen using $FFD2 as described below. The examples above, using Y as an offset, are more applicable to storing, say, items in a database or printing hardcopy.

Nonetheless, if you are printing out many columns of numbers and need a subroutine to space your printout correctly, you might want to use a subroutine which will add ten to the Y offset each time you call the subroutine:

```
5000  TYA
5001  CLC
5002  ADC #10
5004  TAY
5005  RTS
```

This subroutine directly adds ten to the Y register whenever you JSR $5000. However, it's more typical to rely on $FFD2 for screen printing since it will keep track of the cursor position for you. Just LDA with whatever character you want printed and then JSR $FFD2, and it will be printed at the next available space.

You can see that moving over ten spaces could be accomplished by LDA #32:JSR $FFD2 performed ten times. The 32 is the blank character. However, here, too, there is a more practical method.

*Anything you can print from BASIC you can print from ML.* So, all the cursor control characters can be printed, CLR screen, backspace, anything. Most control characters can be entered into LADS directly by typing #"*c* where *c* is the control code you desire:

```
5000  LDA #"c
5001  JSR  $FFD2
```

Alternatively, you can put the actual Commodore ASCII value into the accumulator prior to JSR $FFD2. One way to find out the ASCII value to, for example, clear the screen, you could go to BASIC and type CHR$(" ") to get it. There is a complete list of Commodore 128 ASCII in Appendix G. Here is a list of the control characters:

| Dec | Hex | Uppercase/Graphics Set Lowercase/Uppercase Set |
|---|---|---|
| 2 | 02 | underline on[1] |
| 5 | 05 | white |
| 7 | 07 | bell tone[2] |
| 9 | 09 | tab[2] |
| 10 | 0A | linefeed[2] |
| 13 | 0D | RETURN |
| 14 | 0E | switch to lowercase |
| 15 | 0F | flash on[1] |
| 17 | 11 | cursor down |
| 18 | 12 | reverse on |
| 19 | 13 | home |
| 20 | 14 | delete |
| 24 | 18 | TAB set/clear[2] |
| 27 | 1B | ESCape |
| 28 | 1C | red |
| 29 | 1D | cursor right |
| 30 | 1E | green |
| 31 | 1F | blue |
| 32 | 20 | space |
| 129 | 81 | orange[3] |
| | | dark purple[1] |
| 130 | 82 | underline off[1] |
| 142 | 8E | switch to uppercase |
| 143 | 8F | flash off[1] |
| 144 | 90 | black |
| 145 | 91 | cursor up |
| 146 | 92 | reverse off |
| 147 | 93 | clear screen |
| 148 | 94 | insert |
| 149 | 95 | brown[3] |
| | | dark yellow[1] |
| 150 | 96 | light red |
| 151 | 97 | dark gray[3] |
| | | dark cyan[1] |
| 152 | 98 | medium gray |
| 153 | 99 | light green |
| 154 | 9A | light blue |
| 155 | 9B | light gray |
| 156 | 9C | purple |
| 157 | 9D | cursor left |
| 158 | 9E | yellow |
| 159 | 9F | cyan |

**Notes**

1. 80-column display only
2. 128 mode only
3. 40-column display only

# Chapter 10

# The 128 Environment

# The 128 Environment

Let's take a tour of some of the capabilities of this potent machine. We'll discover switches and modes that you can tap which will turbocharge your ML programs.

## Versatile Escapes

First off, your ML programs can control the screen by invoking the ESCape key sequences.

Do you need to delete the current line, the line whereon the cursor sits? From BASIC, you would hit the ESC key, let it go, then type D. To do this from within an ML program:

```
LDA #"D:JSR $C01E
```

$C01E is a subroutine which activates the escape sequences. You must be in bank 15 for this to work. If your ML program is going to utilize built-in routines like this, you must either switch in bank 15 at the start of your program and leave it active (as does LADS) or switch it in just before you access a subroutine like the one at $C01E.

You switch in bank 15 by:

```
LDA #0:STA $FF00
```

This is the first thing LADS does prior to assembling your source code because LADS uses a number of built-in ROM routines.

Here is a list of the other escape sequences; there's one for every letter of the alphabet. To use them, just replace the D in the example above with the appropriate letter.

A Turn on autoinsert mode
B Current cursor position becomes bottom of screen window
C Turn off autoinsert mode
D Delete the line where the cursor is
E Make cursor not flash
F Make cursor flash
G Enable beep sound
H Prevent beep from sounding
I Insert line
J Move cursor to the start of the current line
K Move cursor to the end of the current line
L Permit scrolling

M Prevent scrolling
N Make screen white-on-black (80-column screen only)
O Turn off insert, reverse, or quote modes
P Erase from cursor to the start of the current line
Q Erase from cursor to the end of the current line
R Turn on black-on-white mode (80-column screen only)
S Change to square cursor (80-column screen)
T Current cursor position becomes top of screen window
U Change to underline cursor (80-column screen)
V Cause scroll upward
W Cause scroll downward
X Switch between a 40- or 80-column TV monitor
Y Make TAB every eight columns
Z Remove all TABs
@ Clear the screen from the cursor to the bottom

## Many Memories

The 128 has a total of 16 memory configurations, called *banks.* Each bank is 64K large, but that doesn't mean that the 128 has 16 separate 64K blocks of memory. Rather, the banks are just different 64K selections from the smorgasbord of RAM, ROM, and input/output chips in the computer. Two banks, 0 and 1, are mostly RAM, and you can do with them what you will—the RAM in each bank comes from a separate 64K block of RAM. Other banks are mixtures of RAM and ROM. Special locations like low memory and $FFD0 and other registers are common to all banks so that communication is possible between the banks (*something* has to be unvarying).

How are these banks best visualized? Clearly they aren't all there all the time. You are always only "in" one bank at a time. You might think of it as if you are in charge of lighting a play and you've got a box with 16 buttons, one for each bank, labeled 0 through 15.

Onstage, there are 16 different performers, each with different talents and different shapes (although as you can see in the list of banks above, there are some which look like the others in places). In any case, when the play starts, you can turn a spotlight on any performer you wish. But, the rule is that only one performer can be lit at a time. So, if you turn on bank 0, you are, in effect, turning the light off one other bank, the one previously lit.

In other words, you're confined to *serial,* not *parallel,* lighting effects. However, you can be very fast with a series of switches. You can even switch between banks so quickly that the illusion is created that more than one is active at once. By using JSR, JMP, CMP, LDA, and STA *LONG* commands (see Chapter 11), you can access distant banks without even explicitly switching out of your home bank. The lighting will flicker imperceptibly for the briefest moment when you use one of the *LONG* Kernal routines.

## Memory in the Monitor

When in the monitor (via F8 directly from BASIC mode or a BRK instruction that stops an ML program in progress), you can save, load, modify memory, and many other things (see Chapter 3). Normally, you use four-character hex numbers to indicate where you want things to happen:

**M 0B00**

Or you can leave off leading zeros:

**M B00**

followed by RETURN will show you what's in the memory locations following address $B00 in *bank 0*. Bank 0 is the default when you just give the monitor a number between 0 and FFFF (0–65535 decimal). To access other banks, you need to add a digit between 1 and F (1–15 decimal) which will put you in touch with any of the banks you thus select. To see memory at B00 bank 1, type M 10B00. To see bank 14, type M E0B00, and so on, for any of the banks. In practice, bank 0, bank 1, and bank 15 are the most commonly used. Bank 0 is the monitor's default, bank 1 has 64K of free RAM memory, and bank 15 puts all the I/O, BASIC, and Kernal routines at your disposal. Here's what each bank gives you when referenced via the monitor:

| Bank | Memory Configuration |
|---|---|
| 0 | RAM 0 |
| 1 | RAM 1 |
| 2 | RAM 2 |
| 3 | RAM 3 |
| 4 | Internal ROM, RAM 0, Input/Output Chips |
| 5 | Internal ROM, RAM 1, Input/Output Chips |
| 6 | Internal ROM, RAM 2, Input/Output Chips |
| 7 | Internal ROM, RAM 3, Input/Output Chips |
| 8 | External ROM, RAM 0, Input/Output Chips |
| 9 | External ROM, RAM 1, Input/Output Chips |
| A | External ROM, RAM 2, Input/Output Chips |

| | |
|---|---|
| B | External ROM, RAM 3, Input/Output Chips |
| C | Kernal, 1/2 Internal, RAM 0, Input/Output |
| D | Kernal, 1/2 External, RAM 0, Input/Output |
| E | Kernal, BASIC, RAM 0, Character ROM |
| F | Kernal, BASIC, RAM 0, Input/Output |

Its name implies that the Commodore 128 has 128K of RAM, and you may be wondering how that relates to the information above. Interestingly, the 128 is actually designed like a 256K computer with only half of its memory installed. That memory is in two separate 64K blocks, RAM 0 and RAM 1. The other two blocks, RAM 2 and RAM 3, are empty. In the 128, the phantom banks behave as mirror images of RAM 0 and RAM 1, respectively. Thus, banks 0 and 2 are identical, as are banks 9 and B. Thus, until the Commodore 256 comes along, the following banks *should not be used:* 2, 3, 6, 7, A and B. Internal ROM refers to an empty socket inside the 128 which may, in the future, hold ROM chips with built-in software, similar to the "productivity package" in the earlier Commodore Plus/4 model. External ROM refers to ROM in cartridges plugged into the memory expansion port. These can be ignored for now, so the only banks you really need to know are 0, 1, and 15 (and occasionally 14 if you need access to the character ROM—when designing custom character sets, for example).

If you use some BASIC ROM routines, you'll need a bank that invokes it. If you want to use the Kernal (the jump table into operating system, BASIC, and I/O routines), you'll have to have that as well. In sum, you should probably call in bank 15 at the start of your ML program and have it all. You don't put a 15 into the switching register to get bank 15—you put a 0 into it. LDA #0:STA $FF00 will create bank 15, and you can then freely access any routines you might need; you'll have the full complement of Commodore routines at your disposal. If you need more RAM, switch in and out of bank 1. (Don't worry why 0 calls in bank 15; we'll explain forthwith.) But remember that the RAM portion of bank 15 comes from the same place as bank 0, the RAM 0 block. That is, address $2000 in bank 0 and $2000 in bank 15 *both refer to the same memory location*. If you put a routine at $2000 in bank 0, then try to put another routine at that address in bank 15, you'll overwrite the original routine.

Or, best, use the long-distance JSR, CMP, LDA, and so on, special features which can quickly reach outside the current bank. There is a way to go into other banks without switching. We'll get to that soon. For most ML, just remember that you'll want to set bank 15 as the environment. And, a good place to store things is in the 64K RAM available in bank 1. The other banks are only very rarely useful for most ML programming.

## Manipulating Memory

To understand how the 128 organizes its memory, you must visualize that the 8502 chip can address only 64K of memory at any given time. Any single instruction can only, for example, LDA 65535 or, in hex, LDA $FFFF. You cannot LDA higher. Zero to 65535 is the range of possible addressing for an eight-bit chip.

How then is it possible to call this the 128 and say that you can use 128K of RAM for your programming?

The answer is that the computer has a facility for switching between those zones of memory called *banks*. When you're programming in BASIC, your program can reside in one 64K area of memory while its variables reside in another 64K area. In ML, you can cause banks to be *switched* in and out of range of the chip. This switching is accomplished by storing different numbers into location $FF00.

There are some considerations. It would be ungainly to keep switching whole banks when you only wanted to use, say, bank 1 as storage space. The easier way to access this bank is to use special LDA and STA instructions which can reach into it without your switching banks in your program. We'll get to these special instructions in a minute.

When you turn on the computer, it defaults to bank 0 RAM. However, if you are programming in ML and intend to make use of the Kernal, I/0, and BASIC routines (and most ML programs do), you'll want to switch to bank 15 and stay there. Bank 15 is the normal environment for ML programmers because it gives you some RAM, but it also provides access to all the important ROM routines, too. LADS switches in bank 15 right at the start (see the Eval subprogram in Appendix D). You switch in bank 15 by LDA #0:STA $FF00, and that's it. Thereafter, unless you put something else into $FF00, you'll be in bank 15, and all BASIC's routines and the Kernal and I/O routines will be at your disposal.

Obviously, you couldn't switch banks if *all* 64K always switched when you changed banks. $FF00, for example, has to be available to any bank. It can't change. Neither, for other reasons, can zero page change. You can count on these locations to be common to any bank. But we're programming in ML, and we're not concerned here with banks which involve CPM, cartridge memory, or such. So, we need only worry about bank 15, our usual configuration, and banks 0 and 1 wherein we'll find lots of RAM with which to make good use.

How can you store something in bank 1 RAM, then call in bank 15 with all its ROM? Won't the heavy information in bank 15 crush or cover over what you put into bank 1? No. bank 1 really is a different memory area; you just can't access it at the same time that you access bank 15 (except for the memory zones they have in common). So, STA LONG to bank 1 while you're in bank 15. The things you STA will still be there when you go to LDA LONG or when you switch banks.

### Coming In from the Keyboard

If you need to test keys being pressed, you'll have to ask location $D4 (212 decimal). Unhappily, this location does not yield the ASCII code. Carriage return is not 13. The letter *A* is not 65. It's another code altogether, the "keyboard matrix code." You don't need to deal with this. If you want your ML program to detect a particular key being pressed, find out its "matrix code" by running this simple BASIC program:

**10 PRINT PEEK(212);:GOTO 10**

and while it runs, press the key you're interested in. The numbers on the screen will be the code for that key. Then you can:

**LDA 212:CMP #**whatever code**:BEQ FOUNDIT**

to handle a case where some particular key was pressed. Notice that while no key is pressed, the number 88 is always in address 212. That's useful. You can see if *any* key is pressed by:

**LDA 212:CMP #88:BEQ NOKEY**

and continue on with your program since the user hasn't touched the keyboard.

By the way, the letter *A* is 10, and the carriage return key is 1 in the 128's keyboard matrix code. Don't worry about what the matrix means or how it is calculated. Just run the little BASIC program above if you want to pause your space invaders game when the player holds down the P key. It'll tell you what P sticks into location 212 and can CMP for it and JSR to a subroutine that pauses until any other key is pressed (when 212 contains something besides the number 88.)

### The Speed Switch

One of the most exciting and valuable features of the 128 is the fact that you can make the 128 run twice as fast as normal—go from 1 to 2 megahertz. The speed is controlled by the register at $D030. It normally contains $FC. If you LDA #$FF:STA $D030, you switch on the turbocharger and things only take half as long to compute. A 40-column display will blank out during this speedup. You shouldn't speed things up during access to disk or printer or tape, but it's well worth using in other circumstances.

LADS uses this speed switch. For example, when using a 1571 disk, LADS can assemble a large program, 72K of source code, in two minutes, 25 seconds. Pass one takes 55 seconds; pass two takes 90 seconds. These measurements were taken with LADS assembling itself.

# Chapter 11

# Built-in Routines

# Built-in Routines

Commodore machines, since the start, have made a sensible provision for upgrading software after the arrival of a new model. Because many programmers will want to access the canned ROM routines like PRINT for their own purposes, it would be much easier for software manufacturers and programmers in general if the addresses of the most popular ROM routines were to remain stable. Commodore has made a provision so that this will happen.

In the original Commodore PET, JSR $FFD2 printed the character in the accumulator. In the 128, Commodore's latest machine, it is the same. There is a whole list of such addresses, high up in ROM memory, which has remained trustworthy throughout the years and has simplified the job of transporting software when new models and new machines are introduced. This list is called the Kernal.

The Kernal list is a series of JMP $*NNNN* instructions. The *NNNN* will point to the actual address, in that particular machine, where, say, PRINT is really accomplished. You don't need to bother with the *NNNN* when using the Kernal, just JSR to the Kernal routine and your program will be directed to the appropriate ROM address. Here are the useful Kernal routines for the 128.

You should be in bank 15 to access the 128's Kernal routines. LDA #0:STA $FF00 will accomplish this; put it at the start of your ML program if you're going to be using BASIC or Kernal ROM routines.

### Set 2,8,1

$FFBA establishes preconditions for communication with a peripheral by setting up the file number, device number, and secondary address. It works together with the next two routines described immediately below. It establishes the 2,8,1 part of BASIC's OPEN 2,8,1, "FILENAME" and, thus, you have accomplished one third of the job of opening a file (or loading or saving) when you've JSRed to $FFBA. You put the file number (2, in our example above) into the accumulator, the device number (8, for disk, in the example) into X, and the secondary address (the example's 1) into Y. Then JSR $FFBA.

Here's how to set things up for an OPEN 2,8,1:

**LDA #2:LDX #8:LDY #1:JSR $FFBA**

To see this (and the two companion routines below) in action, prior to a LOAD, see the Open1 subprogram in LADS (Appendix D). If you are calling the printer, use 4,4,255.

## Set Filename

$FFBD also sets things up prior to an OPEN, SAVE, or LOAD. This tells the OPEN, SAVE, or LOAD where to find the filename for the command. You put the length of the name into the accumulator, the LSB of the name into X, the MSB into Y. Then JSR $FFBD.

Here's how you would establish the name:

**LDA #4:LDX #<FILENAME:LDY #>FILENAME:JSR $FFBD**
**FILENAME .BYTE "NAME"**

Note that if you are communicating with the printer, there will be no filename. However, you should still JSR to $FFBD, but give a zero as the length.

## Set Bank Number

$FF68 is the third precondition to opening, loading, or saving. It establishes which bank you want to have involved with the I/O. Do you want to load into bank 1? Or save from bank 0? You must tell the computer prior to I/O. Also, this routine tells the computer which bank holds the *filename* set up by the previous routine ($FFBD).

So, put the memory bank (1–15) into the accumulator, and the bank where the filename is into X. Then JSR $FF68. See the SAVE routine in Open1 in LADS to follow how the filename and bank are handled prior to a save from bank 1 (even though LADS resides in bank 15).

## OPEN

$FFC0 opens a file on disk or tape. After you've performed the three precondition JSRs above, you can just JSR $FFC0 and start working with it (pulling in or sending out bytes). To see the four Kernal calls thus far described working in concert, please look at the LOAD or SAVE routine in LADS's Open1 subprogram. The filename to which those examples refer is held in the Tables subprogram.

Just as in BASIC, you can also pass commands to the disk via OPEN 15,8,15 "V0:", where the item in quotes (set up just as if it were a filename) instructs the disk to, in this case, validate the disk.

### CLOSE

$FFC3 closes a file. When you want to perform a CLOSE, put the file number into the accumulator and JSR $FFC3. LADS closes down files during its shutdown routine in the Eval subprogram (lines 4390–4540) just prior to returning control of the computer to BASIC.

Note that you don't need to CLOSE after LOAD or SAVE.

### INPUT#

$FFC6 establishes a channel to a peripheral for input. You put the file number into the X register and JSR $FFC6. It's the equivalent of the #2 in INPUT#2,A$. This is used any time you want to get a byte from an already opened disk file. It would be followed by the GET routine (below). Without establishing this channel, all input comes, by default, from the keyboard. When you finish and wish to restore the default conditions, you must JSR to CLEARCHANNELS (below).

### OUTPUT#

$FFC9 establishes a channel to a peripheral for output. You put the file number into the X register and JSR $FFC9. It's the equivalent of the #3 in PRINT#3,A$. It's used any time you want to send a byte to an already opened disk file. It would be followed by $FFD2, the PRINT routine. Without establishing this channel, all output goes, by default, to the screen. Thus, for *each* character that you are printing to the printer, you must LDA #4:JSR $FFC9:LDA CHARACTER:JSR $FFD2:JSR CLEARCHANNELS. To see this in action, see the printer routines in the second half of the LADS Printops subprogram.

### Restore Default I/O (Screen and Keyboard)

$FFCC clears the channels which were established by the preceding two routines. It restores the keyboard as the default for input and the screen as the default for output.

## INPUT

$FFCF is an important routine. It's the equivalent of PRINT, but in the other direction—it INPUTs characters from the keyboard, or, if a file and channel have been opened for input from the disk, it pulls the next character off the file, leaving it in the accumulator for you to do with as you wish (store to a buffer, encode, look for a particular key, and so on). A disk file will be read sequentially, one byte at a time, by repeatedly JSR $FFCF because the disk will remember which was the last byte pulled off the file. Also, you can read sequential, program, or other kinds of files in this fashion. If you haven't opened a channel to a disk file, the routine will read from the keyboard until it detects a carriage return.

## PRINT

$FFD2 is perhaps the most famous Commodore Kernal routine and you'll use it extensively. It parallels the INPUT routine above, except it PRINTs characters—it goes in the other direction; it's the *O* in I/O.

What you put into the accumulator will be printed to the screen, or disk or printer (if you've opened files and channels to those devices as described above). Obviously, opening a channel to print to the keyboard is as useless as opening a channel to input from the printer. Some peripherals are, by nature, insensitive to input or output.

If you intend to print directly to the screen, you can use $C00C which operates just like $FFD2, but is slightly faster. FFD2 eventually gets to C00C, but it does a number of things first which are unrelated to screen printing.

A third method of printing which some people find useful is similar to immediate addressing. You JSR $FA17, and the 128 will look for the message you want printed *immediately following this JSR in your code.* You must end the message with a zero to show where it finishes. The computer will print the message and then pick up the next instruction just following the embedded message. Here's an example which combines traditional PRINT with this new method we're calling PRINTIM, for *print immediate*:

**Program 11-1. Embedded PRINT**

```
10 *= $B00
20 .S
30 .O
40 ;     EMBEDDED PRINT
50 ;
60 PRINTIM = $FA17;  PRINT IMMEDIATE
70 PRINT = $FFD2
80 ;
90 LDA #0:STA $FF00;  SET BANK 15
100 LDA #"A:JSR PRINT;  NORMAL PRINT
110 JSR PRINTIM;        PRINT WHAT IMMEDIATELY FOLLOWS
120 .BYTE "BCDEFG":.BYTE 0; ZERO DELIMITER ENDS MESSAGE
130 LDA #"H:JSR PRINT;  NORMAL PRINT
140 RTS
```

Although this routine might at first glance seem attractive, it is probably better to cluster all your messages at the end of your ML program as described under PRINT in Chapter 9. One reason is that this is an eccentric method of writing ML and is possible with only a few operating systems. You couldn't run this on the 64, for instance.

But a more important reason is that you won't be able to debug your program as easily because embedded messages will not, of course, disassemble.

## LOAD

$FFD5 loads a program file into memory. You set it up the way you would set up access to a sequential file (described above) by establishing the file parameters, the filename, and the bank wherein the name resides and the bank to which you wish the program loaded. The parameters are set as 0,8,1 for normal loading:

**LDA #0:LDX #8:LDY #1:JSR FFBA**

sets the parameters for a LOAD from disk. It would be 0,1,1 for tape.

This routine will also VERIFY. If, just prior to JSR $FFD5, you put a zero into the accumulator, LOAD will take place. Any other number in the accumulator will cause a VERIFY. (There was an error if, after JSR $FFD5, the carry flag is set. So you can BCS to an error-handling routine. All disk or tape access can be tested in this fashion for errors. The accumulator will contain an error code as well.)

Following LOAD, Y holds the MSB of the ending address and X, the LSB.

To see the steps involved in loading a program file into bank 1, see LOAD in the Open1 LADS subprogram. In addition to setting a zero into the accumulator (to LOAD, not VERIFY) just prior to JSR $FFD5, you can also put the LSB into X, the MSB into Y of a target address. In this way, you can force a LOAD to an address other than that from which the program was originally saved. To trigger this forced load, you must use a secondary address of 0; that is, the value you load into the Y register before you call the routine to set the file parameters ($FFBA) must be 0 instead of the 1 shown in the example above. Then:

```
LDA #0; cause LOAD
LDX #0; LSB
LDY #$80; MSB
JSR  $FFD5
```

will cause the program to be loaded at address $8000, regardless of where it was saved from. Normally, BASIC programs are saved from $1C00.

## SAVE

$FFD8 saves a program to disk or tape. It's quite similar to the way you load and is illustrated, like LOAD, in the LADS Open1 subprogram. Set the filename (see $FFBD above); set the bank number (see $FF68 above); set the file parameters (see $FFBA above). The accumulator is unused in this routine; Y holds 8 for disk or 1 for tape, and X, holding the secondary address, is only used for tape SAVEs. Then load the pointer to the starting address of the program you want saved into the accumulator. There is a pointer to the normal start of BASIC programs at $2D, so, unless you are saving something other than a BASIC program, LDA #$2D. Put the ending address (there's a pointer at $2F holding this address) into X (LSB) and Y (MSB) and JSR $FFD8. To establish the ending address: LDX $2F:LDY $30.

## Test RUN/STOP Key

$FFE1 checks the RUN/STOP key. If it's being pressed, the Z flag will be set, so you can JSR $FFE1:BEQ STOPKEYDOWN. This is one way to let the user exit your ML program. See line 690 in the Eval subprogram of LADS.

## GET

$FFE4 GETs a character. This is a way to get a keypress *in the Commodore ASCII code* from the keyboard. Unlike polling location $D4, where you get the keyboard matrix value of a pressed key, JSR $FFE4 leaves a printable ASCII character code in the accumulator. It will return a zero if no key is pressed:

```
GETKEY JSR $FFE4
BEQ  GETKEY
CMP  #13
BEQ  CARRIAGE
CMP  #65
BEQ  CHARA
CMP  #66:BEQ CHARB
CMP  #"C:BEQ CHARC
CMP  #"D:BEQ CHARD
```

shows how to accept input from the user and branch to appropriate subroutines depending on which key the user selected. You can use this to allow selection from a menu (CMP #"1 if the 1 key is pressed) or to build your own customized input routine which, for example, might refuse to recognize any numbers and, upon detecting one, would BEQ GETKEY to wait for a correct key. And, to make $FFE4 especially convenient, you can directly print whatever ASCII value is returned:

```
LOOP JSR $FFE4; GET KEYPRESS
BEQ LOOP; 0 MEANS NO KEY WAS PRESSED, SO TRY AGAIN
JSR $FFD2; ECHO THE CHARACTER TO SCREEN
```

### Cursor Control

$FFF0 allows you to find out where the cursor is on the screen or to move it to a different location. If you are using the 128's windowing facility, the positions will reference the start address of the window.

The carry flag is used to determine whether you intend to read or move the cursor. SEC if you want to read. CLC if you want to move.

To move the cursor down three lines and over five positions, you first read its position by SEC:JSR $FFF0. Then, you set it up to move down three lines by INX:INX:INX and over five columns by INY:INY:INY:INY:INY and CLC:JSR $FFF0 to send the cursor to its new place on the screen. The carry will be set if there was an error, so you can BCS ERROROUTINE after JSR $FFF0 to check.

This routine has obvious applications for screen formatting, TAB, and PRINTAT routines. It could also be used to govern some kinds of games where character graphics are on the move around the screen.

*The routines described so far (except for Set Bank Number and Print Immediate) are Commodore Kernal routines and, therefore, can be used in 64 mode as well as 128 mode. However, the following routines are new, created to access some of the features unique to the 128.*

## GO 64

$FF4D sends you into 64 mode, with no hope of returning. JMP to it and you cannot regain control via ML. It's as if you typed GO 64 from BASIC and answered Y when asked ARE YOU SURE? The machine transforms itself into a 64 and the transformation cannot be reversed without resetting the computer.

## Customize Function Keys

$FF65 changes the command available via one of the function keys. You can customize a function key to print whatever you want onscreen and, if it's a command, perform a carriage return to activate the command. Function keys operate using a principle similar to the "dynamic keyboard" technique in use for years on Commodore computers. *Dynamic keyboard* refers to stuffing the keyboard buffer with the required command and then, when the computer regains control, the buffer is emptied to the screen just as if the user had typed in whatever was in the buffer. This can, among other things, cause a BASIC program to modify itself (if you include a line number at the start of the message and end with a carriage return).

To program a function key, you have the accumulator point to a pointer in zero page which has the LSB, MSB, and bank number of the string which you want printed when the function key is pressed. So, if you set up:

**FA 00**
**FB 30**
**FC 0F**

that would point to a string at $3000 in bank 15. Waiting at address 3000 might be LIST with a carriage return. In LADS, you would:

**LDA #<F8:STA $FA:LDA #>F8:STA $FB:LDA #15:STA $FC**

to set up the pointer and have, at the location we'll label F8:

**F8 .BYTE "LIST":.BYTE 13**

Then, you put the length of your string into Y which, in this example, is 5. Finally, put the function key you want to modify into X (8, in this example), and then JSR $FF65. The complete LADS source code to accomplish this is

```
LDA #0:STA $FF00; SWITCH INTO BANK 15
LDA #<F8:STA $FA:LDA #>F8:STA $FB:LDA #15:STA $FC; SET
UP POINTER TO F8
LDA #$FA:LDY #5:LDX #8:JSR $FF65; CREATE FUNCTION
KEY #8
F8 .BYTE "LIST":.BYTE 13
```

The normal function keys are numbered 1 through 8. You can also customize the SHIFT–RUN/STOP key by putting 9 into X, or the HELP key with a 10 in X prior to JSRing (these two keys cannot be changed via the KEY command in BASIC. It's possible only in ML).

## Bank Number Code

$FF6B lets you know the proper code for accessing a memory bank. You may have noticed that you LDA #0:STA $FF00 to select bank *fifteen,* not bank zero as you might expect. When setting the $FF00 register, you have to use the code, but when indicating a bank in most other routines (far JSR, LDA, etc., and FF65 above) you give the actual bank number.

If you have a problem accessing a bank, it may be that you need to use the bank code rather than the bank's actual number. In that case, try LDX #BANKNUMBER:JSR $FF6B:BRK, and the accumulator will hold the bank code for that bank number. To find out what bank code to store in $FF00 to switch to bank 14:

**LDX #14:JSR $FF6B:BRK**

and the accumulator will have the answer. Try substituting that number for the actual bank number in your routine and see if it works. However, other than $FF00 and some few registers right above it, the actual bank number will work and you needn't bother with any of this special coding.

## Long-Distance Access

### JSR Long

$FF6E will JSR to an ML routine in a bank other than the one you're currently in. There are several such long-distance routines which will be described below. They use the *actual bank number* and also set up pointers in zero page. Some preparations are necessary. First we must save the registers and the status register:

**STA 6:STX 7:STY 8:PHP:PLA:STA 5**

accomplishes that. Then we announce that we want to JSR to bank 1 at address $4000:

**LDA #1:STA 2:LDA #$40:STA 3:LDA #0:STA 4**

and we can now JSR $FF6E, and the ML routine in bank 1 at address $4000 will RTS back to our current bank just like any other subroutine. However, we'll need to mirror image the save-registers routine above to restore stability:

**LDA 5:PHA:LDA 6:LDX 7:LDY 8:PLP**

This makes a JSR long-distance nondestructive to the current environment, like $FFD2. Registers and the flags are unaffected by the JSR because we saved and restored them.

### JMP Long

$FF71 is a JMP long-distance. It works precisely like the JSR described above except that, like any JMP, there is no automatic return.

### LDA Long

$FF74 is a long-distance LDA *(NN)*,Y and, as with JSR long-distance described above, must set up a few things before being activated. You put the pointer to the address in the accumulator and the bank number in X. Presumably, Y is being used by you as an index as it normally would be in indirect Y addressing.

If you want to load the byte at address $4000 of bank 1 (you're not in bank 1 or you wouldn't need to load long-distance):

**LDA #0:STA $FC:LDA #$40:STA $FD; to set up the pointer**
**LDA $FC; to point to the pointer**
**LDX #1; point to the bank**
**JSR $FF74; causes LDA ($FC),Y from bank 1**

## STA Long

$FF77 is a long-distance STA *(NN)*,Y and operates like LDA described just above. You put the byte you want stored into the accumulator and the bank number into X. However, you must also store the pointer ($FC in our example below) into $2B9:

First set up the pointer:

**LDA #0:STA $FC:LDA #$40:STA $FD:LDA #$FC:STA $2B9**

Then put the byte you want stored into the accumulator:

**LDA #45**

And put the bank number into X:

**LDX #1**

And:

**JSR $FF77**

Remember that, as always, Y is an offset, so if it's not holding a zero when you JSR $FF77, its value will be added to $4000 to determine exactly where in bank 1 the 45 in the accumulator will be stored.

When the .D pseudo-op is invoked in LADS, it stores object code to bank 1 and uses this long-distance STA.

## CMP Long

$FF7A compares—CMP *(NN)*,Y—long-distance. You set up a pointer in zero page and store the pointer's address in $2C8 (as described above for the long-distance STA). Then you put the byte to be compared into the accumulator and the bank number into X. Y holds the offset, if any, as is usual with indirect Y addressing.

Then JSR $FF7A and the flags will be set according to the result of the comparison as normal. You can BEQ, BNE, BCC, BCS as you normally would after a CMP test.

# Appendices

# 8502 Instruction Set

Here are the 56 mnemonics, the 56 instructions you can give the 8502 (or 6502 or 6510) chip. Each of these instructions is described below in several ways: what it does, what major uses it has in ML programming, what addressing modes it can use, what flags it affects, its opcode (hex/decimal), and the number of bytes it uses up.

## ADC

**What it does:** Adds byte in memory to the byte in the accumulator, plus the carry flag if set. Sets the carry flag if result exceeds 255. The result is left in the accumulator.

**Major uses:** Adds two numbers together. If the carry flag is set prior to an ADC, the resulting number will be *one* greater than the total of the two numbers being added (the carry is added to the result). Thus, one always clears the carry (CLC) before beginning any addition operation. Following an ADC, a set (up) carry flag indicates that the result exceeded one byte's capacity (was greater than 255), so you can chain-add bytes by subsequent ADCs without any further CLCs (see "Multibyte Addition" in Appendix E).

Other flags affected by addition include the V (overflow) flag. This flag is rarely of any interest to the programmer. It merely indicates that a result became larger than could be held within bits 0–6. In other words, the result "overflowed" into bit 7, the highest bit in a byte. Of greater importance is the fact that the Z flag is set if the result of an addition is zero. Also the N flag is set if bit 7 is set. This N flag is called the "negative" flag because you can manipulate bytes thinking of the seventh bit as a sign (+ or −) to accomplish "signed arithmetic" if you want to. In this mode, each byte can hold a maximum value of 127 (since the seventh bit is used to reveal the number's sign). The B branching instruction's relative addressing mode uses this kind of arithmetic.

ADC can be used following an SED which puts the 8502 into "decimal mode." Here's an example. Note that the number 75 is *decimal* after you SED:

**SED**
**CLC**
**LDA #$75**
**ADC #$05** This will result in 80.
**CLD** Always get rid of decimal mode as soon as you've finished.

Attractive as it sounds, the decimal mode isn't of much real value to the programmer. LADS will let you work in decimal if you want to without requiring that you enter the 8502's mode. Just leave off the $, and LADS will handle the decimal numbers for you.

**Addressing modes:**

| Name | Format | Opcode | Bytes Used |
|---|---|---|---|
| Immediate | ADC #15 | $69/105 | 2 |
| Zero Page | ADC 15 | $65/101 | 2 |
| Zero Page,X | ADC 15,X | $75/117 | 2 |
| Absolute | ADC 1500 | $6D/109 | 3 |
| Absolute,X | ADC 1500,X | $7D/125 | 3 |
| Absolute,Y | ADC 1500,Y | $79/121 | 3 |
| Indirect,X | ADC (15,X) | $61/97 | 2 |
| Indirect,Y | ADC (15),Y | $71/113 | 2 |

**Affected flags:** N Z C V

## AND

**What it does:** Logical ANDs the byte in memory with the byte in the accumulator. The result is left in the accumulator. All bits in both bytes are compared, and if both bits are one, the result is one. If either or both bits are zero, the result is zero.

**Major uses:** Most of the time, AND is used to turn bits off. Let's say that you are pulling in numbers higher than 128 (10000000 and higher) and you want to "unshift" them and print them as lowercase letters. You can then put a zero into the seventh bit of your "mask" and then AND the mask with the number being unshifted:

**LDA ?** Test number
**AND #$7F** 01111111

(If *either* bit is zero, the result will be zero. So the seventh bit of the test number is turned off here, and all the other bits in the test number are unaffected.)

**Addressing modes:**

| Name | Format | Opcode | Bytes Used |
|---|---|---|---|
| Immediate | AND #15 | $29/41 | 2 |
| Zero Page | AND 15 | $25/37 | 2 |
| Zero Page,X | AND 15,X | $35/53 | 2 |
| Absolute | AND 1500 | $2D/45 | 3 |
| Absolute,X | AND 1500,X | $3D/61 | 3 |
| Absolute,Y | AND 1500,Y | $39/57 | 3 |
| Indirect,X | AND (15,X) | $21/33 | 2 |
| Indirect,Y | AND (15),Y | $31/49 | 2 |

**Affected flags:** N Z

## ASL

**What it does:** Shifts the bits in a byte to the left by 1. This byte can be in the accumulator or in memory, depending on the addressing mode. The shift moves the seventh bit into the carry flag and shoves a zero into the zeroth bit.

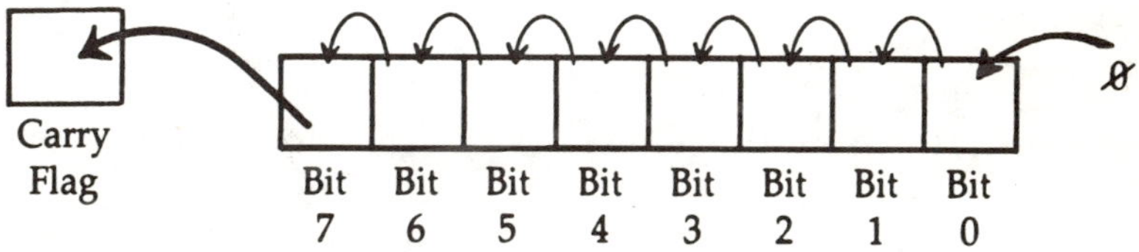


**Major uses:** Allows you to multiply a number by 2. Numbers bigger than 255 can be manipulated using ASL with ROL (see "Multiplication" in Appendix E).

A secondary use is to move the lower four bits in a byte (a four-bit unit is often called a *nybble*) into the higher four bits. The lower bits are replaced by zeros, since ASL stuffs zeros into the zeroth bit of a byte. You move the lower to the higher nybble of a byte by ASL ASL ASL ASL.

**Addressing modes:**

| Name | Format | Opcode | Bytes Used |
|---|---|---|---|
| Accumulator | ASL | $0A/10 | 1 |
| Zero Page | ASL 15 | $06/6 | 2 |
| Zero Page,X | ASL 15,X | $16/22 | 2 |
| Absolute | ASL 1500 | $0E/14 | 3 |
| Absolute,X | ASL 1500,X | $1E/30 | 3 |

**Affected flags:** N Z C

## BCC

**What it does:** Branches up to 127 bytes forward or 128 bytes backward from the address of the following instruction if the carry flag is clear. In effect, it branches if the *first* item (the accumulator contents) is lower than the *second*, as in LDA #149:CMP #150 or LDA #15: SBC #22. The comparison or subtraction would clear the carry and, the cleared carry then triggering BCC, a branch would take place.

**Major uses:** For testing the results of CMP or ADC or other operations which affect the carry flag. IF-THEN or ON-GOTO type structures in ML can involve the BCC test. It is similar to BASIC's < instruction.

**Addressing modes:**

| Name | Format | Opcode | Bytes Used |
|---|---|---|---|
| Relative | BCC addr. | $90/144 | 2 |

**Affected flags:** None

## BCS

**What it does:** Branches up to 127 bytes forward or 128 bytes backward from the address of the following instruction if the carry flag is set. It branches if the *first* item (the accumulator contents) is higher than or equal to the *second*, as in LDA #249:CMP #150 or LDA #85:SBC #22. The comparison or subtraction would set the carry and, the carry then triggering BCS, a branch would take place.

**Major uses:** For testing the results of LDA or ADC or other operations which affect the carry flag. IF-THEN or ON-GOTO type structures in ML can involve the BCC test. It is similar to BASIC's >= instruction.

**Addressing modes:**

| Name | Format | Opcode | Bytes Used |
|---|---|---|---|
| Relative | BCS addr. | $B0/176 | 2 |

**Affected flags:** None

## BEQ

**What it does:** Branches up to 127 bytes forward or 128 bytes backward from the address of the following instruction if the zero flag (Z) is set. In other words, it branches if an action on two bytes results in a zero, as in LDA #150: CMP #150 or LDA #22: SBC #22. These actions would set the zero flag, so the branch would take place.

**Major uses:** For testing the results of LDA or ADC or other operations which affect the carry flag. IF-THEN or ON-GOTO type structures in ML can involve the BEQ test. It is similar to BASIC's = instruction.

**Addressing modes:**

| Name | Format | Opcode | Bytes Used |
|---|---|---|---|
| Relative | BEQ addr. | $F0/240 | 2 |

**Affected flags:** None

## BIT

**What it does:** Tests the bits in the byte in memory against the bits in the byte held in the accumulator. The bytes (memory and accumulator) are unaffected. BIT merely sets flags. The Z flag is set as if an accumulator AND memory had been performed. The V flag and the N flag receive *copies* of the sixth and seventh bits of the tested number.

**Major uses:** Although BIT has the advantage of not having any effect on the tested numbers, it is infrequently used because you cannot employ the immediate addressing mode with it. Other tests (CMP and AND, for example) can be used instead.

**Addressing modes:**

| Name | Format | Opcode | Bytes Used |
|---|---|---|---|
| Zero Page | BIT 15 | $24/36 | 2 |
| Absolute | BIT 1500 | $2C/44 | 3 |

**Affected flags:** N Z V

## BMI

**What it does:** Branches up to 127 bytes forward or 128 bytes backward from the address of the following instruction if the negative (N) flag is set. In effect, it branches if the seventh bit has been set by the most recent event: LDA #150 or LDA #128 would set the seventh bit. These actions would set the N flag, signifying that a *minus number* is present if you are using signed arithmetic or that there is a *shifted character* (or a BASIC keyword) if you are thinking of a byte in terms of the ASCII code.

**Major uses:** Testing for BASIC keywords, shifted ASCII, or graphics symbols. Testing for + or − in signed arithmetic.

**Addressing modes:**

| Name | Format | Opcode | Bytes Used |
|---|---|---|---|
| Relative | BMI addr. | $30/48 | 2 |

**Affected flags:** None

## BNE

**What it does:** Branches up to 127 bytes forward or 128 bytes backward from the address of the following instruction if the zero flag is clear. In other words, it branches if the result of the most recent event is not zero, as in LDA #150: SBC #120 or LDA #128: CMP #125. These actions would clear the Z flag, signifying that a result was not zero.

**Major uses:** The reverse of BEQ. BNE means Branch if Not Equal. Since a CMP subtracts one number from another to perform its comparison, a zero result means that they are equal. Any other result will trigger a BNE (not equal). Like the other B branch instructions, it has uses in IF-THEN, ON-GOTO type structures and is used as a way to exit loops (for example, BNE will branch back to the start of a loop until a zero delimiter is encountered at the end of a text message). BNE is like BASIC's <> instruction.

**Addressing modes:**

| Name | Format | Opcode | Bytes Used |
|---|---|---|---|
| Relative | BNE addr. | $D0/208 | 2 |

**Affected flags:** None

## BPL

**What it does:** Branches up to 127 bytes forward or 128 bytes backward from the address of the following instruction if the N flag is clear. In effect, it branches if the seventh bit is clear in the most recent event, as in LDA #12 or LDA #127.

These actions would clear the N flag, signifying that a *plus number* (or zero) is present in signed arithmetic mode.

**Major uses:** For testing the results of LDA or ADC or other operations which affect the negative (N) flag. IF-THEN or ON-GOTO type structures in ML can involve the BCC test. It is the opposite of the BMI instruction. BPL can be used for tests of "unshifted" ASCII characters and other bytes which have the seventh bit off and so are lower than 128 (0XXXXXXX).

**Addressing modes:**

| Name | Format | Opcode | Bytes Used |
|---|---|---|---|
| Relative | BPL addr. | $10/16 | 2 |

**Affected flags:** None

## BRK

**What it does:** Causes a forced interrupt. This interrupt cannot be masked (prevented) by setting the I (interrupt) flag within the status register. If there is a Break Interrupt Vector (a vector is like a pointer) in the computer, it may point to a resident monitor if the computer has one. The PC and the status register are saved on the stack. The PC points to the location of the BRK + 2.

**Major uses:** Debugging an ML program can often start with a sprinkling of BRKs into suspicious locations within the code. The ML is executed, a BRK stops execution and drops you into the monitor, you examine registers or tables or variables to see if they are as they should be at this point in the execution, and then you restart execution from the breakpoint. This instruction is essentially identical to the actions and uses of the STOP command in BASIC.

**Addressing modes:**

| Name | Format | Opcode | Bytes Used |
|---|---|---|---|
| Implied | BRK | $00/0 | 1 |

**Affected flags:** Break (B) flag is set.

## BVC

**What it does:** Branches up to 127 bytes forward or 128 bytes backward from the address of the following instruction if the V (overflow) flag is clear.

**Major uses:** None. In practice, few programmers use "signed" arithmetic where the seventh bit is devoted to indicating a positive or negative number (a set seventh bit means a negative number). The V flag has the job of notifying you when you've added, say, 120 + 30, and have therefore set the seventh bit via an "overflow" (a result greater than 127). The result of your addition of two positive numbers should not be seen as a negative number, but the seventh bit *is* set. The V flag can be tested and will then reveal that your answer is still positive, but an overflow took place.

**Addressing modes:**

| Name | Format | Opcode | Bytes Used |
|---|---|---|---|
| Relative | BVC addr. | $50/80 | 2 |

**Affected flags:** None

## BVS

**What it does:** Branches up to 127 bytes forward or 128 bytes backward from the address of the following instruction if the V (overflow) flag is set.

**Major uses:** None; see BVC above.

**Addressing modes:**

| Name | Format | Opcode | Bytes Used |
|---|---|---|---|
| Relative | BVS addr. | $70/112 | 2 |

**Affected flags:** None

## CLC

**What it does:** Clears the carry flag (puts a zero into it).

**Major uses:** Always used before any addition (ADC). If there are to be a series of additions (multiple-byte addition), only the first ADC is preceded by CLC since the carry feature is necessary. There might be a carry, and the result will be incorrect if it is not taken into account.

The 8502 does not offer an addition instruction without

the carry feature. Thus, you must always clear it before the first ADC so that a carry won't be accidentally added.

**Addressing modes:**

| Name | Format | Opcode | Bytes Used |
|---|---|---|---|
| Implied | CLC | $18/24 | 1 |

**Affected flags:** Carry (C) flag is set to zero.

## CLD

**What it does:** Clears the decimal mode flag (puts a zero into it).

**Major uses:** This clears the flag which forces the chip into "decimal mode." On some computers, it's necessary to CLD at the start of an ML program because the D flag can be in an indeterminate state when you SYS to your ML routine. However, this isn't necessary on the 128. Commodore computers thoughtfully execute a CLD when first turned on as well as upon entry to monitor modes (PET/CBM and 128 models) and when the SYS command occurs.

For further detail about the 8502's decimal mode, see SED below.

**Addressing modes:**

| Name | Format | Opcode | Bytes Used |
|---|---|---|---|
| Implied | CLD | $D8/216 | 1 |

**Affected flags:** Decimal (D) flag is set to zero.

## CLI

**What it does:** Clears the interrupt-disable flag. All interrupts will therefore be serviced (including maskable ones).

**Major uses:** To restore normal interrupt routine processing following a temporary suspension of interrupts for the purpose of redirecting the interrupt vector. For more detail, see SEI below.

**Addressing modes:**

| Name | Format | Opcode | Bytes Used |
|---|---|---|---|
| Implied | CLI | $58/88 | 1 |

**Affected flags:** Interrupt (I) flag is set to zero.

## CLV

**What it does:** Clears the overflow flag (puts a zero into it).
**Major uses:** None; see BVC above.

**Addressing modes:**

| Name | Format | Opcode | Bytes Used |
|---|---|---|---|
| Implied | CLV | $B8/184 | 1 |

**Affected flags:** Overflow (V) flag is set to zero.

## CMP

**What it does:** Compares the byte in memory to the byte in the accumulator. Three flags are affected, but the bytes in memory and in the accumulator are undisturbed. A CMP is actually a subtraction of the byte in memory from the byte in the accumulator. Therefore, if you LDA #15:CMP #15, the result (of the subtraction) will be zero, and BEQ would be triggered since the CMP would have set the Z flag.

**Major uses:** This is an important instruction in ML. It is central to IF-THEN and ON-GOTO type structures. In combination with the B branching instructions like BEQ, CMP allows the 8502 chip to make decisions, to take alternative pathways depending on comparisons. CMP throws the N, Z, or C flag up or down. Then a B instruction can branch, depending on the condition of a flag.

Often, an action will affect flags by itself, and a CMP will not be necessary. For example, LDA #15 will put a zero into the N flag (seventh bit not set) and will put a zero into the Z flag (the result was not zero). LDA does not affect the C flag. In any event, you could LDA #15: BPL TARGET, and the branch would take effect. However, if you LDA $20 and need to know if the byte loaded is *precisely* $0D, you must CMP #$0D:BEQ TARGET. So, while CMP is sometimes not absolutely necessary, it will never hurt to include it prior to branching.

Another important branch decision is based on > or < situations. In this case, you use BCC and BCS to test the C (carry) flag. And you've got to keep in mind the *order* of the numbers being compared. The memory byte is compared to the byte sitting in the accumulator. The structure is accumulator value *is less than* memory (BCC is triggered because the carry flag was cleared). Or accumulator value *is more than or equal to* memory (BCS is triggered because the carry flag was set). Here's an example. If you want to find out if the number in the accumulator is less than $40, just CMP #$40:BCC LESSTHAN:

**LDA #75**
**CMP #$40; IS IT LESS THAN $40?**
**BCC LESSTHAN**

One final comment about the useful BCC/BCS tests following CMP: It's easy to remember that BCC means *less than* and BCS means *more than or equal* if you notice that C is less than S in the alphabet.

The other flag affected by CMPs is the N flag. Its uses are limited since it merely reports the status of the seventh bit; BPL triggers if that bit is clear, BMI triggers if it's set. However, that seventh bit does show whether the number is greater than (or equal to) or less than 128, and you can apply this information to the ASCII code or to look for BASIC keywords or to search databases (BPL and BMI are used by LADS's database search routines in the Array subprogram). Nevertheless, since LDA and many other instructions affect the N flag, you can often directly BPL or BMI without any need to CMP first.

**Addressing modes:**

| Name | Format | Opcode | Bytes Used |
|---|---|---|---|
| Immediate | CMP #15 | $C9/201 | 2 |
| Zero Page | CMP 15 | $C5/197 | 2 |
| Zero Page,X | CMP 15,X | $D5/213 | 2 |
| Absolute | CMP 1500 | $CD/205 | 3 |
| Absolute,X | CMP 1500,X | $DD/221 | 3 |
| Absolute,Y | CMP 1500,Y | $D9/217 | 3 |
| Indirect,X | CMP (15,X) | $C1/193 | 2 |
| Indirect,Y | CMP (15),Y | $D1/209 | 2 |

**Affected flags:** N Z C

## CPX

**What it does:** Compares the byte in memory to the byte in the X register. Three flags are affected, but the bytes in memory and in the X register are undisturbed. A CPX is actually a subtraction of the byte in memory from the byte in the X register. Therefore, if you LDA #15:CPX #15, the result (of the subtraction) will be zero, and BEQ would be triggered since the CPX would have set the Z flag.

**Major uses:** X is generally used as an index, a counter within loops. Though the Y register is often preferred as an index since it can serve for the very useful indirect Y addressing mode (LDA (15),Y), the X register is nevertheless pressed into service when more than one index is necessary or when Y is busy with other tasks.

In any case, the flags, conditions, and purposes of CPX are quite similar to CMP (the equivalent comparison instruction for the accumulator). For further information on the various possible comparisons (greater than, equal, less than, not equal), see CMP above.

**Addressing modes:**

| Name | Format | Opcode | Bytes Used |
|---|---|---|---|
| Immediate | CPX #15 | $E0/224 | 2 |
| Zero Page | CPX 15 | $E4/228 | 2 |
| Absolute | CPX 1500 | $EC/236 | 3 |

**Affected flags:** N Z C

## CPY

**What it does:** Compares the byte in memory to the byte in the Y register. Three flags are affected, but the bytes in memory and in the Y register are undisturbed. A CPX is actually a subtraction of the byte in memory from the byte in the Y register. Therefore, if you LDA #15: CPY #15, the result (of the subtraction) will be zero, and BEQ would be triggered since the CPY would have set the Z flag.

**Major uses:** Y is the most popular index, the most heavily used counter within loops since it can serve two purposes: It permits the very useful indirect Y addressing mode—LDA (15),Y—and can simultaneously maintain a count of loop events.

See CMP above for a detailed discussion of the various branch comparisons which CPY can implement.

**Addressing modes:**

| Name | Format | Opcode | Bytes Used |
|---|---|---|---|
| Immediate | CPY #15 | $C0/192 | 2 |
| Zero Page | CPY 15 | $C4/196 | 2 |
| Absolute | CPY 1500 | $CC/204 | 3 |

**Affected flags:** N Z C

## DEC

**What it does:** Reduces the value of a byte in memory by 1. The N and Z flags are affected.

**Major uses:** A useful alternative to SBC when you are reducing the value of a memory address. DEC is simpler and shorter than SBC, and although DEC doesn't affect the C flag, you can still decrement double-byte numbers (see "Decrement Double-Byte Numbers" in Appendix E).

The other main use for DEC is to control a memory index when the X and Y registers are too busy to provide this service. For example, you could define, say, address $505 as a counter for a loop structure. Then LOOP STA $8000:DEC $505:BEQ END:JMP LOOP. This structure would continue storing A into $8000 until address $505 was decremented to zero. This imitates DEX or DEY and allows you to set up as many nested loop structures (loops within loops) as you wish.

**Addressing modes:**

| Name | Format | Opcode | Bytes Used |
|---|---|---|---|
| Zero Page | DEC 15 | $C6/198 | 2 |
| Zero Page,X | DEC 15,X | $D6/214 | 2 |
| Absolute | DEC 1500 | $CE/206 | 3 |
| Absolute,X | DEC 1500,X | $DE/222 | 3 |

**Affected flags:** N Z

## DEX

**What it does:** Reduces the X register by 1.

**Major uses:** Used as a counter (an index) within loops. Normally, you LDX with some number (the number of times you want the loop executed) and then DEX:BEQ END as a way of counting events and exiting the loop at the right time.

**Addressing modes:**

| Name | Format | Opcode | Bytes Used |
|---|---|---|---|
| Implied | DEX | $CA/202 | 1 |

**Affected flags:** N Z

## DEY

**What it does:** Reduces the Y register by 1.

**Major uses:** Like DEX, DEY is often used as a counter for loop structures. But DEY is the more common of the two since the Y register can simultaneously serve two purposes within a loop by permitting the very popular indirect Y addressing mode. A common way to print a screen message (the ASCII form of the message is at $5000 in this example, and the message ends with zero): LDY #0:LOOP LDA $5000,Y:BEQ END:STA SCREEN,Y:INY:JMP LOOP:END and continue with the program.

**Addressing modes:**

| Name | Format | Opcode | Bytes Used |
|---|---|---|---|
| Implied | DEY | $88/136 | 1 |

**Affected flags:** N Z

## EOR

**What it does:** Exclusive-ORs a byte in memory with the accumulator. Each bit in memory is compared with each bit in the accumulator, and the bits are then set (given a one) if *one of the compared bits* is one. However, bits are cleared if both are zero or if both are one. The bits in the byte held in the accumulator are the only ones affected by this comparison.

**Major uses:** EOR doesn't have too many uses. Its main value is to *toggle* a bit. If a bit is clear (is a zero), it will be set (to a one); if a bit is set, it will be cleared. For example, if you want to reverse the current state of the sixth bit in a given byte: LDA BYTE:EOR #$40:STA BYTE. This will set bit 6 in BYTE if it was zero (and clear it if it was one). This selective bit toggling could be used to "shift" an unshifted ASCII character via EOR #$80 (1000000). Or if the character were shifted, EOR #$80 would make it lowercase. EOR toggles.

**Addressing modes:**

| Name | Format | Opcode | Bytes Used |
|---|---|---|---|
| Immediate | EOR #15 | $49/73 | 2 |
| Zero Page | EOR 15 | $45/69 | 2 |
| Zero Page,X | EOR 15,X | $55/85 | 2 |
| Absolute | EOR 1500 | $4D/77 | 3 |
| Absolute,X | EOR 1500,X | $5D/93 | 3 |
| Absolute,Y | EOR 1500,Y | $59/89 | 3 |
| Indirect,X | EOR (15,X) | $41/65 | 2 |
| Indirect,Y | EOR (15),Y | $51/81 | 2 |

**Affected flags:** N Z

## INC

**What it does:** Increases the value of a byte in memory by 1.

**Major uses:** Used exactly as DEC (see DEC above), except it counts up instead of down. For raising address pointers or supplementing the X and Y registers as loop indexes.

**Addressing modes:**

| Name | Format | Opcode | Bytes Used |
|---|---|---|---|
| Zero Page | INC 15 | $E6/230 | 2 |
| Zero Page,X | INC 15,X | $F6/246 | 2 |
| Absolute | INC 1500 | $EE/238 | 3 |
| Absolute,X | INC 1500,X | $FE/254 | 3 |

**Affected flags:** N Z

## INX

**What it does:** Increases the X register by 1.

**Major uses:** Used exactly as DEX (see DEX above), except it counts up instead of down. For loop indexing.

**Addressing modes:**

| Name | Format | Opcode | Bytes Used |
|---|---|---|---|
| Implied | INX | $E8/232 | 1 |

**Affected flags:** N Z

## INY

**What it does:** Increases the Y register by 1.

**Major uses:** Used exactly as DEY (see DEY above), except it counts up instead of down. For loop indexing and working with the indirect Y addressing mode—LDA (15),Y.

**Addressing modes:**

| Name | Format | Opcode | Bytes Used |
|---|---|---|---|
| Implied | INY | $C8/200 | 1 |

**Affected flags:** N Z

## JMP

**What it does:** Jumps to any location in memory.

**Major uses:** Branching long range. It is the equivalent of BASIC's GOTO instruction. The bytes in the program counter are replaced with the address (the argument) following the JMP instruction and, therefore, program execution continues from this new address.

Indirect jumping—JMP (1500)—is not recommended, although some programmers find it useful. It allows you to set up a table of jump targets and bounce off them indirectly. For example, if you had placed the numbers $00 $04 in addresses $88 and $89, a JMP ($0088) instruction would send the program to whatever ML routine was located in address $0400. Unfortunately, if you should locate one of your pointers on the edge of a *page* (for example, $00FF or $17FF), this indirect JMP addressing mode reveals its great weakness. There is a bug which causes the jump to travel to the wrong place—JMP ($00FF) picks up the first byte of the pointer from $00FF, but the second byte of the pointer will be incorrectly taken from $0000. With JMP ($17FF), the second byte of the pointer would come from what's in address $1700.

Since there is this bug and since there are no compelling reasons to set up JMP tables, you might want to forget you ever heard of indirect jumping.

**Addressing modes:**

| Name | Format | Opcode | Bytes Used |
|---|---|---|---|
| Absolute | JMP 1500 | $4C/76 | 3 |
| Indirect | JMP (1500) | $6C/108 | 3 |

**Affected flags:** None

## JSR

**What it does:** Jumps to a subroutine anywhere in memory. Saves the PC (Program Counter) address, plus three, of the JSR instruction by pushing it onto the stack. The next RTS in the program will then pull that address off the stack and return to the instruction following the JSR.

**Major uses:** As the direct equivalent of BASIC's GOSUB command, JSR is heavily used in ML programming to send control to a subroutine and then (via RTS) to return and pick up where you left off. The larger and more sophisticated a program becomes, the more often JSR will be invoked. In LADS, whenever something is printed to screen or printer, you'll often see a chain of JSRs performing necessary tasks: JSR PRNTCR: JSR PRNTSA:JSR PRNTSPACE:JSR PRNTNUM:JSR PRNTSPACE. This JSR chain prints a carriage return, the current assembly address, a space, a number, and another space.

Another thing you might notice in LADS and other ML programs is a PLA:PLA pair. Since JSR stuffs the correct return address onto the stack before leaving for a subroutine, you need to do something about that return address if you later decide *not to RTS* back to the position of the JSR in the program. This might be the case if you *usually* want to RTS, but in some particular cases, you don't. For those cases, you can take control of program flow by removing the return address from the stack (PLA:PLA will clean off the two-byte address) and then performing a direct JMP to wherever you want to go.

If you JMP out of a subroutine without PLA:PLA, you could easily overflow the stack and crash the program.

**Addressing modes:**

| Name | Format | Opcode | Bytes Used |
|---|---|---|---|
| Absolute | JSR 1500 | $20/32 | 3 |

**Affected flags:** None

## LDA

**What it does:** Loads the accumulator with a byte from memory. *Copy* might be a better word than *load,* since the byte in memory is unaffected by the transfer.

**Major uses:** The busiest place in the computer. Bytes coming in from disk, tape, or keyboard all flow through the accumulator, as do bytes on their way to screen or peripherals.

Also, because the accumulator differs in some important ways from the X and Y registers, the accumulator is used by ML programmers in a different way from the other registers.

Since INY/DEY and INX/DEX make those registers useful as counters for loops (the accumulator couldn't be conveniently employed as an index; there is no INA instruction), the accumulator is the main temporary storage register for bytes during their manipulation in an ML program. ML programming, in fact, can be defined as essentially the rapid, organized maneuvering of single bytes in memory. And it is the accumulator where these bytes often briefly rest before being sent elsewhere.

**Addressing modes:**

| Name | Format | Opcode | Bytes Used |
|---|---|---|---|
| Immediate | LDA #15 | $A9/169 | 2 |
| Zero Page | LDA 15 | $A5/165 | 2 |
| Zero Page,X | LDA 15,X | $B5/181 | 2 |
| Absolute | LDA 1500 | $AD/173 | 3 |
| Absolute,X | LDA 1500,X | $BD/189 | 3 |
| Absolute,Y | LDA 1500,Y | $B9/185 | 3 |
| Indirect,X | LDA (15,X) | $A1/161 | 2 |
| Indirect,Y | LDA (15),Y | $B1/177 | 2 |

**Affected flags:** N Z

## LDX

**What it does:** Loads the X register with a byte from memory.

**Major uses:** The X register can perform many of the tasks that the accumulator performs, but it is generally used as an index for loops. In preparation for its role as an index, LDX puts a value into the register.

**Addressing modes:**

| Name | Format | Opcode | Bytes Used |
|---|---|---|---|
| Immediate | LDX #15 | $A2/162 | 2 |
| Zero Page | LDX 15 | $A6/166 | 2 |
| Zero Page,Y | LDX 15,Y | $B6/182 | 2 |
| Absolute | LDX 1500 | $AE/174 | 3 |
| Absolute,Y | LDX 1500,Y | $BE/190 | 3 |

**Affected flags:** N Z

## LDY

**What it does:** Loads the Y register with a byte from memory.

**Major uses:** The Y register can perform many of the tasks that the accumulator performs, but it is generally used as an index for loops. In preparation for its role as an index, LDY puts a value into the register.

**Addressing modes:**

| Name | Format | Opcode | Bytes Used |
|---|---|---|---|
| Immediate | LDY #15 | $A0/160 | 2 |
| Zero Page | LDY 15 | $A4/164 | 2 |
| Zero Page,X | LDY 15,X | $B4/180 | 2 |
| Absolute | LDY 1500 | $AC/172 | 3 |
| Absolute,X | LDY 1500,X | $BC/188 | 3 |

**Affected flags:** N Z

## LSR

**What it does:** Shifts the bits in the accumulator or in a byte in memory to the right by one bit. A zero is stuffed into bit 7, and bit 0 is put into the carry flag.

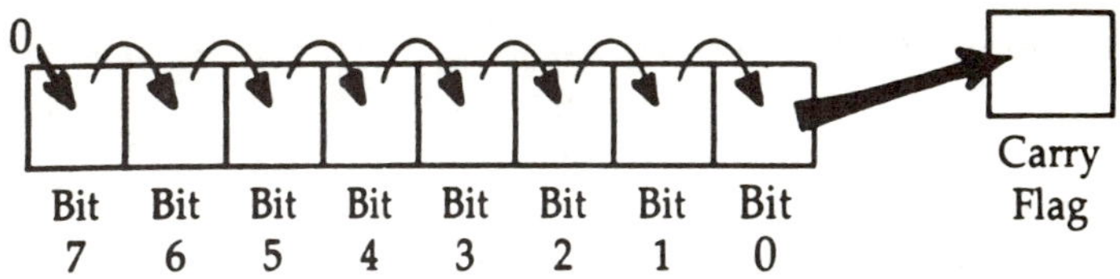


**Major uses:** To divide a byte by 2. In combination with the ROR instruction, LSR can divide a two-byte or larger number (see Appendix E).

LSR:LSR:LSR:LSR will put the high four bits (the high nybble) into the low nybble (with the high nybble replaced by the zeros being stuffed into the seventh bit and then shifted to the right).

**Addressing modes:**

| Name | Format | Opcode | Bytes Used |
|---|---|---|---|
| Accumulator | LSR | $4A/74 | 2 |
| Zero Page | LSR 15 | $46/70 | 2 |
| Zero Page,X | LSR 15,X | $56/86 | 2 |
| Absolute | LSR 1500 | $4E/78 | 3 |
| Absolute,X | LSR 1500,X | $5E/94 | 3 |

**Affected flags:** N Z C

# NOP

**What it does:** Nothing; NO oPeration.

**Major uses:** Debugging. When setting breakpoints with BRK, you will often discover that a breakpoint, when examined, passes the test. That is, there is nothing wrong at that place in the program. So, to allow the program to execute to the next breakpoint, you cover the BRK with a NOP. Then, when you run the program, the computer will slide over the NOP with no effect on the program. Three NOPs could cover a JSR *XXXX*, and you could see the effect on the program when that particular JSR is eliminated.

**Addressing modes:**

| Name | Format | Opcode | Bytes Used |
|---|---|---|---|
| Implied | NOP | $EA/234 | 1 |

**Affected flags:** None

# ORA

**What it does:** Logically ORs a byte in memory with the byte in the accumulator. The result is in the accumulator. An OR results in a one if either the bit in memory or the bit in the accumulator is one.

**Major uses:** Like an AND mask which turns bits off, ORA masks can be used to turn bits on. For example, if you wanted to "shift" an ASCII character by setting the seventh bit, you could LDA CHARACTER:ORA #$80. The number $80 in binary is 10000000, so all the bits in CHARACTER which are ORed with zeros here will be left unchanged. (If a bit in CHARACTER is a one, it stays a one. If it is a zero, it stays zero.) But the one in the seventh bit of $80 will cause a zero in the CHARACTER to turn into a one. (If CHARACTER already has a one in its seventh bit, it will remain a one.)

**Addressing modes:**

| Name | Format | Opcode | Bytes Used |
|---|---|---|---|
| Immediate | ORA #15 | $09/9 | 2 |
| Zero Page | ORA 15 | $05/5 | 2 |
| Zero Page,X | ORA 15,X | $15/21 | 2 |
| Absolute | ORA 1500 | $0D/13 | 3 |
| Absolute,X | ORA 1500,X | $1D/29 | 3 |
| Absolute,Y | ORA 1500,Y | $19/25 | 3 |
| Indirect,X | ORA (15,X) | $01/1 | 2 |
| Indirect,Y | ORA (15),Y | $11/17 | 2 |

**Affected flags:** N Z

## PHA

**What it does:** Pushes the accumulator onto the stack.

**Major uses:** To temporarily *(very temporarily)* save the byte in the accumulator. If you are within a particular subroutine and you need to save a value for a brief time, you can PHA it. But beware that you must PLA it back into the accumulator *before any RTS* so that it won't misdirect the computer to the wrong RTS address. All RTS addresses are saved on the stack. Probably a safer way to temporarily save a value (a number) would be to STA TEMP or put it in some other temporary variable that you've set aside to hold things. Also, the values of A, X, and Y need to be temporarily saved, and the programmer will combine TYA and TXA with several PHAs to stuff all three registers onto the stack. But, again, matching PLAs must restore the stack as soon as possible and certainly prior to any RTS.

**Addressing modes:**

| Name | Format | Opcode | Bytes Used |
|---|---|---|---|
| Implied | PHA | $48/72 | 1 |

**Affected flags:** None

## PHP

**What it does:** Pushes the "processor status" onto the top of the stack. This byte is the status register, the byte which holds all the flags: N Z C I D V.

**Major uses:** To temporarily, *very temporarily,* save the state of the flags. If you need to preserve all current conditions for a minute (see description of PHA above), you may also want to preserve the status register as well. You must, however, restore the status register byte and clean up the stack by using a PLP before the next RTS.

**Addressing modes:**

| Name | Format | Opcode | Bytes Used |
|---|---|---|---|
| Implied | PHP | $08/8 | 1 |

**Affected flags:** None

## PLA

**What it does:** Pulls the top byte off the stack and puts it into the accumulator.

**Major uses:** To restore a number which was temporarily stored on top of the stack (with the PHA instruction). It is the opposite action of PHA (see above). Note that PLA does affect the N and Z flags. Each PHA must be matched by a corresponding PLA if the stack is to correctly maintain RTS addresses, which is the main purpose of the stack.

**Addressing modes:**

| Name | Format | Opcode | Bytes Used |
|---|---|---|---|
| Implied | PLA | $68/104 | 1 |

**Affected flags:** N Z

## PLP

**What it does:** Pulls the top byte off the stack and puts it into the status register (where the flags are). PLP is a mnemonic for PuLl Processor status.

**Major uses:** To restore the condition of the flags after the status register has been temporarily stored on top of the stack (with the PHP instruction). It is the opposite action of PHP (see above). PLP, of course, affects *all* the flags. Any PHP must be matched by a corresponding PLP if the stack is to correctly maintain RTS addresses, which is the main purpose of the stack.

**Addressing modes:**

| **Name** | **Format** | **Opcode** | **Bytes Used** |
|---|---|---|---|
| Implied | PLP | $28/40 | 1 |

**Affected flags:** All

## ROL

**What it does:** Rotates the bits in the accumulator or in a byte in memory to the left by one bit. A rotate left (as opposed to an ASL, Arithmetic Shift Left) moves bit 7 to the carry, *moves the carry into bit 0,* and every other bit moves one position to its left. (ASL operates quite similarly, except it always puts a zero into bit 0.)

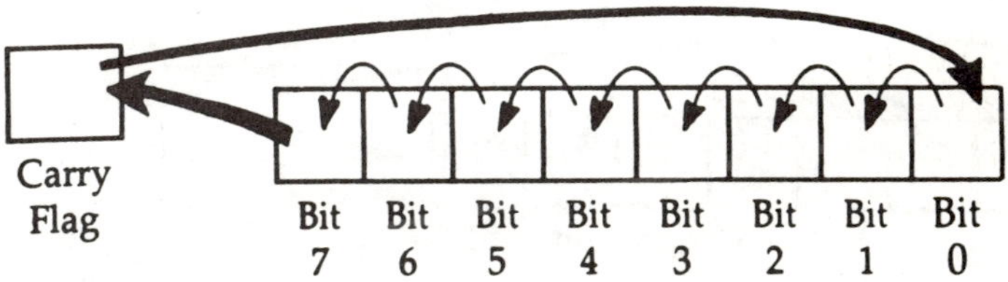


**Major uses:** To multiply a byte by 2. ROL can be used with ASL to multiply multiple-byte numbers since ROL pulls any carry into bit 0. If an ASL resulted in a carry, it would be thus taken into account in the next higher byte in a multiple-byte number. (See Appendix E.)

Notice how the act of moving columns of binary numbers to the left has the effect of multiplying by 2:

**0010** The number 2 in binary
**0100** The number 4

This same effect can be observed with decimal numbers, except the columns represent powers of 10:

**0010** The number 10 in decimal
**0100** The number 100

**Addressing modes:**

| Name | Format | Opcode | Bytes Used |
|---|---|---|---|
| Accumulator | ROL | $2A/42 | 1 |
| Zero Page | ROL 15 | $26/38 | 2 |
| Zero Page,X | ROL 15,X | $36/54 | 2 |
| Absolute | ROL 1500 | $2E/46 | 3 |
| Absolute,X | ROL 1500,X | $3E/62 | 3 |

**Affected flags:** N Z C

## ROR

**What it does:** Rotates the bits in the accumulator or in a byte in memory to the right by one bit. A rotate right (as opposed to an LSR, Logical Shift Right) moves bit 0 into the carry, *moves the carry into bit 7,* and every other bit moves one position to its right. (LSR operates quite similarly, except it always puts a zero into bit 7.)

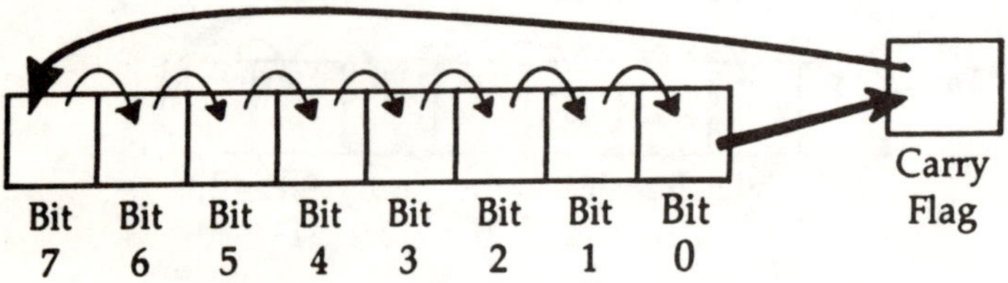


**Major uses:** To divide a byte by 2. ROR can be used with LSR to divide multiple-byte numbers since ROR puts any carry into bit 7. If an LSR resulted in a carry, it would be thus taken into account in the next lower byte in a multiple-byte number. (See Appendix E.)

Notice how the act of moving columns of binary numbers to the right has the effect of dividing by 2:

**1000** The number 8 in binary
**0100** The number 4

This same effect can be observed with decimal numbers, except the columns represent powers of 10:

**1000** The number 1000 in decimal
**0100** The number 100

**Addressing modes:**

| Name | Format | Opcode | Bytes Used |
|---|---|---|---|
| Accumulator | ROR | $6A/106 | 1 |
| Zero Page | ROR 15 | $66/102 | 2 |
| Zero Page,X | ROR 15,X | $76/118 | 2 |
| Absolute | ROR 1500 | $6E/110 | 3 |
| Absolute,X | ROR 1500,X | $7E/126 | 3 |

**Affected flags:** N Z C

## RTI

**What it does:** Returns from an interrupt.

**Major uses:** None. You might want to add your own routines to your machine's normal interrupt routines (see SEI below), but you won't be *generating* actual interrupts of your own. Consequently, you cannot ReTurn from Interrupts you never create.

**Addressing modes:**

| Name | Format | Opcode | Bytes Used |
|---|---|---|---|
| Implied | RTI | $40/64 | 1 |

**Affected flags:** All (status register is retrieved from the stack)

## RTS

**What it does:** Returns from a subroutine jump (caused by JSR).

**Major uses:** Automatically picks off the two top bytes on the stack and places them into the program counter. This reverses the actions taken by JSR (which put the program counter bytes onto the stack just before leaving for a subroutine). When RTS puts the return bytes into the program counter, the next event in the computer's world will be the instruction following the JSR which stuffed the return address onto the stack in the first place.

**Addressing modes:**

| Name | Format | Opcode | Bytes Used |
|---|---|---|---|
| Implied | RTS | $60/96 | 1 |

**Affected flags:** None

## SBC

**What it does:** Subtracts a byte in memory *from* the byte in the accumulator, and "borrows" if necessary. If a "borrow" takes place, the carry flag is cleared (set to zero). Thus, you always SEC (set the carry flag) before an SBC operation so that you can tell if you need a "borrow." In other words, when an SBC operation clears the carry flag, it means that the byte in memory was *larger* than the byte in the accumulator. And since memory is subtracted from the accumulator in an SBC operation, if memory is the larger number, we must "borrow."

**Major uses:** Subtracts one number from another.

**Addressing modes:**

| Name | Format | Opcode | Bytes Used |
|---|---|---|---|
| Immediate | SBC #15 | $E9/233 | 2 |
| Zero Page | SBC 15 | $E5/229 | 2 |
| Zero Page,X | SBC 15,X | $F5/245 | 2 |
| Absolute | SBC 1500 | $ED/237 | 3 |
| Absolute,X | SBC 1500,X | $FD/253 | 3 |
| Absolute,Y | SBC 1500,Y | $F9/249 | 3 |
| Indirect,X | SBC (15,X) | $E1/225 | 2 |
| Indirect,Y | SBC (15),Y | $F1/241 | 2 |

**Affected flags:** N Z C V

## SEC

**What it does:** Sets the carry (C) flag (in the processor status register byte).

**Major uses:** This instruction is always used before any SBC operation to show if the result of the subtraction was negative (if the accumulator contained a smaller number than the byte in memory being subtracted from it). See SBC above.

**Addressing modes:**

| Name | Format | Opcode | Bytes Used |
|---|---|---|---|
| Implied | SEC | $38/56 | 1 |

**Affected flags:** C

## SED

**What it does:** Sets the decimal (D) flag (in the processor status register byte).

**Major uses:** Setting this flag puts the 8502 into decimal arithmetic mode. This mode can be easier to use when you are inputting or outputting decimal numbers (from the user of a program or to the screen). Simple addition and subtraction can be performed in decimal mode, but most programmers ignore this feature since more complicated math requires that you remain in the normal binary state of the 8502.

*Note:* Commodore computers automatically clear this mode when powered on or when entering ML via SYS. However, Apple and Atari computers can enter ML in an indeterminate state. Since there is a possibility that the D flag might be set (causing havoc) on entry to an ML routine, it is sometimes suggested that Apple and Atari owners use the CLD instruction at the start of any ML program they write. Fortunately Commodore users do not need to worry about this, but all ML programmers must CLD following any deliberate use of the decimal mode (see SED).

**Addressing modes:**

| Name | Format | Opcode | Bytes Used |
|---|---|---|---|
| Implied | SED | $F8/248 | 1 |

**Affected flags:** D

## SEI

**What it does:** Sets the interrupt disable flag (the I flag) in the processor status byte. When this flag is up, the 8502 will not acknowledge or act upon interrupt attempts (except a few nonmaskable interrupts which can take control in spite of this flag, like a reset of the entire computer). The operating systems of most computers will regularly interrupt the activities of the chip for necessary, high-priority tasks such as updating an internal clock, displaying things on the TV, receiving signals from the keyboard, and so forth. These interruptions of whatever the chip is doing normally occur 60 times every second. To find out what housekeeping routines your computer interrupts the chip to accomplish, look at the pointer in $FFFE/FFFF. It gives the starting address of the maskable interrupt routines.

**Major uses:** You can alter a RAM pointer so that it sends these interrupts to *your own ML routine,* and your routine then would conclude by pointing to the normal interrupt routines.

In this way, you can add something you want (a click sound for each keystroke? the time of day on the screen?) to the normal actions of your operating system. The advantage of this method over normal SYSing is that your interrupt-driven routine is essentially transparent to whatever else you are doing (in whatever language). Your customization appears to have become part of the computer's ordinary habits.

However, if you try to alter the RAM pointer *while the other interrupts are active,* you will point away from the normal housekeeping routines in ROM, crashing the computer. This is where SEI comes in. You disable the interrupts while you LDA STA LDA STA the new pointer. Then CLI turns the interrupt back on and nothing is disturbed.

Interrupt processing is a whole subcategory of ML programming and has been widely discussed in magazine articles. Look there if you need more detail.

**Addressing modes:**

| Name | Format | Opcode | Bytes Used |
|---|---|---|---|
| Implied | SEI | $78/120 | 1 |

**Affected flags:** I

## STA

**What it does:** Stores the byte in the accumulator into memory.

**Major uses:** Can serve many purposes and is among the most used instructions. Many other instructions leave their results in the accumulator (ADC/SBC and logical operations like ORA), after which they are stored in memory with STA.

**Addressing modes:**

| Name | Format | Opcode | Bytes Used |
|---|---|---|---|
| Zero Page | STA 15 | $85/133 | 2 |
| Zero Page,X | STA 15,X | $95/149 | 2 |
| Absolute | STA 1500 | $8D/141 | 3 |
| Absolute,X | STA 1500,X | $9D/157 | 3 |
| Absolute,Y | STA 1500,Y | $99/153 | 3 |
| Indirect,X | STA (15,X) | $81/129 | 2 |
| Indirect,Y | STA (15),Y | $91/145 | 2 |

**Affected flags:** None

## STX

**What it does:** Stores the byte in the X register into memory.

**Major uses:** Copies the byte in X into a byte in memory.

**Addressing modes:**

| Name | Format | Opcode | Bytes Used |
|---|---|---|---|
| Zero Page | STX 15 | $86/134 | 2 |
| Zero Page,Y | STX 15,Y | $96/150 | 2 |
| Absolute | STX 1500 | $8E/142 | 3 |

**Affected flags:** None

## STY

**What it does:** Stores the byte in the Y register into memory.

**Major uses:** Copies the byte in Y into a byte in memory.

**Addressing modes:**

| Name | Format | Opcode | Bytes Used |
|---|---|---|---|
| Zero Page | STY 15 | $84/132 | 2 |
| Zero Page,X | STY 15,X | $94/148 | 2 |
| Absolute | STY 1500 | $8C/140 | 3 |

**Affected flags:** None

## TAX

**What it does:** Transfers the byte in the accumulator to the X register.

**Major uses:** Sometimes you can copy the byte in the accumulator into the X register as a way of briefly storing the byte until it's needed again by the accumulator. If X is currently unused, TAX is a convenient alternative to PHA (another temporary storage method).

However, since X is often employed as a loop counter, TAX is a relatively rarely used instruction.

**Addressing modes:**

| Name | Format | Opcode | Bytes Used |
|---|---|---|---|
| Implied | TAX | $AA/170 | 1 |

**Affected flags:** N Z

## TAY

**What it does:** Transfers the byte in the accumulator to the Y register.

**Major uses:** Sometimes you can copy the byte in the accumulator into the Y register as a way of briefly storing the byte until it's needed again by the accumulator. If Y is currently unused, TAY is a convenient alternative to PHA (another temporary storage method).

However, since Y is quite often employed as a loop counter, TAY is a relatively rarely used instruction.

**Addressing modes:**

| Name | Format | Opcode | Bytes Used |
|---|---|---|---|
| Implied | TAY | $A8/168 | 1 |

**Affected flags:** N Z

## TSX

**What it does:** Transfers the stack pointer to the X register.

**Major uses:** The stack pointer is a byte in the 8502 chip which points to where a new value (number) can be added to the stack. The stack pointer would be "raised" by two, for example, when you JSR and the two bytes of the program counter are pushed onto the stack. The next available space on the stack thus becomes two higher than it was previously. By contrast, an RTS will pull a two-byte return address off the stack, freeing up some space, and the stack pointer would then be "lowered" by two.

The stack pointer is always added to $0100 since the stack is located between addresses $0100 and $01FF.

**Addressing modes:**

| Name | Format | Opcode | Bytes Used |
|---|---|---|---|
| Implied | TSX | $BA/186 | 1 |

**Affected flags:** N Z

## TXA

**What it does:** Transfers the byte in the X register to the accumulator.

**Major uses:** There are times, after X has been used as a counter, when you'll want to compute something using the value of the counter. And you'll therefore need to transfer the byte in X to the accumulator. For example, if you search the screen for character $75:

```
CHARACTER = $75:SCREEN = $0400
LDX #0
LOOP LDA SCREEN,X:CMP #CHARACTER:BEQ MORE:INX
BEQ NOTFOUND
                           ; this prevents an endless loop
MORE TXA                   ; you now know the character's location
NOTFOUND BRK
```

In this example, we want to perform some action based on the location of the character. Perhaps we want to remember the location in a variable for later reference. This will require that we transfer the value of X to the accumulator so that it can be added to the SCREEN start address.

**Addressing modes:**

| Name | Format | Opcode | Bytes Used |
|---|---|---|---|
| Implied | TXA | $8A/138 | 1 |

**Affected flags:** N Z

## TXS

**What it does:** Transfers the byte in X register into the stack pointer.

**Major uses:** Alters where, in the stack, the current "here's storage space" is pointed to. There are no common uses for this instruction.

**Addressing modes:**

| Name | Format | Opcode | Bytes Used |
|---|---|---|---|
| Implied | TXS | $9A/154 | 1 |

**Affected flags:** None

## TYA

**What it does:** Transfers the byte in the Y register to the accumulator.

**Major uses:** See TXA.

**Addressing modes:**

| Name | Format | Opcode | Bytes Used |
|---|---|---|---|
| Implied | TYA | $98/152 | 1 |

**Affected flags:** N Z

Appendix B

# How to Use LADS

This appendix represents a step-by-step explanation of how to assemble machine language programs using the LADS assembler. As you familiarize yourself with its features and practice using it, you will perhaps discover things about the assembler which you'd want to modify to suit your own programming style. For example, if you find that you would prefer to reword the error messages, simply change them in the Tables subprogram and run LADS through itself to produce a new-generation LADS. For a discussion on creating custom versions of LADS, see the end of this appendix.

Here, however, is a description of the features which are built into LADS.

## General Instructions for Using LADS

LADS assembles from *source files.* They are particularly easy and convenient to create: Just turn on your computer and pretend you're writing a BASIC program. LADS works with source files created exactly the way you would write a BASIC program. You use line numbers, you can use colons, you can insert new line numbers or delete. The only difference is that you're writing ML, so you use ML commands rather than BASIC commands. Here's an example you can type in and try. Turn on your 128 (or press the RESET button) and type this in:

```
10 *= 2816
15 .S
16 .O
20 LDA #66:LDY #65
30 JSR $FFD2
40 TYA:JSR $FFD2
```

As you can see, it's quite similar to writing a BASIC program. You use line numbers, colons, and whatever programmer's aids (such as automatic line numbering) that you ordinarily use to write BASIC itself. But notice that if you use colons you should keep the instructions tight against the colons. (LDA #22 : LDY #0 would confuse LADS. Spaces following a colon won't cause any problems, but it's best to make a habit of leaving no spaces around colons.)

Now you're ready to assemble. Type BLOAD "LADS and press RETURN. Then type SYS 10000 to activate LADS. It will assemble your program, storing the resulting ML *object code* (the runnable ML program) starting at address 2816, and then return you to BASIC mode with the familiar READY. If you are using a 40-column screen, it will temporarily go blank during the actual assembly because LADS switches to 2 megahertz for extra speed. This won't affect anything, but you'll not see things onscreen during an assembly.

This example program is supposed to print the characters *BA* on your screen. To test it, enter SYS 2816. To change things, just LIST your source code and, perhaps, change the character being printed:

```
20 LDA #66:LDY #$43;  $43 IS HEX FOR 67, THE ASCII CODE
                      FOR "C"
```

and hit RETURN, just as you would to adjust a BASIC program line. Now we've asked to have the letters *BC* printed on the screen. Again, activate LADS assembly by typing SYS 10000, and then test the results by SYS 2816. It's as simple as that.

But LADS has many other features you'll find useful as you program. For example, if you've typed in the "Loader" program (Appendix F) or bought LADS on disk and have a 1571 disk drive, LADS will automatically boot into the 128 when you power up or reset. It will also redefine the F1, F2, F3, and F5 keys to run or reload LADS at the press of a key, to SYS 2816 ($B00, the start of many of the examples in this book), and to invoke AUTO 10 line numbering.

The F1 key will SYS 10000 and should be used when you're using LADS as we did in the example above. Use F3 to BLOAD in a fresh copy of LADS if it should get corrupted and fail to respond. Users of the 1571 disk drive might want to change the two BLOADs to BOOTs in the Loader for greater convenience; 1541 users should leave it as BLOAD.

### Few Rules

There are very few absolute rules when using LADS, but one is that you *must provide the starting address,* the address where you want the ML program to begin in the computer's memory. You signify this with the *= symbol, which means "Program Counter equals." LADS expects to find this *= symbol as the first thing in your source code. When LADS sees *=, it sets the program counter to the number following the equal sign. Remember also that there must be a space between the = and the starting address: *= 2816, not *=2816.

Also notice that you can use either decimal or hexadecimal numbers interchangeably in LADS. Line 20 is hex in the example above for the number #$43, but the 66 is decimal. It's up to you which kind of numbers you want to use at any given time.

### Features

There are a number of *pseudo-ops* available in LADS. Pseudo-ops are direct instructions to the assembler which make things easier for the programmer. The .S in line 15 in the example above is such an instruction. It tells LADS to print the results of an assembly to the screen. The .O causes LADS to send the results of the assembly, the object code, to RAM memory.

If you add line 17 to our test program, you will cause the listing to be in decimal instead of hex:

```
10 *= 2816
15 .S
16 .O
17 .NH
```

The pseudo-op .NH means *no hex,* and causes the listing to change from hex to decimal.

You can add REM-like comments by using a semicolon. And you can turn the screen listing *off* with .NS, anytime. Turn it on or off as much as you want. This can be an especially useful switch if you don't need to see an entire listing, but just want to see how a small section or sections of your program are assembling. Also, using .S will slow up the assembly process. The .S and .NS screen listings are most helpful as a kind of disassembly on the fly:

```
10 *= 2816
15 .S
16 .O
17 .NH
20 LDA #66:LDY #65
25 .NS
30 JSR $FFD2
40 TYA:JSR $FFD2
```

For more complete listings and more extensive debugging, you would want to activate printer listings so you can more easily study the flow of things and make notes or corrections. You turn on printer listings with .P and turn them off with .NP. When you use .P, it automatically turns on .S, so you'll see screen listings even if you didn't include .S.

Because source code comments would clutter up a screen listing, particularly a 40-column screen, comments are suppressed when you use .S. However, comments are reproduced when you use .P for printer listings. Also, if you are using a Cardco interface with a 1541 disk drive, the .P printout might stall. Should this happen, turn off the disk drive and the printout will proceed.

To have the ML stored into memory during assembly, use .O; to switch off these POKEs to memory, use .NO.

The pseudo-ops which turn the printer on and off; direct object code to disk, screen, and RAM; or switch between hex and decimal printout can be switched on and off within your source code wherever convenient. For example, you can turn on your printer anywhere within the program by inserting .P and turn it off anywhere with .NP. Among other things, this would allow you to specify that only a particular section of a large program be printed out. This can come in very handy if you're working on a long program where there would be a significant wait if you had to print out the whole thing.

*Always put pseudo-ops on a line by themselves.* Any other programming code can be put on a line in any fashion (divided by colons: LDA 15:STA 27:INY), but pseudo-ops should be the only things on their lines. (The .BYTE pseudo-op, described below, is an exception—it can be on a multiple-statement line.)

**100 .P .S** Wrong
**100 .P** Right
**110 .S** Right

And remember to keep your instructions right next to the colons, no spaces:

**100 LDA #15 : STA 5000 : INY** Wrong
**100 LDA #15:STA 5000:INY** Right

You have now learned all you will need to know about LADS to create and assemble the examples in this book. What follows are additional, more advanced features of LADS.

### More Sophisticated Features

Here's a summary of all the commands you can give LADS:

| | |
|---|---|
| **.P** | Turn on printer listing of object code (.S will also be activated). |
| **.NP** | Turn off printer listing of object code. |
| **.O** | Turn on POKEs to memory. Object code is stored into RAM *during* assembly. |
| **.NO** | Turn off POKEs to memory. |
| **.D** ***sourcefilename objectfilename*** | Read source code from *sourcefilename* and store object code to *objectfilename* on disk following assembly. Use no quotes around the filenames (.O will also be activated). |
| **.FILE** ***filename*** | Necessary when you use .D. Links one source file to the next in a chain so that they will all assemble together as a single large source program (end the chain with .END pseudo-op). |
| **.END** ***filename*** | Necessary when you use .D. Links the last source file to first source file in a chain. If you are not assembling a chain of files (rather, are assembling from a single file), you must still give *its* filename as the .END so that the assembler knows where to go for the second pass. Any source code must have .END as the last line in the program, whether the source code is contained within a single disk file or spread across a multiple-file chain. |
| **.S** | Turn on screen listing during assembly. |
| **.NS** | Turn off screen listing during assembly. |
| **.H** | Turn on hexadecimal output for screen or printer listing. |
| **.NH** | Turn off hexadecimal output for screen or printer listing (as a result, the listings are in decimal). |

| | |
|---|---|
| *= | Set program counter to new address. |
| + | Add a value to a label. |
| #"*c* | ASCII value of character *c* (typeable characters only, no control codes). |
| **#<*label*** | Least significant byte (LSB) of *label*. |
| **#>*label*** | Most significant byte (MSB) of *label*. |
| **.BYTE *N N*** | Insert single-byte decimal numbers directly into object code. |
| **.BYTE *"CCCCC*** | Insert characters directly into object code. |

## A Stable Buffer

The pseudo-op *= is always the first item in any ML source code program. It tells the computer where you want your program stored. However, *= can be used within a program too, to change the storage addresses dynamically. This is useful mainly when you want to create data tables. The subprogram Tables in LADS source code is an example of a data table. (A subprogram is one of the source code files which, when linked together, form an entire ML program. We'll describe linking shortly.)

Most programmers locate an ML program's tables, nonzero page variables, buffers, and messages at the high end of the ML program the way LADS does with its Tables subprogram. Since you don't know what the highest RAM address will be while you're writing a program, you can force your data tables to always reside at the same high address by setting *= to some address, perhaps 4K above the starting address. This gives you space to write the program below the tables without moving the tables up higher in RAM memory each time you add to the source code.

The advantage of stabilizing the location of your tables is that you can easily PEEK them, and this greatly assists debugging. You'll always know exactly where buffers and variables are going to end up in memory after an assembly—regardless of the changes you make in the program. After your program is debugged and running perfectly, you can remove the *= and assemble one last time, closing up the gap between the program and its tables.

Here's an example. Suppose you write:

```
10 *= $5000
20 STA BUFFER
30 *= $6000
40 BUFFER .BYTE 0 0 0 0 0 0 0 0 0 0 0 0 0 0 0 0 0 0
```

This creates an ML opcode instruction (STA buffer) at address $5000 (the starting address of this particular example ML program), but places the buffer itself at $6000. When you add additional instructions after STA buffer, the location of the buffer itself will remain at address $6000. This means that you can write an entire program (smaller than $1000 bytes) without having to worry that the location of the buffer is being bumped up higher each time you add new instructions, new code. It's high enough so that it remains stable at $6000, and you can debug the program more easily. You can always check whether something is being correctly sent into the buffer by just looking at $6000 from the monitor.

This fragment of code illustrates two other features of LADS. You can use the pseudo-op .BYTE to set aside some space in memory (the zeros above just make space to hold other things in a "buffer" during the execution of an ML program). You can also use .BYTE to define specific numbers in memory:

```
.BYTE 65 66 67 68
```

This would put these numbers (*always use decimal numbers between 0 and 255 with this pseudo-op*) into memory at the location of the .BYTE instruction; .BYTE can also handle text and any control characters (such as cursor up) except screen clear. An easy way to create messages that you want to print to the screen is to use the .BYTE pseudo-op and surround text with quotes:

```
500 FIRSTLETTERS .BYTE "ABCD":.BYTE 0
```

Then, if you wanted to print this message, you could write:

```
 2 *= $0B00
 5 LDY #0
10 LOOP LDA FIRSTLETTERS,Y
20 BEQ ENDMESSAGE
30 STA $0400,Y; location of screen RAM
40 INY
50 JMP LOOP
```

**60 ENDMESSAGE RTS; finished printout**
**500 FIRSTLETTERS .BYTE "ABCD:.BYTE 0**

Note that using the second set of quotation marks is optional with the .BYTE pseudo-op: You can use either **.BYTE "ABCD:.BYTE 0** or **.BYTE "ABCD":.BYTE 0**. To POKE numbers instead of characters, just leave out the quotation marks: **.BYTE 10 15 75**. And since these numeric values are being POKEd directly into bytes in memory, remember that they cannot be larger than 255. It's like BASIC's POKE statement.

Another convenient pseudo-op looks like this: #". It is used when you want to specify a character instead of a number for immediate addressing. Say, you need to print a comma to the screen. You could LDA #44 (the ASCII code for a comma) and JSR PRINT.

But if you don't remember that a comma is the number 44 in the ASCII code, and you don't want to look it up, LADS will do it for you. Just use a quotation mark after the # symbol: LDA #", (followed by the character you're after, in this case, the comma). The correct value for the character will be inserted into your object code. To print the letter *A*, you would LDA #"A and proceed to print it with JSR $FFD2. Any character you type after the quotation mark will be translated into Commodore ASCII for you. Remember that the #" pseudo-op gives you the screen *print* code, not the screen POKE code. If you try to POKE the character directly on the 40-column screen with STA $0400, you'll get a shifted version of whatever character you requested. Also, #" cannot translate cursor or control codes. If you want to clear the screen, you'll need to look up clear screen on the ASCII chart in Appendix G. Clear screen is 147, so you'd use LDA #147:JSR PRINT to accomplish that.

## Labels

You probably noticed in the example above how many English *words* were used to write the source code: FIRSTLETTERS, ENDMESSAGE, LOOP. These are used pretty much as variables are used in BASIC. But there are some special advantages in ML. You give subroutines *names* rather than line numbers and that helps document and structure your program. Also, these words, called *labels*, can be of any length. And, unlike BASIC which sees only the first two characters as significant, each label is entirely significant in LADS. So,

SCREEN and SCORE are distinct labels and will not be confused.

With LADS, as with other assemblers that permit labels, you need not refer to locations in memory or numeric values by using numbers. And you'll find that labels are far easier to use.

In the example above, line 10 starts off with the word LOOP. This means that you can use the word LOOP later to refer to that location (see line 50). That's quite a convenience: The assembler remembers where the word LOOP is used, and you need not refer to an actual memory *address;* you can refer to the label instead. This kind of label is called a *PC-type* (for Program Counter) or *address-type* label.

The other type of label is defined with an assembly convention called an *equate* (an equal sign). This is quite similar to the way that BASIC allows you to assign value to words—it's called "assigning variables" when you do it in BASIC. In ML, the = pseudo-op works pretty much the way the = sign does in BASIC, and these "equates" should be put at the very start of an ML program. (See the Defs subprogram in Appendix D.) Here's an example of equates, located at the start of the program, in lines 10 and 20:

```
5 *= $0B00
10 SCREEN = $0400; the location of the first byte in RAM of the
   screen
20 LETTERA = $41; the letter A
30 ; ------------------------
40 START LDA #LETTERA; notice "START" (an address-type
   label)
50 STA SCREEN; 40-COLUMN MODE ONLY
60 RTS
```

Line 10 assigns the number $0400 (1024 decimal) to the word SCREEN. Anytime thereafter that you use the word SCREEN, LADS will substitute $0400 when it assembles your ML program. Line 20 "equates" the word LETTERA to the number $41. So, when you LDA #LETTERA in line 40, the assembler will put a $41 into your program. (Notice that, like BASIC, LADS requires equate labels to be a single word. You couldn't use LETTER A, since that's two words.)

Line 30 is just a REMark. The semicolon tells the assembler that what follows on that line is to be ignored. Nevertheless, blank lines or graphic dividers like line 30 can help to visually separate subroutines, tables, and equates from your actual ML program. In this case, we've used line 30 to separate the section of the program which defines labels (lines 10–20) from the program proper (lines 40–60). All this makes it easier to read and understand your source code later.

Remember that in BASIC only the first two letters of a variable name are significant. So, SCREEN and SCORE are taken to be identical variables. LADS, however, offers you the advantage of seeing *all* letters within a label as significant. SCREEN and SCREEN1 *are* different labels to LADS. Of course, you cannot use the *same* label to mark two different addresses or values. You can't use the same label for two different equates because that would be meaningless:

```
SCREEN = $0400
SCREEN = $0500
```

Nor should you define two different addresses within the ML program using the same label:

```
10 LOOP  LDA 12
20       BEQ LOOP
30       BNE LOOP
40 LOOP  RTS
```

LADS would have no way of knowing, in lines 20 and 30, to which LOOP you intended to branch. Don't be concerned, however, about keeping track of what labels you may have already used. When you assemble, LADS will report any duplicate labels and tell you which line numbers they occurred in. Then you can easily make up new labels where necessary:

```
40 LOOP1
```

or

```
40 NEWLOOP
```

Notice that lines 20 and 30, although they both contain the label LOOP, do not cause any problems. That's because they are only referring to the label, not defining it. Labels are defined only when they occur as the first thing following a line number or a colon. You can use them to *refer* to the defined locations or values as often as you want.

A related labeling error will also be flagged by LADS. If LADS reports this to you:

```
560 NUMBURS LDA 12     UNDEFINED LABEL
```

you would need to look at line 560. Usually, this is caused by a typo. You meant to type NUMBERS as your label and later referred to NUMBERS (which would generate an UNDEFINED LABEL error message of its own). Again, just LIST 560, and type 560 NUMBERS LDA 12 to make things right.

If your source code contains a label with nothing following it:

**560 NUMBERS**

or

**570 NUMBERS:INY**

you'll see a NAKED LABEL error message. Line 560 is meaningless because the line is blank following the label. It defines nothing. Line 570 is meaningless for the same reason because a colon separates statements and is therefore the logical equivalent of an end-of-line.

### Automatic Math

There are times when you will want to have LADS do addition for you. That's where the + pseudo-op comes in. If you write "label+1", you will add 1 to the value of the label. Here's how it works:

```
10 *= $B00
20 HIMEM = 57; top-of-memory pointer.
30 ;----------------------------
40 LDA #0:STA HIMEM:LDA #$50:STA HIMEM+1
```

Here we are putting a new location into the top-of-memory pointer which the computer uses to decide where it can store things in bank 1. (Doing that could protect an ML program which resides above the address stored in this pointer.) Like all pointers, it uses two bytes. If we want to store $5000 into this pointer, we store the lower half (the least significant byte) into MEMTOP. We'll want to put the number $50 into the most significant byte of the pointer—but we don't need to waste time making a new label. It's just one higher in memory than MEMTOP, hence, MEMTOP+1.

You'll also want to use the + pseudo-op command in constructions like this:

```
10 *= $B00
15 SCREEN = $0400
17 ;----------------------------
20 LDA #32; the blank character
30 LDY #0
```

```
40 START STA SCREEN,Y
50 STA SCREEN+256,Y
60 STA SCREEN+512,Y
70 STA SCREEN+768,Y
80 INY
90 BNE START
```

This is the fastest way to fill memory with a given byte. In this case we're clearing out the screen RAM by filling it with blanks (in the 40-column mode only). As you can see, it's easy to indicate multiples of 256 by just adding them to the label SCREEN. Any time you want to add a number to a label, just attach + and the number, but don't leave any spaces between the label, the + and the number:

```
LDA (LABEL + 22),Y   Wrong
LDA (LABEL+22),Y     Right
```

A similar pseudo-op command is the #<. This refers to the least significant byte of a *label.* For example,

```
10 *= $0B00
20 SCREEN = $0400
25 SCREENPOINTER = $FB
30 ;-------------------
40 LDA #<SCREEN; LSB (least significant byte of the label
   SCREEN, $00)
50 STA SCREENPOINTER
60 LDA #>SCREEN; MSB (most significant byte of the label
   SCREEN, $04)
70 STA SCREENPOINTER+1
```

Line 40 is the equivalent of LDA #$00 and line 60 is the equivalent of LDA #$04, but using #< and #> allows you to break a label into its bytes conveniently without having to know the actual value of the label.

You'll find this technique used several times in the LADS source code. It puts the LSB (least signficant byte) or the MSB (most signficant byte) of a label into the LSB or MSB of a pointer which, in effect, creates the pointer (makes it point to the label). In the example above, we want to set up a pointer that will hold the address of the screen RAM. We've called this pointer SCREENPOINTER, and we want to put $00 (the LSB of SCREEN) into SCREENPOINTER. So, we extract the LSB of SCREEN in line 40 by using # combined with the less-than symbol. We complete the job of creating the pointer by using the greater-than symbol to fetch the MSB:

**60 LDA #>SCREEN:STA SCREENPOINTER+1**

Notice that these symbols must be attached to the label; *no space is allowed.* For example, LDA #> SCREEN would create problems. This LSB or MSB extraction from a label is something you'll need to do from time to time. The #< and #> pseudo-ops do it for you.

## Chained Files

LADS has two distinct personalities. So far we've been discussing LADS as it comes out of the can, its native state when you, or the Loader, BLOAD it in from disk. It assembles and stores the results on screen (with .S), in RAM in bank 15 (.O), or to the printer (.P). Let's call this mode RAMLADS since it works exclusively in RAM.

This personality is most useful for testing routines which are short enough for the source code to fit between $1C00 (the default start of BASIC text area) and $2710 where the LADS assembler starts in memory. But when source code gets fairly large, it will either overwrite LADS, or LADS itself, which stores labels during assembly moving down from $2710, will overwrite the source code. In short, assembling source code about 1K or longer will cause the source code and LADS to compete for the same memory space and interfere with each other.

For these larger programs, you should store your source code on disk and, by using the .D pseudo-op at the start of the source code, tell LADS to look on the disk drive for material to assemble. (Cassette tape users will not be able to switch DISKLADS on with the .D pseudo-op. They must use RAMLADS and then save object code to tape via the monitor. See SAVE in Chapter 3.)

When you insert .D into your source code, LADS transforms itself; it modifies its actual structure and turns its attention to the disk drive for source code. Let's call this second personality DISKLADS. DISKLADS offers several benefits when large programs are involved.

It is sometimes convenient to create several source code subprograms, to break the ML program source code into several pieces. An example of this is the LADS source code itself. It's divided into a number of program files: Array, Equate, Math, Pseudo, and so on. This way, you don't need to load the entire source code into the computer's memory when you just want to work on a particular part of it. It also allows you to assemble source code far larger than could fit into available RAM. For example, LADS itself, with all its comments, has source code which is 72K large. By the way, this creates an interesting ratio between source and object code: After assembly, LADS boils down to about 5K of runnable object code.

When using DISKLADS, you link the separate source code files together into a chain. In the last line of each subprogram you want to link, you put the linking pseudo-op .FILE *NAME* (use no quotes) to tell the assembler which subprogram to assemble next. Subprograms, chained together in this fashion, will be treated *as if they were one large program.*

The final subprogram in the chain ends with the special pseudo-op .END *NAME,* and this time the name is the filename of the first of the subprograms, the subprogram which begins the chain. It's like stringing pearls and then, at the end, tying thread so that the last pearl is next to the first, to form a necklace.

Notice however that when you turn on DISKLADS with .D, you *always* need to include the .END pseudo-op, even if you are assembling from just one, unlinked, source code file. In that case (where you're working with a solo file), you don't use any linking .FILE pseudo-ops. Instead, refer the file to itself with .END *NAME* where you list the solo file's name.

Here's an illustration of how three subprograms would be linked to form a complete program:

```
 5 *= 2816
10 ; FIRSTSOURCE--first program in chain
20 ;its first line must contain the start address
30 .D FIRSTSOURCE FIRSTOBJECT
40 LDA #20
50 STA $0400
60 .FILE SECOND
```

Then you save this subprogram to disk (it's handy to let the first remark line in each subprogram identify the subprogram's filename):

**DSAVE "FIRSTSOURCE**

Next, you create SECOND, the next link in the chain. But here, you use no starting address; you enter no *= since only one start address is needed for any program:

```
10 ; SECOND (IT'S A GOOD IDEA TO PUT THE NAME OF
   THE FILE HERE)
20 INY:INX:DEY:DEX
30 .FILE THIRD
DSAVE "SECOND
```

Now write the final subprogram, ending it with the clasp pseudo-op .END *NAME* which links this last subprogram to the first:

```
10 ; THIRD
20 LDA #191:STA $0400
30 .END FIRSTSOURCE
DSAVE "THIRD
```

When you want to assemble this linked source code, if the first file in the chain isn't already in RAM memory, you **DLOAD "FIRSTSOURCE** to show LADS the .D. Then press F1 or type SYS 10000, and LADS will take it from there.

The format for .D is

**.D *sourcename objectname***

RAMLADS will see the .D and change itself into DISKLADS. After you've once transformed RAMLADS into this new personality, it will locate source code on the disk files and store object code to bank 1. After it has finished the assembly, LADS will save (with replace) the object code to the disk under the name you gave for the object file after .D. In our three-file example above, LADS will save a file named FIRSTOBJECT. Finally, LADS will reload itself and, thus, change back into its RAMLADS personality. In other words, LADS responds appropriately if there is .D in the source code. If it doesn't find one, it remains RAM-oriented.

DISKLADS operates somewhat differently from RAMLADS. DISKLADS always switches on the .O pseudo-op and saves the object code to RAM in *bank 1*. Thus (unlike RAMLADS where you have to find a safe place to store object code when using .O), with DISKLADS you can create an ML program that resides *anywhere* between $0000 and $FFFF (0–65535 decimal), and it will not interfere with LADS or BASIC or anything else since it's being stored into the pure RAM of bank 1. (Remember, though, that extremely low RAM—$0000–$03FF—is shared between banks.) Thus, your source and object codes can be huge, as large as a RAM bank.

Then, when assembly is finished, the object code is stored to disk under the name you gave with .D (FIRSTOBJECT in the example above). Use no quotation marks around filenames for .D or .END or .FILE. If you forget to put .END or .FILE when you've used .D, LADS will remind you that it now needs these linking commands. If you want to go back to assembling smaller routines with RAMLADS, just start typing in source code, but avoid .D. LADS changes personality only when triggered with .D. Naturally, you don't use .FILE or .END with RAMLADS.

When DISKLADS has finished assembling the example above by the disk method, there will be an ML program on disk called FIRSTOBJECT. You can BLOAD it and SYS 2816 (that was the start address we gave this program), and the newly assembled ML program will execute. Note that even though LADS saved it to disk from bank 1, it will BLOAD into bank 0 unless you specify otherwise with the BLOAD command. Also, DISKLADS always does a Save–with–Replace, and this allows you to keep testing versions without having to rename each one. If you want to preserve a version, be sure to RENAME it before assembling; it will be replaced at the end of the assembly. You can always stop any assembly at any time with the RUN/STOP key. If a file is being loaded when you press RUN/STOP, just hold down the RUN/STOP key until disk access finishes. Since no object code is saved to disk until assembly is finished, any previous version of object code will remain unreplaced on the disk.

While LADS is assembling in either mode, it will report any errors by ringing the bell, displaying the line number wherein the error occurred, and showing the offending source code in reverse video. After assembly, it will tell you the total number of errors, if any.

LADS also prints the starting address in hex of each file, and DISKLADS prints LOADING when bringing the file in from disk, and blanks the line while actually assembling.

### Rules for LADS

Here are the rules you need to follow when writing ML for LADS to assemble:

1. *In general, all equate labels (labels using an equal sign) should be defined at the start of your program.*

While this isn't absolutely necessary for labels with numbers above 255 (see SCREEN in the example below), it *is* the best programming practice. It makes it easier for you to modify your programs and simplifies debugging. LADS itself locates all its equate labels in the subprogram Defs (Appendix D), the first subprogram in its chain of source code files.

What's more, it is *necessary* that any equate label with a value lower than 256 be defined before any ML mnemonics reference that label. So, to be on the safe side, just get into the habit of putting all equate labels at the very start of your programs:

```
10 *= 2816
20 ARRAYPOINTER = $FB; (251 decimal), a zero page address
30 OTHERPOINTER = $FD; (253 decimal), another zero page
   address
40 ;-----------------------
50 LDY #0:LDA $1
60 STA ARRAYPOINTER,Y
70 SCREEN = $0400
```

Notice that it's permissible to define the label SCREEN anywhere in your program. It's not a zero page address. You do have to be careful, however, with zero page addresses (addresses lower than 255). So most ML programmers make it a habit to define all their equates at the start of their source code.

2. *Put only one pseudo-op on a line.*

Don't use a colon to put two pseudo-ops on a single line:

```
10 *= 864
20 .O:.NH   Wrong
30 .O       Right
40 .NH      Right
```

The main exception to this is the .BYTE pseudo-op. Normally, you'll set up messages with a zero at their ends to *delimit* them, to show that the message is complete. When you delimit messages with a zero, you don't need to know the length of the message; you just branch when you come upon a zero:

```
10 *= 2816
20 SCREEN = $0400
30 ;---------------------
```

**40 LDY #0**
**50 LOOP LDA MESSAGE,Y:BEQ END; loading a zero signals end of message.**
**60 STA SCREEN,Y:INY: JMP LOOP; LADS ignores spaces after colon.**
**70 ; ---------- message area here ----------**
**80 MESSAGE .BYTE "PRINT THIS ON SCREEN":.BYTE 0**

Any embedded pseudo-ops like + or = or #> can be used on multiple-statement lines. The pseudo-ops which should be on a line by themselves are the I/O (input/output) instructions which direct communication to disk, screen, or printer, like .P, .S, .D, .END, and so forth. It's also important to put .D at the *start* of your source code.

Generally, it's important that you space things correctly. Avoid leading spaces before semicolons (see lines 50 and 60 above for correct use of semicolons. Everything on a line following a semicolon is ignored, so spaces *after* the semicolon are fine. Also, if you wrote **SCREEN= 864**, LADS would think that your label was *screen=* instead of *screen*. So you need that space between the label and the equal sign. Likewise, you need to put *a single space* between labels, mnemonics, and arguments:

**LOOP LDA MESSAGE**

Running them together will confuse LADS.

**LOOPLDA MESSAGE**

and

**LOOP LDAMESSAGE**

are wrong.

Spaces within remarks are ignored. In fact, LADS ignores everything within remarks, everything following a semicolon on a line (see line 70). Thus, the semicolon should come after anything you want assembled. You couldn't rearrange line 50 above by putting the BEQ END after the remark message. It would be ignored because it followed the semicolon.

Errant spacing, while it sometimes won't assemble correctly, is generally not fatal. LADS can ignore some spacing errors and will report error messages when it finds others. LOOPLDA would result in an UNDEFINED LABEL error message, for example. But it's a good idea to get into the habit of putting colons and semicolons right up against source code, with no extra spaces.

When using the text form of .BYTE, it's up to you whether you use a close quote:

**50 MESSAGE .BYTE "PRINT THIS"** Right
**60 MESSAGE .BYTE "PRINT THIS** Also right

3. *The first character of any label must be a letter, not a number.*

LADS knows when it comes upon a label because a number starts with a number; a label starts with a letter of the alphabet:

```
10 *= $B00
20 LABEL = 255
30 LDA LABEL
40 LDA 255
```

Lines 30 and 40 accomplish the same thing and are correctly written. It would confuse LADS, however, if you wrote

**20 5LABEL = 255** Wrong

since the number 5 at the start of the word LABEL would signal the assembler that it had come upon a number, not a label. You can use numbers anywhere else in a label name—just don't put a number at the start of the name. Also avoid using symbols like #, <, >, and *, and other punctuation, shifted letters, or graphics symbols within labels. Stick with ordinary alphanumerics:

**10 5LABEL** Wrong
**20 LABEL15** Right
**30 *LABEL*** Wrong

4. *Move the program counter forward, never backward.*

The *= pseudo-op should be used to make space in memory. If you set the PC below its current address, you would be writing over previously assembled code:

**10 *= $B00**
**20 LDA #15**
**30 *= $B50** Right

**10 *= $B10**
**20 LDA #15**
**30 *= $B00** Wrong; you'll assemble right over the LDA #15.

**Modifying LADS**

LADS is, of course, itself a machine language program. This book and the optional disk include all the source code for LADS. It's heavily commented, so you can understand how the assembler works and locate things you want to modify.

To change LADS, to customize your assembler, you'll have to have typed in all the source code (or purchased this book's disk). Be sure to make a couple of backup disks in case the first attempts at improvements are less than entirely successful. Then, modify one or more of the subprograms such as Eval or Indisk, and SCRATCH the earlier subprogram(s) on disk and BLOAD or BOOT LADS. For additional safety, RENAME "LADS" TO "OLDLADS" so that you'll have a working version of the assembler for any emergencies. Next, DLOAD "DEFS128", which is LADS's starting subprogram, and SYS 10000. LADS will then create a new version of itself with your modifications incorporated and save it to disk under the name LADS.

LADS can assemble its own source code because, to an assembler, source code is source code. It doesn't have any problems with self-regeneration nor does it harbor any proscriptions against what is, after all, the ethically ambiguous act of cloning.

Appendix C

# Commodore 128 Memory Map

## 0–255 ($0000–$00FF) Zero Page

The numbers in brackets ([ ]) following each entry are the corresponding Commodore 64 locations. An asterisk in brackets ([*]) indicates that the location is identical in the 64. All addresses are listed in both decimal and hexadecimal

| | | |
|---|---|---|
| 0 | $00 | 8502 I/O port data direction register [*] |
| 1 | $01 | 8502 I/O port data register [*] |
| 2 | $02 | Bank value storage for JMPFAR and JSRFAR |
| 3–4 | $03–$04 | Program counter storage for JMPFAR and JSRFAR |
| 5 | $05 | Status register storage for JMPFAR and JSRFAR |
| 6 | $06 | Accumulator storage for JMPFAR and JSRFAR |
| 7 | $07 | X register storage for JMPFAR and JSRFAR |
| 8 | $08 | Y register storage for JMPFAR and JSRFAR |
| 45–46 | $2D–$2E | Pointer to start of BASIC program text (in bank 0) [43–44/$2B–$2C] |
| 47–48 | $2F–$30 | Pointer to start of variables (in bank 1) [45–46/$2D–$2E] |
| 49–50 | $31–$32 | Pointer to start of arrays (in bank 1) [47–48/$2F–$30] |
| 51–52 | $33–$34 | Pointer to start of free memory (in bank 1) [49–50/$31–$32] |
| 53–54 | $35–$36 | Pointer to bottom of dynamic string storage (in bank 1) [51–52/$33–$34] |
| 55–56 | $37–$38 | Pointer to most recently used string (in bank 1) [53–54/$35–$36] |
| 57–58 | $39–$3A | Pointer to top of dynamic string storage (in bank 1) [55–56/$37–$38] |
| 59–60 | $3B–$3C | Current BASIC line number [57–58/$39–$3A] |
| 61–62 | $3D–$3E | Pointer to current BASIC text character [122–123/$7A–$7B] |
| 65–66 | $41–$42 | Current DATA line number [63–64/$3F–$40] |
| 67–68 | $43–$44 | Pointer to current DATA item [65–66/$41–$42] |
| 71–72 | $47–$48 | Pointer to current BASIC variable name [69–70/$47–$48] |
| 73–74 | $49–$4A | Pointer to current variable contents |
| 99–104 | $63–$68 | Floating-point accumulator 1 (FAC1) [97–102/$61–$66] |
| 106–111 | $6A–$6F | Floating-point accumulator 2 (FAC2) [105–110/$69–$6E] |
| 125–126 | $7D–$7E | Pointer into BASIC runtime stack at $0800–$09FF |
| 144 | $90 | Status byte for tape and serial I/O [*] |
| 145 | $91 | STOP key flag (127 = RUN/STOP key pressed) [*] |
| 152 | $98 | Number of files currently opened [*] |

| | | |
|---|---|---|
| 153 | $99 | Current input device [*] |
| 154 | $9A | Current output device [*] |
| 157 | $9D | Kernal message flag (192 = Kernal control and error messages displayed, 128 = only control messages displayed, 64 = only error messages displayed, 0 = no messages displayed) [*] |
| 160–162 | $A0–$A2 | Software jiffy clock [*] |
| 172–173 | $AC–$AD | Working pointer for LOAD, SAVE, and VERIFY [*] |
| 174–175 | $AE–$AF | Ending address for LOAD, SAVE, and VERIFY [*] |
| 178–179 | $B2–$B3 | Pointer to cassette buffer [*] |
| 183 | $B7 | Length of current filename [*] |
| 184 | $B8 | Current logical file number (channel) [*] |
| 185 | $B9 | Current secondary address [*] |
| 186 | $BA | Current device number [*] |
| 187–188 | $BB–$BC | Address of current filename [*] |
| 193–195 | $C1–$C2 | Starting address for SAVE, LOAD, and VERIFY [*] |
| 195–196 | $C3–$C4 | Starting address of memory to be loaded or saved to tape [*]<br>Also used as a pointer during block memory moves |
| 198 | $C6 | Bank for current LOAD, SAVE, or VERIFY operation |
| 199 | $C7 | Bank where current filename is found |
| 200–201 | $C8–$C9 | Pointer to RS-232 input buffer [247–248/$F7–$F8] |
| 202–203 | $CA–$CB | Pointer to RS-232 output buffer [249–250/$F9–$FA] |
| 204–204 | $CC–$CD | Pointer to current keyboard lookup table (in ROM) [243–244/$F3–$F4] |
| 208 | $D0 | Number of characters in keyboard buffer [198/$C6] |
| 211 | $D3 | Current SHIFT, CONTROL, Commodore, and ALT key status [653/028D] |
| 212 | $D4 | Matrix coordinate of current key pressed [203/$CB] |
| 213 | $D5 | Matrix coordinate of last key pressed [197/$C5] |
| 215 | $D7 | Screen width flag (0 = 40 columns, 128 = 80 columns) |
| 216 | $D8 | Text/graphics mode flag for 40-column screen:<br>224 = graphic 4 (split multicolor bitmapped and text)<br>160 = graphic 3 (multicolor bitmapped)<br>96 = graphic 2 (split bitmapped and text)<br>32 = graphic 1 (bitmapped)<br>0 = graphic 0 (text) |
| 217 | $D9 | Shadow register for CHREN bit of location $01 (4 = I/O block at $D000–$DFFF, 0 = character ROM at $D000–$DFFF) |
| 224–225 | $E0–$E1 | Pointer to current text screen line [209–210/$D1–$D2] |
| 226–227 | $E2–$E3 | Pointer to current color (attribute) line [243–244/$F3–$F4] |
| 228 | $E4 | Bottom line of current window |
| 229 | $E5 | Top line of current window |
| 230 | $E6 | Left margin of current window |
| 231 | $E7 | Right margin of current window |
| 232 | $E8 | Line for input [201/$C9] |

| | | |
|---|---|---|
| 233 | $E9 | Starting logical column for input [202/$CA] |
| 234 | $EA | Ending logical column for input [200/$C8] |
| 235 | $EB | Current cursor line [214/$D6] |
| 236 | $EC | Current cursor column [211/$D3] |
| 237 | $ED | Maximum number of lines in screen |
| 238 | $EE | Maximum number of columns in a line [213/$D5] |
| 243 | $F3 | Reverse mode flag (if nonzero, characters are printed in reverse video) [199/$C7] |
| 244 | $F4 | Quote mode flag (if nonzero, quote mode is in effect) [212/$D4] |
| 245 | $F5 | Insert mode flag (if nonzero, number of inserts pending) [216/$D8] |
| 247 | $F7 | Enable/disable character set switching with SHIFT-Commodore (128 = disable switching, 0 = enable switching) [657/$0291] |
| 248 | $F8 | Enable/disable screen scrolling (128 = no scrolling, 0 = allow scrolling) |
| 251–254 | $FB–$FE | Unused [251–254/$FB–$FE] |

**256–511 ($0100–$01FF) Page One—System Stack**

**512–1023 ($0200–$03FF) Common RAM Vectors and Routines**

| | | |
|---|---|---|
| 512–673 | $0200–$02A1 | BASIC input buffer (161 bytes) [512–600/$0200–$0258] |
| 674–686 | $02A2–$02AE | INDFET routine to get a character from any bank |
| 687–701 | $02AF–$02BD | INDSTA routine to store a character in any bank |
| 702–716 | $02BE–$02CC | INDCMP routine to compare characters in any banks |
| 717–738 | $02CD–$02E2 | JSRFAR routine to jump to a subroutine in any bank and return to the calling bank |
| 739–761 | $02E3–$02F9 | JMPFAR routine to jump to a routine in any bank without return |
| 768–769 | $0300–$0301 | IERROR vector to BASIC error message routine [*] |
| 770–771 | $0302–$0303 | IMAIN vector to main BASIC immediate mode loop [*] |
| 772–773 | $0304–$0305 | ICRNCH vector to routine that tokenizes a line of BASIC text [*] |
| 774–775 | $0306–$0307 | IQPLOP vector to routine that lists a token as characters [*] |
| 776–777 | $0308–$0309 | IGONE vector to routine that executes a BASIC statement token [*] |
| 778–779 | $030A–$030B | IEVAL vector to routine that evaluates an arithmetic expression [*] |
| 780–781 | $030C–$030D | Vector to routine that tokenizes a two-byte token |
| 782–783 | $030E–$030F | Vector to routine that lists a two-byte token as characters |
| 784–785 | $0310–$0311 | Vector to routine that executes a two-byte BASIC statement token |
| 788–789 | $0314–$0315 | CINV vector to IRQ handler routine [*] |

| | | |
|---|---|---|
| 790–791 | \$0316–\$0317 | CBINV vector to BRK handler routine [*] |
| 792–793 | \$0318–\$0319 | NMINV vector to NMI handler routine [*] |
| 794–795 | \$031A–\$031B | IOPEN vector to the Kernal OPEN routine [*] |
| 796–797 | \$031C–\$031D | ICLOSE vector to the Kernal CLOSE routine [*] |
| 798–799 | \$031E–\$031F | ICHKIN vector to the Kernal CHKIN routine [*] |
| 800–801 | \$0320–\$0321 | ICKOUT vector to the Kernal CKOUT routine [*] |
| 802–803 | \$0322–\$0323 | ICLRCH vector to the Kernal CHRCH routine [*] |
| 804–804 | \$0324–\$0325 | IBASIN vector to the Kernal BASIN routine [*] |
| 806–807 | \$0326–\$0327 | IBSOUT vector to the Kernal BSOUT routine [*] |
| 808–809 | \$0328–\$0329 | ISTOP vector to the Kernal STOP routine [*] |
| 810–811 | \$032A–\$032B | IGETIN vector to the Kernal GETIN routine [*] |
| 812–813 | \$032C–\$032D | ICLALL vector to the Kernal CLALL routine [*] |
| 816–817 | \$0330–\$0331 | ILOAD vector to the Kernal LOAD routine [*] |
| 818–819 | \$0332–\$0333 | ISAVE vector to the Kernal SAVE routine [*] |
| 842–851 | \$034A–\$0353 | Keyboard input buffer [631–640/\$0277–\$0280] |
| 866–875 | \$0362–036B | Table of logical file numbers [601–610/\$0259–\$0262] |
| 876–885 | \$036C–\$0375 | Table of device numbers for open files [611–620/\$0263–\$026C] |
| 886–895 | \$0376–\$037F | Table of secondary addresses for open files [621–630/\$026D–\$0276] |
| 896–926 | \$0380–\$039E | Routine to get next character of BASIC program text from bank 0 (CHRGET) [115–138/\$73–\$8A] |
| 902 | \$0386 | Entry point in CHRGET to retrieve previous character (CHRGOT) [121/\$79] |
| 927–938 | \$039F–\$03AA | Indirect fetch from bank 0 for ROM routines |
| 939–950 | \$03AB–\$03B6 | Indirect fetch from bank 1 for ROM routines |
| 951–959 | \$03B7–\$03BF | Fetch from bank 1 for ROM routines; uses \$24–\$25 as pointer |
| 960–968 | \$03C0–\$03C8 | Fetch from bank 0 for ROM routines; uses \$26–\$27 as pointer |
| 969–977 | \$03C9–\$03D1 | Fetch from bank 0 for ROM routines; uses \$3D–\$3E as pointer |

**1024–2047 (\$0400–\$07FF) Bank 0: 40-Column Text Screen Memory**

**2048–7167 (\$0800–\$1BFF) Bank 0: BASIC and Kernal Working Storage**

| | | |
|---|---|---|
| 2048–2559 | \$0800–\$09FF | BASIC stack: pointers for DO-LOOP, BEGIN-BEND, etc. |
| 2560–2561 | \$0A00–\$0A01 | System restore vector (points to BASIC warm-start routine) |
| 2562 | \$0A02 | Flag to indicate that system vector has been initialized |
| 2563 | \$0A03 | PAL/NTSC flag (0 = NTSC video, 1 = PAL video) [678/\$02A6] |
| 2565–2566 | \$0A05–\$0A06 | Pointer to bottom of memory used for program text (in bank 0) [641–642/\$0281–\$0282] |
| 2567–2568 | \$0A07–\$0A08 | Pointer to top of memory used for variables (in bank 1) [643–644/\$0283–\$0284] |

| | | |
|---|---|---|
| 2576 | $0A10 | RS-232 control register [659/$0293] |
| 2577 | $0A11 | RS-232 command register [660/$0294] |
| 2578–2579 | $0A12–$0A13 | RS-232 user-defined baud rate [661–662/$0295–$0296] |
| 2580 | $0A14 | RS-232 status register [663/$0297] |
| 2582–2583 | $0A16–$0A17 | RS-232 baud timing constant value [665–666/$0299–$029A] |
| 2584 | $0A18 | Index to last character in the RS-232 input buffer [667/$029B] |
| 2585 | $0A19 | Index to first character in the RS-232 input buffer [668/$029C] |
| 2586 | $0A1A | Index to last character in the RS-232 output buffer [669/$029D] |
| 2587 | $0A1B | Index to first character in the RS-232 output buffer [670/$029E] |
| 2592 | $0A20 | Maximum number of characters in the keyboard buffer [649/$0289] |
| 2594 | $0A22 | Enable/disable key repeating (128 = all keys repeat, 64 = no keys repeat, 0 = space, INST/DEL, and cursor keys delete) [650/$028A] |
| 2624–2687 | $0A40–$0A7F | Storage area for screen editor variables during 40/80-column screen display exchanges |
| 2752 | $0AC0 | Number of function ROMs present |
| 2753–2756 | $0AC1–$0AC4 | Table of function ROM identifier bytes |
| 2816–3007 | $0B00–$0BBF | Cassette buffer [828–1019/$33C–$03FB] |
| 2816–3071 | $0B00–$0BFF | Holds image of boot sector during disk boot |
| 3072–3327 | $0C00–$0CFF | RS-232 input buffer |
| 3328–3583 | $0D00–$0DFF | RS-232 output buffer |
| 3584–4095 | $0E00–$0FFF | Sprite definition area |
| 4096–4105 | $1000–$1009 | Table of indexes to function key definitions |
| 4106–4351 | $100A–$10FF | Storage area for function key definitions |
| 4616 | $1208 | Error number for last error |
| 4617–4618 | $1209–$120A | Line number where last error occurred |
| 4624–4625 | $1210–$1211 | Pointer to end of BASIC program text (in bank 0) |
| 4626–4627 | $1212–$1214 | Pointer to top of memory for BASIC program text (in bank 0) |
| 4632–4634 | $1218–$121A | JSR and address for USR statement |

**2024–65279 ($0800–$FEFF) Bank 1: BASIC Variable Storage**

**7168–65279 ($1C00–$FEFF) Bank 0: BASIC Program Text Storage**

**7168–16383 ($1C00–$3FFF) Bank 0: 40-Column High-Resolution Screen and Color Memory (if used)**

| | | |
|---|---|---|
| 7168–8191 | $1C00–$1FFF | Color memory for bitmapped screen |
| 8192–16383 | $2000–$3FFF | Bitmap for high-resolution screen |

**16348–45055 ($4000–$AFFF) BASIC ROM**

| | | |
|---|---|---|
| 16343 | $4000 | BASIC cold-start vector |
| 16346 | $4003 | BASIC warm-start vector |
| 16349 | $4006 | BASIC IRQ entry vector |

### 45056–49151 ($B000–$BFFF) Machine Language Monitor ROM

| | | |
|---|---|---|
| 45056 | $B000 | Monitor cold-start vector |
| 45059 | $B003 | Monitor BRK entry vector |

### 49152–53247 ($C000–$CFFF) Screen Editor ROM

Editor Jump Table

| | | |
|---|---|---|
| 49152 | $C000 | Initialize screen editor and video chips (Kernal CINT) |
| 49155 | $C003 | Display a character |
| 49158 | $C006 | Get a key from keyboard buffer (GETIN from keyboard) |
| 49161 | $C009 | Get a character from the screen (BASIN from screen) |
| 49164 | $C00C | Print a character on the screen (BSOUT to screen) |
| 49167 | $C00F | Return number of lines and columns in current window (Kernal SCRORG) |
| 49170 | $C012 | Scan keyboard for keypress (Kernal KEY) |
| 49173 | $C015 | Check for key repeat |
| 49176 | $C018 | Read or set cursor position (Kernal PLOT) |
| 49179 | $C01B | Move cursor on 80-column screen |
| 49182 | $C01E | Handle ESC key sequences |
| 49185 | $C021 | Define a programmable key (Kernal PFKEY) |
| 49188 | $C024 | Editor IRQ entry vector |
| 49191 | $C027 | Initialize character set for 80-column display (Kernal DLCHR) |
| 49194 | $C02A | Switch between 40- and 80-column displays (Kernal SWAPPER) |
| 49197 | $C02D | Set window boundaries |

### 53248–57343 ($D000–$DFFF) Character ROM

| | | |
|---|---|---|
| 53248–54271 | $D000–$D3FF | Uppercase/graphics set definitions (normal) |
| 54272–55295 | $D400–$D7FF | Uppercase/graphics set definitions (reverse video) |
| 55296–56319 | $D800–$DBFF | Lowercase/uppercase set definitions (normal) |
| 56320–57343 | $DC00–$DFFF | Lowercase/uppercase set definitions (reverse video) |

### 53248–57343 ($D000–$DFFF) I/O Block

| | | |
|---|---|---|
| 53248–53296 | $D000–$D030 | VIC 40-column video chip |
| 54272–54300 | $D400–$D41C | SID sound chip |
| 54528–54539 | $D500–$D50B | MMU memory management chip |
| 54784–54785 | $D600–$D601 | 8563 80-column video chip |
| 55296–56319 | $D800–$DBFF | Color memory for 40-column screen |
| 56320–56335 | $DC00–$DC0F | CIA input/output chip 1 |
| 56576–56591 | $DD00–$DD0F | CIA input/output chip 2 |

| | | |
|---|---|---|
| 56832–57087 | $DE00–$DEFF | Expansion I/O slot (unused) |
| 57088–57098 | $DF00–$DF0A | REC expansion memory controller chip in memory expansion module |

**57344–65535 ($E000–$FFFF) Kernal ROM**

New Kernal Jump Table Entries for the 128

| | | | |
|---|---|---|---|
| 65351 | $FF47 | SPIN_SPOUT | Set serial ports for fast input or output |
| 65354 | $FF4A | CLOSE_ALL | Close all files to a device |
| 65357 | $FF4D | C64MODE | Enter 64 mode |
| 65360 | $FF50 | DMA_CALL | Send command to DMA device |
| 65363 | $FF53 | BOOT_CALL | Boot a program from disk |
| 65366 | $FF56 | PHOENIX | Initialize function ROM cartridges |
| 65369 | $FF59 | LKUPLA | Look up logical file number in file tables |
| 65372 | $FF5C | LKUPSA | Look up secondary address in file tables |
| 65375 | $FF5F | SWAPPER | Switch between 40- and 80-column displays |
| 65378 | $FF62 | DLCHR | Initialize character set for 80-column display |
| 65381 | $FF65 | PFKEY | Assign a string to a function key |
| 65384 | $FF68 | SETBNK | Set banks for I/O operations |
| 65387 | $FF6B | GETCFG | Get byte to configure MMU for any bank |
| 65390 | $FF6E | JSRFAR | Jump to a subroutine in any bank, with return to the calling bank |
| 65393 | $FF71 | JMPFAR | Jump to a routine in any bank, with no return to the calling bank |
| 65396 | $FF74 | INDFET | Load a byte from an address (offset of Y) in any bank |
| 65399 | $FF77 | INDSTA | Store a byte to an address (offset of Y) in any bank |
| 65402 | $FF7A | INDCMP | Compare a byte to the contents of an address (offset of Y) in any bank |
| 65405 | $FF7D | PRIMM | Print the string in memory immediately following the JSR to this routine |

Standard Commodore Kernal Jump Table
(Also found on the Commodore 64, VIC-20, 16, and Plus/4)

| | | | |
|---|---|---|---|
| 65409 | $FF81 | CINT | Initialize screen editor and video chips |
| 65412 | $FF84 | IOINIT | Initialize I/O devices |
| 65415 | $FF87 | RAMTAS | Initialize RAM and buffers |
| 65418 | $FF8A | RESTOR | Restore default values for Kernal indirect RAM vectors |
| 65421 | $FF8D | VECTOR | Set or copy Kernal indirect RAM vectors |
| 65424 | $FF90 | SETMSG | Enable or disable Kernal messages |
| 65427 | $FF93 | SECND | Send secondary address |
| 65430 | $FF96 | TKSA | Send secondary address to talker |
| 65433 | $FF99 | MEMTOP | Set or read top of RAM |
| 65436 | $FF9C | MEMBOT | Set or read bottom of RAM |
| 65439 | $FF9F | KEY | Read the keyboard |
| 65442 | $FFA2 | SETTMO | Enable/disable IEEE timeouts (unused in the 128) |
| 65445 | $FFA5 | ACPTR | Input a byte from the serial bus |
| 65448 | $FFA8 | CIOUT | Output a device to the serial bus |

| | | | |
|---|---|---|---|
| 65451 | $FFAB | UNTLK | Send untalk command to serial device |
| 65454 | $FFAE | UNLSN | Send unlisten command to serial device |
| 65457 | $FFB1 | LISTN | Send listen command to serial device |
| 65460 | $FFB4 | TALK | Send talk command to serial device |
| 65453 | $FFB7 | READSS | Read the I/O status |
| 65466 | $FFBA | SETLFS | Set channel, device number, and secondary address |
| 65469 | $FFBD | SETNAM | Specify length and address of current filename |
| 65472 | $FFC0 | OPEN | Open a logical file |
| 65475 | $FFC3 | CLOSE | Close a logical file |
| 65478 | $FFC6 | CHKIN | Set a specified channel for input |
| 65481 | $FFC9 | CKOUT | Set a specified channel for output |
| 65484 | $FFCC | CLRCH | Clear all channels |
| 65487 | $FFCF | BASIN | Retrieve a byte from the input channel |
| 65490 | $FFD2 | BSOUT | Send a byte to the output channel |
| 65493 | $FFD5 | LOAD | Load or verify data from device |
| 65496 | $FFD8 | SAVE | Save contents of memory to a device |
| 65499 | $FFDB | SETTIM | Set jiffy clock |
| 65502 | $FFDE | RDTIM | Read jiffy clock |
| 65505 | $FFE1 | STOP | Read RUN/STOP key status |
| 65508 | $FFE4 | GETIN | Get a byte from the input buffer |
| 65511 | $FFE7 | CLALL | Close all files and channels |
| 65514 | $FFEA | UDTIM | Update jiffy clock |
| 65517 | $FFED | SCRORG | Get size of current screen window |
| 65520 | $FFF0 | PLOT | Set or read cursor position |
| 65523 | $FFF3 | IOBASE | Get location of I/O block |

**65280–65284 ($FF00–$FF04) Common MMU Registers**

# LADS Source Code

The source code for LADS (Label Assembly Development System) is divided into 13 sections, each of which accomplishes a particular task for the assembler. All subroutines and most individual instructions are commented. If you are interested in studying or customizing the assembler, here is a brief overview of functions of the various sections:

- **Defs.** All the labels for zero page pointers and ROM routines used by the assembler are defined here.
- **Eval.** The main routine. Most other sections of the assembler are called from within Eval to perform their various services. Eval starts assembly (line 30) and ends assembly (line 4260). In between, Eval takes each line of source code apart, determining the intended addressing mode.
- **Equate.** Builds the database of labels during the assembler's first pass through the source code.
- **Array.** Searches through the label database on the second pass and locates a label name and its numeric value.
- **Open1.** Loads or saves disk files when DISKLADS is invoked with .D
- **Findmn.** A search routine to look through the list of 8502 mnemonics (in Tables below) to find the correct opcode.
- **Getsa.** Locates the start address as the first thing in the source code. Also contains the byte-by-byte source code reading routine, CHARIN.
- **Valdec.** Transforms ASCII numerals from the source code into integers. Thus, the *characters* 2 5 become the *number* 25 after Valdec finishes with them.
- **Indisk.** The main input routine. Each line of source code is brought in, analyzed in various ways, and prepared for Eval.
- **Math.** Handles the + pseudo-op.
- **Printops.** Keeps track of our location within the object code and formats screen and printer output in various ways.
- **Pseudo.** Handles all pseudo-ops except + *= and .BYTE. The .D section transforms RAMLADS into DISKLADS.
- **Tables.** LADS's internal database. Contains lookup tables of mnemonics, opcodes, and addressing-mode categories. Includes flags, pointers, error messages, and registers used by various routines.

## Program D-1. Defs

```
10 *= 10000
31 .D DEFS128 LADS
40 ; "DEFS128"  EQUATES AND DEFINITIONS FOR COMMODORE 128
50 ;---------------------  MACHINE SPECIFIC ZERO PAGE EQUATES -----------
60 RAMSTART = $2D; BASIC'S START OF RAM MEMORY NEXT
70 BMEMTOP = $39; BASIC'S TOP OF RAM MEMORY
80 ST = $90; STATUS WORD FOR DISK/TAPE I/O
90 LOADFLAG = $0C; FLAG WHICH SHOWS LOAD OR VERIFY (0 = LOAD)
110 FNAMEPTR = $BB; POINTER TO FILENAME LOCATION IN RAM.
120 FNUM = $B8; CURRENT FILE NUMBER FOR OPEN, GET & PUT CHARS TO DEVICE
130 FSECOND = $B9; CURRENT SECONDARY ADDRESS FOR OPEN
140 FDEV = $BA; DEVICE NUMBER (8 FOR COMMODORE DISK)
150 CURPOS = $EC; POSITION OF CURSOR ON A GIVEN SCREEN LINE.
160 ;---------------------  LADS INTERNAL ZERO PAGE EQUATES -----------
170 TEMP = $87:SA = $FA:MEMTOP = $FC:PARRAY = $89:PMEM = $41:KSTOR = $8E
175 ;A = 100:X = 101:Y = 102
180 ;------------------  MACHINE SPECIFIC ROM EQUATES -----------
190 BABUF = $0200; BASIC'S INPUT BUFFER
200 TOBASIC = $4003; GO BACK TO BASIC
210 KEYWDS = $4417; START OF /WORD TABLE IN BASIC
220 OUTNUM = $8E32; PRINTS OUT A (MSB), X (LSB) NUMBER
230 OPEN = $FFC0; OPENS A FILE  (3 BYTES PAST NORMAL OPEN IN ROM).
235 SETMEM = $FF00; MEMORY REGISTER TO SWITCH IN ROM
236 SETADDRESSES = $FFBA
237 SETNAME = $FFBD
250 CHKOUT = $FFC9; OPENS CHANNEL FOR WRITE (FILE# IN X)
270 PRINT = $FFD2; SENDS OUT ONE BYTE
280 LOAD = $FFD5; LOAD A BASIC PROGRAM FILE (SOURCE CODE FILE) INTO RAM.
290 CLRCHN = $FFCC; RESTORES DEFAULT I/O
300 CLOSE = $FFC3; CLOSE FILE (FILE# IN A)
```

# ONCE SOLD TALES

www.oncesoldtales.com

Item Name: 128 Machine Language for Beginners by Mansfield, Richard
SKU: AAPK3482 T09 2507:82
Description: A good exlibrary copy. Softly worn around edges. All pages and cover clear of markings. Binding solid and tight. Creased.
Quantity: 1
Price: 23.13
Shipping Fee: 3.99
Purchase Date: 4/2/2010 6:05:53 AM
Venue: Amazon.com
Amazon.com Order ID: 002-3212100-2706649
OST Order ID: 1005997

Buyer: Robert G. Higgins
Shipped to:
ROBERT G. HIGGINS
2299 W 4240 S
SALT LAKE CITY UT 84119-5341

Shipped From:
Once Sold Tales
22430 72nd Ave S
Kent, WA 98032
United States

```
310 STOP = $FFE1; TESTS STOP KEY, RETURNS TO BASIC IF PRESSED.
320 SCREEN = $0400; ADDRESS OF 1ST BYTE OF SCREEN RAM
330 ;------------------
350 .FILE EVAL
```

**Program D-2. Eval**

```
10 ; "EVAL"  MAIN EVALUATION ROUTINE
20 ;-------------------------------------------------------------
30 START LDA #0; SWITCH IN BANK 15
35 STA $FF00:STA EFLAG
40 LDY #48
50 STRTLP STA OP,Y;      -- LOOP TO CLEAR FLAGS --
60 DEY
70 BNE STRTLP; --------
80 LDA #<START; STORE BOTTOM OF LADS INTO TOP OF ARRAY/MEMORY.  PROTECT IT.
90 STA MEMTOP
100 STA BMEMTOP
110 STA ARRAYTOP
120 LDA #>START
130 STA MEMTOP+1
140 STA BMEMTOP+1
150 STA ARRAYTOP+1;--------
160 LDA #1;              -- SET DEFAULTS --
170 ; HERE YOU CAN SET ANY ADDITIONAL DEFAULTS YOU WISH
180 STA HXFLAG; TURN ON HEX LISTING FLAG
350 T1 NOP:NOP:NOP;JSR LOAD1; BRING IN READ FILE (SOURCE CODE FILE ON DISK) TO BANK
360 ;------------------  RE-ENTRY POINT FOR PASS 2 -------
370 SMORE JSR MEMSA; POINT DISKFILE TO 1ST CHARACTER IN SOURCE CODE
380 LDA #0
```

```
390 STA ENDFLAG; SET LADS-IS-OVER FLAG TO DOWN
400 JSR INDISK; GET A SINGLE LINE OF SOURCE CODE
410 LDA PASS; IF 2ND PASS
420 BNE STARTLINE;          THEN JUMP OVER PRINTING OF LADS NAME
430 LDA #147:JSR PRINT; CLEAR SCREEN
440 LDA #230; PRINT BLOCK GRAPHICS SYMBOL
450 JSR PRINT
460 LDA #76;          L
470 JSR PRINT
480 LDA #65;          A
490 JSR PRINT
500 LDA #68;          D
510 JSR PRINT
520 LDA #83;          S
530 JSR PRINT
540 JSR PRNTCR:JSR PRNTCR:JSR PRNTCR
550 CKHEX LDA HEXFLAG; IF START ADDRESS NUMBER IS HEX, IT'S ALREADY TRANSLATED
560 BNE STAR1
570 LDA #<LABEL; IN THE LABEL BUFFER IS SOMETHING LIKE: *= 864
580 STA TEMP; PUT THE ADDRESS OF THE BUFFER INTO THE POINTER CALLED TEMP
590 LDA #>LABEL
600 STA TEMP+1
610 JSR VALDEC; TURN ASCII NUMBER INTO A TWO-BYTE INTEGER IN "RESULT"
620 STAR1 LDA RESULT;     -- STORE OBJECT CODE'S STARTING ADDRESS IN SA,TA --
630 STA SA
640 STA TA
650 LDA RESULT+1
660 STA SA+1
670 STA TA+1
675 ;----------------
680 ;----------------   ENTRY POINT FOR EACH NEW LINE OF SOURCE CODE  ----
690 STARTLINE JSR STOP:BNE EVIND
```

```
695 JMP FINI; RESPOND TO STOP KEY PRESSED, ABORT ASSEMBLY.
700 ;-----------------
710 ;-----------------
720 EVIND LDA ENDFLAG:BEQ MOREIND:JMP FINI:MOREIND JSR INDISK
730 LDA #0
740 STA EXPRESSF; SET DOWN THE FLAG THAT SIGNALS A LABEL ARGUMENT LIKE LDA P
750 STA BUFLAG; SET DOWN THE FLAG THAT SIGNALS # OR ( DURING ARRAY CHECK.
760 LDY PASS;ON PASS 1, WE WON'T PRINT LINE NUMBERS, ADDR. OR ANYTHING
770 BNE MOREEV
780 JMP MOE4
790 MOREEV STY LOCFLAG; ZERO ADDRESS-TYPE LABEL FLAG (LIKE: LABEL INY)
800 ;                   THIS IS FOR THE INLINE SUBROUTINE BELOW.
810 LDA SFLAG; SHOULD WE PRINT TO THE SCREEN
820 BEQ MX; IF NOT, SKIP THIS PART
830 JSR PRNTLINE; PRINT LINE NUMBER
840 JSR PRNTSPACE; PRINT SPACE
850 JSR PRNTSA; PRINT PC (PROGRAM COUNTER)."SA" IS THE VARIABLE.
860 JSR PRNTSPACE
870 MX LDA PLUSFLAG; DO WE HAVE A + PSEUDO OP
880 BEQ MOE4; IF NOT SKIP
890 JSR MATH; IF SO, HANDLE IT IN SUBPROGRAM "MATH"
900 MOE4 JMP FINDMN; LOOK UP MNEMONIC (OR, NOT FINDING ONE, IT'S A LABEL)
910 ; --------  EVALUATE ARGUMENT
920 EVAR LDA TP
930 BEQ TP1JMP; CHECK TYPE, IF 0, NO ARGUMENT
940 CMP #3; IF NOT TYPE 3, THEN CONTINUE EVALUATION
950 BNE EVGO
960 LDA #1; OTHERWISE, REPLACE 3 WITH 1 IN TP (TYPE)
970 STA TP
980 LDA LABEL+3; IS THERE SOMETHING (NOT A ZERO) IN 4TH POSITION
990 BNE EVGO; EVGO = ARGUMENT (IF NOT, THERE'S NO ARGUMENT,IT'S IMPLIED)
```

```
1ØØØ LDA #8; OTHERWISE, RAISE OP (OPCODE) BY 8
1Ø1Ø CLC
1Ø2Ø ADC OP
1Ø3Ø STA OP
1Ø4Ø TP1JMP JMP TP1; AND JUMP TO TYPE 1 (SINGLE BYTE TYPES)
1Ø5Ø ;------------------
1Ø6Ø EQLABEL LDA PASS; MOE4 FOUND IT TO BE A LABEL, NOT A MNEMONIC
1Ø7Ø BEQ EQLAB1; ON PASS 1 WE DON'T CARE WHICH KIND OF LABEL IT IS SO WE
1Ø8Ø LDY #255; GO DOWN AND STORE IT IN THE ARRAY (VIA EQLAB1)
1Ø9Ø EVX1 INY; BUT ON PASS 2, WE NEED TO DECIDE IF IT'S A PC ADDRESS TYPE
11ØØ LDA LABEL,Y; LABEL (LIKE: LABEL INY) OR AN EQUATE TYPE (LABEL = 15)
111Ø BEQ GONOAR; SO IN THIS LOOP WE LOOK FOR A BLANK WHILE STORING THE
112Ø STA FILEN,Y; LABEL NAME IN THE "FILEN" BUFFER. IF WE FIND A Ø, IT'S
113Ø CMP #32; A NAKED LABEL (NO ARGUMENT TO IT) WHICH CAUSES US TO PRINT
114Ø BNE EVX1;OUT THAT ERROR MESSAGE (AT NOAR, IN EQUATE).OTHERWISE, WE FIND A
115Ø INY; BLANK AND FALL THROUGH TO THIS LINE.
116Ø LDA LABEL,Y; WE RAISE Y BY 1 AND CHECK FOR AN = SIGN.
117Ø CMP #$3D
118Ø BNE NOTEQ; IF NOT, IT'S A PC ADDRESS TYPE (SO SET LOCFLAG)
119Ø JMP INLINE; IF SO,WAS = TYPE SO IGNORE IT (ON PASS 2) ----------
12ØØ NOTEQ LDX #Ø
121Ø STX LOCFLAG;(SHOWS PRINTOUT TO DO THIS TYPE OF LABEL ON SCREEN/PRINTER)
122Ø TXA; PUT A ZERO IN AT THE END OF THE LABEL NAME (AS A DELIMITER)
123Ø STA FILEN,Y; NOW WE HAVE TO MOVE THE ARGUMENT PORTION OF THIS LINE
124Ø EVX5 LDA LABEL,Y; OVER TO THE START OF THE "LABEL" BUFFER FOR FURTHER
125Ø BEQ EVX4; ANALYSIS (Ø DELIMITER HERE)
126Ø STA LABEL,X; WE CAN IGNORE THE PC LABEL (THIS IS PASS 2), BUT WE
127Ø INX; NEED TO EVALUATE THE REST OF THE LINE FOLLOWING THAT LABEL.
128Ø INY
129Ø JMP EVX5;-------------------
13ØØ EVX4 STA LABEL,X
131Ø JMP MOE4; JUMP TO CONTINUE EVALUATION
```

```
1320 GONOAR JSR NOAR; PRINT NO ARGUMENT MESSAGE (A SPRINGBOARD);----------
1330 EQLAB1 JSR EQUATE; PUT LABEL AND ITS VALUE INTO THE ARRAY (PASS 1)
1340 JMP MOE4; CONTINUE EVALUATION
1350 ;------------------- TRANSLATE ARGUMENT LABELS INTO NUMBERS
1360 EVEXLAB LDA BUFFER; IS THIS 1ST CHARACTER ALPHABETIC (>64)
1370 CMP #64
1380 BCS EVE1; IF SO, GO DOWN TO FIND ITS VALUE.
1390 LDA BUFFER+1; IF NOT, IT MUST HAVE BEEN A ( OR # SYMBOL
1400 INC BUFLAG; TO TELL ARRAY THAT ( OR # WAS FOUND (AND TO IGNORE THEM)
1410 EVE1 EOR #$80; SET 7TH BIT IN 1ST CHAR. (TO MATCH ARRAY STORAGE METHOD)
1420 STA WORK; SAVE IT HERE TEMPORARILY TO COMPARE WITH ARRAY WORDS
1430 JSR ARRAY;  EVAL. EXPRESSION LABEL, SHIFTED 1ST CHAR.
1440 JMP L340; THEN CONTINUE ON WITH EVALUATION (AFTER VALUE IS IN "RESULT")
1450 ;--------------- IS ARGUMENT NUMERIC OR A LABEL
1460 EVGO LDY #0
1470 STY EXPRESSF; TURN OFF THE "IT'S A LABEL" FLAG
1472 ;------------------- ERROR TRAP FOR NAKED MNEMONICS ----------------
1474 LDA LABEL+3:CMP #32:BEQ GVEG:JMP L700; (TEST FOR "INC:" TYPE ERROR)
1480 GVEG LDA LABEL+4,Y; CHECK 5TH CHAR. (LDA NAME OR LDA 25) (THE "N" OR "2")
1490 CMP #65; IF LESS THAN 65 (ASCII FOR "A") THEN IT'S A NUMBER
1500 BCC EVMO2A
1510 INC EXPRESSF; >65 = ALPHABETIC ARG (LABEL) SO RAISE THIS FLAG
1520 EVMO2A STA BUFFER,Y; STORE 1ST CHAR. OF ARGUMENT IN "BUFFER" BUFFER
1530 INY
1540 LDA LABEL+4,Y; LOOK AT 2ND CHAR. IN THE ARGUMENT
1550 BEQ EVMO3; IF ZERO, WE'RE AT THE END SO MOVE ON
1560 STA BUFFER,Y; OTHERWISE, STORE 2ND CHAR.
1570 CMP #65; IF LOWER THAN 65, DON'T RAISE LABEL-ARGUMENT FLAG
1580 BCC EVMO2
1590 INC EXPRESSF; IF HIGHER, DO RAISE IT
1600 EVMO2 INY; NOW MOVE REST OF ARGUMENT UP TO "BUFFER" BUFFER
```

```
1610 LDA LABEL+4,Y; LOOP TO MOVE THE ARGUMENT INTO THE BUFFER
1620 BEQ EVMO3; EVMO3 TAKES OVER AFTER END OF ARGUMENT IS REACHED
1630 STA BUFFER,Y
1640 JMP EVMO2; RETURN FOR MORE ARGUMENT CHARACTERS.
1650 ;---------------
1660 EVMO3 DEY
1670 STY ARGSIZE; REMEMBER NUMBER OF CHARACTERS IN ARGUMENT
1680 LDA HEXFLAG; IF IT'S HEX, INDISK SUBPROGRAM ALREADY TRANSLATED IT FOR US
1690 BNE L340; SO GO ON TO EVALUATE ADDRESS MODE.
1700 LDA EXPRESSF; IF IT'S A LABEL (NOT A NUMBER) THEN GO TO THE ROUTINE
1710 BNE EVEXLAB; WHICH EVALUATES EXPRESSION (ARGUMENT) LABELS, "EVEXLAB"
1720 ; ----------  CALCULATE ARGUMENT'S VALUE (IF IT'S A DECIMAL NUMBER)
1730 LDA #<BUFFER; MAKE "TEMP" POINTER POINT TO "BUFFER"
1740 STA TEMP
1750 LDA #>BUFFER
1760 STA TEMP+1
1770 LDY #0
1780 LDA BUFFER; IS 1ST CHARACTER HIGHER THAN 48 (ASCII FOR THE NUMBER ZERO)
1790 CMP #48
1800 BCS MCAL; IF SO, SKIP THIS PART
1810 CLC; IF NOT, THE 1ST CHARACTER MUST BE # OR ( ..... SO WE NEED TO
1820 INC TEMP; MAKE "TEMP" POINT 1 CHARACTER HIGHER IN "BUFFER" TO
1830 BCC MCAL; AVOID HAVING THE ASCII TO INTEGER SUBROUTINE THINK THAT THE
1840 INC TEMP+1; NUMBER STARTS WITH A # OR ( --- THAT WOULD MESS THINGS UP.
1850 MCAL LDA (TEMP),Y; NOW LOOK FOR THE END OF THE NUMBER:  -----------
1860 BEQ MCAL1; IT COULD END WITH A 0 (DELIMITER) OR
1870 CMP #41; WITH A ) LEFT PARENTHESIS OR
1880 BEQ MCAL1
1890 CMP #44; WITH A , COMMA (AS IN: 15,Y) OR
1900 BEQ MCAL1
1910 CMP #32; WITH BLANK SPACE (AS IN: #15  ;COMMENT)
1920 BEQ MCAL1
```

```
1930 INY; IF WE'VE NOT YET FOUND ONE OF THESE 4 THINGS, CONTINUE LOOKING
1940 JMP MCAL;-----------------------------
1950 MCAL1 PHA; SAVE ACCUMULATOR
1960 TYA
1970 PHA;SAVE Y REGISTER(BY NOW, Y IS POINTING AT THE SPACE JUST AFTER THE #)
1980 LDA #0; PUT DELIMITER ZERO INTO BUFFER JUST FOLLOWING NUMBER.
1990 STA (TEMP),Y
2000 JSR VALDEC;GO TO THE ASCII-NUMBER-TO-INTEGER-NUMBER-IN-"RESULT" ROUTINE
2010 PLA; RESTORE THE A AND Y REGISTERS
2020 TAY
2030 PLA
2040 STA (TEMP),Y; RESTORE "," OR ")" TO THE BUFFER (FOR THE ADDR. ANALYSIS)
2045 ;
2050 ;---------  ANALYZE THE ARGUMENT TO DETERMINE ADDRESSING MODE ------
2055 ;
2060 ; (THIS ESSENTIALLY AMOUNTS TO MODIFYING THE ORIGINAL OPCODE TO
2070 ;  REFLECT THE CORRECT ADDRESSING MODE.  ADJUSTMENTS TO THE OPCODE "OP"
2080 ;  APPEAR RATHER FREQUENTLY FROM HERE ON.  THEIR LOGIC WILL NOT BE
2090 ;  COMMENTED.  ADDING 4,8,16, OR 24 TO AN "OP" IS BASED ON THE
2100 ;  RELATIONSHIPS WITHIN THE OPCODE TABLE.
2110 ;
2120 L340 LDA BUFFER; 1ST CHAR. OF THE ARGUMENT (THE "#" IN LDA #15)
2130 CMP #35
2140 BEQ JIMMED; # SYMBOL FOUND (SO IMMEDIATE MODE).  BRANCH TO SPRINGBOARD
2150 CMP #40; IS IT A "(" LEFT PARENTHESIS.  IF SO, GO TO INDIRECT ADDR.
2160 BEQ INDIR
2170 LDA TP; IS IT A RELATIVE ADDR. MODE (LIKE BNE, BEQ).
2180 CMP #8
2190 BEQ REL; IF SO, GO TO WHERE THEY ARE HANDLED.
2200 CMP #3; ADD 8 TO OP AT THIS POINT IF IT'S A TYPE 3
2210 BNE EVMO5
```

```
2220 LDA #8
2230 CLC
2240 ADC OP
2250 STA OP
2260 JMP TP1; AND JUMP TO THE SINGLE BYTE TYPES (IMPLIED ADDRESSING)
2270 INDIR LDY ARGSIZE; HANDLE INDIRECT ADDRESSING-------------------
2280 LDA BUFFER,Y; LOOK AT THE LAST CHARACTER IN THE ARGUMENT.
2290 CMP #41; IS IT A ")" LEFT PARENTHESIS
2300 BEQ MINDIR; IF SO, HANDLE THAT TYPE.
2310 LDA TP
2320 CMP #1; IF TYPE 1, ADD 16 AT THIS POINT TO OPCODE
2330 BNE MINDIR
2340 LDA #16
2350 CLC
2360 ADC OP
2370 STA OP
2380 MINDIR LDA TP; TYPE 6 IS A JUMP INSTRUCTION
2390 CMP #6
2400 BEQ JJUMP; SO GO TO THE JUMP-HANDLING ROUTINE
2410 JMP TWOS; OTHERWISE, IT MUST BE A 2-BYTE TYPE SO PRINT/POKE IT.;-------
2420 JIMMED JMP IMMED; SPRINGBOARD TO IMMEDIATE MODE TYPES.
2430 ;------------------------------ HANDLE RELATIVE ADDRESS (BNE) TYPES
2440 REL LDA PASS; ON PASS 1, DON'T BOTHER, JUST INCREASE PC BY 2
2450 BNE MREL
2460 JMP TWOS
2470 MREL SEC; ON PASS 2, SUBTRACT PC FROM ARGUMENT TO GET REL. BRANCH
2480 LDA RESULT
2490 SBC SA
2500 PHA; SAVE LOW BYTE ANSWER
2510 LDA RESULT+1
2520 SBC SA+1
2530 BCS FOR; IF ARGUMENT > CURRENT PC, THEN IT'S A BRANCH FORWARD
```

```
254Ø CMP #$FF
255Ø BEQ MPXS
256Ø PLA
257Ø JMP DOBERR
258Ø MPXS PLA; OTHERWISE, CHECK FOR OUT OF RANGE BRANCH ATTEMPT
259Ø BPL BERR; OUT OF RANGE (PRINT ERROR MESSAGE "BERR")
26ØØ JMP RELM; AND JUMP TO REL CONCLUSION ROUTINE
261Ø FOR BEQ MPXS1; CHECK FORWARD BRANCH OUT OF RANGE
262Ø PLA
263Ø JMP DOBERR
264Ø MPXS1 PLA
265Ø BPL RELM; WITHIN RANGE-----------------------
266Ø BERR JMP DOBERR; PRINT "BRANCH OUT OF RANGE" ERROR MESSAGE
267Ø RELM SEC; FINISH UP REL. ADDR. TYPE --------------------
268Ø SBC #2; CORRECT FOR THE FACT THAT BRANCHES ARE CALCULATED FROM THE
269Ø STA RESULT; INSTRUCTION FOLLOWING THEM:  BNE LOOP:LDA 15 WOULD BE
27ØØ LDA #Ø;     CALCULATED FROM THE PC OF THE LDA 15
271Ø STA RESULT+1
272Ø JMP TWOS; NOW GO TO THE 2-BYTE PRINT/POKE (WITH CORRECT ARGUMENT)
273Ø ;------------------------------ CONTINUE ADDR. MODE ANALYSIS
274Ø EVMO5 LDY ARGSIZE
275Ø DEY
276Ø LDA BUFFER,Y; LOOK AT LAST CHARACTER OF ARGUMENT
277Ø CMP #44; IF IT'S NOT A COMMA, THEN THIS MUST BE A JUMP INSTRUCTION
278Ø BNE JJUMP; SO GO TO THE JUMP-HANDLING ROUTINE
279Ø INY
28ØØ JMP XYTYPE; OTHERWISE, IT MUST BE A ,X OR ,Y TYPE;---------------
281Ø JJUMP LDA OP; HANDLE JMP MNEMONIC
282Ø CMP #76; IF THE OPCODE ISN'T 76, IT'S NOT A JUMP
283Ø BNE MEV; SO LOOK FOR SOMETHING ELSE
284Ø JMP JUMP; NOW SPRINGBOARD TO THE JUMP-HANDLING ROUTINE.----------
```

```
2850 MEV LDA RESULT+1; IF HIGH BYTE OF RESULT ISN'T ZERO (ZERO PG. ADDR)
2860 BNE PREPTHREES; THEN GO TO THE 3-BYTE INSTRUCTIONS
2870 LDA TP; OTHERWISE, IT'S ZERO PAGE MODE
2875 CMP #9:BEQ PREPTHREES; HANDLE JSRS INTO ZERO PAGE
2880 CMP #6; IF HIGHER THAN TYPE 6, IT'S AN ORDINARY 2-BYTE TYPE
2890 BCS TWOS; SO GO THERE.
2900 CMP #2; IF TYPE 2, ALSO GO THERE.
2910 BEQ TWOS
2920 LDA #4; OTHERWISE, ADD 4 TO OPCODE AND FALL THROUGH INTO TWO-BYTE TYPE
2930 CLC
2940 ADC OP
2950 STA OP
2960 ;------------------------------  2 BYTE TYPES (LIKE LDA 12)
2970 TWOS JSR FORMAT; PRINT/POKE OPCODE
2980 JSR PRINT2; THEN PRINT/POKE ARGUMENT
2990 JMP INLINE; AND FINALLY PREPARE TO FETCH NEW LINE OF SOURCECODE
3000 ;------------------------------  HANDLE JMP
3010 JUMP LDY ARGSIZE; IS IT JMP 1500 OR JMP
3020 LDA BUFFER,Y;  )  AT THE END PROVES IT'S AN INDIRECT JUMP SO
3030 CMP #41
3040 BNE JUMO
3050 LDA #108;          WE MUST CHANGE THE OPCODE FROM 76 TO 108
3060 STA OP
3070 JUMO JMP THREES; TREAT IT AS A NORMAL 3-BYTE INSTRUCTION
3080 ;------------------------------ IMMEDIATE ADDRESSING (# TYPE)
3090 IMMED LDA BUFFER+1
3100 CMP #""; IS THIS A CHARACTER LOAD PSEUDO-OP LIKE: LDA #"A
3110 BNE IMMEDX
3120 LDA BUFFER+2; IF SO, PUT THE ASCII CHAR. INTO "RESULT" (ARGUMENT)
3130 STA RESULT
3140 IMMEDX LDA TP
```

```
3150 CMP #1
3160 BNE TWOS; IF IT'S TYPE 1, ADJUST OPCODE BY ADDING 8 TO IT.
3170 LDA #8
3180 CLC:ADC OP:STA OP
3190 JMP TWOS
3200 ;---------------------------------- 1 BYTE TYPES
3210 TP1 JSR FORMAT; JUST POKE OPCODE FOR THESE, THERE'S NO ARGUMENT
3220 JMP INLINE;
3230 ;---------------------------------- 3 BYTE TYPES
3240 PREPTHREES LDA TP; SEVERAL OPCODE ADJUSTMENTS (BASED ON TYPE)
3250 CMP #2
3260 BEQ PTT
3270 CMP #7;
3280 BNE PT1
3290 PTT LDA OP
3300 CLC
3310 ADC #8
3320 STA OP
3330 JMP THREES
3340 PT1 CMP #6
3350 BCS THREES
3360 LDA OP
3370 CLC
3380 ADC #12
3390 STA OP
3400 THREES JSR FORMAT; PRINT/POKE OPCODE
3410 JSR PRINT3; PRINT/POKE 2 BYTES OF THE ARGUMENT
3420 ;------------------------------------- PREPARE TO GET A NEW LINE
3430 ;PRINT MAIN INPUT AND COMMENTS, THEN TO STARTLINE
3440 INLINE LDA PASS; ON PASS 1, IGNORE THIS WHOLE PRINTOUT THING.
3450 BNE NLOX1
```

```
346Ø JMP JST
347Ø NLOX1 LDA SFLAG; LIKEWISE, IF SCREENFLAG IS DOWN, IGNORE.
348Ø BNE NLOX
349Ø JMP JST
35ØØ NLOX LDA LOCFLAG; ANY PC ADDRESS LABEL TO PRINT
351Ø BNE PRMMX1; NO LOC TO PRINT
352Ø LDA PRINTFLAG; PRINT TO PRINTER
353Ø BEQ PRMM
354Ø LDA #2Ø
355Ø SEC
356Ø SBC CURPOS; SUBTRACT CURRENT CURSOR POSITION
357Ø STA A; MOVE THE CURSOR TO 2ØTH COLUMN ON THE SCREEN
358Ø JSR CLRCHN; PREPARE PRINTER TO PRINT BLANKS
359Ø LDX #4
36ØØ JSR CHKOUT
361Ø LDY A
362Ø BPL PRXM1
363Ø LDY #2
364Ø JMP PRMLOP
365Ø PRXM1 LDA #32
366Ø PRMLOP JSR PRINT;---------------- PRINT BLANKS TO PRINTER
367Ø DEY
368Ø BNE PRMLOP; PRINT MORE BLANKS TO PRINTER;---------------
369Ø JSR CLRCHN; RESTORE NORMAL I/O
37ØØ LDX #1
371Ø JSR CHKIN
372Ø PRMM LDA #2Ø; PUT 2Ø INTO CURRENT SCREEN CURSOR POSITION
373Ø STA CURPOS
374Ø LDA #<FILEN; POINT "TEMP" TO PC ADDRESS LABEL FOR PRINTOUT
375Ø STA TEMP
376Ø LDA #>FILEN
377Ø STA TEMP+1
```

```
3780 JSR PRNTMESS; PRINT LOCATION LABEL;----------
3790 PRMMX1 LDA #30; MOVE CURSOR TO 30TH COLUMN
3800 SEC
3810 SBC CURPOS
3820 STA X; SAVE OFFSET FROM CURRENT POSITION (30-POSITION) FOR PRINTER
3830 LDA #30
3840 STA CURPOS; SET SCREEN CURSOR POSITION TO 30
3850 LDA PRINTFLAG; DO WE NEED TO PRINT BLANKS TO THE PRINTER
3860 BEQ PRMMFIN
3870 JSR CLRCHN; ALERT PRINTER TO RECEIVE BLANKS
3880 LDX #4
3890 JSR CHKOUT
3900 LDY X
3910 BEQ PXMX; HANDLE NO BLANKS (IGNORE)
3920 BMI PXMX; HANDLE TOO MANY BLANKS (>127) (IGNORE)
3930 LDA #32
3940 PRMLOPX JSR PRINT; PRINT BLANKS TO PRINTER FOR FORMATTING--------
3950 DEY
3960 BNE PRMLOPX; PRINT MORE BLANKS----------
3970 PXMX JSR CLRCHN; RESTORE NORMAL I/O
4000 PRMMFIN JSR PRNTINPUT; PRINT MAIN INPUT BUFFER (BULK OF SOURCE LINE)
4010 LDA BYTFLAG; IS THERE A < OR > PSEUDO-OP TO PRINT --------------
4020 BEQ PRXM; HANDLE < AND >
4030 CMP #1; 1 IN BYTFLAG MEANS <
4040 BNE MO5
4050 LDA #60
4060 JMP PRMO
4070 MO5 LDA #62; PRINT >
4080 PRMO JSR PRINT
4090 JSR PTP1; PRINT > OR <.  PTP1 IS TO PRINTER----------
4100 PRXM LDA BABFLAG; IS THERE ANY COMMENT TO PRINT (SOMETHING FOLLOWING ;)
```

```
4110 BEQ RETTX; IF NOT, SKIP THIS.
4120 JSR PRNTSPACE; PRINT A SPACE--------  PRINT COMMENTS FIELD ----------
4130 LDA #59; PRINT A SEMICOLON
4140 JSR PRINT
4150 LDA #<BABUF; POINT "TEMP" TO THE COMMENTS BUFFER "BABUF"
4160 STA TEMP
4170 LDA #>BABUF
4180 STA TEMP+1
4190 JSR PRNTMESS; PRINT WHAT'S IN THE COMMENTS BUFFER
4200 RETTX JSR PRNTCR; PRINT CARRIAGE RETURN
4210 LDA ENDFLAG; IF ENDFLAG IS UP, JUMP TO THE SHUTDOWN ROUTINE
4220 BNE FINI
4230 JST JMP STARTLINE; OTHERWISE GO BACK UP TO GET THE NEXT SOURCE LINE.
4240 ;------------------------------------ THE END OF A PASS (1 OR 2)
4250 FINI LDA PASS
4260 BNE FIN; IF IT'S PASS 2, SHUT EVERYTHING DOWN.
4270 INC PASS
4280 LDA TA; PUT THE ORIGINAL START ADDR. INTO THE PC PROGRAM COUNTER (SA)
4290 STA SA
4300 LDA TA+1
4310 STA SA+1
4360 JMP SMORE; PASS 1 FINISHED, START PASS 2 (ENTRY POINT FOR PASS 2)------
4370 ;
4380 ;-------------------- SHUT DOWN LADS OPERATIONS AND RETURN TO BASIC ------
4390 FIN JSR CLRCHN; RESTORE NORMAL I/O
4400 LDA #<ERN:STA TEMP:LDA #>ERN:STA TEMP+1:JSR PRNTCR
4410 JSR PRNTSPACE:JSR PRNTSPACE:LDX EFLAG:LDA #0:JSR PRNTNUM:JSR PRNTMESS
4440 LDA PRINTFLAG; IS THE PRINTER ACTIVE
4450 BEQ FINFIN; IF NOT, JUST RETURN TO BASIC
4460 JSR CLRCHN; OTHERWISE SHUT DOWN PRINTER, GRACEFULLY.
4470 LDX #4
```

```
4480 JSR CHKOUT
4490 LDA #13;        BY PRINTING A CARRIAGE RETURN
4500 JSR PRINT
4510 JSR CLRCHN
4520 LDA #4
4530 JSR CLOSE
4540 FINFIN LDA #$FC:STA $D030:LDA #0:STA $FF00
4545 BACK LDA CYCLEFLAG:BEQ REALEND; DON'T RELOAD LADS IF RAMLADS
4546 LDA #4:STA FNAMELEN:LDA #76:STA FILEN:LDA #65:STA FILEN+1
4547 LDA #68:STA FILEN+2:LDA #83:STA FILEN+3:JSR LOAD2
4548 LDA #145:JSR PRINT:NOP:NOP:NOP:LDA #"D:JSR $C01E:LDA #"@:JSR $C01E
4549 REALEND JMP TOBASIC; RETURN TO BASIC
4550 ;
4560 ;-----------------------------------  ,X OR ,Y ADDRESSING TYPE
4570 XYTYPE LDA BUFFER,Y; LOOK AT LAST CHAR. IN ARGUMENT
4580 CMP #88; IS IT AN X
4590 BEQ L720
4600 DEY; OTHERWISE, LOOK AT THE 3RD CHAR. FROM END OF ARGUMENT
4610 DEY
4620 LDA BUFFER,Y; IS IT A  )  LEFT PARENTHESIS
4630 CMP #41
4640 BNE ZEROY; IF NOT, IT'S NOT AN INDIRECT ADDR. MODE
4650 JMP INDIR; IF SO, IT IS AN INDIRECT ADDRESSING MODE
4660 ZEROY LDA RESULT+1; CHECK HIGH BYTE OF RESULT (ZERO PG. OR NOT)
4670 BNE L680; ZERO Y TYPE
4680 LDA TP; ADJUST OPCODE BASED ON TYPE
4690 CMP #2
4700 BEQ L730
4710 CMP #5
4720 BEQ L730
4730 CMP #1
```

```
4740 BEQ L760
4750 L680 LDA TP
4760 CMP #1
4770 BNE L690
4780 LDA OP
4790 CLC
4800 ADC #24
4810 STA OP
4820 JMP THREES
4830 L690 LDA TP
4840 CMP #5
4850 BEQ M6
4860 LDA #$31
4870 JSR P
4880 JMP L700
4890 M6 LDA OP
4900 CLC
4910 ADC #28
4920 STA OP
4930 JMP THREES
4940 ;----------- PRINT A SYNTAX ERROR MESSAGE ------------------
4950 L700 JSR ERRING; RING ERROR BELL AND TURN ON REVERSE CHARACTERS
4960 JSR PRNTLINE; PRINT LINE NUMBER
4970 LDA #<MERROR; POINT "TEMP" TO SYNTAX ERROR MESSAGE
4980 STA TEMP
4990 LDA #>MERROR
5000 STA TEMP+1
5010 JSR PRNTMESS:JSR PRNTCR; PRINT THE MESSAGE
5020 JMP INLINE; GO TO THE GET-THE-NEXT-LINE ROUTINE
5030 ;----------------------------- CONTINUE ANALYSIS OF ADDR. MODE
5040 L720 LDA RESULT+1; MAKE FURTHER ADJUSTMENTS TO OPCODE
5050 BNE L780; NOT ZERO PAGE
```

```
5060 L730 LDA TP
5070 CMP #2
5080 BNE L740
5090 LDA #16
5100 CLC
5110 ADC OP
5120 STA OP
5130 JMP TWOS
5140 L740 CMP #1
5150 BEQ L759
5160 CMP #3
5170 BEQ L759
5180 CMP #5
5190 BEQ L759
5200 L750 LDA #$32
5210 JSR P
5220 JMP L700
5230 L759 LDA #20
5240 CLC
5250 ADC OP
5260 STA OP
5270 ; ------------------- ZERO PAGE Y ERROR TRAP -----------------------
5271 L760 LDA BUFFER+2,Y:CMP #89:BNE ML760
5272 LDA OP:CMP #182:BEQ ML760; IS THE MNEMONIC LDX (IF SO, MODE IS CORRECT)
5273 JMP L680; IF NOT, JUMP TO MAKE IT (LDA $0015,Y) ABSOLUTE Y
5274 ML760 JMP TWOS
5275 ;---------------------------------
5280 L780 LDA TP
5290 CMP #2
5300 BNE L790
5310 LDA #24
```

```
5320 CLC
5330 ADC OP
5340 STA OP
5350 JMP THREES
5360 L790 CMP #1
5370 BEQ L809
5380 CMP #3
5390 BEQ L809
5400 CMP #5
5410 BEQ L809
5420 L800 LDA #$33
5430 JSR P
5440 JMP L700
5450 L809 LDA #28
5460 CLC
5470 ADC OP
5480 STA OP
5490 JMP THREES;    END OF ADDR. MODE EVALUATIONS AND ADJUSTMENTS
5500 ;
5510 ;-------------------- ERROR REPORTING FOR DEBUGGING (PRINTS PC)
5520 P STA A; WHEN YOU INSERT A "JSR P" INTO YOUR SOURCE CODE, THIS ROUTINE
5530 STY Y; WILL PRINT THE PC FROM WHICH YOU JSR'ED.
5540 STX X:JSR PRNTCR; WILL REVEAL THE JSR ADDR.
5550 LDA #$BA; PRINT A GRAPHICS SYMBOL TO SIGNAL THAT THE PC IS TO FOLLOW
5560 JSR PRINT
5570 PLA; SAVE THE RTS ADDRESS (TO KEEP THE STACK INTACT)
5580 TAX
5590 PLA
5600 TAY
5610 TYA
5620 PHA
```

```
5630 TXA
5640 PHA
5650 TYA
5660 JSR OUTNUM; PRINT THE PC ADDRESS.
5670 JSR PRNTCR:LDA A; RESTORE THE REGISTERS.
5680 LDY Y
5690 LDX X
5700 RTS
5710 ;--------------------------
5720 CLEANLAB LDY #0; FILLS MAIN INPUT BUFFER ("LABEL") WITH ZERO. CLEANS IT.
5730 TYA
5740 CLEMORE STA LABEL,Y
5750 INY
5760 CPY #80
5770 BNE CLEMORE
5780 RTS
5790 ; ---------PRINT BRANCH OUT OF RANGE ERROR MESSAGE--------------
5800 DOBERR JSR PRNTCR; PRINT "BRANCH OUT OF RANGE" ERROR MESSAGE
5810 JSR ERRING
5820 JSR PRNTLINE; PRINT THE LINE NUMBER
5830 LDA #<MBOR; POINT "TEMP" TO THE ERROR MESSAGE "MBOR"
5840 STA TEMP; (MESSAGE BRANCH OUT OF RANGE, MBOR)
5850 LDA #>MBOR
5860 STA TEMP+1
5870 JSR PRNTMESS; PRINT THE MESSAGE
5880 JSR PRNTCR; PRINT A CARRIAGE RETURN AND
5890 JMP TWOS; BUNGLE AS AN ORDINARY 2-BYTE EVENT (TO KEEP PC CORRECT)
5900 ;--------------------------
5910 .FILE EQUATE
```

### Program D-3. Equate

```
10 ; "EQUATE"  EVALUATE LABELS
20 ; COULD BE EITHER PC (ADDRESS) TYPE OR EQUATE TYPE.  STORE IN ARRAY.
25 ; FORMAT--NAME/2-BYTE INTEGER VALUE/NAME/2-BYTE VALUE/ETC...
3Ø ;-------------
4Ø EQUATE LDY #255; PREPARE Y TO ZERO AT START OF LOOP
5Ø EQ1 INY; Y GOES TO ZERO 1ST TIME THROUGH LOOP
6Ø LDA LABEL,Y; LOOK AT THE WORD, THE LABEL
7Ø BEQ NOAR; END OF LINE (SO THERE'S A NAKED LABEL, NOTHING FOLLOWS IT)
8Ø CMP #32; FOUND A SPACE, SO RAISE Y BY 2 AND SET LABEL SIZE (LABSIZE)
9Ø BNE EQ1; OTHERWISE, KEEP LOOKING FOR A SPACE.
1ØØ INY
11Ø INY
12Ø STY LABSIZE
13Ø ;-------------------- LOWER MEMTOP POINTER WITHIN ARRAY (BY LABEL SIZE)
14Ø SUBMEM SEC; SUBTRACT LABEL SIZE FROM ARRAY POINTER TO MAKE ROOM FOR LABEL
15Ø LDA MEMTOP
16Ø SBC LABSIZE
17Ø STA MEMTOP
18Ø LDA MEMTOP+1
19Ø SBC #Ø
2ØØ STA MEMTOP+1;--------------
2Ø5 ;SHIFT 7TH BIT OF 1ST CHAR. TO SIGNIFY START OF LABEL'S NAME
21Ø LDY #Ø
22Ø LDA LABEL,Y
23Ø EOR #$8Ø
24Ø STA (MEMTOP),Y; STORE SHIFTED 1ST LETTER
25Ø EQ3 INY
26Ø LDA LABEL,Y; IF SPACE, STOP STORING LABEL NAME IN ARRAY.
27Ø CMP #32
28Ø BEQ EQ2
```

```
290 STA (MEMTOP),Y; OTHERWISE, PUT NEXT LETTER INTO ARRAY &
300 JMP EQ3; CONTINUE.
310 EQ2 INY; NOW CHECK FOR = (SIGNIFYING EQUATE TYPE) (LABEL = 15)
320 LDA LABEL,Y
330 CMP #$3D; IF EQUATE TYPE, GO TO FIND ITS VALUE.
340 BEQ EQUAL
350 DEY; OTHERWISE, IT'S PC TYPE (LABEL LDA 15)
360 LDA SA; SO THE PC VARIABLE (SA) CONTAINS THE VALUE OF THIS LABEL
370 STA (MEMTOP),Y; STORE IT RIGHT AFTER LABEL NAME WITHIN ARRAY.
380 INY
390 LDA SA+1
400 STA (MEMTOP),Y
410 LDX LABSIZE; NOW, USING LABELSIZE AS INDEX, ERASE THE PC-TYPE LABEL
420 DEX;         FROM THE BUFFER.  FOR EXAMPLE, (LABEL LDA 15) NOW
430 LDY #0;      BECOMES (LDA 15).  THE LABEL NAME IS COVERED OVER
440 EQ5 LDA LABEL,X; TO PREPARE THE REST OF THE LINE TO BE ANALYZED
450 BEQ EQ4; NORMALLY BY EVAL.
460 STA LABEL,Y
470 INX
480 INY
490 JMP EQ5
500 EQ4 STA LABEL,Y
510 RTS; RETURN TO EVAL --------------------------
520 NOAR JSR PRNTCR:JSR PRNTLINE;NAKED LABEL FOUND (NO ARGUMENT) SO
525 JSR ERRING
530 LDA #<NOARG; RING BELL AND PRINT NAKED LABEL ERROR MESSAGE.
540 STA TEMP
550 LDA #>NOARG
560 STA TEMP+1
570 JSR PRNTMESS:JSR PRNTCR
580 JMP EQRET; RETURN TO EVAL-----------------------
```

```
584 ;
585 ;--------------- HANDLE EQUATE TYPES HERE (LABEL = 15)
590 EQUAL DEY
600 STY LABPTR; TELLS US HOW FAR FROM MEMTOP WE SHOULD STORE ARGUMENT VALUE
610 LDA HEXFLAG; HEX NUMBERS ALREADY HANDLED BY INDISK ROUTINE, SO SKIP OVER.
620 BNE FINEQ; HEX FLAG UP, SO GO TO EQUATE EXIT ROUTINE BELOW.
630 INY; OTHERWISE, WE NEED TO FIGURE OUT THE ARGUMENT (LABEL = 15)
640 INY; THERE ARE THREE CHARS. ( = ) BETWEEN LABEL & ARGUMENT, SO
650 INY; INY THRICE.
660 STY WORK+1; POINT TO LOCATION OF ASCII NUMBER (IN LABEL BUFFER)
670 LDA #<LABEL; SET UP TEMP POINTER TO POINT TO ASCII NUMBER
680 CLC
690 ADC WORK+1
700 STA TEMP
710 LDA #>LABEL
720 ADC #0
730 STA TEMP+1
740 JSR VALDEC; CALCULATE ASCII NUMBER VALUE AND STORE IN RESULT
750 FINEQ LDY LABPTR; STORE INTEGER VALUE JUST AFTER LABEL NAME IN ARRAY
760 LDA RESULT
770 STA (MEMTOP),Y
780 LDA RESULT+1
790 INY
800 STA (MEMTOP),Y
810 EQRET PLA;PULL OFF THE RTS (FROM EVAL) AND JUMP DIRECTLY TO INLINE
820 PLA;      IGNORING ANY FURTHER EVALUATION OF THIS LINE SINCE EQUATE TYPE
830 JMP INLINE; LABELS ARE FOLLOWED BY NOTHING TO EVALUATE
840 .FILE ARRAY
```

### Program D-4. Array

```
10 ; "ARRAY" LOOKS THROUGH LABEL TABLE AND PUTS VALUE IN RESULT.
20 ;  (USED IN BOTH PASS 1 AND PASS 2)
30 ARRAY LDA ARRAYTOP;PUT TOP-OF-ARRAY VALUE INTO THE DYNAMIC POINTER (PARRAY)
40 STA PARRAY; IN OTHER WORDS, MAKE PARRAY POINT TO THE HIGHEST WORD IN THE
50 LDA ARRAYTOP+1; LABEL ARRAY
60 STA PARRAY+1
70 JSR DECPAR
80 LDA #$FF; SET UP FOR BMI TEST IF NO MATCH FOUND
90 STA FOUNDFLAG
100 STARTLK SEC; START LOOKING FOR LABEL NAME
110 LDA MEMTOP; CHECK TO SEE IF WE'RE AT THE BOTTOM OF THE ARRAY
120 SBC PARRAY
130 LDA MEMTOP+1
140 SBC PARRAY+1
150 BCS ADONE; IF SO, CHECK IF WE FOUND THE LABEL (OR FOUND IT TWICE)
160 LDX #0; SET LABEL NAME SIZE COUNTER TO ZERO
170 SEC; GO DOWN 2 BYTES IN MEMORY (PAST THE INTEGER VALUE OF A LABEL)
180 LDA PARRAY
190 SBC #2
200 STA PARRAY
210 LDA PARRAY+1
220 SBC #0
230 STA PARRAY+1
240 LDY #0
250 ;---------------------------
260 LPAR LDA (PARRAY),Y; LOOK FOR A 7TH BIT SET (START OF LABEL NAME)
270 BMI FOUNDONE; IF YES, WE'VE GOT TO THE START OF A NAME.
280 LDA PARRAY; OTHERWISE GO DOWN 1 BYTE IN ARRAY
290 BNE MDECX
```

```
300 DEC PARRAY+1
310 MDECX DEC PARRAY
320 INX; INCREASE LABEL NAME SIZE COUNTER
330 JMP LPAR
340 ;----------------------
350 FOUNDONE LDA PARRAY; WE'VE LOCATED A LABEL NAME IN THE ARRAY
360 STA PT; REMEMBER IT'S STARTING LOCATION
370 LDA PARRAY+1
380 STA PT+1
390 LDA (PARRAY),Y
400 CMP WORK; COMPARE THE 1ST LETTER WITH THE 1ST LETTER OF THE TARGET WORD
410 BEQ LKMORE; LOOK MORE CLOSELY AT THE WORD, IF 1ST LETTER MATCHED
420 JMP STARTOVER; IF IT DIDN'T MATCH, GO DOWN IN THE TABLE & FIND NEXT WORD.
430 ;--------------------------
440 LKMORE INX; RAISE LENGTH COUNTER BY 1
450 STX WORK+1; REMEMBER IT
460 LDX #1
470 LDA BUFLAG;THIS MEANS THAT # OR ( COME BEFORE THE NAME IN THE BUFFER
480 BEQ LKM1; IF THEY DON'T WE DON'T NEED TO RAISE Y IN ORDER TO IGNORE THEM
490 INY
500 JSR DECPAR; LOWER THE INDEX TO COMPENSATE FOR THE INY
510 ;
520 LKM1 INY
530 LDA BUFFER,Y; CHECK BUFFER-HELD LABEL
540 BEQ FOUNDIT; IF WE'RE AT THE END OF THE WORD (Ø), THEN WE'VE FOUND A MATCH
550 CMP #48; OR THERE'S A MATCH IF IT'S A CHARACTER LOWER THAN ASCII Ø (,OR+)
560 BCC FOUNDIT
570 ; NOT YET THE END OF THE "BUFFER" HELD LABEL
580 INX
590 CMP (PARRAY),Y; IF ARRAY WORD STILL AGREES WITH BUFFER WORD, THEN
600 BEQ LKM1; CONTINUE LOOKING AT THESE WORDS
```

```
610 ;----------------------------  NO MATCH, SO LOOK AT NEXT WORD DOWN -----
620 STARTOVER LDA PT; PUT PREVIOUS WORD'S START ADDR. INTO POINTER
630 STA PARRAY
640 LDA PT+1
650 STA PARRAY+1
660 JSR DECPAR; LOWER POINTER BY 1 (STARTLK WILL LOWER IT ALSO, BELOW VALUE)
670 JMP STARTLK; TRY ANOTHER WORD IN THE ARRAY
680 ;-----------------------
690 ADONE LDA FOUNDFLAG
700 BMI AD1; DIDN'T FIND THE LABEL
710 RTS; ALL IS WELL.  RETURN TO EVAL.
720 AD1 LDA PASS
730 BNE AD1X; 2ND PASS-- GO AHEAD AND PRINT ERROR MESSAGE
740 BEQ ADONE1; ON 1ST PASS, MIGHT NOT YET BE DEFINED (RAISE INCSA/2S OR 3S)
750 AD1X JSR ERRING; LABEL NOT IN TABLE.  (TREAT IT AS A 2-BYTE ADDRESS)
760 JSR PRNTLINE
770 JSR PRNTSPACE
780 LDA #<NOLAB
790 STA TEMP
800 LDA #>NOLAB
810 STA TEMP+1
820 JSR PRNTMESS; RING BELL AND PRINT NOT FOUND MESSAGE
830 JSR PRNTCR
840 ADONE1 PLA
850 PLA;
860 LDA OP
870 AND #31
880 CMP #16
890 BEQ ADO2; CHECK IF BRANCH INSTRUCT.
900 LDA BYTFLAG
910 BNE ADO2; < OR > PSEUDO
920 JMP THREES
```

```
930 ADO2 JMP TWOS
940 ;
950 FOUNDIT CPX WORK+1;CHECK LABEL LENGTH AGAINST TARGET WORD LENGTH
960 BEQ FOUNDF; THEY MUST EQUAL TO SIGNIFY A MATCH. (PRINT/PRIN WOULD FAIL)
970 JMP STARTOVER; FAILED MATCH
980 FOUNDF INC FOUNDFLAG; RAISE FLAG TO ZERO (FIRST MATCH)
990 BEQ FOFX; IF HIGHER THAN Ø, PRINT DUPLICATION LABEL ERROR MESSAGE
1000 JSR DUPLAB
1010 FOFX LDY WORK+1
1020 LDA BUFLAG; COMPENSATE FOR # AND (
1030 BEQ FOF
1040 INY
1050 FOF LDA (PARRAY),Y; PUT TABLE LABEL'S VALUE IN RESULT
1060 STA RESULT
1070 INY
1080 LDA (PARRAY),Y
1090 STA RESULT+1
1100 LDA BYTFLAG
1110 BEQ CMPMO; IS IT > OR < PSEUDOPRINT
1120 CMP #2
1130 BNE AREND
1140 LDA RESULT+1; STORE HIGH BYTE INTO LOW BYTE
1150 STA RESULT
1160 CMPMO LDA PLUSFLAG; DO ADDITION + PSEUDO OP
1170 BEQ AREND
1180 CLC; ADD THE + NUMBER "ADDNUM" TO RESULT
1190 LDA ADDNUM
1200 ADC RESULT
1210 STA RESULT
1220 LDA ADDNUM+1
1230 ADC RESULT+1
1240 STA RESULT+1
```

```
1250 AREND LDA PASS; ON 2ND PASS, CHECK FOR DUPS
1260 BNE ARENX
1270 RTS; GO BACK TO EVAL
1280 ARENX JMP STARTOVER; ON PASS 2, LOOK FOR DUPS (SO CONTINUE IN ARRAY)
1290 ;------------------------------
1300 DECPAR LDA PARRAY; LOWER ARRAY POINTER BY 1
1310 BNE MDEC
1320 DEC PARRAY+1
1330 MDEC DEC PARRAY
1340 RTS
1350 ; ------------------
1360 DUPLAB JSR ERRING; RING BELL AND PRINT DUP LABEL MESSAGE
1370 LDA #<MDUPLAB
1380 STA TEMP
1390 LDA #>MDUPLAB
1400 STA TEMP+1
1410 JSR PRNTMESS
1420 JSR PRNTCR
1430 RTS;----------------------------------
1440 .FILE OPEN1
```

**Program D-5. Open1**

```
400 ; "OPEN1"   ---------- INPUT/OUTPUT --------------
470 ;-------------------------
480 ; LOAD "NAME"  (LOADS A PROGRAM FILE, A SOURCE CODE FILE INTO RAM)
490 ;-------------------------
500 LOAD1 LDA #0:STA $FF00:LDA #$FC:STA $D030; BANK 15/SLOW SPEED
505 JSR CLRCHN:LDA FNAMELEN:LDX #<FILEN:LDY #>FILEN
510 JSR SETNAME; POINT TO FILENAME
```

```
520 LDA #Ø:TAX:JSR $FF68; SETBANK TO Ø
530 LDA #Ø:LDX #8:TAY
540 JSR SETADDRESSES
550 LDA #Ø:TAX:LDY #$8Ø:JSR LOAD:BCS FERROR; SET TARGET ADDRESS TO $8ØØØ
610 JSR CLRCHN:LDA #Ø:STA $FFØØ
615 GOROUND LDA #$ØØ:STA PMEM:LDA #$8Ø:STA PMEM+1; POINT TO $8ØØØ FOR SOURCE
617 NIP LDA #$FC:STA $DØ3Ø:LDA #145:JSR PRINT:LDA #"D:JSR $CØ1E; CURSOR UP
618 LDA #145:JSR PRINT:LDA #"D:JSR $CØ1E:LDA #"@:JSR $CØ1E; CLEAR TO BOTTOM
620 RTS
630 FERROR JSR ERRING; DISK ERROR
640 LDA #$FC:STA $DØ3Ø:JMP TOBASIC
660 ;------------------------
1000 ; SAVE1 "NAME"  (SAVES RAM SOURCE CODE RESULTS TO A DISK FILE)
1001 ;------------------------
1005 SAV1 LDA #Ø:STA $FFØØ:LDA #$FC:STA $DØ3Ø; BANK 15/SLOW SPEED
1006 LDA #145:JSR PRINT:JSR PRINT:LDA #"D:JSR $CØ1E; CURSOR UP/CLEAR LINE
1010 LDA DNAMELEN:LDX #<DFILEN:LDY #>DFILEN
1020 JSR SETNAME; POINT TO FILENAME
1030 LDA #$Ø1:LDX #Ø:JSR $FF68; SET BANK TO 1
1040 LDA #Ø:LDX #8:LDY #Ø
1050 JSR SETADDRESSES
1055 LDA TA:STA TEMP:LDA TA+1:STA TEMP+1; SET UP TOP OF CODE POINTER
1060 LDA #<TEMP:LDX SA:LDY SA+1:JSR $FFD8:BCS FERROR
1070 JSR CLRCHN:LDA #Ø:STA $FFØØ
1080 JMP FINI;------------------------
2000 OPEN4 LDA #Ø:JSR SETNAME; OPEN FILE TO PRINTER
2010 LDX #Ø:JSR $FF68
2020 LDX #4:TXA:LDY #255:JSR SETADDRESSES
2030 JSR OPEN:BCS PRERROR
2040 JSR CLRCHN
2050 RTS
2060 PRERROR JSR PRINT; ERROR OPENING TO PRINTER;------------------------
```

```
2070 LDA ST
2080 BNE PREND
2090 JSR CHARIN
2100 BNE PRERROR
2110 PREND JSR ERRING:LDA #$FC:STA $D030:JMP TOBASIC;--------------------
6000 LOAD2 LDA FNAMELEN; LOAD LADS BACK IN AFTER ASSEMBLY IS OVER
6010 LDX #<FILEN:LDY #>FILEN:JSR SETNAME:LDA #0:LDX #0:JSR $FF68
6020 LDX #8:LDY #$FF:JSR SETADDRESSES:LDA #0:JSR LOAD:BCS LERR
6030 JSR CLRCHN:LDA #0:STA $FF00:RTS
6040 LERR JSR ERRING:LDA #$FC:STA $D030:JMP TOBASIC
6090 .FILE FINDMN
```

### Program D-6. Findmn

```
10 ; "FINDMN" -- LOOKS THROUGH MNEMONICS FOR MATCH TO LABEL.
20 ; WE JMP TO THIS FROM EVAL.  & JMP BACK TO 1 OF 2 LOCATIONS (JMP FOR SPEED)
30 FINDMN LDY #0
40 LDX #255; PREPARE X TO GO TO ZERO AT START OF LOOP
50 LOOP INX; X RAISED TO ZERO AT START OF LOOP
60 LDA MNEMONICS,Y; LOOK IN TABLE OF MNEMONICS
70 CMP LABEL; COMPARE IT TO 1ST SAVE. OF WORD IN LABEL BUFFER
80 BEQ MORE; IF =, COMPARE 2ND LETTERS OF TABLE VS. BUFFER
90 INY; OTHERWISE GO UP THREE IN THE TABLE TO FIND THE NEXT MNEMONIC
100 INY
110 INY
120 CPX #57; HAVE WE CHECKED ALL 56 MNEMONICS.
130 BNE LOOP; IF NOT, CONTINUE TRYING TO FIND A MATCH
140 NOMATCH JMP EQLABEL; DIDN'T FIND A MATCH (SO GO BACK TO EVAL)
150 MORE INY; COMPARE 2ND LETTER
160 LDA MNEMONICS,Y
170 CMP LABEL+1
```

```
180 BEQ MORE1; IF =, GO ON TO COMPARE 3RD AND FINAL LETTER
190 INY
200 INY
210 BNE LOOP; 2ND LETTER DIDN'T MATCH, TRY NEXT MNEMONIC (Y <> 0)
220 BEQ NOMATCH ; IF Y = 0, WE'VE GONE PAST TABLE (RETURN TO EVAL)
230 MORE1 INY; COMPARE 3RD LETTER
240 LDA MNEMONICS,Y
250 CMP LABEL+2
260 BEQ FOUND; IF 3RD LETTERS ARE =, WE'VE FOUND OUR MATCH
270 INY
280 BNE LOOP; OTHERWISE TRY NEXT MNEMONIC
290 BEQ NOMATCH
300 FOUND LDA LABEL+3; THE 4TH CHAR. MUST BE A BLANK FOR THIS TO BE A MNEMONIC
310 CMP #32
320 BEQ FO1; IF SO, STORE DATA ABOUT THIS MNEMONIC & RETURN TO EVAL.
330 CMP #0; OR IF END OF LINE, IT WOULD BE AN IMPLIED ADDR. MNEMONIC LIKE INY
340 BNE NOMATCH; OTHERWISE, NO MATCH FOUND (IT'S NOT A MNEMONIC).
350 FO1 LDA TYPES,X; STORE ADDR. TYPE.
360 STA TP
370 LDY OPS,X; STORE OPCODE
380 STY OP
390 END JMP EVAR; MATCH FOUND SO JUMP TO EVAR ROUTINE IN EVAL
400 .FILE GETSA
```

**Program D-7. Getsa**

```
5 ;"GETSA"---------------- POINTS TO START ADDRESS OF ENTIRE SOURCE CODE ---
10 MEMSA LDA #$00:STA PMEM:LDA #$1C:STA PMEM+1
20 T2 JSR CHARIN:JSR CHARIN:JSR CHARIN:JSR CHARIN; ADD 4 TO PMEM TO POINT TO *=
30 JSR CHARIN:CMP #172:BEQ MMSA
```

```
40 LDA #<MNOSTART:STA TEMP:LDA #>MNOSTART:STA TEMP+1:JSR PRNTMESS
50 JMP FIN; GO BACK TO BASIC VIA ROUTINE WITHIN EVAL
60 MMSA RTS
65 ;--------- MAIN SINGLE-BYTE INPUT FETCH ROUTINE -------------------
70 CHARIN INC PMEM:BNE INCP1:INC PMEM+1; NOPS REPLACED WITH LONG LOAD FOR DISKLADS
80 INCP1 STY Y:LDY #0:LDA (PMEM),Y:NOP:NOP:NOP:NOP:NOP:PHP:LDY Y:PLP:RTS
90 CHKIN RTS; REPLACES DISK ROUTINE IN DEFS
100 .FILE VALDEC
```

**Program D-8. Valdec**

```
10 ; "VALDEC"  TRANSLATE ASCII INPUT TO A TWO-BYTE INTEGER IN RESULT
15 ;
20 ;  SETUP/TEMP MUST POINT TO ASCII NUMBER (WHICH ENDS IN ZERO).
30 ;  RESULTS/ RESULT HOLDS 2-BYTE RESULT
40 ; -------------------------
50 VALDEC LDY #0
55 ; READ ASCII FROM LEFT TO RIGHT--INCREMENTING Y --(TO FIND LENGTH)
60 VGETZERO LDA (TEMP),Y
70 BEQ VZERO; 0 DELIMITER FOUND
80 INY
90 JMP VGETZERO;---------------  (FOR EXAMPLE, ASSUME ASCII IS "15")
110 VZERO STY VREND; SAVE LENGTH OF ASCII NUMBER  (IN THE EXAMPLE, LEN = 2)
120 DEY
130 LDA #0; CLEAN "RESULT" VARIABLE (SET TO 0)
140 STA RESULT
150 STA RESULT+1
160 LDX #1; USE "X" VARIABLE AS A MULTIPLY-X10-HOW-MANY-TIMES COUNTER
170 STX X
180 VALLOOP LDA (TEMP),Y; LOAD IN THE RIGHTMOST ASCII CHARACTER (EX: "5")
```

```
190 AND #$ØF; AS ASCII, 5 = $35.  O STRIP OFF THE 3, LEAVING THE 5.
200 STA RADD; STORE IN MULTIPLICATION REGISTER
210 STA TSTORE; STORE IN "REMEMBER IT" REGISTER
220 LDA #Ø; PUT Ø IN BOTH THESE REGISTERS (IN THEIR HIGH BYTES)
230 STA RADD+1
240 STA TSTORE+1;----------------- MULTIPLY X1Ø AS MUCH AS NECESSARY------
250 VLOOP DEX; LOWER THE COUNTER. (IN THE EXAMPLE, X NOW = Ø FOR 1ST CHAR)
260 BEQ VGOON; SO WE DON'T JSR TO THE X1Ø SUBROUTINE IN THIS CASE)
270 JSR TEN; OTHERWISE,WE'D MULTIPLY THE NUMBER X1Ø AS MANY TIMES AS NECESSARY
280 LDA RADD; MOVE RESULT OF MULTIPLICATION INTO STORAGE REGISTER
290 STA TSTORE
300 LDA RADD+1
310 STA TSTORE+1; SAVING RESULTS OF MOST RECENT MULTIPLICATION
320 JMP VLOOP; CONTINUE MULTIPLYING X1Ø UNTIL X IS DOWN TO ZERO.--------
330 VGOON INC X; RAISE X BY 1 (SINCE WE'RE MOVING LEFT AND EACH NUMBER WILL
335 ;                            BE 1ØX THE ONE TO ITS RIGHT).
340 LDX X
350 JSR VALADD; ADD RADD TO RESULT (ADD IN RESULTS OF THE MULTIPLICATION)
360 DEY; MOVE INDEX OVER BY 1 (TO POINT TO NEXT ASCII CHAR. TO THE LEFT)
370 DEC VREND; LOWER LENGTH POINTER.  IF IT'S NOT YET ZERO, THEN
380 BNE VALLOOP; CONTINUE PROCESSING THIS ASCII NUMBER
390 RTS; OTHERWISE RETURN TO CALLER.
400 ;---------------   MULTIPLY BY 1Ø
410 TEN CLC
420 ASL RADD;       MULTIPLY RADD X 4
430 ROL RADD+1
440 ASL RADD
450 ROL RADD+1;---------------
460 CLC
470 LDA TSTORE;PULL OUT ORIGINAL NUMBER AND ADD IT TO RESULT OF X4 (GIVING X5)
480 ADC RADD
490 STA RADD
```

```
500 LDA TSTORE+1
510 ADC RADD+1
520 STA RADD+1;------------ NOW, MULTIPLY X2.  ((N*4+N)*2) IS N*10
530 ASL RADD
540 ROL RADD+1
550 RTS
560 ;------------- ADD RESULTS OF THE MULTIPLICATION TO THE INTEGER ANSWER
570 VALADD CLC
580 LDA RADD
590 ADC RESULT
600 STA RESULT
610 LDA RADD+1
620 ADC RESULT+1
630 STA RESULT+1
640 RTS
650 .FILE INDISK
```

## Program D-9. Indisk

```
10 ; "INDISK" MAIN GET-INPUT-FROM-SOURCE CODE ROUTINE
20 ;SETUP/EXPECTS SA TO POINT TO 1ST CHAR IN A NEW LINE (OR BEYOND COLON)
30 ;RESULTS/EITHER FLAGS END OF PROG. OR FILLS LABEL+ WITH LINE OF CODE
40 ;-----------------
50 INDISK JSR CLEANLAB; FILL LABEL WITH ZEROS (ROUTINE IN EVAL)
60 LDY #0:STY Y
70 STY HEXFLAG; PUT HEXFLAG DOWN
80 STY BABFLAG; PUT COMMENTS FLAG DOWN
90 STY BYTFLAG; PUT FLAG SHOWING < OR > DOWN
100 STY PLUSFLAG; PUT ARITHMETIC PSEUDO OP (+) FLAG DOWN
110 LDA COLFLAG; IF THERE WAS A COLON JUST PRIOR TO THIS, REMOVE ANY BLANKS
```

```
120 BNE NOBLANKS; (THIS TAKES CARE OF: INY:  LDA 15:    LDX 17 TYPE ERRORS)
130 JSR CHARIN; OTHERWISE, PULL IN THE 1ST CHARACTER (FROM BANK 1 RAM)
140 STA LINEN; STORE LOW BYTE OF LINE NUMBER
150 JSR CHARIN
160 STA LINEN+1; STORE HIGH BYTE OF LINE NUMBER
170 NOBLANKS JSR CHARIN; ROUTINE TO ELIMINATE BLANKS FOLLOWING A COLON
175 BNE COOLOOK
176 JSR ENDPRO; THIS HANDLES COLONS PLACED ACCIDENTALLY AT END OF LINE
177 PLA:PLA:JMP STARTLINE
180 COOLOOK CMP #32; (OR FOLLOWING A LINE NUMBER)
190 BEQ NOBLANKS;---------------------------
200 JMP MOI1; SKIP TO CHECK FOR COLON (IT'S EQUIVALENT TO AN END OF LINE Ø)
210 STINDISK JSR CHARIN; ENTRY POINT WITHIN LINE (NOT AT START OF LINE)
220 MOINDI BNE MOI1; IF NOT ZERO, LOOK FOR COLON
230 JMP ENDPRO; FOUND A Ø END OF LINE. CHECK FOR END OF PROGRAM (3 ZEROS)
240 MOI1 CMP #58; IS IT A COLON
250 BNE XMO1; IF NOT, CHECK FOR SEMICOLON
260 JMP COLON; FOUND A COLON
270 XMO1 CMP #59; IS IT A SEMICOLON
280 BNE COMOA; IF NOT CONTINUE ON
290 STY A; FOUND A SEMICOLON (REM)
300 LDA PRINTFLAG; IF PRINTOUT NOT REQUESTED, THEN DON'T STORE THE REMARKS
310 BEQ PULLRX
320 STA BABFLAG; SET UP PRINT COMMENTS FLAG (A MUST BE > Ø AT THIS POINT)
330 LDA A; OTHERWISE, CHECK Y (SAVED ABOVE).  IF ZERO, IS A SEMICOLON AT
340 BEQ PUX; START OF THE LINE (NO LABELS OR MNEMONICS, JUST A BIG COMMENT)
350 JSR PULLREST; OTHERWISE SAVE COMMENTS FOLLOWING THE SEMICOLON
360 JMP MPULL; AND THEN RETURN TO EVAL ---------------------------
370 PUX JSR CHARIN; PUT NON-COMMENT DATA INTO LABEL BUFFER
380 BEQ PUX1; END OF LINE, SO EXIT
390 CMP #127; 7TH BIT NOT SET (SO IT'S NOT A KEYWORD IN BASIC)
400 BCC PUX2
```

```
410 JSR KEYWORD; IT IS A KEYWORD, SO EXTEND IT OUT AS AN ASCII WORD
420 PUX2 STA LABEL,Y; PUT THE CHAR. INTO THE MAIN BUFFER
430 INY
440 JMP PUX; RETURN TO LOOP FOR MORE CHARACTERS---------------------
450 PUX1 JSR PRNTLINE; PRINT THE LINE NUMBER
460 JSR PRNTSPACE; PRINT A SPACE
470 JSR PRNTINPUT; PRINT THE CHARACTERS IN THE LABEL BUFFER (MAIN BUFFER)
480 JSR PRNTCR; PRINT A CARRIAGE RETURN
490 LDA #Ø; SET A VARIABLE TO ZERO TO SIGNIFY NOTHING FOR EVAL TO EVALUATE
500 STA A
510 JMP MPULL; GO TO EXIT ROUTINE--------------------------------
520 PULLREST STA BABFLAG; PUT REMARKS INTO BABUF (BUFFER FOR COMMENTS)
530 ;                     THIS ROUTINE REMOVES (AND SAVES) COMMENTS
540 STA A; SET A VARIABLE TO SIGNIFY NOTHING FOR EVAL TO EVALUATE
550 LDY #Ø; SET OFFSET TO BABUF BUFFER FOR FILLING WITH COMMENTS
560 PAX1 JSR CHARIN; GET CHARACTER
570 BNE PAX; IF NOT ZERO, CONTINUE
580 STA BABUF,Y; OTHERWISE, WE'RE AT THE END OF THE COMMENT
590 LDY A
600 RTS; Y MUST HOLD OFFSET FOR ZERO FILL (ENDPRO)-----------------
610 PAX BPL PAXA; NOT A KEYWORD (7TH BIT NOT SET)
620 JSR KEYWAD; OTHERWISE, EXTEND KEYWORD INTO AN ASCII STRING
630 PAXA STA BABUF,Y; STORE CHAR. IN REMARK BUFFER
640 INY
650 JMP PAX1; RETURN TO LOOP TO GET ANOTHER CHARACTER--------------
660 PULLRX JSR CHARIN; JUST PULL IN REMARK CHARACTERS, IGNORING THEM
670 BEQ MPULL; LOOKING FOR THE END OF LINE ZERO
680 JMP PULLRX;-------------------------
690 MPULL JSR ENDPRO; CHECK FOR END OF PROGRAM AND THEN
700 LDA A; SEE IF Y = Ø.  IF SO, THE SEMICOLON WAS AT THE START OF A LINE
710 BNE MPULL1
```

```
720 PLA; Y = Ø SO JUMP BACK TO EVAL TO PREPARE TO GET NEXT LINE
730 PLA
740 JMP STARTLINE; SEMI AT START SO RETURN TO EVAL TO GET NEXT LINE---------
750 MPULL1 RTS; SEMICOLON, BUT NOT AT START OF LINE (RETURN TO CALLER)
760 COMOA CMP #177
770 BEQ HI; FOUND >
780 CMP #179
790 BEQ LO; FOUND <
800 CMP #170
810 BNE COMO
820 INC PLUSFLAG; FOUND +
830 COMO CMP #172
840 BNE COMO1
850 JMP STAR; FOUND *
860 COMO1 CMP #46
870 BEQ PSEUDOO; FOUND PSEUDO-OP
880 CMP #36
890 BEQ HEXX; FOUND HEX NUMBER
900 CMP #127; NOT A KEYWORD (7TH BIT NOT UP)
910 BCC ADDLAB
920 JSR KEYWORD; FOUND KEYWORD, SO EXTEND IT INTO AN ASCII STRING
930 ADDLAB STA LABEL,Y; PUT THE CHARACTER INTO THE MAIN BUFFER AND
940 INY; RAISE THE POINTER AND
950 JMP STINDISK; RETURN TO GET ANOTHER CHARACTER (BUT NOT A LINE NUMBER)
960 ;----------------------
970 COLON STA COLFLAG; SIGNIFY COLON BY SETTING COLFLAG
980 RTS;----------------------
990 PSEUDOO JMP PSEUDOJ; SPRINGBOARD TO PSEUDO-OP HANDLING ROUTINES
1000 HEXX STA LABEL,Y; SPRINGBOARD TO HEX NUMBER TRANSLATOR
1010 INY
1020 JMP HEX
```

```
1220 ;------------------ HANDLE > AND < PSEUDO-OPS
1230 HI LDA #2;       THE BYTFLAG HAS 3 POSSIBLE STATES:
1240 STA BYTFLAG;           Ø = LINE DOESN'T CONTAIN A > OR < PSEUDO
1250 JMP STINDISK;          1 = < (LOW BYTE) TYPE
1260 LO LDA #1;             2 = > (HIGH BYTE) TYPE
1270 STA BYTFLAG;       (ACTION IS TAKEN ON THIS PSEUDO-OP WITHIN THE
1280 JMP STINDISK;          EQUATE SUBPROGRAM).  O WE FETCH THE NEXT CHAR.
1290 ;------------------ HANDLE THE *= PSEUDO-OP (CHANGE THE PC)
1300 STAR JSR STINDISK
1325 LDA #$18:JSR PRINT
1330 LDA #42; PRINT *
1340 JSR PRINT
1350 JSR PRNTINPUT; PRINT STRING IN LABEL BUFFER
1360 JSR PRNTCR; PRINT CARRIAGE RETURN
1370 STARN LDA HEXFLAG; IF HEX, THE ARGUMENT HAS ALREADY BEEN FIGURED
1380 BNE STARR; SO JUMP OVER THIS NEXT PART
1390 LDY #Ø
1400 STAF LDA LABEL,Y
1410 CMP #32
1420 BEQ STAF1
1430 INY
1440 JMP STAF; FIND NUMBER (BY LOOKING FOR THE BLANK: *= 15)
1450 STAF1 INY
1460 STY TEMP; POINT TO ASCII NUMBER
1470 LDA #<LABEL
1480 CLC
1490 ADC TEMP
1500 STA TEMP
1510 LDA #>LABEL
1520 ADC #Ø
1530 STA TEMP+1
```

```
1540 JSR VALDEC; TRANSLATE ASCII NUMBER INTO INTEGER (IN RESULT)
1600 STARR LDA RESULT; PUT THE ARGUMENT OF *= INTO THE PC (SA)
1610 STA SA
1620 LDA RESULT+1
1630 STA SA+1
1640 PLA; PULL OFF THE RTS AND
1650 PLA
1660 JMP STARTLINE; RETURN TO EVAL FOR THE NEXT LINE OF CODE
1670 ;------------------ IS THIS THE END OF THE ENTIRE SOURCE CODE
1680 ENDPRO STA LABEL,Y; PUT THE ZERO (THAT SENT US HERE) INTO THE MAIN BUFFER
1690 INY
1700 CPY #80
1710 BNE ENDPRO; FILL REST OF BUFFER WITH 00S
1720 STA LABEL,Y
1730 JSR CHARIN; PULL IN THE NEXT 2 BYTES.  IF THEY ARE BOTH ZEROS, THEN
1740 JSR CHARIN; WE HAVE, IN FACT, FOUND THE END OF OUR SOURCE CODE FILE
1750 BEQ INEND; AND WE BEQ TO INEND
1760 LDA #0; OTHERWISE WE PUT THE COLFLAG (COLON) DOWN, BECAUSE THIS IS
1770 STA COLFLAG; AN END OF LINE CONDITION, NOT A COLON
1780 RTS; AND RETURN TO CALLER
1790 INEND LDA DISKFLAG:BEQ DEND:JMP SOUREND
1800 DEND LDA #1:STA ENDFLAG;SET END OF SOURCE CODE FLAG
1810 RTS; AND RETURN TO CALLER
1820 ;----------------------- CHANGE A HEX NUMBER TO A 2-BYTE INTEGER
1830 ; PULL IN NEXT FEW BYTES, TURNING THEM INTO AN INTEGER IN RESULT
1840 HEX LDX #0; PUTS INTEGER EQUIVALENT OF INCOMING HEX INTO RESULT
1850 H1 STX X:JSR CHARIN:PHP:LDX X:PLP
1860 BEQ DECI; END OF LINE (SO STOP LOOKING)
1870 CMP #58
1880 BEQ DECI; COLON (SO STOP LOOKING)
1890 CMP #32
```

```
1900 BEQ H1; BLANK CHARACTER SO KEEP LOOKING FOR END OF LINE
1910 CMP #59
1920 BEQ DECI; SEMICOLON (SO STOP LOOKING)
1930 CMP #44
1940 BEQ DECIT; COMMA (SO STOP LOOKING, BUT GO TO A DIFFERENT PLACE)
1950 CMP #41; (THIS "DIFFERENT PLACE" HANDLES A NOT-END-OF-LINE CONDITION).
1960 BEQ DECIT; CLOSE PARENTHESIS ) (SO STOP LOOKING)
1970 STA HEXBUF,X; OTHERWISE, PUT THE ASCII-STYLE-HEX CHAR. IN BUFFER AND
1980 INX; RAISE THE INDEX AND
1990 STA LABEL,Y; ALSO STORE IT INTO MAIN BUFFER FOR PRINTOUT AND
2000 INY; RAISE THIS INDEX TOO
2010 JMP H1; THEN KEEP ON PUTTING HEX NUMBER INTO HEXBUFFER-----------
2020 DECIT STX HEXLEN; SAVE LENGTH OF ASCII-HEX NUMBER
2030 STA LABEL,Y; FINISH STORING CHARS. INTO MAIN BUFFER (, OR ) IN THIS CASE)
2040 INY
2050 JSR STARTHEX; TRANSLATE ASCII-HEX NUMBER INTO INTEGER IN RESULT VARIABLE
2060 JMP STINDISK; RETURN TO PULL IN REST OF THE LINE;-----------
2070 DECI STA A; SAVE THE END OF LINE, COLON, OR SEMICOLON CHAR. FOR LATER
2080 LDA #0
2090 STX HEXLEN; SAVE LENGTH OF ASCII-HEX NUMBER
2100 STA LABEL,Y; FINISH STORING CHARS. INTO MAIN BUFFER (0 IN THIS CASE)
2110 JSR STARTHEX; TRANSLATE ASCII-HEX NUMBER INTO INTEGER IN RESULT VARIABLE
2120 LDA A; RETRIEVE 0 OR COLON OR SEMICOLON AND GO BACK UP TO MOINDI WHICH
2130 JMP MOINDI;----------------- BEHAVES ACCORDING TO WHICH SYMBOL A HOLDS.
2140 STARTHEX LDA #0;----------------- HEX-ASCII TO INTEGER TRANSLATOR------
2150 STA RESULT; SET RESULT TO ZERO
2160 STA RESULT+1
2170 TAX; SET X TO ZERO
2180 HXLOOP ASL RESULT; SHIFT AND ROLL (MOVES 2-BYTE BITS TO THE LEFT)-----
2190 ROL RESULT+1; DOING THIS 8 TIMES HAS THE EFFECT OF BRINGING IN
2200 ASL RESULT; THE ASCII NUMBER, 1 BYTE AT A TIME, AND TRANSFORMING IT
```

```
2210 ROL RESULT+1; INTO A 2-BYTE INTEGER WITHIN THIS 2-BYTE VARIABLE WE'RE
2220 ASL RESULT; CALLING "RESULT."
2230 ROL RESULT+1
2240 ASL RESULT
2250 ROL RESULT+1
2260 LDA HEXBUF,X; GET A BYTE FROM THE ASCII-HEX NUMBER
2270 CMP #65; IF IT'S LOWER THAN 65, IT'S NOT AN ALPHABETIC (A-F) HEX NUMBER
2280 BCC HXMORE; SO DON'T SUBTRACT 7 FROM IT
2290 SBC #7; BUT IF IT'S > 65, THEN -7.   = 65.  65-7 = 58.
2300 HXMORE AND #15; WHEN YOU 58 AND 15, YOU GET 10 (THE VALUE OF A)
2310 ORA RESULT; #15 (00001111) AND #58 (00111010)  = 00001010 (TEN)
2320 STA RESULT; PUT THE BYTE INTO RESULT
2330 INX; RAISE THE INDEX
2340 CPX HEXLEN; ARE WE AT THE END OF OUR ASCII-HEX NUMBER
2350 BNE HXLOOP; IF NOT, CONTINUE
2360 INC HEXFLAG; IF SO, RAISE HEXFLAG (TO SHOW RESULT HAS THE ANSWER)
2370 LDA #1; AND RETURN TO CALLER
2380 RTS
2390 ;-----------------------
2400 ; HANDLE PSEUDOS.  (.BYTE TYPES)
2410 PSEUDOJ CPY #0; IF Y = 0 THEN IT'S NOT A PC LABEL LIKE (LABEL .BYTE 0 0)
2420 BEQ PSE2
2430 LDX PASS; OTHERWISE, ON 1ST PASS, STORE LABEL NAME AND PC ADDR. IN ARRAY
2440 BNE PSE2
2450 PHA; SAVE A AND Y REGISTERS
2460 TYA
2470 PHA
2480 JSR EQUATE; NAME AND PC ADDR. STORED IN ARRAY
2490 PLA; PULL OUT A AND Y REGISTERS (RESTORE THEM)
2500 TAY
2510 PLA
```

```
2520 PSE2 STA LABEL,Y; STORE . CHAR.
2530 INY
2540 JSR CHARIN; GET CHAR. FOLLOWING THE PERIOD (.)
2550 STA LABEL,Y
2560 INY
2570 CMP #66; IS IT "B" FOR .BYTE
2580 BNE PSEUD1; WASN'T .BYTE
2590 LDA #0; RESET FLAG WHICH WILL DISTINGUISH BETWEEN .BYTE 0 AND .BYTE "A
2600 STA BNUMFLAG; " TYPE, OR 00 08 15 172 TYPE (THE TWO .BYTE TYPES)
2610 LDA PASS; PRINT NOTHING TO SCREEN ON PASS 1
2620 BEQ CLB
2630 STY YY; SAVE Y REGISTER (OUR INDEX)
2640 ;                          NOW WE REPLICATE THE ACTIONS OF INLINE (IN EVAL)
2650 LDA SFLAG; SHOULD WE PRINT TO SCREEN
2660 BEQ CLB; NO
2670 JSR PRNTLINE; YES, PRINT LINE NUMBER
2680 JSR PRNTSPACE; PRINT SPACE
2690 JSR PRNTSA; PRINT PC ADDRESS
2700 JSR PRNTSPACE; PRINT SPACE
2710 LDY YY; RECOVER Y INDEX
2720 CLB JSR CHARIN; PULL IN CHARACTER FROM BANK 0
2730 STA LABEL,Y; STORE IN MAIN BUFFER
2740 INY
2750 CMP #32; IS IT A SPACE
2760 BNE CLB; IF NOT, CONTINUE PULLING IN MORE CHARACTERS------------
2770 JSR CHARIN; (WE'RE LOOKING FOR THE 1ST SPACE AFTER .BYTE)
2780 STA LABEL,Y; STORE FOR PRINTING
2790 INY
2800 CMP #34; IS THE CHARACTER A QUOTE (").IF SO, IT'S A .BYTE "ABCD TYPE
2810 BNE BNUMWERK; OTHERWISE IT'S NOT THE " TYPE
2820 BY1 JSR CHARIN;----------  HANDLE ASCII STRING .BYTE TYPES
```

```
2830 BNE BY2
2840 JMP BENDPRO; FOUND A Ø END OF LINE (OR PROGRAM)
2850 BY2 CMP #58; FOUND A COLON "END OF LINE"
2860 BNE BY2X
2870 JMP BEN1; FOUND A COLON
2880 BY2X CMP #59; FOUND A SEMICOLON "END OF LINE"
2890 BNE BY3
2900 JSR PULLREST; STORE COMMENTS IN COMMENT BUFFER (BABUF)
2910 LDX PRINTFLAG; IF NO PRINTOUT REQUESTED, THEN
2920 STX BABFLAG; DON'T PRINT COMMENTS
2930 JMP BENDPRO; A SEMICOLON SO END THIS ROUTINE IN THAT WAY.
2940 BY3 CMP #34; HAVE WE FOUND A CONCLUDING QUOTE (")
2950 BNE BY3X
2960 JMP BY1; FOUND A " SO IGNORE IT
2970 BY3X LDX PASS; ON PASS 1, JUST RAISE PC COUNTER (INCSA); DON'T POKE IT.
2980 BNE PSLOOP
2990 JSR INCSA
3000 JMP BY1;------------------
3010 PSEUD1 JMP PSEUDO; SOME OTHER PSEUDO TYPE, NOT .BYTE (A SPRINGBOARD)
3020 PSLOOP STA LABEL,Y; STORE A CHARACTER IN MAIN BUFFER;-------------
3030 TAX
3040 STY Y; SAVE Y INDEX
3050 JSR POKEIT; PASS 2, SO POKE IT INTO MEMORY (THE ASCII CHARACTER)
3060 LDY Y; RESTORE Y
3070 INY; RAISE INDEX AND
3080 JMP BY1; GET NEXT CHARACTER
3090 BNUMWERK LDX #Ø;-------- HANDLE .BYTE 1 2 3 (NUMERIC TYPE)
3100 STX BFLAG; PUT DOWN BFLAG (END OF LINE SIGNAL)
3110 STA NUBUF,X; WE'RE BORROWING THE NUBUF FOR THIS ROUTINE.
3120 INX
3130 WERK1 LDA BFLAG; IF BFLAG IS UP, WE'RE DONE.
3140 BNE BBEND; SO GO TO END ROUTINE
```

```
3150 WK0 STX X:JSR CHARIN:PHP:LDX X:PLP; OTHERWISE, GET A CHARACTER
3160 BEQ BSFLAG; IF ZERO (END OF LINE) SET BFLAG UP.
3170 CMP #58; LIKEWISE IF COLON
3180 BEQ BSFLAG
3190 CMP #59; SEMICOLON REQUIRES THAT WE FIRST FILL THE COMMENT BUFFER
3200 BNE WK1;        BEFORE SETTING THE BFLAG (IN THE BSFLAG ROUTINE)
3210 JSR PULLREST; HERE'S WHERE THE COMMENT BUFFER IS FILLED
3220 LDX PRINTFLAG; IF NO PRINTOUT REQUESTED, THEN
3230 STX BABFLAG; DON'T PRINT COMMENTS
3240 JMP BSFLAG; FOUND SEMICOLON
3250 WK1 STA BUFM; PUT CHAR. INTO "BUFM" BUFFER
3260 LDA PASS; ON PASS 1, RAISE THE PC ONLY (INCSA), NO POKES
3270 BNE WERK5
3280 LDA BUFM
3290 CMP #32; IS IT A SPACE
3300 BNE WERK1; IF NOT, RETURN FOR MORE OF THE NUMBER (0 VS 555)
3310 JSR INCSA; RAISE PC COUNTER BY 1
3320 JMP WERK1; GET NEXT NUMBER
3330 WERK5 LDA BUFM; PUT CHAR. INTO PRINTOUT MAIN BUFFER
3340 STA LABEL,Y
3350 INY
3360 CMP #32; IS IT A SPACE
3370 BEQ WERK2
3380 CMP #0; IS IT END OF LINE
3390 BEQ WERK2
3400 CMP #58; IS IT COLON
3410 BEQ WERK2
3420 STA NUBUF,X; OTHERWISE, STORE IT
3430 INX
3440 JMP WERK1; AND RETURN FOR MORE OF THE NUMBER----------------
3450 BSFLAG INC BFLAG; RAISE UP THE END OF LINE FLAG
```

```
3460 STA BUFM+1; SAVE COLON, SEMICOLON, OR WHATEVER FOR LATER USE
3470 JMP WK1; RETURN FOR MORE (BUT THIS TIME IT WILL END LINE);---------
3480 WERK2 LDA #<NUBUF; POINT TO THE ASCII NUMBER STORED IN BABUF
3490 STA TEMP
3500 LDA #>NUBUF
3510 STA TEMP+1
3520 STY Y
3530 JSR VALDEC; TURN THE ASCII INTO AN INTEGER IN RESULT
3540 LDX RESULT
3550 JSR POKEIT; POKE THE RESULT INTO MEMORY (OR DISK OBJECT FILE)
3560 LDY Y; ERASE THE NUMBER IN HEXBUF
3570 LDA #0
3580 LDX #5
3590 CLEX STA NUBUF,X
3600 DEX
3610 BNE CLEX
3620 JMP WERK1; AND THEN RETURN TO FETCH THE NEXT NUMBER;--------------
3630 BBEND LDA PASS; END .BYTE LINE.  ON PASS 1, RAISE PC (POKEIT RAISES IT
3640 BNE BBEND1;                      ON PASS 2).
3650 JSR INCSA
3660 BBEND1 LDA BUFM+1; IF END OF LINE SIGNAL WAS A COLON, THEN
3670 CMP #58
3680 BEQ BEN1; DON'T LOOK FOR LINE NUMBER OR END OF SOURCE CODE FILE (ENDPRO)
3690 BENDPRO JSR ENDPRO
3700 BEN1 STA COLFLAG; SET IT (COLON) OR NOT (ENDPRO RETURNS WITH 0 IN A)
3710 INC LOCFLAG; RAISE PRINT-A-PC-LABEL FLAG
3720 PLA; PULL RTS FROM STACK
3730 PLA
3740 LDA PASS; ON PASS 1, DON'T PRINT ANY COMMENTS
3750 BEQ NOPR
3760 LDA SFLAG; IF SCREENFLAG IS DOWN, DON'T PRINT ANY COMMENTS
```

```
3770 BEQ NOPR
3780 JMP PRMMFIN; BACK TO EVAL (WHERE COMMENTS ARE PRINTED)
3790 NOPR JMP STARTLINE; BACK TO EVAL (BYPASSING PRINTOUT)
4080 ;---------------------- BELOW. THIS STORES KEYWORDS TO COMMENT BUFFER
4090 KEYWAD PHA; SEE KEYWORD BELOW. THIS STORES KEYWORDS TO COMMENT BUFFER
4100 LDA #<BABUF:STA AUT+1:LDA #>BABUF:STA AUT+2:PLA:JSR KEYWORD
4110 RESTKEY PHA:LDA #<LABEL:STA AUT+1:LDA #>LABEL:STA AUT+2:PLA:RTS
4270 ;------------------
4271 SOUREND LDA #<DMES:STA TEMP:LDA #>DMES:STA TEMP+1:JSR PRNTMESS:JMP FIN
4330 ;-------- TRANSLATE A SINGLE-BYTE KEYWORD TOKEN INTO ASCII STRING
4340 KEYWORD STY A:SEC; FIND NUMBER OF KEYWORD (IS IT 1ST, 5TH, OR WHAT)
4350 SBC #$7F
4362 LDY #$17:STY KSTOR:LDY #$44:STY KSTOR+1
4370 CMP #$4F:BNE KM
4372 LDY #$C9:STY KSTOR:LDY #$46:STY KSTOR+1:JSR CHARIN:TAY:DEY:TYA:JMP KM1
4380 KM CMP #$7F:BNE KM1
4381 LDY #$09:STY KSTOR:LDY #$46:STY KSTOR+1:JSR CHARIN:TAY:DEY:TYA
4382 KM1 TAX:LDY #0
4390 KLP DEX:BEQ FOUNDK
4400 FINDSHIFT LDA (KSTOR),Y:PHA:INC KSTOR:BNE SKP:INC KSTOR+1:SKP PLA
4410 BPL FINDSHIFT
4420 BMI KLP
4422 FOUNDK LDX A:LDY #0
4430 FOUNDK1 LDA (KSTOR),Y:BMI DNN
4440 AUT STA LABEL,X:INY:INX:BNE FOUNDK1
4450 DNN AND #$7F:STX Y:LDY Y:RTS
4460 YY .BYTE 0; TEMPORARY HOLDING PLACE FOR Y
4500 .FILE MATH
```

## Program D-10. Math

```
10 ; "MATH"  THIS ROUTINE HANDLES +   IT COMES FROM EVAL AFTER INDISK
20 ; IT LEAVES THE INTENDED ADDITION IN THE VARIABLE "ADDNUM"
30 ; (ADDNUM IS ADDED TO "RESULT" IN THE VALDEC SUBPROGRAM)
40 MATH LDY #Ø; SET INDEXES TO ZERO
50 LDX #Ø
60 MATH1 LDA LABEL,Y; LOOK FOR LOCATION OF "+" SYMBOL--------
70 CMP #43
80 BEQ MATH2
90 INY
100 JMP MATH1;------------- NOW POINT TO 1ST NUMBER FOLLOWING +
110 MATH2 INY
120 LDA LABEL,Y
130 JSR RANGECK; CHECK TO SEE IF THIS IS BETWEEN 48 - 58 (ASCII FOR Ø-9)
140 BCS VALIT; IF NOT, EXIT THIS ROUTINE (WE'VE STORED THE NUMBER AND HAVE
150 STA HEXBUF,X; LOCATED SOMETHING OTHER THAN AN ASCII NUMBER)
160 INX; KEEP STORING VALID ASCII NUMBERS IN HEXBUF BUFFER
170 JMP MATH2;-------------------
180 RANGECK CMP #58;-------------- IS THIS >47 AND <58
190 BCS MATH3
200 SEC
210 SBC #48
220 SEC
230 SBC #208; IS IT > 47 & < 58
240 MATH3 RTS
250 VALIT LDA #Ø;---------- TURN IT FROM ASCII INTO A 2-BYTE INTEGER
260 STA HEXBUF,X; PUT ZERO AT END OF ASCII NUMBER (AS DELIMITER)
270 LDA #<HEXBUF; POINT "TEMP" POINTER TO ASCII NUMBER IN BUFFER
280 STA TEMP
290 LDA #>HEXBUF
```

```
300 STA TEMP+1
310 JSR VALDEC; ROUTINE WHICH TURNS ASCII NUMBER INTO INTEGER IN "RESULT"
320 LDA RESULT; MOVE RESULT TO TEMPORARY ADDITION VARIABLE, "ADDNUM"
330 STA ADDNUM
340 LDA RESULT+1
350 STA ADDNUM+1
360 RTS; RETURN TO CALLER
370 .FILE PRINTOPS
```

### Program D-11. Printops

```
10 ; "PRINTOPS"   PRINTS & POKES VALUES (BOTH OPCODES & ARGUMENTS)
20 FORMAT LDA PASS; ON PASS 2, IGNORE INCSA (RAISES PC) SINCE
30 BNE PRM; ON PASS 2, WE JSR TO POKEIT (IT GOES TO INCSA)
40 JSR INCSA; BUT ON PASS 1, WE DON'T PRINT OR POKE ANYTHING, WE JUST
50 RTS; RAISE THE PC AND RETURN --------------
60 PRM LDA SFLAG; SHOULD WE PRINT TO SCREEN
70 BEQ PRMX; IF NOT, SKIP THIS NEXT PART (PRINT TO SCREEN)
80 JSR CLRCHN; OTHERWISE, RESET NORMAL I/O CONDITION
110 LDX OP; LOAD THE OPCODE
120 JSR PRNTNUM; PRINT IT
130 JSR PRNTSPACE; PRINT A SPACE
140 PRMX LDX OP;----------- NOW POKE THE OPCODE INTO RAM/DISK MEMORY
150 JSR POKEIT
160 RTS;----------------------------------------
170 ; PRINT TWO BYTES (THE OPCODE AND A 1-BYTE ARGUMENT)-----------------
180 PRINT2 LDA PASS; ON PASS 2, WE SKIP INCSA (SEE LINE 20 ABOVE)
190 BNE P2M
200 JSR INCSA
210 RTS;--------------------
```

```
220 P2M LDA SFLAG; IF SCREEN PRINT FLAG IS DOWN, SKIP PRINTING TO SCREEN
230 BEQ P2MX
240 LDX RESULT; OTHERWISE PRINT THE LOW-BYTE OF "RESULT" (THE ARGUMENT)
250 JSR PRNTNUM
260 P2MX LDX RESULT; AND ALSO POKE THE LOW-BYTE TO RAM BANK 1
270 JMP POKEIT; A JMP TO POKEIT WILL RTS US BACK TO THE CALLER------------
280 ; PRINT THREE BYTES (THE OPCODE AND A 2-BYTE ARGUMENT)-----------------
290 PRINT3 LDA PASS; ON PASS 2, SKIP INCSA (SEE LINE 20 ABOVE)
300 BNE P3M
310 JSR INCSA; RAISE PC BY 2
320 JSR INCSA
330 RTS;--------------------
340 P3M LDA SFLAG; SHOULD WE PRINT TO SCREEN
350 BEQ P3MX
360 LDX RESULT; PRINT AND POKE LOW BYTE OF ARGUMENT
370 JSR PRNTNUM
380 P3MX LDX RESULT
390 JSR POKEIT
400 LDA SFLAG; SHOULD WE PRINT TO SCREEN
410 BEQ P3MXX
420 LDA HXFLAG; ARE WE PRINTING OPCODES AND ARGUMENTS IN HEX
430 BEQ P3MX2; IF SO, DON'T PRINT A SPACE HERE
440 JSR PRNTSPACE; OTHERWISE, PRINT A SPACE
450 P3MX2 LDX RESULT+1; PRINT AND POKE THE HIGH BYTE OF THE ARGUMENT
460 JSR PRNTNUM
470 P3MXX LDX RESULT+1
480 JMP POKEIT; AND A JUMP TO POKEIT WILL RTS US BACK TO CALLER
490 POKEIT STX WORK+1;-------------POKE IN A BYTE TO RAM ---------------
500 LDA POKEFLAG; ARE WE SUPPOSED TO POKE TO RAM
510 BEQ INCSA; IF NOT, SKIP IT
515 T3 NOP:NOP:NOP:NOP:NOP;LDA #<SA:STA $02B9; STA(LONG) REPLACES NOPS
520 LDY #0; OTHERWISE, SEND THE BYTE TO RAM MEMORY AT CURRENT PC ADDRESS (SA)
```

```
530 T4 TXA:STA (SA),Y
541 NOP:NOP:NOP;JSR $FF77 IF DISKLADS FOR LONG STORE
650 INCSA CLC;------------------- RAISE THE PC COUNTER (SA) BY 1 --------
660 INC SA:BNE RDS:INC SA+1
720 RDS RTS
730 ;----------------------- PRINTOUT ROUTINES (TO SCREEN) ----------
740 PRNTMESS LDY #Ø; PRINT A MESSAGE (ERRORS USUALLY) TO THE SCREEN
750 MESSLOOP LDA (TEMP),Y; THESE MESSAGES ARE DELIMITED BY Ø AND ARE POINTED
760 BEQ MESSDONE; TO BY THE VARIABLE "TEMP"
770 JSR $C72D;  FAST PRINT TO SCREEN
780 JSR PTP; AFTER PRINTING A CHARACTER TO SCREEN, CHECK TO SEE IF IT SHOULD
790 INY;                     ALSO BE PRINTED TO THE PRINTER
800 JMP MESSLOOP
810 MESSDONE RTS;----------------------------
820 PRNTSPACE LDA #32; PRINT A SPACE CHARACTER
830 JSR $C72D; FAST PRINT TO SCREEN
840 JSR PTP; SEE IF IT SHOULD ALSO GO TO THE PRINTER
850 RTS;---------------------------------------
860 PRNTNUM STX X; PRINT A NUMBER (LOW BYTE IN X, HIGH BYTE IN A)
870 LDA HXFLAG; IF WE'RE PRINTING IN HEX, NOT DECIMAL, THEN
880 BEQ PRNTNUMD; USE THE HEXPRINT SUBROUTINE.  OTHERWISE, GO TO PRNTNUMD
890 TXA
900 JSR HEXPRINT
910 JSR PTPNU; CHECK IF NUMBER SHOULD BE PRINTED TO PRINTER AS WELL
920 LDX X; RESTORE NUMBER IN X BEFORE
930 RTS; RETURNING TO CALLER-------------------------
940 PRNTNUMD LDA #Ø; PRINT A DECIMAL NUMBER
950 JSR OUTNUM; BASIC'S LINE NUMBER PRINTOUT ROUTINE
960 JSR PTPNU; SHOULD WE ALSO PRINT IT TO PRINTER
970 LDX X; RESTORE VALUE IN X BEFORE
980 RTS; RETURNING TO THE CALLER ---------------------------------
```

```
990 PRNTSA LDA HXFLAG; PRINT THE SA (PC, PROGRAM COUNTER)
1000 BEQ PRNTSAD; IF NOT HEX PRINTOUT, THEN USE DECIMAL ROUTINE BELOW
1010 LDA SA+1; OTHERWISE, PRINT LOW AND HIGH BYTES OF SA (AS HEX)
1020 JSR HEXPRINT; HIGH BYTE 1ST
1030 LDA SA
1040 JSR HEXPRINT
1050 JSR PTPSA; SHOULD WE ALSO PRINT SA TO PRINTER
1060 RTS;-----------------
1070 PRNTSAD LDX SA; PRINT SA (DECIMAL VERSION)
1080 LDA SA+1
1090 JSR OUTNUM
1100 JSR PTPSA; PRINT TO PRINTER, TOO
1110 RTS;--------------------------------------------------
1120 PRNTCR LDA #13;                         PRINT A CARRIAGE RETURN
1130 JSR $C72D; FAST PRINT TO SCREEN
1140 JSR PTP; SHOULD WE DO IT ON THE PRINTER TOO
1150 RTS;--------------------------------------------------
1160 PRNTLINE LDX LINEN;                     PRINT A SOURCE CODE LINE NUMBER
1170 LDA LINEN+1
1180 JSR OUTNUM; BASIC ROUTINE (LOW BYTE IN X, HIGH IN A)
1190 JSR PTPLI; SHOULD WE ALSO PRINT LINE NUMBER TO PRINTER
1200 RTS; -------------------------------------------------
1210 PRNTINPUT LDA #<LABEL;                  PRINT CONTENTS OF MAIN INPUT
1220 STA TEMP;                               BUFFER ("LABEL")
1230 LDA #>LABEL; POINT "TEMP" TO THE BUFFER AND THEN
1240 STA TEMP+1
1250 JSR PRNTMESS; USE GENERAL MESSAGE PRINTING ROUTINE
1260 RTS
1270 ;-------------------------   ERROR PRINTOUT PREPARATIONS
1280 ERRING LDA #7; RING BELL
1290 JSR PRINT:JSR PRINT:JSR PRINT
1300 LDA #18; TURN ON REVERSE PRINTING TO HIGHLIGHT ERROR
```

```
1310 JSR PRINT
1320 JSR PRNTINPUT; PRINT CONTENTS OF MAIN INPUT BUFFER
1330 LDA #13; PRINT A CARRIAGE RETURN
1340 JSR PRINT:INC EFLAG
1350 RTS
1360 ;------------------------------------- PRINTOUT (TO PRINTER)
1370 ;(PTP PRINTS A SINGLE CHARACTER TO THE PRINTER).
1380 PTP JSR SAVEEM:LDX PASS; ON PASS 1, DO NO PRINTING TO PRINTER
1390 BNE PTP1
1400 LDX X:RTS
1410 PTP1 LDX PRINTFLAG; IF PRINTFLAG IS DOWN, DO NOTHING, RETURN TO CALLER
1420 BNE MPTP
1430 LDX X:RTS;---------
1440 MPTP JSR CLRCHN;
1460 LDX #4
1470 JSR CHKOUT
1480 LDA A; RECOVER A
1490 JSR PRINT; PRINT TO PRINTER
1500 JSR CLRCHN; RESTORE NORMAL I/O
1530 RETT JSR GETEM;RECOVER REGS
1540 RTS; RETURN TO CALLER
1550 ;--------------------   NUMBERS TO PRINTER
1560 PTPNU JSR SAVEEM:LDX PASS; SAME LOGIC AS LINES 1350+ ABOVE
1570 BNE PTPN1
1580 LDX X:RTS
1590 PTPN1 LDX PRINTFLAG
1600 BNE MPTPN
1610 LDX X:RTS
1620 MPTPN JSR SAVEEM:JSR CLRCHN
1630 LDX #4
1640 JSR CHKOUT
```

```
165Ø LDA HXFLAG; HEX OR DECIMAL MODE
166Ø BEQ MPTPND
167Ø LDA X
168Ø JSR HEXPRINT
169Ø JMP FINPTP
17ØØ MPTPND LDA #Ø
171Ø LDX X
172Ø JSR OUTNUM
173Ø FINPTP JSR CLRCHN:JSR GETEM
176Ø RTS
177Ø ;------------------- SA TO PRINTER
178Ø PTPSA JSR SAVEEM:LDX PASS; SAME LOGIC AS LINES 135Ø+ ABOVE
179Ø BNE PTPS1
18ØØ LDX X:RTS
181Ø PTPS1 LDX PRINTFLAG
182Ø BNE MPTPSA
183Ø LDX X:RTS
184Ø MPTPSA JSR CLRCHN
185Ø LDX #4
186Ø JSR CHKOUT
187Ø LDX HXFLAG; HEX OR DECIMAL PRINTOUT
188Ø BEQ MPTPSAD
189Ø LDA SA+1
19ØØ JSR HEXPRINT
191Ø LDA SA
192Ø JSR HEXPRINT
193Ø JMP FINPTPSA
194Ø MPTPSAD LDA SA+1
195Ø LDX SA
196Ø JSR OUTNUM
197Ø FINPTPSA JSR CLRCHN:JSR GETEM
2ØØØ RTS
```

```
2010 ;------------------ LINE NUMBER TO PRINTER
2020 PTPLI JSR SAVEEM:LDX PASS; SAME LOGIC AS LINES 1350+ ABOVE
2030 BNE PTPL1
2040 LDX X:RTS
2050 PTPL1 LDX PRINTFLAG
2060 BNE MPTPL
2070 LDX X:RTS
2080 MPTPL JSR CLRCHN
2090 LDX #4
2100 JSR CHKOUT
2110 LDA LINEN+1
2120 LDX LINEN
2130 JSR OUTNUM
2140 JSR CLRCHN:JSR GETEM
2170 RTS
2180 ;-------------------------------------- HEX NUMBER PRINTOUT
2190 ; PRINT THE NUMBER IN THE ACCUMULATOR AS A HEX DIGIT (AS ASCII CHARS.)
2200 HEXPRINT PHA; STORE NUMBER
2210 AND #$0F; CLEAR HIGH BITS (10101111 BECOMES 00001111, FOR EXAMPLE)
2220 TAY; NOW WE KNOW WHICH POSITION IN THE STRING OF HEX NUMBERS ("HEXA")
2230 LDA HEXA,Y; THIS NUMBER IS.  SO PULL IT OUT AS AN ASCII CHARACTER
2240 ; (HEXA LOOKS LIKE THIS: "0123456789ABCDEF")
2250 TAX; SAVE LOW-BITS VALUE INTO X
2260 PLA; PULL OUT THE ORIGINAL NUMBER, BUT THIS TIME
2270 LSR;SHIFT RIGHT 4 TIMES (MOVING THE 4 HIGH BITS INTO THE 4 LOW BITS AREA)
2280 LSR; (10101111 BECOMES 00001010, FOR EXAMPLE)
2290 LSR
2300 LSR
2310 TAY; AGAIN, PUT POSITION OF THIS VALUE INTO THE Y INDEX
2320 LDA HEXA,Y; PULL OUT THE RIGHT ASCII CHARACTER FROM "HEXA" STRING
2330 JSR PRINT; PRINT HIGH VALUE (FIRST) (A HOLDS HIGH VALUE AFTER LINE 2280)
```

```
2340 TXA; (X HELD LOW VALUE AFTER LINE 2210)
2350 JSR PRINT; PRINT LOW VALUE
2360 RTS; RETURN TO CALLER
2370 SAVEEM STA A:STY Y:RTS
2380 GETEM LDA A:LDY Y:RTS
2500 .FILE PSEUDO
```

### Program D-12. Pseudo

```
10 ; "PSEUDO" HANDLE ALL PSEUDOPS EXCEPT .BYTE
15 ;
20 ; JMP HERE FROM INDISK
30 ; (INDISK WAS JSR'ED TO FROM EVAL). / Y HOLDS POINTER TO LABEL
40 ; -------------------------
50 PSEUDO CMP #70; IS IT "F" FOR .FILE
60 BNE PSE1
70 JSR FILE; F MEANS GO TO NEXT LINKED FILE -----------------
80 GOBACK PLA; RETURN TO EVAL TO GET NEXT LINE
90 PLA
100 JMP STARTLINE;-------------------------
110 PSE1 CMP #128; IS IT .END
120 BNE PSEE
130 JSR PEND; 128 IS TOKEN FOR END (END OF CHAIN PSEUDO)
140 JMP GOBACK; RETURN TO EVAL
150 PSEE CMP #68; IS IT "D" FOR .DISK (CREATE OBJECT CODE FILE ON DISK)
160 BNE PSEE1
170 JMP PDISK; OPEN FILE ON DISK FOR OBJECT CODE STORAGE
180 PSEE1 CMP #80; IS IT "P" FOR .P (PRINTER OUTPUT)
190 BNE PSEE2
200 JMP PPRINTER; TURN ON PRINTER LISTING
210 PSEE2 CMP #78; IS IT "N" FOR .NH OR .NS OR SOME OTHER "TURN IT OFF"
```

```
220 BNE PSEE3
230 JMP NIX; TURN SOMETHING OFF
240 PSEE3 CMP #79; IS IT "O" FOR OUTPUT (POKE OBJECT CODE INTO RAM)
250 BNE PSEE4
260 JMP OPON; START POKING OBJECT CODE (DEFAULT)
270 PSEE4 CMP #83; IS IT "S" FOR PRINT TO SCREEN
280 BNE PSEE5
290 JMP SCREIN; TURN ON SCREEN PRINTING
300 PSEE5 CMP #72; IS IT "H" FOR HEX NUMBERS DURING PRINTOUTS
310 BNE PSE9;
320 JMP HEXIT; TURN ON HEX PRINTING
330 ;-------------------------  PRINT ERROR MESSAGE (NO SUCH PSEUDO-OP)
340 PSE9 STA LABEL,Y; STORE CHAR. FOR PRINTOUT
350 JSR PRNTLINE
360 JSR PRNTSPACE
370 JSR PRNTSA
380 JSR ERRING
390 JSR PRNTINPUT
400 LDA #<MERROR
410 STA TEMP
420 LDA #>MERROR
430 STA TEMP+1
440 JSR PRNTMESS
450 JSR PRNTCR
460 JMP PULLINE; PULL IN (& IGNORE) REST OF LINE, THEN BACK TO EVAL
470 ;-------------------------  HANDLE .FILE PSEUDO-OP ----------------
480 FILE JSR CHARIN
490 CMP #32; LOOK FOR END OF THE WORD .FILE (TO LOCATE FILENAME)
500 BEQ FI0
510 JMP FILE; CONTINUE LOOKING FOR BLANK
520 FI0 LDY #0
530 FI1 JSR CHARIN
```

```
540 CMP #0; END OF LINE
550 BEQ FI2
560 CMP #127; KEYWORD, SO STRETCH IT OUT
570 BCC FII1
580 JSR KEYWORD
590 FII1 STA LABEL,Y; STORE CHAR. OF FILENAME
600 INY
610 JMP FI1; CONTINUE STORING FILENAME IN MAIN BUFFER (LABEL)
620 FI2 STY FNAMELEN; STORE FILENAME LENGTH
630 LDY #0
640 FILO LDA LABEL,Y;------- PUT FILENAME INTO PROPER BUFFER (FILEN)
650 BEQ FILO1
660 STA FILEN,Y
670 INY
680 JMP FILO
710 FILO1 JSR PRNTSA; PRINT THE FILENAME
720 JSR PRNTSPACE
730 FI5 JSR PRNTINPUT
740 JSR PRNTCR; CARRIAGE RETURN
750 JSR LOAD1; LOAD NEXT LINKED FILE ON DISK (FOR CONTINUED READING OF SOURCE)
760 JSR CHARIN
810 LDX #0
820 STX ENDFLAG; SET END OF PROGRAM FLAG TO ZERO
830 RTS
840 ;------------------------- HANDLE .END PSEUDO-OP ---------
850 PEND LDA PASS:BEQ DONK:JMP PEND1
858 DONK LDA #46; PRINT OUT .END
860 JSR PRINT
870 LDA #69
880 JSR PRINT
890 LDA #78
```

```
900 JSR PRINT
910 LDA #68
920 JSR PRINT
930 LDA #32
940 JSR PRINT
950 JSR CHARIN
960 JSR FIØ; GET FILENAME, ETC. JUST AS .FILE PSEUDO-OP DOES
970 LDA PASS; ON PASS 1, DON'T SET THE ENDFLAG UP.
980 BEQ PEND1; BUT ON PASS 2, IT'S NECESSARY (TO END THE ENTIRE PROGRAM)
990 INC ENDFLAG
1000 PEND1 INC PASS; RAISE PASS FROM PASS 1 TO PASS 2
1005 LDA PASS:CMP #2:BNE MORS4:JMP DFINI
1010 MORS4 LDA TA; PUT ORIGINAL START ADDRESS BACK INTO PC (SA) FOR RESTART OF
1020 STA SA; ASSEMBLY ON PASS 2.
1030 LDA TA+1
1040 STA SA+1
1050 JSR INDISK; SET UP NEXT LINE
1060 RTS
1070 ;-------------------- HANDLE .D FILENAME/FILENAME: SOURCE/OBJECT CODE FILENAMES
1071 PDISK INC POKEFLAG:INC CYCLEFLAG:INC DISKFLAG
1072 PLW JSR CHARIN:CMP #32:BEQ PLW:LDY #Ø:CMP #127:BCC PDIX1:JMP DK
1075 PDLOOP1 JSR CHARIN:CMP #32:BEQ PD11
1076 PDLO3 CMP #127; IT'S A KEYWORD (WITHIN THE FILENAME) IF >127
1077 BCC PDIX1
1078 DK STY YY:PHA:JSR KEYWORD:PLA:LDY YY:JSR SOURCEWORD
1079 PDIX1 STA LABEL,Y; KEEP STORING FILENAME INTO PRINTOUT BUFFER (LABEL)
1080 STA FILEN,Y; AS WELL AS LOAD1 BUFFER (FILEN)
1081 INY
1082 JMP PDLOOP1; KEEP STORING FILENAME;------------------
1083 PD11 STY FNAMELEN
1100 ;POINT TO OBJECT FILENAME -------
```

```
1110 STA LABEL,Y
1120 LDY #Ø; SET UP SAVE WITH REPLACE
1122 LDA #"@:STA DFILEN,Y:INY:LDA #"Ø:STA DFILEN,Y:INY:LDA #58:STA DFILEN,Y:INY
1130 PDLOOP JSR CHARIN
1140 BEQ PD1; END OF LINE
1150 CMP #127; IT'S A KEYWORD (WITHIN THE FILENAME) IF >127
1160 BCC PDIX:PHA; MAKE KEYWORD DETOKENIZING ROUTINE POINT TO DFILEN
1162 LDA #<DFILEN:STA AUT+1:LDA #>DFILEN:STA AUT+2:PLA
1170 STY Y:JSR KEYWORD:JSR RESTKEY:LDY Y
1180 PDIX CMP #32:BEQ PDLOOP:STA LABEL,Y; KEEP STORING FILENAME FOR PRINTOUT
1190 STA DFILEN,Y; AS WELL AS SAVE1 BUFFER (DFILEN)
1200 INY
1210 JMP PDLOOP; KEEP STORING FILENAME;------------------
1220 PULLJ JSR PULLINE;-------- SPRINGBOARD TO IGNORE FILENAME
1230 PD1 STY DNAMELEN
1500 JSR ENDPRO; GET NEXT LINE NUMBER
1530 LDX #Ø
1535 STX ENDFLAG; RESET END OF PROGRAM FLAG
1540 ; TRANSFORM FROM RAMLADS INTO DISKLADS  ----------------
1541 CHA LDY #Ø:LDA TRANSF,Y:STA T1,Y:INY:LDA TRANSF,Y:STA T1,Y:INY:LDA TRANSF,Y
1542 STA T1,Y:INY
1543 LDA #$8Ø:STA MEMSA+5
1544 LDA #$EA:STA T2:STA T2+1:STA T2+2
1545 LDA TRANSF,Y:INY:STA INCP1+5:LDA TRANSF,Y:INY:STA INCP1+6
1546 LDA TRANSF,Y:INY:STA INCP1+7:LDA TRANSF,Y:INY:STA INCP1+8
1547 LDA TRANSF,Y:INY:STA INCP1+9:LDA TRANSF,Y:INY:STA INCP1+1Ø
1548 LDA TRANSF,Y:INY:STA INCP1+11
1549 LDA TRANSF,Y:INY:STA T3:LDA TRANSF,Y:INY:STA T3+1:LDA TRANSF,Y:INY
155Ø STA T3+2:LDA TRANSF,Y:INY:STA T3+3:LDA TRANSF,Y:INY:STA T3+4
1551 LDA TRANSF,Y:INY:STA T4+1:LDA TRANSF,Y:INY:STA T4+2:LDA TRANSF,Y:INY
1552 STA T4+3:LDA TRANSF,Y:INY:STA T4+4:LDA TRANSF,Y:STA T4+5
1553 LDA #$EA:LDX #Ø:MLML STA EVIND,X:INX:CPX #8:BNE MLML:LDA #$FF:STA NIP+1
```

```
1554 PLA:PLA:LDA CYCLEFLAG:CMP #1:BEQ RESTART
1555 JMP STARTLINE; AND RETURN TO EVAL TO GET NEXT LINE
1556 RESTART LDA #145:JSR PRINT:JSR PRINT
1557 LDA #"D:JSR $CØ1E:JSR LOAD1:JMP SMORE
156Ø ;------------------------ HANDLE .P (PRINTER) PSEUDO-OP -------
157Ø PPRINTER LDA PASS; ON PASS 1, DO NO PRINTER OUTPUT
158Ø BEQ PULLINE; GET RID OF REST OF LINE AND GO ON.
159Ø JSR OPEN4; PASS 2, SO OPEN PRINTER TO HEAR FROM COMPUTER
16ØØ INC PRINTFLAG; RAISE PRINTER OUTPUT FLAG (SO PRINT WILL SEND BYTES TO
161Ø JSR CLRCHN;                THE PRINTER AS WELL AS THE SCREEN).
162Ø LDA #1:STA SFLAG
164Ø ;--------------------- SUCTION ROUTINE.  GET RID OF REST OF A LINE
165Ø PULLINE JSR CHARIN; IGNORE ALL BYTES, JUST LOCATE NEXT LINE
166Ø BEQ ENDPULL; ZERO END OF LINE SHOULD GO TO ENDPRO FOR NEXT LINE #
167Ø CMP #58; WHEREAS A COLON END OF LINE SKIPS THAT STEP
168Ø BEQ ENDPULR; (COLON)
169Ø JMP PULLINE; NEITHER COLON NOR ZERO (SO PULL IN MORE CHARACTERS)
17ØØ ENDPULL JSR ENDPRO
171Ø ENDPULR PLA; PULL RTS OFF STACK
172Ø PLA
173Ø LDX #Ø
174Ø STX ENDFLAG; SET ENDFLAG DOWN
175Ø JMP STARTLINE; RETURN TO EVAL (TO GET NEXT LINE OF SOURCE CODE)
176Ø ;------------------------ HANDLE .O (POKE BYTES TO RAM) PSEUDO-OP
182Ø OPON LDA #1
183Ø STA POKEFLAG; RAISE POKE-TO-RAM FLAG
184Ø JMP PULLINE; IGNORE REST OF LINE
185Ø ;------------------------ HANDLE .N(SOMETHING),TURN-IT-OFF PSEUDO-OPS
186Ø NIX LDA PASS; ON PASS 1, DON'T BOTHER WITH ANY OF THIS
187Ø BEQ PULLINE
188Ø JSR CHARIN; ON PASS 2, SEE WHICH THING IS BEING TURNED OFF
189Ø CMP #8Ø; IS IT ".NP" TO "NOT PRINT TO PRINTER"
```

```
1900 BEQ NIXPRINT
1910 CMP #79; IS IT ".NO" TO "NOT POKE OBJECT BYTES TO RAM"
1920 BEQ NIXOP
1930 CMP #83; IS IT ".NS" TO "NOT PRINT TO SCREEN"
1940 BEQ NIXSCREEN
1950 CMP #72; IS IT ".NH" TO "NOT PRINTOUT HEX" (THUS SWITCH TO DECIMAL)
1960 BEQ NIXHEX
1970 ;--------------------------- TURN OFF PRINTER OUTPUT
1980 NIXPRINT LDA #46; PRINT ".NP" TO SCREEN
1990 JSR PRINT
2000 LDA #78; "N"
2010 JSR PRINT
2020 LDA #80; "P"
2030 JSR PRINT
2040 JSR PRNTCR; CARRIAGE RETURN
2050 DEC PRINTFLAG; LOWER PRINT-TO-SCREEN FLAG
2060 JSR CLRCHN; TURN OFF PRINTER
2070 LDX #4
2080 JSR CHKOUT
2090 LDA #13
2100 JSR PRINT
2110 LDA #4
2120 JSR CLOSE
2130 JSR CLRCHN
2140 LDX #1; RESTORE NORMAL I/O
2150 JSR CHKIN
2160 JMP PULLINE; IGNORE REST OF LINE (AND RETURN TO EVAL)
2170 ;--------------------------- STOP POKEING OBJECT BYTES TO RAM
2180 NIXOP LDA #46; PRINT ".NO"
2190 JSR PRINT
2200 LDA #78;      "N"
2210 JSR PRINT
```

```
2220 LDA #79;        "O"
2230 JSR PRINT
2240 JSR PRNTCR;CARRIAGE RETURN
2250 LDA #0
2260 STA POKEFLAG; TURN OFF POKE FLAG
2270 JMP PULLINE; IGNORE REST OF LINE (AND RETURN TO EVAL)
2280 ;--------------------------- STOP HEX PRINTOUTS (START DECIMAL)
2290 NIXHEX LDA #46; PRINT ".NH"
2300 JSR PRINT
2310 LDA #78;        "N"
2320 JSR PRINT
2330 LDA #72;        "H"
2340 JSR PRINT
2350 JSR PRNTCR; CARRIAGE RETURN
2360 LDA #0
2370 STA HXFLAG; PUT HEXFLAG DOWN
2380 JMP PULLINE; IGNORE REST OF LINE (AND RETURN TO EVAL)
2390 ;--------------------------- STOP SCREEN PRINTOUTS
2400 NIXSCREEN LDA #46; PRINT ".NS"
2410 JSR PRINT
2420 LDA #78;        "N"
2430 JSR PRINT
2440 LDA #83;        "S"
2450 JSR PRINT
2460 JSR PRNTCR;CARRIAGE RETURN
2470 LDA #0
2480 STA SFLAG; PUT DOWN SCREEN PRINTOUT FLAG
2490 JMP PULLINE; IGNORE REST OF LINE (AND RETURN TO EVAL)
2500 ;---------------------------  DISK ERROR DETECTION ROUTINE --------
2510 DISERR LDX ST; CHECK DISK STATUS VARIABLE (COMPUTER SPECIFIC)
2520 BNE MODIER; IF NOT ZERO, THERE IS SOME FAULT IN THE DISK I/O
```

```
2530 RTS;----------
2540 MODIER LDA #0; PRINT OUT ERROR MESSAGE
2550 JSR PRNTNUM
2560 JSR PRNTSPACE
2570 LDA #<MDISER
2580 STA TEMP; POINT TO DISK ERROR MESSAGE
2590 LDA #>MDISER
2600 STA TEMP+1
2610 JSR ERRING; RING BELL
2620 JSR PRNTMESS; PRINT ERROR MESSAGE
2630 PLA; PULL RTS OFF STACK
2640 PLA
2650 JMP FIN; SHUT DOWN ENTIRE LADS OPERATION
2660 ;--------------- HANDLE .S PSEUDO-OP (TURN ON SCREEN PRINTOUT)
2670 SCREIN LDA PASS:BEQ SCREX:LDA #46; PRINT ".S"
2680 JSR PRINT
2690 LDA #83;        "S"
2700 JSR PRINT
2710 JSR PRNTCR; CARRIAGE RETURN
2740 LDA #1; OTHERWISE, RAISE SCREEN PRINTOUT (LISTING) FLAG
2750 STA SFLAG
2760 SCREX JMP PULLINE; IGNORE REST OF LINE (AND RETURN TO EVAL)
2770 ;-------------- HANDLE .H PSEUDO-OP (HEX NUMBERS DURING PRINTOUT)
2780 HEXIT LDA #46; PRINT ".H"
2790 JSR PRINT
2800 LDA #72;       "H"
2810 JSR PRINT
2820 JSR PRNTCR; CARRIAGE RETURN
2830 LDA #1
2840 STA HXFLAG; SET HEXFLAG UP
2850 JMP PULLINE; IGNORE REST OF LINE (AND RETURN TO EVAL)
```

```
2860 DFINI LDA DISKFLAG:BEQ DONEF; END OF ASSEMBLY----------
2870 JSR SAV1; SAVE OBJECT CODE
2880 DONEF JMP FINI; RETURN TO BASIC
4000 SOURCEWORD PHA; MAKE KEYWORD DETOKENIZING ROUTINE POINT TO FILEN
4010 LDA #<FILEN:STA AUT+1:LDA #>FILEN:STA AUT+2:PLA
4020 JSR KEYWORD:JSR RESTKEY:RTS
5000 .FILE TABLES
```

### Program D-13. Tables

```
10 ; "TABLES"
15 ;
20 ;  TABLE OF MNEMONICS AND PARALLEL TABLE OF OPCODE/ADDRESS TYPE DATA
30 ;  BUFFERS AND MESSAGES, FLAGS, POINTERS, REGISTERS
40 ;-------------------------  MNEMONICS, TYPES, ADDRESS MODE OPCODES
50 MNEMONICS .BYTE "LDALDYJSRRTSBCSBEQBCCCMP
60 .BYTE "BNELDXJMPSTASTYSTXINYDEY
70 .BYTE "DEXDECINXINCCPYCPXSBCSEC
80 .BYTE "ADCCLCTAXTAYTXATYAPHAPLA
90 .BYTE "BRKBMIBPLANDORAEORBITBVC
100 .BYTE "BVSROLRORLSRCLDCLIASLPHP
110 .BYTE "PLPRTISEDSEITSXTXSCLVNOP
120 TYPES .BYTE 1 5 9 0 8 8 8 1
130 .BYTE 8 5 6 1 2 2 0 0
140 .BYTE 0 2 0 2 4 4 1 0
150 .BYTE 1 0 0 0 0 0 0 0
160 .BYTE 0 8 8 1 1 1 7 8
170 .BYTE 8 3 3 3 0 0 3 0
180 .BYTE 0 0 0 0 0 0 0 0
190 OPS .BYTE 161 160 32 96 176 240 144 193
```

```
200 .BYTE 208 162 76 129 132 134 200 136
210 .BYTE 202 198 232 230 192 224 225 56
220 .BYTE 97 24 170 168 138 152 72 104
230 .BYTE 0 48 16 33 1 65 36 80
240 .BYTE 112 34 98 66 216 88 2 8
250 .BYTE 40 64 248 120 186 154 184 234
260 ;--------------------  HEX ROUTINE TABLE  ------------------
270 HEXA .BYTE "0123456789ABCDEF"
280 ;--------------------  BUFFERS ------------------------------
290 LABEL .BYTE 0 0 0 0 0 0 0 0 0 0 0 0 0 0 0 0 0 0 0 0 0
300 BUFFER .BYTE 0 0 0 0 0 0 0 0 0 0 0 0 0 0 0 0 0 0 0 0
310 BUFM .BYTE 0 0 0 0 0 0 0 0 0 0 0 0 0 0 0 0 0 0 0 0
320 HEXBUF .BYTE 0 0 0 0 0 0 0 0 0 0 0 0 0 0 0 0 0 0 0 0 0
330 FILEN .BYTE 0 0 0 0 0 0 0 0 0 0 0 0 0 0 0 0
340 NUBUF .BYTE 0 0 0 0 0 0 0
345 DFILEN .BYTE 0 0 0 0 0 0 0 0 0 0 0 0 0 0 0 0
350 ;-----  REGISTERS USED BY VALDEC -------
360 RADD .BYTE 0 0;TEMPORARY REGISTER FOR DOUBLE ADDITION
370 VREND .BYTE 0; TEMP REG TO HOLD END OF PROGRAM COUNTER
380 TSTORE .BYTE 0 0; TEMPORARY REGISTER FOR MULTIPLY
390 ;---- MESSAGES TO PRINT TO SCREEN -------------------------
400 MNOSTART .BYTE "NO START ADDRESS":.BYTE 0
410 MBOR .BYTE "-------------------- BRANCH OUT OF RANGE":.BYTE 0
420 NOLAB .BYTE "UNDEFINED LABEL":.BYTE 0
430 NOARG .BYTE "          NAKED LABEL":.BYTE 0
440 MDISER .BYTE "      <<<<<<<< DISK ERROR >>>>>>>> ":.BYTE 0
450 MDUPLAB .BYTE "      -- DUPLICATED LABEL -- ":.BYTE 0
460 MERROR .BYTE "      -- SYNTAX ERROR -- ":.BYTE 0
461 DMES .BYTE "  .FILE OR .END REQUIRED ":.BYTE 0
470 ;-----------  FLAGS, POINTERS, REGISTERS  --------------------
480 OP .BYTE 0;         OPCODE
```

```
490 TP .BYTE Ø;           TYPE
500 TA .BYTE Ø Ø;           START ADDRESS
510 LINEN .BYTE Ø Ø;        CURRENT LINE #
520 ENDFLAG .BYTE Ø;      END-OF-PROG FLAG
530 WORK .BYTE Ø Ø;         TEMP WORK AREA
540 RESULT .BYTE Ø Ø;       TEMP ANSWER AREA
550 ARGN .BYTE Ø Ø;         VALUE OF ARGUMENT
560 ARGSIZE .BYTE Ø;      LENGTH OF ARGUMENT
570 EXPRESSF .BYTE Ø;     IS IT AN EXPRESS LABEL
580 HEXFLAG .BYTE Ø;      HEX NUMBER FLAG
590 HEXLEN .BYTE Ø;       LENGTH OF HEX NUMBER
593 FNAMELEN .BYTE Ø;     SOURCE CODE FILE NAME
594 DNAMELEN .BYTE Ø;     OBJECT CODE FILE NAME
600 NUMSIZE .BYTE Ø;      LENGTH OF ASCII NUMBER IN BUFFER (FOR VALDEC)
610 KEYNUM .BYTE Ø;       POSITION OF KEYWORD IN BASIC'S TABLE
620 LABSIZE .BYTE Ø;      SIZE OF LABEL (EQUATE TYPE)
630 LABPTR .BYTE Ø Ø;       POINTS TO ARRAY POSITION FOR ARG STORAGE
640 ARRAYTOP .BYTE Ø Ø;     TOP OF ARRAYS--SAME AS MEMTOP BEFORE LABELS.
650 BUFLAG .BYTE Ø;       AVOID # OR ( DURING ARRAYS ANALYSIS
660 PASS .BYTE Ø;         WHICH PASS WE'RE ON.
665 A .BYTE Ø:X .BYTE Ø:Y .BYTE Ø; TEMPORARY REGISTER STORAGE
680 PT .BYTE Ø Ø;           TEMPORARILY HOLDS PARRAY (IN "ARRAY") 2-BYTE
690 BNUMFLAG .BYTE Ø;     FOR .BYTE IN "INDISK"
700 BFLAG .BYTE Ø Ø;        FOR NUMWERK IN "INDISK"
710 ADDNUM .BYTE Ø Ø;       NUMBER TO ADD FOR + PSEUDO
720 PLUSFLAG .BYTE Ø;     FLAG SHOWS THAT + PSEUDO HAPPENED.
730 BYTFLAG .BYTE Ø;      SHOWS THAT < OR > HAPPENED.
740 DISKFLAG .BYTE Ø;     SHOWS TO SEND BYTES TO DISK OBJECT FILE
750 PRINTFLAG .BYTE Ø;    SHOWS TO SEND BYTES TO PRINTER
760 POKEFLAG .BYTE Ø;     SHOWS TO SEND BYTES TO MEMORY (OBJECT CODE)
770 COLFLAG .BYTE Ø;      ENCOUNTERED A COLON (USED BY INDISK)
```

```
780 FOUNDFLAG .BYTE Ø;  DUPLICATED LABEL NAME (USED BY ARRAY)
790 SFLAG .BYTE Ø;      SHOWS TO SEND SOURCECODE TO SCREEN
800 HXFLAG .BYTE Ø;     SHOWS TO PRINT SA AND OPCODES IN HEX
810 LOCFLAG .BYTE Ø;    SHOWS TO PRINT A PC ADDRESS LABEL
820 BABFLAG .BYTE Ø;    SHOWS TO PRINT A REM AFTER PRNTINPUT IN EVAL
830 ;--------------- SUBSTITUTIONS TO CHANGE RAMLADS INTO DISKLADS
835 TRANSF JSR LOAD1:LDA #<PMEM:LDX #Ø:JSR $FF74:LDA #<SA:STA $Ø2B9:LDX #1:JSR $FF7
836 CYCLEFLAG .BYTE Ø;  RAMLADS VS. DISKLADS (SET BY .D IN PSEUDO)
837 EFLAG .BYTE Ø;     ERROR COUNT
838 ERN .BYTE " ERRORS":.BYTE Ø; ERROR MESSAGE
845 ; NOW LINK UP WITH 1ST FILE ("DEFS") TO PERMIT 2ND PASS.
850 ;
860 .END DEFS128
```

Appendix E

# Library of Subroutines

Here is a collection of techniques you'll need to use in many of your ML programs. Those techniques which are not inherently easy to understand are followed by an explanation.

## Increment and Decrement Double-Byte Numbers

You'll often want to raise or lower a number by 1. To *increment* a number, you add 1 to it: Incrementing 5 results in 6. *Decrementing* lowers a number by 1. Single-byte numbers are easy; you just use INC or DEC. But you'll often want to increment two-byte numbers which hold addresses, game scores, pointers, or some other number which requires two bytes. Two bytes, ganged together and seen as a single number, can hold values from 0 ($0000) up to 65535 ($FFFF). Here's how to raise a two-byte number by 1, to increment it:

(Let's assume that the number you want to increment or decrement is located in addresses $0605 and $0606, and the ML program segment performing the action is located at $5000.)

```
5000  INCREMENT INC $0605   Raise the low byte.
5003  BNE GOFORTH           If not zero, leave high byte alone.
5005  INC $0606             Raise high byte.
5008  GOFORTH...            Continue with program.
```

The trick in this routine is the BNE. If the low byte isn't raised to 0 (from 255), we don't need to add a carry to the high byte, so we jump over it. However, if the low byte does turn into a 0, the high byte must then be raised. This is similar to the way an ordinary decimal increment creates a carry when you add 1 to 9 (or to 99 or 999). The lower number turns to 0, and the next column over is raised by 1.

To double-decrement, you need an extra step. The reason it's more complicated is that the 8502 chip has no way to test if you've crossed over to $FF, down from $00. BNE and BEQ will test if something is 0, but nothing tests for $FF. (The N flag *is* turned on when you go from $00 to $FF, and BPL or BMI could test it.) The problem with it, though, is that the N flag isn't limited to sensing $FF. It is sensitive to *any* number higher than 127 decimal ($7F).

So, here's the way to handle double-deckers:

```
5000 LDA $0605               Load in the low byte, affecting the
                             zero flag.
5003 BNE FIXLOWBYTE          If it's not zero, lower it, skipping
                             high byte.
5005 DEC $0606               Zero in low byte forces this.
5008 FIXLOWBYTE DEC $0605    Always dec the low byte.
```

Here we *always* lower the low byte, but lower the high byte only when the low byte is found to be zero. If you think about it, that's the way any subtraction would work.

## Comparison

Comparing a single-byte against another single-byte is easily achieved with CMP. Double-byte comparison can be handled this way:

(Assume that the numbers you want to compare are located in addresses $0605,0606 and $0700,0701. The ML program segment performing the comparison is located at $5000.)

```
5000  SEC
5001  LDA  $0605  Low byte of first number
5004  SBC  $0700  Low byte of second number
5007  STA  $0800  Temporary holding place for this result
500A  LDA  $0606  High byte of first number
500D  SBC  $0701  High byte of second number, leave result in A
5010  ORA  $0800  Results in zero if A and $0800 were both zero
```

The flags in the status register are left in various states after this routine—you can test them with the B instructions and branch according to the results. The ORA sets the Z (zero) flag if the results of the first subtraction (left in $0800) and the second subtraction (in A, the accumulator) were both zero. This would happen only if the two numbers tested were identical, and BEQ would test for this (Branch if EQual).

If the first number is lower than the second, the carry flag would have been cleared, so BCC (Branch if Carry Clear) will test for that possibility. If the first number is higher than the second, BCS (Branch if Carry Set) will be true. You can therefore branch with BEQ for =, BCC for <, and BCS for >. Just keep in mind which number you're considering the *first* and which the *second* in this test.

## Double-Byte Addition

CLC ADC and SEC SBC will add and subtract one-byte numbers. To add two-byte numbers, use:

(Assume that the numbers you want to add are located in addresses $0605,0606 and $0700,0701. The ML program segment performing the addition is located at $5000.)

```
5000  CLC            Always do this before any addition.
5001  LDA  $0605
5004  ADC  $0700
5007  STA  $0605     The result will be left in $0605,0606.
500A  LDA  $0606
500D  ADC  $0701
5010  STA  $0606
```

It's not necessary to put the result on top of the number in $0605,0606—you can put it anywhere. But you'll often be adding a particular value to another and not needing the original any longer—adding ten points to a score for every blasted alien is an example. If this were the case, following the logic of the routine above, you would have a 10 in $0701,0702:

```
0701 0A  The ten points you get for hitting an alien
0702 00
```

You'd want that 10 to remain undisturbed throughout the game. The score, however, keeps changing during the game and, held in $0605,0606, it can be covered over, replaced with each addition.

## Double-Byte Subtraction

This is quite similar to double-byte addition. Since subtracting one number from another is also a comparison of those two numbers, you could combine subtraction with the double-byte comparison routine above (using ORA). In any event, this is the way to subtract double-byte numbers. Be sure to keep straight which number is being subtracted from the other. We'll call the number *being subtracted* the *second number.*

(Assume that the number you want to subtract—the "second number"—is located in addresses $0700,0701, and that the number it is being subtracted from—the "first number"—is held in $0605,0606. The result will be left in $0605,0606. The ML program segment performing the subtraction is located at $5000.)

```
5000  SEC                Always do this before any subtraction
5001  LDA  $0605         Low byte of first number
5004  SBC  $0700         Low byte of second number
5007  STA  $0605         Result will be left in $0605,0606
500A  LDA  $0606         High byte of first number
500D  SBC  $0701         High byte of second number
5010  STA  $0606         High byte of final result
```

## Multibyte Addition and Subtraction

Using the methods for adding and subtracting illustrated above, you can manipulate larger numbers than can be held within two bytes (65535 is the largest possible two-byte integer). Here's how to subtract one four-byte-long number from another. The locations and conditions are the same as for the two-byte subtraction example above, except the "first number" (the *minuend*) is held in the four-byte chain, $0605,0606,0607,0608, and the "second number" (the *subtrahend*, the number being subtracted from the first number) is in $0700,0701,0702,0703.

Also observe that the most significant byte is held in $0703 and $0608. We'll use the Y register for indirect Y addressing, four bytes in zero page as pointers to the two numbers, and the X register as a counter to make sure that all four bytes are dealt with. This means that X must be loaded with the length of the chains we're subtracting—in this case, 4.

```
5000  LDX  #4               Length of the byte chains.
5002  LDY  #0               Set Y...
5004  SEC                   always before subtraction.
5005  LOOP LDA (FIRST),Y
5007  SBC  (SECOND),Y
5009  STA  (FIRST),Y        The answer will be left in $0605–$0608.
500B  INY                   Raise index to chains.
500C  DEX                   Lower counter.
5010  BNE  LOOP             Haven't yet done all four bytes.
```

Before this will work, the pointers in zero page must have been set up to allow the indirect Y addressing. This is one way to do it:

```
2000  FIRST = $FB        Define zero page pointers at $FB and $FD.
2000  SECOND = $FD
2000  SETUP LDA #5       Set up pointer to $0605.
2002  STA  FIRST
2004  LDA  #6
2006  STA  FIRST+1
```

```
2008  LDA  #0          Set up pointer to $0700.
200A  STA  SECOND
200C  LDA  #7
200E  STA  SECOND+1
```

## Multiplication

### × 2

ASL (no argument used, "accumulator addressing mode") will multiply the number in the accumulator by 2.

### × 3

To multiply by 3, use a temporary variable byte we'll call TEMP.

```
5000  STA  TEMP  Put the number into the variable.
5003  ASL        Multiply it by 2.
5004  ADC  TEMP  (X * 2 + X = X * 3)—the answer is in A.
```

### × 4

To multiply by 4, just ASL twice.

```
5000  ASL  * 2
5001  ASL  * 2 again
```

### × 4 (Two Byte)

To multiply a two-byte integer by 4, use a two-byte variable we'll call TEMP and TEMP+1.

```
5000  ASL  TEMP     Multiply the low byte by 2...
5003  ROL  TEMP+1   moving any carry into the high byte.
5006  ASL  TEMP     Multiply the low byte by 2 again.
5009  ROL  TEMP+1   Again acknowledge any carry.
```

### × 10

To multiply a two-byte integer by 10, use an additional two-byte variable we'll call STORE.

```
5000                 First, put the number into STORE for
                     safekeeping.
5000  LDA  TEMP:STA  STORE:LDA TEMP+1:STA STORE+1
500C                 Then multiply it by 4.
500C  ASL  TEMP      Multiply the low byte by 2...
500F  ROL  TEMP+1    moving any carry into the high byte.
5012  ASL  TEMP      Multiply the low byte by 2 again.
5015  ROL  TEMP+1;   Again acknowledge any carry.
5018                 Then add the original, resulting in X * 5.
```

```
5018  LDA  STORE
501B  ADC  TEMP
501E  STA  TEMP
5021  LDA  STORE+1
501D  ADC  TEMP+1
5024  STA  TEMP+1
5027                    Then just multiply by 2 since (5 * 2 = 10)
5027  ASL  TEMP
502A  ROL  TEMP+1
```

### × ?

To multiply a two-byte integer by other odd values, just use a similar combination of addition and multiplication which results in the correct amount of multiplication.

### × 100

To multiply a two-byte integer by 100, just go through the above subroutine twice.

### × 256

To multiply a one-byte integer by 256, just transform it into a two-byte integer.

```
5000  LDA  TEMP
5003  STA  TEMP+1
5006  LDA  #0
5008  STA  TEMP
```

## Division

### ÷ 2

LSR (no argument used, "accumulator addressing mode") will divide the number in the accumulator by 2.

### ÷ 4

To divide by 4, just LSR twice.

```
5000  LSR   / 2
5001  LSR   / 2 again
```

### ÷ 4 (Two Byte)

To divide a two-byte integer, called TEMP, by 2:

```
5000  LSR  TEMP+1  Shift high byte right...
5001  ROR  TEMP    pulling any carry into the low byte.
```

Appendix F

# Typing In LADS

LADS is a very long program. The directions for typing it in are listed below. For those who prefer not to type it in, it can be purchased on disk, along with many of the other programs in this book, by calling COMPUTE! Publications toll-free at 1-800-346-6767 (in New York, call 1-212-887-8525) or by using the coupon in the back of this book. Be sure to state that you want the disk for the book *128 Machine Language for Beginners.*

In order to make it as easy as possible to type in LADS, we've included two program entry aids written in BASIC: "The Automatic Proofreader" and "MLX." To assist you in understanding how to enter these programs, COMPUTE! has established the following listing conventions.

Generally, BASIC program listings like the one for MLX will contain words within braces which spell out any special characters: {DOWN} means to press the cursor-down key; {5 SPACES} means to press the space bar five times.

To indicate that a key should be *shifted* (press the key while holding down the SHIFT key), the key will be underlined in our listings. For example, S means to type the S key while holding the SHIFT key. This would appear on your screen as a heart symbol. If you find an underlined key enclosed in braces (for example, {10 N}), you should type the key as many times as indicated. In that case, you would enter ten shifted N's.

If a key is enclosed in special brackets, [< >], you should hold down the *Commodore key* while pressing the key inside the special brackets. (The Commodore key is the key in the lower left corner of the keyboard.) Again, if the key is preceded by a number, you should press the key as many times as indicated; [<9@>] means type Commodore-@ nine times.

Refer to Figure F-1 when entering cursor and color control keys:

**Figure F-1. Keyboard Conventions**

| When You Read: | Press: | See: | When You Read: | Press: | See: |
|---|---|---|---|---|---|
| {CLR} | SHIFT CLR/HOME | | {C= 1} | COMMODORE 1 | |
| {HOME} | CLR/HOME | | {C= 2} | COMMODORE 2 | |
| {UP} | SHIFT ↑ CRSR ↓ | | {C= 3} | COMMODORE 3 | |
| {DOWN} | ↑ CRSR ↓ | | {C= 4} | COMMODORE 4 | |
| {LEFT} | SHIFT ← CRSR → | | {C= 5} | COMMODORE 5 | |
| {RIGHT} | ← CRSR → | | {C= 6} | COMMODORE 6 | |
| {RVS} | CTRL 9 | | {C= 7} | COMMODORE 7 | |
| {OFF} | CTRL 0 | | {C= 8} | COMMODORE 8 | |
| {BLK} | CTRL 1 | | { F1 } | f1 | |
| {WHT} | CTRL 2 | | { F2 } | SHIFT f1 | |
| {RED} | CTRL 3 | | { F3 } | f3 | |
| {CYN} | CTRL 4 | | { F4 } | SHIFT f3 | |
| {PUR} | CTRL 5 | | { F5 } | f5 | |
| {GRN} | CTRL 6 | | { F6 } | SHIFT f5 | |
| {BLU} | CTRL 7 | | { F7 } | f7 | |
| {YEL} | CTRL 8 | | { F8 } | SHIFT f7 | |
| | | | ← | ← | |
| | | | ↑ | SHIFT ↑ | |

## Typing In LADS

Before you can enter LADS, you must first enter the "Machine Language Editor" program (MLX), Program F-2. MLX will allow you to enter the LADS object code without a mistake. It is therefore extremely important that MLX be entered correctly. To assist you in typing in MLX you should use "The Automatic Proofreader." Here are the steps you should follow to enter LADS.

1. Read the directions for using the Automatic Proofreader below.
2. Type in Program F-1, the Automatic Proofreader, and save it to disk or tape.
3. Activate the Automatic Proofreader and type in and save Program F-2, MLX, checking each line with the Automatic Proofreader as you finish typing it in.

4. Read the directions for using MLX.
5. Run MLX and begin entering the object code for LADS, Program F-3.
6. When you have finished entering the LADS object code, use the Save option of MLX to save a copy.
7. You are now ready to BLOAD LADS.
8. Type in and save Program F-4, using the filename LOADER. If you have a 1571 disk drive, use the "Autoboot Maker" utility from the Test/Demo Disk that came with the 1571 drive to make "Loader" run when you turn on your system.

## The Automatic Proofreader

Philip I. Nelson

"The Automatic Proofreader" helps you type in program listings without typing mistakes. It's a short error-checking program that conceals itself in memory and adheres to your Commodore's operating system. Each time you press RETURN to enter a program line, the Proofreader displays a two-letter checksum in reverse video at the top of your screen. If the checksum on your screen doesn't match the one in the printed listing, you've typed the line incorrectly—it's that simple. You don't have to use the Proofreader to enter printed listings, but doing so greatly reduces your chances of making a typo.

### Getting Started

First, type in the Automatic Proofreader program *exactly* as it appears in the listing. Since the Proofreader can't check itself, type carefully to avoid mistakes. Don't omit any lines, even if they contain unfamiliar commands or you think they don't apply to your computer. As soon as you're finished typing the Proofreader, save at least two copies on disk or tape before running it the first time. This is very important because the Proofreader erases the BASIC portion of itself when you run it, leaving only the machine language portion in memory.

When that's done, type RUN and press RETURN. After announcing which computer it's running on, the Proofreader installs the ML routine in memory, displays the message PROOFREADER ACTIVE, erases the BASIC portion of itself, and ends. If you type LIST and press RETURN, you'll see that no BASIC program remains in memory. The computer is ready for you to type in a new BASIC program.

## Entering Programs

Once the Proofreader is active, you can begin typing in a BASIC program as usual. Every time you finish typing a line and press RETURN, the Proofreader displays a two-letter checksum (reverse-video letters) in the upper left corner of the screen. Compare this checksum with the two-letter checksum printed to the left of the corresponding line in the program listing. If the letters match, it's almost certain the line was typed correctly. If the letters don't match, check for your mistake and correct the line.

The Proofreader ignores spaces that aren't enclosed in quotation marks, so you can omit spaces (or add extra ones) between keywords and still see a matching checksum. For example, these two lines generate the same checksum:

```
10 PRINT"THIS IS BASIC"
10 PRINT           "THIS IS BASIC"
```

However, since spaces inside quotation marks are almost always significant, the Proofreader pays attention to them. For instance, these two lines generate different checksums:

```
10 PRINT"THIS IS BASIC"
10 PRINT"THIS ISBA     SIC"
```

A common typing mistake is transposition—typing two successive characters in the wrong order, like PIRNT instead of PRINT or 64378 instead of 64738. A checksum program that adds up the values of all the characters in a line can't possibly detect transposition errors (it can only tell whether the right characters are present, regardless of what order they're in). Because the Proofreader computes the checksum with a more sophisticated formula, it is also sensitive to the *position* of each character within the line and thus catches transposition errors.

The Proofreader does *not* accept keyword abbreviations (for example, ? instead of PRINT). If you prefer to use abbreviations, you can still check the line with the Proofreader: Simply LIST the line after typing it, move the cursor back onto the line, and press RETURN. LISTing the line substitutes the full keyword for the abbreviation and allows the Proofreader to work properly. The same technique works for rechecking a program you've already typed in: Reload the program, LIST several lines on the screen, and press RETURN over them.

*Do not use any GRAPHIC commands while the Proofreader is active*. When you activate a command like GRAPHIC 1, the computer moves everything at the start of BASIC program space—including the Proofreader—to another memory area, causing the Proofreader to crash. The same thing happens if you run any program that contains a GRAPHIC command. The Proofreader deallocates any graphics areas before installing itself in memory, but you are responsible for seeing that the computer remains in this configuration.

Though the Proofreader doesn't interfere with other BASIC operations, it's always a good idea to disable it before running any other program. Some programs may need the space occupied by the Proofreader's ML routine or may create other memory conflicts. However, the Proofreader is purposely made difficult to dislodge: It's not affected by tape or disk operations, or by pressing RUN/STOP–RESTORE. The simplest way to disable it is to turn the computer off, then on again.

## Machine Language Editor, MLX

Ottis R. Cowper

"MLX" is a new way to enter long machine language programs without a lot of fuss. MLX lets you enter the numbers from a special list that looks similar to BASIC DATA statements. It checks your typing on a line-by-line basis. It won't let you enter invalid characters or let you continue if there's a mistake in a line. It won't even let you enter a line or digit out of sequence.

### Using MLX

Type in and save some copies of MLX (you'll want to use it to enter future ML programs from other COMPUTE! publications). When you're ready to enter "LADS Object Code," Program F-3, load and run MLX. It asks you for a starting address and an ending address. These addresses are

**Starting Address: 2710**
**Ending Address: 3D27**

If you're unfamiliar with machine language, the addresses (and all other values you enter in MLX) may appear strange. Instead of the usual decimal numbers you're accustomed to, these numbers are in *hexadecimal*—a base 16 numbering system commonly used by ML programmers. Hexadecimal—hex for short—includes the numbers 0–9 and the letters A–F. But don't worry—even if you know nothing about ML or hex, you should have no trouble using MLX.

After you enter the starting and ending addresses, MLX will offer you the option of clearing the workspace. Choose this option if you're starting to enter LADS for the first time. If you're continuing to enter LADS that you partially typed from a previous session, don't choose this option.

It's not necessary to know more about this option to use MLX, but here's an explanation if you're interested: When you first run MLX, the workspace area contains random values. Clearing the workspace fills it with zeros. This makes it easier to find where you left off if you enter the listing in multiple sittings. However, clearing the workspace is useful only before you first begin entering a listing; there's no need to clear it before you reload to continue entering a partially typed listing.

When you save your work with MLX, it stores the entire contents of the data buffer. If you clear the workspace before starting, the incomplete portion of the listing is filled with zeros when saved and thus refilled with zeros when reloaded. If you don't clear the workspace when first starting, the incomplete portion of the listing is filled with random data. Whether or not you clear the workspace before you reload, this random data will refill the unfinished part of the listing when you load your previous work. The rule, then, is to use the clear workspace feature before you begin entering data from a listing and not to bother with it afterward.

At this point, MLX presents a menu of commands:

**E**nter data
**D**isplay data
**L**oad data
**S**ave file
**C**atalog disk
**Q**uit

## Entering a Listing

To begin entering data, press E. You'll be asked for the address at which you wish to begin entering data. (If you pressed E by mistake, you can return to the command menu by pressing RETURN.) When you begin typing LADS, you should enter the starting address here. If you're typing LADS in multiple sittings, you should enter the address where you left off typing at the end of the previous session. In any case, make sure the address you enter corresponds to the address of a line of the LADS MLX listing. Otherwise, you'll be unable to enter the data correctly.

After you enter the address, you'll see that address appear as a prompt with a nonblinking cursor. Now you're ready to enter data. Type in all nine numbers on that line, beginning with the first two-digit number after the colon (:). Each line represents eight data bytes and a checksum. Although an MLX-format listing appears similar to the "hex dump" machine language listings you may be accustomed to, the extra checksum number on the end allows MLX to check your typing. (You *can* enter the data from an MLX listing using the built-in monitor if the rightmost column of data is omitted, but we recommend against it. It's much easier to let MLX do the proofreading and error checking for you.)

Only the numbers 0–9 and the letters A–F can be typed in. If you press any other key (with some exceptions noted below), you'll hear a warning buzz. To simplify typing, MLX redefines the function keys and the + and − keys on the numeric keypad so that you can enter data one-handed. Figure F-2 shows the keypad configuration supported by MLX.

MLX checks for transposed characters. If you're supposed to type in *A0* and instead enter *0A*, MLX will catch your mistake. To correct typing mistakes before finishing a line, use the INST/DEL key to delete the character to the left of the cursor. (The cursor-left key also deletes.) If you mess up a line really badly, press CLR/HOME to start the line over.

The RETURN key is also active, but only before any data is typed on a line. Pressing RETURN at this point returns you to the command menu. After you type a character of data, MLX disables RETURN until the cursor returns to the start of a line. Remember, you can press CLR/HOME to get to a line number prompt quickly.

**Figure F-2. Keypad for 128 MLX**

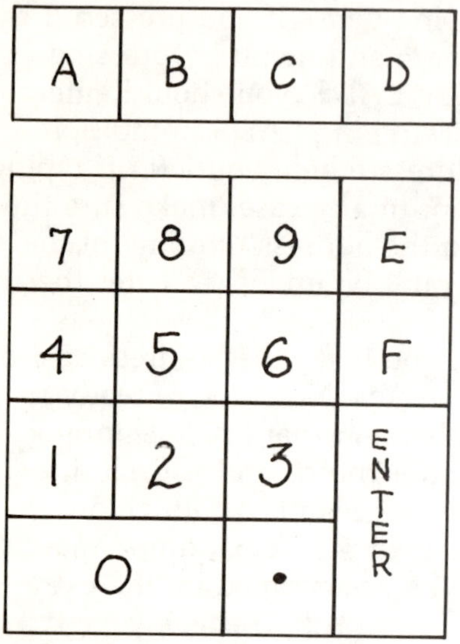


### Beep Or Buzz

When you enter a line, MLX recalculates the checksum from the eight bytes and the address and compares this value to the number from the ninth column. If the values match, you'll hear a pleasant beep to indicate that the line was entered correctly. The data is then added to the workspace area, and the prompt for the next line of data appears. But if MLX detects a typing error, you'll hear a low buzz and see an error message. MLX will then redisplay the line for editing.

To make corrections in a line that MLX has redisplayed for editing, compare the line on the screen with the one printed in the listing, then move the cursor to the mistake and type the correct key. The cursor-left and -right keys provide the normal cursor controls. (The INST/DEL key now works as an alternative cursor-left key.) You cannot move left beyond the first character in the line. If you try to move beyond the rightmost character, you'll reenter the line. During editing, RETURN is active; pressing it tells MLX to recheck the line. You can press the CLR/HOME key to clear the entire line if you want to start from scratch, or if you want to get to a line number prompt to use RETURN to get back to the menu.

After you have entered the last number on the last line of the listing, MLX automatically moves to the Save option.

### Other MLX Functions

The second menu choice, DISPLAY DATA, examines memory and shows the contents in the same format as the program listing (including the checksum). When you press D, MLX asks you for a starting address. Be sure that the starting address you give corresponds to a line number in the listing. Otherwise, the display will be meaningless. MLX displays program lines until it reaches the end of the program, at which point the menu is redisplayed. You can pause the scrolling display by pressing the space bar. (MLX finishes printing the current line before halting.) To resume scrolling, press the space bar again. To break out of the display and return to the menu before the ending address is reached, press RETURN.

Two more menu selections let you save programs and load them back into the computer. These are SAVE FILE and LOAD FILE; their operation is quite straightforward. When you press S or L, MLX asks you for the filename. (Again, pressing RETURN at this prompt without entering anything returns you to the command menu.) Next, MLX asks you to press either D or T to select disk or tape.

You'll notice the disk drive starting and stopping several times during a save. Don't panic; this is normal behavior. MLX opens and writes to the file instead of using the usual SAVE command. (Loads, on the other hand, operate at normal speed—thanks to the relocating feature of BASIC 7.0's BLOAD command.) Remember that MLX saves the entire workspace area from the starting address to the ending address, so the save or load may take longer than you might expect if you've entered only a small amount of data from a long listing. When saving a partially completed listing, make sure to note the address where you stopped typing so that you'll know where to resume entry when you reload.

### Error Alert

MLX reports any errors detected during the save or load and displays the standard error messages. (Tape users should bear in mind that the Commodore 128 is never able to detect errors when saving to tape.) MLX also has three special load error messages:

- INCORRECT STARTING ADDRESS, which means the file you're trying to load does not have the starting address you specified when you ran MLX. In this case, no data will be loaded.
- LOAD ENDED AT *address*, which means the file you're trying to load ends before the ending address you specified when you started MLX. The data from the file is loaded, but it ends at the address specified in the error message.
- TRUNCATED AT ENDING ADDRESS, which means the file you're trying to load extends beyond the ending address you specified when you started MLX. The data from the file is loaded, but only up to the specified ending address.

If you see one of these messages and feel certain that you've loaded the right file, exit and rerun MLX, being careful to enter the correct starting and ending addresses.

If you wish to check which programs are on a disk, select the C option from the command menu for a directory. You can use the 128's NO SCROLL key to pause the display. Afterwards, press any key to return to the menu.

The Quit menu option has the obvious effect—it stops MLX and enters BASIC. The RUN/STOP key is trapped, so the Q option lets you exit the program without turning off the computer. (Of course, RUN/STOP–RESTORE also gets you out.) You'll be asked for verification; press Y to exit to BASIC or any other key to return to the menu. After quitting, you can type RUN again and reenter MLX without losing your data as long as you don't use the clear workspace option.

### The Finished Product

When you've finished typing all the data for an ML program and saved your work, you're ready to see the results. The instructions for loading and using the finished product vary from program to program. LADS should be loaded using the command **BLOAD"LADS"** or **LOAD"LADS",8,1** for disk (if you have a 1571 disk drive, **BOOT "LADS"** also works) or **LOAD"LADS",1,1** for tape (assuming you used the filename LADS to save the object code through MLX). When you wish to assemble source code once LADS is in memory, just **SYS 10000** (it's best to reload LADS after you have loaded the source code).

### An Ounce of Prevention

By the time you finish typing in the data for a long ML program such as LADS, you'll have many hours invested in the project. Don't take chances—use our Automatic Proofreader to type MLX, and then test your copy *thoroughly* before first using it to enter any significant amount of data. Make sure all the menu options work as they should. Enter fragments of the program starting at several different addresses, then use the Display option to verify that the data has been entered correctly. And be sure to test the Save and Load options several times to insure that you can recall your work from disk or tape. Don't let a simple typing error in MLX cost you several nights of hard work.

## The Loader

This is a suggestion for a LADS "Loader" program (Program F-4) which will boot LADS if you install it on a disk and use the "Autoboot Maker" on the Test/Demo Disk that comes with the 1571 disk drive. It also redefines the F1, F2, F3, and F5 keys in useful ways. F1 will run either version of LADS. You can invoke it anywhere onscreen because it will cursor down and clear the screen before SYS 10000. F3 will boot RAMLADS in case you want a fresh start because LADS in RAM became corrupted. F2 invokes AUTO 10, and F5 performs a SYS 2816 ($B00, the start address of many of the example programs in this book). Each of these functions clears the screen in such a way that you can hit the function key anywhere on the screen; you need not be on a blank line.

The Loader also creates a small bit of source code containing a common template for experimenting with a short routine.

### Program F-1. The Automatic Proofreader

```
10 VEC=PEEK(772)+256*PEEK(773):LO=43:HI=44
20 PRINT "AUTOMATIC PROOFREADER FOR ";:IF VEC=4236
    4 THEN PRINT "C-64"
30 IF VEC=50556 THEN PRINT "VIC-20"
40 IF VEC=35158 THEN GRAPHIC CLR:PRINT "PLUS/4 & 1
    6"
50 IF VEC=17165 THEN LO=45:HI=46:GRAPHIC CLR:PRINT
    "128"
60 SA=(PEEK(LO)+256*PEEK(HI))+6:ADR=SA
```

```
70 FOR J=Ø TO 166:READ BYT:POKE ADR,BYT:ADR=ADR+1:
     CHK=CHK+BYT:NEXT
80 IF CHK<>2Ø57Ø THEN PRINT "*ERROR* CHECK TYPING
     {SPACE}IN DATA STATEMENTS":END
9Ø FOR J=1 TO 5:READ RF,LF,HF:RS=SA+RF:HB=INT(RS/2
     56):LB=RS-(256*HB)
1ØØ CHK=CHK+RF+LF+HF:POKE SA+LF,LB:POKE SA+HF,HB:N
     EXT
11Ø IF CHK<>22Ø54 THEN PRINT "*ERROR* RELOAD PROGR
     AM AND CHECK FINAL LINE":END
12Ø POKE SA+149,PEEK(772):POKE SA+15Ø,PEEK(773)
13Ø IF VEC=17165 THEN POKE SA+14,22:POKE SA+18,23:
     POKESA+29,224:POKESA+139,224
14Ø PRINT CHR$(147);CHR$(17);"PROOFREADER ACTIVE":
     SYS SA
15Ø POKE HI,PEEK(HI)+1:POKE (PEEK(LO)+256*PEEK(HI)
     )-1,Ø:NEW
16Ø DATA 12Ø,169,73,141,4,3,169,3,141,5,3
17Ø DATA 88,96,165,2Ø,133,167,165,21,133,168,169
18Ø DATA Ø,141,Ø,255,162,31,181,199,157,227,3
19Ø DATA 2Ø2,16,248,169,19,32,21Ø,255,169,18,32
2ØØ DATA 21Ø,255,16Ø,Ø,132,18Ø,132,176,136,23Ø,18Ø
21Ø DATA 2ØØ,185,Ø,2,24Ø,46,2Ø1,34,2Ø8,8,72
22Ø DATA 165,176,73,255,133,176,1Ø4,72,2Ø1,32,2Ø8
23Ø DATA 7,165,176,2Ø8,3,1Ø4,2Ø8,226,1Ø4,166,18Ø
24Ø DATA 24,165,167,121,Ø,2,133,167,165,168,1Ø5
25Ø DATA Ø,133,168,2Ø2,2Ø8,239,24Ø,2Ø2,165,167,69
26Ø DATA 168,72,41,15,168,185,211,3,32,21Ø,255
27Ø DATA 1Ø4,74,74,74,74,168,185,211,3,32,21Ø
28Ø DATA 255,162,31,189,227,3,149,199,2Ø2,16,248
29Ø DATA 169,146,32,21Ø,255,76,86,137,65,66,67
3ØØ DATA 68,69,7Ø,71,72,74,75,77,8Ø,81,82,83,88
31Ø DATA 13,2,7,167,31,32,151,116,117,151,128,129,
     167,136,137
```

### Program F-2. MLX

```
AE 1ØØ TRAP 96Ø:POKE 4627,128:DIM NL$,A(7)
XP 11Ø Z2=2:Z4=254:Z5=255:Z6=256:Z7=127:BS=256*PEE
       K(4627):EA=6528Ø
FB 12Ø BE$=CHR$(7):RT$=CHR$(13):DL$=CHR$(2Ø):SP$=C
       HR$(32):LF$=CHR$(157)
KE 13Ø DEF FNHB(A)=INT(A/256):DEF FNLB(A)=A-FNHB(A
       )*256:DEF FNAD(A)=PEEK(A)+256*PEEK(A+1)
JB 14Ø KEY 1,"A":KEY 3,"B":KEY 5,"C":KEY 7,"D":VOL
        15:IF RGR(Ø)=5 THEN FAST
FJ 15Ø PRINT"{CLR}"CHR$(142);CHR$(8):COLOR Ø,15:CO
       LOR 4,15:COLOR 6,15
```

```
GQ 160 PRINT TAB(12)"{RED}{RVS}{2 SPACES}{9 @}
       {2 SPACES}"RT$;TAB(12)"{RVS}{2 SPACES}{OFF}
       {BLU} 128 MLX {RED}{RVS}{2 SPACES}"RT$;TAB(
       12)"{RVS}{13 SPACES}{BLU}"
FE 170 PRINT"{2 DOWN}{3 SPACES}COMPUTE!'S MACHINE
       {SPACE}LANGUAGE EDITOR{2 DOWN}"
DK 180 PRINT"{BLK}STARTING ADDRESS{4}";:GOSUB 260:
       IF AD THEN SA=AD:ELSE 180
FH 190 PRINT"{BLK}{2 SPACES}ENDING ADDRESS{4}";:GO
       SUB 260:IF AD THEN EA=AD:ELSE 190
MF 200 PRINT"{DOWN}{BLK}CLEAR WORKSPACE [Y/N]?{4}"
       :GETKEY A$:IF A$<>"Y" THEN 220
QH 210 PRINT"{DOWN}{BLU}WORKING...";:BANK Ø:FOR A=
       BS TO BS+(EA-SA)+7:POKE A,Ø:NEXT A:PRINT"DO
       NE"
DC 220 PRINT TAB(1Ø)"{DOWN}{BLK}{RVS} MLX COMMAND
       {SPACE}MENU {4}{DOWN}":PRINT TAB(13)"{RVS}E
       {OFF}NTER DATA"RT$;TAB(13)"{RVS}D{OFF}ISPLA
       Y DATA"RT$;TAB(13)"{RVS}L{OFF}OAD FILE"
HB 230 PRINT TAB(13)"{RVS}S{OFF}AVE FILE"RT$;TAB(1
       3)"{RVS}C{OFF}ATALOG DISK"RT$;TAB(13)"{RVS}
       Q{OFF}UIT{DOWN}{BLK}"
AP 240 GETKEY A$:A=INSTR("EDLSCQ",A$):ON A GOTO 34
       Ø,55Ø,64Ø,65Ø,93Ø,94Ø:GOSUB 95Ø:GOTO 24Ø
SX 250 PRINT"STARTING AT";:GOSUB 26Ø:IF(AD<>Ø)OR(A
       $=NL$)THEN RETURN:ELSE 25Ø
BG 260 A$=NL$:INPUT A$:IF LEN(A$)=4 THEN AD=DEC(A$
       )
PP 270 IF AD=Ø THEN BEGIN:IF A$<>NL$ THEN 3ØØ:ELSE
        RETURN:BEND
MA 280 IF AD<SA OR AD>EA THEN 3ØØ
PM 290 IF AD>511 AND AD<6528Ø THEN PRINT BE$;:RETU
       RN
SQ 300 GOSUB 95Ø:PRINT"{RVS} INVALID ADDRESS
       {DOWN}{BLK}":AD=Ø:RETURN
RD 310 CK=FNHB(AD):CK=AD-Z4*CK+Z5*(CK>Z7):GOTO 33Ø
DD 320 CK=CK*Z2+Z5*(CK>Z7)+A
AH 330 CK=CK+Z5*(CK>Z5):RETURN
QD 340 PRINT BE$;"{RVS} ENTER DATA ":GOSUB 25Ø:IF
       {SPACE}A$=NL$ THEN 22Ø
JA 350 BANK Ø:PRINT:F=Ø:OPEN 3,3
BR 360 GOSUB 31Ø:PRINT HEX$(AD)+":";:IF F THEN PRI
       NT L$:PRINT"{UP}{5 RIGHT}";
QA 370 FOR I=Ø TO 24 STEP 3:B$=SP$:FOR J=1 TO 2:IF
        F THEN B$=MID$(L$,I+J,1)
PS 380 PRINT"{RVS}"B$+LF$;:IF I<24 THEN PRINT"
       {OFF}";
RC 390 GETKEY A$:IF (A$>"/" AND A$<":") OR(A$>"@"
       {SPACE}AND A$<"G") THEN 47Ø
AC 400 IF A$="+" THEN A$="E":GOTO 47Ø
```

```
QB 410 IF A$="-" THEN A$="F":GOTO 470
FB 420 IF A$=RT$ AND ((I=0) AND (J=1) OR F) THEN P
       RINT B$;:J=2:NEXT:I=24:GOTO 480
RD 430 IF A$="{HOME}" THEN PRINT B$:J=2:NEXT:I=24:
       NEXT:F=0:GOTO 360
XB 440 IF (A$="{RIGHT}") AND F THEN PRINT B$+LF$;:
       GOTO 470
JP 450 IF A$<>LF$ AND A$<>DL$ OR ((I=0) AND (J=1))
        THEN GOSUB 950:GOTO 390
PS 460 A$=LF$+SP$+LF$:PRINT B$+LF$;:J=2-J:IF J THE
       N PRINT LF$;:I=I-3
GB 470 PRINT A$;:NEXT J:PRINT SP$;
HA 480 NEXT I:PRINT:PRINT"{UP}{5 RIGHT}";:L$="
       {27 SPACES}"
DP 490 FOR I=1 TO 25 STEP 3:GET#3,A$,B$:IF A$=SP$
       {SPACE}THEN I=25:NEXT:CLOSE 3:GOTO 220
BA 500 A$=A$+B$:A=DEC(A$):MID$(L$,I,2)=A$:IF I<25
       {SPACE}THEN GOSUB 320:A(I/3)=A:GET#3,A$
AR 510 NEXT I:IF A<>CK THEN GOSUB 950:PRINT:PRINT"
       {RVS} ERROR: REENTER LINE ":F=1:GOTO 360
DX 520 PRINT BE$:B=BS+AD-SA:FOR I=0 TO 7:POKE B+I,
       A(I):NEXT I
XB 530 F=0:AD=AD+8:IF AD<=EA THEN 360
CA 540 CLOSE 3:PRINT"{DOWN}{BLU}** END OF ENTRY **
       {BLK}{2 DOWN}":GOTO 650
MC 550 PRINT BE$;"{CLR}{DOWN}{RVS} DISPLAY DATA ":
       GOSUB 250:IF A$=NL$ THEN 220
JF 560 BANK 0:PRINT"{DOWN}{BLU}PRESS: {RVS}SPACE
       {OFF} TO PAUSE, {RVS}RETURN{OFF} TO BREAK
       [4]{DOWN}"
XA 570 PRINT HEX$(AD)+":";:GOSUB 310:B=BS+AD-SA
DJ 580 FOR I=B TO B+7:A=PEEK(I):PRINT RIGHT$(HEX$(
       A),2);SP$;:GOSUB 320:NEXT I
XB 590 PRINT"{RVS}";RIGHT$(HEX$(CK),2)
GR 600 F=1:AD=AD+8:IF AD>EA THEN PRINT"{BLU}** END
        OF DATA **":GOTO 220
EB 610 GET A$:IF A$=RT$ THEN PRINT BE$:GOTO 220
QK 620 IF A$=SP$ THEN F=F+1:PRINT BE$;
XS 630 ON F GOTO 570,610,570
RF 640 PRINT BE$"{DOWN}{RVS} LOAD DATA ":OP=1:GOTO
        660
BP 650 PRINT BE$"{DOWN}{RVS} SAVE FILE ":OP=0
DM 660 F=0:F$=NL$:INPUT"FILENAME[4]";F$:IF F$=NL$
       {SPACE}THEN 220
RF 670? PRINT"{DOWN}{BLK}{RVS}T{OFF}APE OR {RVS}D
       {OFF}ISK: [4]";
SQ 680 GETKEY A$:IF A$="T" THEN 850:ELSE IF A$<>"D
       " THEN 680
SP 690 PRINT"DISK{DOWN}":IF OP THEN 760
EH 700 DOPEN#1,(F$+",P"),W:IF DS THEN A$=D$:GOTO 7
       40
```

```
JH 710 BANK Ø:POKE BS-2,FNLB(SA):POKE BS-1,FNHB(SA
       ):PRINT"SAVING ";F$:PRINT
MC 720 FOR A=BS-2 TO BS+EA-SA:PRINT#1,CHR$(PEEK(A)
       );:IF ST THEN A$="DISK WRITE ERROR":GOTO 75
       Ø
GC 730 NEXT A:CLOSE 1:PRINT"{BLU}** SAVE COMPLETED
        WITHOUT ERRORS **":GOTO 22Ø
RA 740 IF DS=63 THEN BEGIN:CLOSE 1:INPUT"{BLK}REPL
       ACE EXISTING FILE [Y/N]{4}";A$:IF A$="Y" TH
       EN SCRATCH(F$):PRINT:GOTO 7ØØ:ELSE PRINT"
       {BLK}":GOTO 66Ø:BEND
GA 750 CLOSE 1:GOSUB 95Ø:PRINT"{BLK}{RVS} ERROR DU
       RING SAVE: {4}":PRINT A$:GOTO 22Ø
FD 760 DOPEN#1,(F$+",P"):IF DS THEN A$=DS$:F=4:CLO
       SE 1:GOTO 79Ø
PX 770 GET#1,A$,B$:CLOSE 1:AD=ASC(A$)+256*ASC(B$):
       IF AD<>SA THEN F=1:GOTO 79Ø
KB 780 PRINT"LOADING ";F$:PRINT:BLOAD(F$),BØ,P(BS)
       :AD=SA+FNAD(174)-BS-1:F=-2*(AD<EA)-3*(AD>EA
       )
RQ 790 IF F THEN 8ØØ:ELSE PRINT"{BLU}** LOAD COMPL
       ETED WITHOUT ERRORS **":GOTO 22Ø
ER 800 GOSUB 95Ø:PRINT"{BLK}{RVS} ERROR DURING LOA
       D: {4}":ON F GOSUB 81Ø,82Ø,83Ø,84Ø:GOTO22Ø
QJ 810 PRINT"INCORRECT STARTING ADDRESS (";HEX$(AD
       );")":RETURN
DP 820 PRINT"LOAD ENDED AT ";HEX$(AD):RETURN
EB 830 PRINT"TRUNCATED AT ENDING ADDRESS ("HEX$(EA
       )")":RETURN
FP 840 PRINT"DISK ERROR ";A$:RETURN
KS 850 PRINT"TAPE":AD=POINTER(F$):BANK 1:A=PEEK(AD
       ):AL=PEEK(AD+1):AH=PEEK(AD+2)
XX 860 BANK 15:SYS DEC("FF68"),Ø,1:SYS DEC("FFBA")
       ,1,1,Ø:SYS DEC("FFBD"),A,AL,AH:SYS DEC("FF9
       Ø"),128:IF OP THEN 89Ø
FG 870 PRINT:A=SA:B=EA+1:GOSUB 92Ø:SYS DEC("E919")
       ,3:PRINT"SAVING ";F$
AB 880 A=BS:B=BS+(EA-SA)+1:GOSUB 92Ø:SYS DEC("EA18
       "):PRINT"{DOWN}{BLU}** TAPE SAVE COMPLETED
       {SPACE}**":GOTO 22Ø
CP 890 SYS DEC("E99A"):PRINT:IF PEEK(2816)=5 THEN
       {SPACE}GOSUB 95Ø:PRINT"{DOWN}{BLK}{RVS} FIL
       E NOT FOUND ":GOTO 22Ø
GQ 900 PRINT"LOADING ...{DOWN}":AD=FNAD(2817):IF A
       D<>SA THEN F=1:GOTO 8ØØ:ELSE AD=FNAD(2819)-
       1:F=-2*(AD<EA)-3*(AD>EA)
SH 910 A=BS:B=BS+(EA-SA)+1:GOSUB 92Ø:SYS DEC("E9FB
       "):IF ST THEN 8ØØ:ELSE 79Ø
XB 920 POKE193,FNLB(A):POKE194,FNHB(A):POKE 174,FN
       LB(B):POKE 175,FNHB(B):RETURN
```

```
CP 930 CATALOG:PRINT"{DOWN}{BLU}** PRESS ANY KEY F
       OR MENU **":GETKEY A$:GOTO 220
MM 940 PRINT BE$"{RVS} QUIT {4}";RT$;"ARE YOU SURE
         [Y/N]?":GETKEY A$:IF A$<>"Y" THEN 220:ELSE
         PRINT"{CLR}":BANK 15:END
JE 950 SOUND 1,500,10:RETURN
AF 960 IF ER=14 AND EL=260 THEN RESUME 300
MK 970 IF ER=14 AND EL=500 THEN RESUME NEXT
KJ 980 IF ER=4 AND EL=780 THEN F=4:A$=DS$:RESUME 8
       00
DQ 990 IF ER=30 THEN RESUME:ELSE PRINT ERR$(ER);"
       {SPACE}ERROR IN LINE";EL
```

### Program F-3. LADS Object Code

*This listing must be entered using the MLX program above.*

**Starting Address: 2710**
**Ending Address: 3D27**

```
2710:A9 00 8D 00 FF 8D 1F 3D 96
2718:A0 30 99 D9 3C 88 D0 FA 34
2720:A9 10 85 FC 85 39 8D F1 E5
2728:3C A9 27 85 FD 85 3A 8D 44
2730:F2 3C A9 01 8D 07 3D EA 3A
2738:EA EA 20 B8 2F A9 00 8D F3
2740:DF 3C 20 88 30 AD F4 3C 78
2748:D0 47 A9 93 20 D2 FF A9 35
2750:E6 20 D2 FF A9 4C 20 D2 06
2758:FF A9 41 20 D2 FF A9 44 69
2760:20 D2 FF A9 53 20 D2 FF CE
2768:20 97 35 20 97 35 20 97 BE
2770:35 AD E8 3C D0 0B A9 85 31
2778:85 87 A9 3B 85 88 20 FB DE
2780:2F AD E2 3C 85 FA 8D DB 01
2788:3C AD E3 3C 85 FB 8D DC B4
2790:3C 20 E1 FF D0 03 4C B1 1E
2798:2A AD DF 3C F0 03 4C B1 05
27A0:2A 20 88 30 A9 00 8D E7 70
27A8:3C 8D F3 3C AC F4 3C D0 3D
27B0:03 4C D0 27 8C 08 3D AD CC
27B8:06 3D F0 0C 20 A0 35 20 46
27C0:51 35 20 79 35 20 51 35 A2
27C8:AD FF 3C F0 03 20 6B 34 28
27D0:4C 6A 2F AD DA 3C F0 17 61
27D8:C9 03 D0 72 A9 01 8D DA 55
27E0:3C AD 88 3B D0 68 A9 08 01
27E8:18 6D D9 3C 8D D9 3C 4C 36
27F0:C7 29 AD F4 3C F0 39 A0 2B
27F8:FF C8 B9 85 3B F0 2E 99 9C
```

```
2800:D7 3B C9 20 D0 F3 C8 B9 E7
2808:85 3B C9 3D D0 03 4C F7 1A
2810:29 A2 00 8E 08 3D 8A 99 6A
2818:D7 3B B9 85 3B F0 08 9D FD
2820:85 3B E8 C8 4C 1A 28 9D 64
2828:85 3B 4C D0 27 20 D5 2C 32
2830:20 77 2C 4C D0 27 AD 9A D1
2838:3B C9 40 B0 06 AD 9B 3B 05
2840:EE F3 3C 49 80 8D E0 3C 59
2848:20 22 2D 4C CF 28 A0 00 FB
2850:8C E7 3C AD 88 3B C9 20 28
2858:F0 03 4C 94 2B B9 89 3B 43
2860:C9 41 90 03 EE E7 3C 99 51
2868:9A 3B C8 B9 89 3B F0 16 BA
2870:99 9A 3B C9 41 90 03 EE 79
2878:E7 3C C8 B9 89 3B F0 06 A1
2880:99 9A 3B 4C 7A 28 88 8C 82
2888:E6 3C AD E8 3C D0 40 AD F2
2890:E7 3C D0 A2 A9 9A 85 87 72
2898:A9 3B 85 88 A0 00 AD 9A C0
28A0:3B C9 30 B0 07 18 E6 87 FF
28A8:90 02 E6 88 B1 87 F0 10 C4
28B0:C9 29 F0 0C C9 2C F0 08 F7
28B8:C9 20 F0 04 C8 4C AC 28 4D
28C0:48 98 48 A9 00 91 87 20 74
28C8:FB 2F 68 A8 68 91 87 AD C0
28D0:9A 3B C9 23 F0 3F C9 28 E8
28D8:F0 17 AD DA 3C C9 08 F0 D4
28E0:37 C9 03 D0 71 A9 08 18 07
28E8:6D D9 3C 8D D9 3C 4C C7 E6
28F0:29 AC E6 3C B9 9A 3B C9 1A
28F8:29 F0 10 AD DA 3C C9 01 53
2900:D0 09 A9 10 18 6D D9 3C 99
2908:8D D9 3C AD DA 3C C9 06 5B
2910:F0 53 4C 8C 29 4C A7 29 F4
2918:AD F4 3C D0 03 4C 8C 29 9E
2920:38 AD E2 3C E5 FA 48 AD 73
2928:E3 3C E5 FB B0 0E C9 FF 49
2930:F0 04 68 4C 5D 2C 68 10 4A
2938:0C 4C 48 29 F0 04 68 4C F3
2940:5D 2C 68 10 03 4C 5D 2C 8A
2948:38 E9 02 8D E2 3C A9 00 A5
2950:8D E3 3C 4C 8C 29 AC E6 F7
2958:3C 88 B9 9A 3B C9 2C D0 F5
2960:04 C8 4C 3F 2B AD D9 3C 64
2968:C9 4C D0 03 4C 95 29 AD B5
2970:E3 3C D0 59 AD DA 3C C9 8E
2978:09 F0 52 C9 06 B0 0D C9 49
2980:02 F0 09 A9 04 18 6D D9 01
2988:3C 8D D9 3C 20 B2 34 20 AF
```

```
2990:D3 34 4C F7 29 AC E6 3C E8
2998:B9 9A 3B C9 29 DØ Ø5 A9 B2
29AØ:6C 8D D9 3C 4C F1 29 AD B5
29A8:9B 3B C9 22 DØ Ø6 AD 9C 89
29BØ:3B 8D E2 3C AD DA 3C C9 3F
29B8:Ø1 DØ D1 A9 Ø8 18 6D D9 E9
29CØ:3C 8D D9 3C 4C 8C 29 2Ø 9A
29C8:B2 34 4C F7 29 AD DA 3C 7C
29DØ:C9 Ø2 FØ Ø4 C9 Ø7 DØ ØC FE
29D8:AD D9 3C 18 69 Ø8 8D D9 E1
29EØ:3C 4C F1 29 C9 Ø6 BØ Ø9 Ø6
29E8:AD D9 3C 18 69 ØC 8D D9 Ø2
29FØ:3C 2Ø B2 34 2Ø ED 34 AD D1
29F8:F4 3C DØ Ø3 4C AE 2A AD 3E
2AØØ:Ø6 3D DØ Ø3 4C AE 2A AD 1Ø
2AØ8:Ø8 3D DØ 3E AD Ø2 3D FØ 8E
2A1Ø:2A A9 14 38 E5 EC 8D F5 DD
2A18:3C 2Ø CC FF A2 Ø4 2Ø C9 5B
2A2Ø:FF AC F5 3C 1Ø Ø5 AØ Ø2 F9
2A28:4C 2D 2A A9 2Ø 2Ø D2 FF F4
2A3Ø:88 DØ FA 2Ø CC FF A2 Ø1 ØB
2A38:2Ø FA 2F A9 14 85 EC A9 16
2A4Ø:D7 85 87 A9 3B 85 88 2Ø 8E
2A48:4Ø 35 A9 1E 38 E5 EC 8D E1
2A5Ø:F6 3C A9 1E 85 EC AD Ø2 83
2A58:3D FØ 1A 2Ø CC FF A2 Ø4 7C
2A6Ø:2Ø C9 FF AC F6 3C FØ ØA 96
2A68:3Ø Ø8 A9 2Ø 2Ø D2 FF 88 E2
2A7Ø:DØ FA 2Ø CC FF 2Ø AD 35 CD
2A78:AD ØØ 3D FØ 11 C9 Ø1 DØ DC
2A8Ø:Ø5 A9 3C 4C 88 2A A9 3E 8C
2A88:2Ø D2 FF 2Ø E1 35 AD Ø9 EB
2A9Ø:3D FØ 13 2Ø 51 35 A9 3B 12
2A98:2Ø D2 FF A9 ØØ 85 87 A9 1B
2AAØ:Ø2 85 88 2Ø 4Ø 35 2Ø 97 19
2AA8:35 AD DF 3C DØ Ø3 4C 91 7F
2ABØ:27 AD F4 3C DØ 1Ø EE F4 FF
2AB8:3C AD DB 3C 85 FA AD DC 26
2ACØ:3C 85 FB 4C 3A 27 2Ø CC 54
2AC8:FF A9 2Ø 85 87 A9 3D 85 C6
2ADØ:88 2Ø 97 35 2Ø 51 35 2Ø 88
2AD8:51 35 AE 1F 3D A9 ØØ 2Ø 9B
2AEØ:5A 35 2Ø 4Ø 35 AD Ø2 3D 59
2AE8:FØ 15 2Ø CC FF A2 Ø4 2Ø 7E
2AFØ:C9 FF A9 ØD 2Ø D2 FF 2Ø 9C
2AF8:CC FF A9 Ø4 2Ø C3 FF A9 E2
2BØØ:FC 8D 3Ø DØ A9 ØØ 8D ØØ B3
2BØ8:FF AD 1E 3D FØ 2E A9 Ø4 F8
2B1Ø:8D EA 3C A9 4C 8D D7 3B 8D
2B18:A9 41 8D D8 3B A9 44 8D 69
```

```
2B2Ø:D9 3B A9 53 8D DA 3B 2Ø ØB
2B28:37 2F A9 91 2Ø D2 FF EA 6B
2B3Ø:EA EA A9 44 2Ø 1E CØ A9 D4
2B38:4Ø 2Ø 1E CØ 4C Ø3 4Ø B9 2F
2B4Ø:9A 3B C9 58 FØ 65 88 88 28
2B48:B9 9A 3B C9 29 DØ Ø3 4C Ø5
2B5Ø:F1 28 AD E3 3C DØ ØF AD 8E
2B58:DA 3C C9 Ø2 FØ 52 C9 Ø5 ED
2B6Ø:FØ 4E C9 Ø1 FØ 7A AD DA B3
2B68:3C C9 Ø1 DØ ØC AD D9 3C 83
2B7Ø:18 69 18 8D D9 3C 4C F1 53
2B78:29 AD DA 3C C9 Ø5 FØ Ø8 3A
2B8Ø:A9 31 2Ø 27 2C 4C 94 2B 55
2B88:AD D9 3C 18 69 1C 8D D9 E5
2B9Ø:3C 4C F1 29 2Ø B9 35 2Ø 5B
2B98:AØ 35 A9 A5 85 87 A9 3C F5
2BAØ:85 88 2Ø 4Ø 35 2Ø 97 35 72
2BA8:4C F7 29 AD E3 3C DØ 44 19
2BBØ:AD DA 3C C9 Ø2 DØ ØC A9 CD
2BB8:1Ø 18 6D D9 3C 8D D9 3C 7Ø
2BCØ:4C 8C 29 C9 Ø1 FØ 1Ø C9 D7
2BC8:Ø3 FØ ØC C9 Ø5 FØ Ø8 A9 AØ
2BDØ:32 2Ø 27 2C 4C 94 2B A9 A4
2BD8:14 18 6D D9 3C 8D D9 3C 92
2BEØ:B9 9C 3B C9 59 DØ ØA AD ØF
2BE8:D9 3C C9 B6 FØ Ø3 4C 66 72
2BFØ:2B 4C 8C 29 AD DA 3C C9 2F
2BF8:Ø2 DØ ØC A9 18 18 6D D9 76
2CØØ:3C 8D D9 3C 4C F1 29 C9 1F
2CØ8:Ø1 FØ 1Ø C9 Ø3 FØ ØC C9 79
2C1Ø:Ø5 FØ Ø8 A9 33 2Ø 27 2C 57
2C18:4C 94 2B A9 1C 18 6D D9 B1
2C2Ø:3C 8D D9 3C 4C F1 29 8D Ø3
2C28:F5 3C 8C F7 3C 8E F6 3C E1
2C3Ø:2Ø 97 35 A9 BA 2Ø D2 FF BB
2C38:68 AA 68 A8 98 48 8A 48 4A
2C4Ø:98 2Ø 32 8E 2Ø 97 35 AD 93
2C48:F5 3C AC F7 3C AE F6 3C 86
2C5Ø:6Ø AØ ØØ 98 99 85 3B C8 AC
2C58:CØ 5Ø DØ F8 6Ø 2Ø 97 35 B6
2C6Ø:2Ø B9 35 2Ø AØ 35 A9 14 21
2C68:85 87 A9 3C 85 88 2Ø 4Ø 2D
2C7Ø:35 2Ø 97 35 4C 8C 29 AØ 39
2C78:FF C8 B9 85 3B FØ 56 C9 A6
2C8Ø:2Ø DØ F6 C8 C8 8C EE 3C 1B
2C88:38 A5 FC ED EE 3C 85 FC 55
2C9Ø:A5 FD E9 ØØ 85 FD AØ ØØ DD
2C98:B9 85 3B 49 8Ø 91 FC C8 38
2CAØ:B9 85 3B C9 2Ø FØ Ø5 91 9B
2CA8:FC 4C 9F 2C C8 B9 85 3B BC
```

```
2CB0:C9 3D F0 3B 88 A5 FA 91 71
2CB8:FC C8 A5 FB 91 FC AE EE 03
2CC0:3C CA A0 00 BD 85 3B F0 69
2CC8:08 99 85 3B E8 C8 4C C4 B7
2CD0:2C 99 85 3B 60 20 97 35 F1
2CD8:20 A0 35 20 B9 35 A9 4D 55
2CE0:85 87 A9 3C 85 88 20 40 A5
2CE8:35 20 97 35 4C 1D 2D 88 E3
2CF0:8C EF 3C AD E8 3C D0 17 DE
2CF8:C8 C8 C8 8C E1 3C A9 85 A2
2D00:18 6D E1 3C 85 87 A9 3B 9A
2D08:69 00 85 88 20 FB 2F AC 4C
2D10:EF 3C AD E2 3C 91 FC AD 25
2D18:E3 3C C8 91 FC 68 68 4C 4C
2D20:F7 29 AD F1 3C 85 89 AD 4E
2D28:F2 3C 85 8A 20 30 2E A9 2C
2D30:FF 8D 05 3D 38 A5 FC E5 9A
2D38:89 A5 FD E5 8A B0 63 A2 5F
2D40:00 38 A5 89 E9 02 85 89 E1
2D48:A5 8A E9 00 85 8A A0 00 EC
2D50:B1 89 30 0C A5 89 D0 02 A3
2D58:C6 8A C6 89 E8 4C 50 2D 70
2D60:A5 89 8D F8 3C A5 8A 8D 4C
2D68:F9 3C B1 89 CD E0 3C F0 F8
2D70:03 4C 92 2D E8 8E E1 3C 06
2D78:A2 01 AD F3 3C F0 04 C8 CF
2D80:20 30 2E C8 B9 9A 3B F0 E8
2D88:53 C9 30 90 4F E8 D1 89 59
2D90:F0 F1 AD F8 3C 85 89 AD DD
2D98:F9 3C 85 8A 20 30 2E 4C C2
2DA0:34 2D AD 05 3D 30 01 60 73
2DA8:AD F4 3C D0 02 F0 17 20 CD
2DB0:B9 35 20 A0 35 20 51 35 45
2DB8:A9 3D 85 87 A9 3C 85 88 32
2DC0:20 40 35 20 97 35 68 68 AE
2DC8:AD D9 3C 29 1F C9 10 F0 BB
2DD0:08 AD 00 3D D0 03 4C F1 8B
2DD8:29 4C 8C 29 EC E1 3C F0 57
2DE0:03 4C 92 2D EE 05 3D F0 EB
2DE8:03 20 39 2E AC E1 3C AD E9
2DF0:F3 3C F0 01 C8 B1 89 8D 30
2DF8:E2 3C C8 B1 89 8D E3 3C 8E
2E00:AD 00 3D F0 0A C9 02 D0 36
2E08:1E AD E3 3C 8D E2 3C AD 3D
2E10:FF 3C F0 13 18 AD FD 3C 7A
2E18:6D E2 3C 8D E2 3C AD FE A6
2E20:3C 6D E3 3C 8D E3 3C AD 58
2E28:F4 3C D0 01 60 4C 92 2D BE
2E30:A5 89 D0 02 C6 8A C6 89 73
2E38:60 20 B9 35 A9 87 85 87 55
```

```
2E40:A9 3C 85 88 20 40 35 20 46
2E48:97 35 60 A9 00 8D 00 FF 9A
2E50:A9 FC 8D 30 D0 20 CC FF 16
2E58:AD EA 3C A2 D7 A0 3B 20 CF
2E60:BD FF A9 00 AA 20 68 FF 77
2E68:A9 00 A2 08 A8 20 BA FF A9
2E70:A9 00 AA A0 80 20 D5 FF 31
2E78:B0 2F 20 CC FF A9 00 8D FD
2E80:00 FF A9 00 85 41 A9 80 17
2E88:85 42 A9 FC 8D 30 D0 A9 B5
2E90:91 20 D2 FF A9 44 20 1E D4
2E98:C0 A9 91 20 D2 FF A9 44 22
2EA0:20 1E C0 A9 40 20 1E C0 C6
2EA8:60 20 B9 35 A9 FC 8D 30 54
2EB0:D0 4C 03 40 A9 00 8D 00 55
2EB8:FF A9 FC 8D 30 D0 A9 91 A1
2EC0:20 D2 FF 20 D2 FF A9 44 12
2EC8:20 1E C0 AD EB 3C A2 EE 34
2ED0:A0 3B 20 BD FF A9 01 A2 77
2ED8:00 20 68 FF A9 00 A2 08 E4
2EE0:A0 00 20 BA FF AD DB 3C E7
2EE8:85 87 AD DC 3C 85 88 A9 20
2EF0:87 A6 FA A4 FB 20 D8 FF 76
2EF8:B0 AF 20 CC FF A9 00 8D 9E
2F00:00 FF 4C B1 2A A9 00 20 1B
2F08:BD FF A2 00 20 68 FF A2 DE
2F10:04 8A A0 FF 20 BA FF 20 33
2F18:C0 FF B0 04 20 CC FF 60 C1
2F20:20 D2 FF A5 90 D0 05 20 8F
2F28:E2 2F D0 F4 20 B9 35 A9 29
2F30:FC 8D 30 D0 4C 03 40 AD 20
2F38:EA 3C A2 D7 A0 3B 20 BD DC
2F40:FF A9 00 A2 00 20 68 FF 84
2F48:A2 08 A0 FF 20 BA FF A9 A3
2F50:00 20 D5 FF B0 09 20 CC 28
2F58:FF A9 00 8D 00 FF 60 20 DA
2F60:B9 35 A9 FC 8D 30 D0 4C 09
2F68:03 40 A0 00 A2 FF E8 B9 0D
2F70:5D 3A CD 85 3B F0 0A C8 98
2F78:C8 C8 E0 39 D0 F0 4C F2 F2
2F80:27 C8 B9 5D 3A CD 86 3B 03
2F88:F0 06 C8 C8 D0 E0 F0 EE 61
2F90:C8 B9 5D 3A CD 87 3B F0 05
2F98:05 C8 D0 D2 F0 E0 AD 88 E1
2FA0:3B C9 20 F0 04 C9 00 D0 3A
2FA8:D5 BD 05 3B 8D DA 3C BC C2
2FB0:3D 3B 8C D9 3C 4C D3 27 8D
2FB8:A9 00 85 41 A9 1C 85 42 BB
2FC0:20 E2 2F 20 E2 2F 20 E2 C6
2FC8:2F 20 E2 2F 20 E2 2F C9 CA
```

```
2FDØ:AC FØ ØE A9 Ø3 85 87 A9 Ø5
2FD8:3C 85 88 2Ø 4Ø 35 4C C6 FF
2FEØ:2A 6Ø E6 41 DØ Ø2 E6 42 FB
2FE8:8C F7 3C AØ ØØ B1 41 EA 51
2FFØ:EA EA EA EA Ø8 AC F7 3C AA
2FF8:28 6Ø 6Ø AØ ØØ B1 87 FØ 6Ø
3ØØØ:Ø4 C8 4C FD 2F 8C ØØ 3C E5
3ØØ8:88 A9 ØØ 8D E2 3C 8D E3 F6
3Ø1Ø:3C A2 Ø1 8E F6 3C B1 87 D3
3Ø18:29 ØF 8D FE 3B 8D Ø1 3C CØ
3Ø2Ø:A9 ØØ 8D FF 3B 8D Ø2 3C 57
3Ø28:CA FØ 12 2Ø 4D 3Ø AD FE F3
3Ø3Ø:3B 8D Ø1 3C AD FF 3B 8D E6
3Ø38:Ø2 3C 4C 28 3Ø EE F6 3C 1C
3Ø4Ø:AE F6 3C 2Ø 74 3Ø 88 CE 83
3Ø48:ØØ 3C DØ CA 6Ø 18 ØE FE FC
3Ø5Ø:3B 2E FF 3B ØE FE 3B 2E 9E
3Ø58:FF 3B 18 AD Ø1 3C 6D FE 38
3Ø6Ø:3B 8D FE 3B AD Ø2 3C 6D BØ
3Ø68:FF 3B 8D FF 3B ØE FE 3B 94
3Ø7Ø:2E FF 3B 6Ø 18 AD FE 3B Ø6
3Ø78:6D E2 3C 8D E2 3C AD FF ØC
3Ø8Ø:3B 6D E3 3C 8D E3 3C 6Ø EE
3Ø88:2Ø 51 2C AØ ØØ 8C F7 3C 3B
3Ø9Ø:8C E8 3C 8C Ø9 3D 8C ØØ 18
3Ø98:3D 8C FF 3C AD Ø4 3D DØ 47
3ØAØ:ØC 2Ø E2 2F 8D DD 3C 2Ø DA
3ØA8:E2 2F 8D DE 3C 2Ø E2 2F 3D
3ØBØ:DØ Ø8 2Ø D8 31 68 68 4C 55
3ØB8:91 27 C9 2Ø FØ EF 4C C9 9Ø
3ØCØ:3Ø 2Ø E2 2F DØ Ø3 4C D8 94
3ØC8:31 C9 3A DØ Ø3 4C 73 31 E9
3ØDØ:C9 3B DØ 73 8C F5 3C AD 98
3ØD8:Ø2 3D FØ 55 8D Ø9 3D AD B5
3ØEØ:F5 3C FØ Ø6 2Ø 11 31 4C BD
3ØE8:39 31 2Ø E2 2F FØ ØE C9 87
3ØFØ:7F 9Ø Ø3 2Ø Ø8 34 99 85 61
3ØF8:3B C8 4C EA 3Ø 2Ø AØ 35 D9
31ØØ:2Ø 51 35 2Ø AD 35 2Ø 97 89
31Ø8:35 A9 ØØ 8D F5 3C 4C 39 BA
311Ø:31 8D Ø9 3D 8D F5 3C AØ CØ
3118:ØØ 2Ø E2 2F DØ Ø7 99 ØØ A7
312Ø:Ø2 AC F5 3C 6Ø 1Ø Ø3 2Ø 9A
3128:DE 33 99 ØØ Ø2 C8 4C 19 DE
313Ø:31 2Ø E2 2F FØ Ø3 4C 31 DF
3138:31 2Ø D8 31 AD F5 3C DØ F7
314Ø:Ø5 68 68 4C 91 27 6Ø C9 C4
3148:B1 FØ 36 C9 B3 FØ 3A C9 C2
315Ø:AA DØ Ø3 EE FF 3C C9 AC BC
3158:DØ Ø3 4C 91 31 C9 2E FØ 84
```

```
3160:16 C9 24 F0 15 C9 7F 90 33
3168:03 20 08 34 99 85 3B C8 BA
3170:4C C1 30 8D 04 3D 60 4C 6A
3178:8C 32 99 85 3B C8 4C FF CE
3180:31 A9 02 8D 00 3D 4C C1 4E
3188:30 A9 01 8D 00 3D 4C C1 B5
3190:30 20 C1 30 A9 18 20 D2 0F
3198:FF A9 2A 20 D2 FF 20 AD 31
31A0:35 20 97 35 AD E8 3C D0 46
31A8:20 A0 00 B9 85 3B C9 20 AB
31B0:F0 04 C8 4C AB 31 C8 84 A2
31B8:87 A9 85 18 65 87 85 87 57
31C0:A9 3B 69 00 85 88 20 FB 7E
31C8:2F AD E2 3C 85 FA AD E3 A5
31D0:3C 85 FB 68 68 4C 91 27 77
31D8:99 85 3B C8 C0 50 D0 F8 3F
31E0:99 85 3B 20 E2 2F 20 E2 D1
31E8:2F F0 06 A9 00 8D 04 3D F5
31F0:60 AD 01 3D F0 03 4C FA 0A
31F8:33 A9 01 8D DF 3C 60 A2 AB
3200:00 8E F6 3C 20 E2 2F 08 9D
3208:AE F6 3C 28 F0 2C C9 3A 91
3210:F0 28 C9 20 F0 EB C9 3B 38
3218:F0 20 C9 2C F0 0F C9 29 79
3220:F0 0B 9D C2 3B E8 99 85 D5
3228:3B C8 4C 01 32 8E E9 3C D1
3230:99 85 3B C8 20 4E 32 4C A1
3238:C1 30 8D F5 3C A9 00 8E B1
3240:E9 3C 99 85 3B 20 4E 32 5D
3248:AD F5 3C 4C C4 30 A9 00 87
3250:8D E2 3C 8D E3 3C AA 0E 08
3258:E2 3C 2E E3 3C 0E E2 3C 5D
3260:2E E3 3C 0E E2 3C 2E E3 85
3268:3C 0E E2 3C 2E E3 3C BD C5
3270:C2 3B C9 41 90 02 E9 07 B9
3278:29 0F 0D E2 3C 8D E2 3C 1F
3280:E8 EC E9 3C D0 D1 EE E8 2A
3288:3C A9 01 60 C0 00 F0 0E 91
3290:AE F4 3C D0 09 48 98 48 01
3298:20 77 2C 68 A8 68 99 85 96
32A0:3B C8 20 E2 2F 99 85 3B 2D
32A8:C8 C9 42 D0 68 A9 00 8D B0
32B0:FA 3C AD F4 3C F0 17 8C 07
32B8:6A 34 AD 06 3D F0 0F 20 61
32C0:A0 35 20 51 35 20 79 35 2E
32C8:20 51 35 AC 6A 34 20 E2 4A
32D0:2F 99 85 3B C8 C9 20 D0 16
32D8:F5 20 E2 2F 99 85 3B C8 B1
32E0:C9 22 D0 45 20 E2 2F D0 DC
32E8:03 4C C3 33 C9 3A D0 03 69
```

```
32FØ:4C C6 33 C9 3B DØ ØC 2Ø 85
32F8:11 31 AE Ø2 3D 8E Ø9 3D 9B
33ØØ:4C C3 33 C9 22 DØ Ø3 4C 27
33Ø8:E4 32 AE F4 3C DØ Ø9 2Ø E9
331Ø:38 35 4C E4 32 4C CD 36 4C
3318:99 85 3B AA 8C F7 3C 2Ø 9B
332Ø:23 35 AC F7 3C C8 4C E4 FC
3328:32 A2 ØØ 8E FB 3C 9D E7 2D
333Ø:3B E8 AD FB 3C DØ 7D 8E 92
3338:F6 3C 2Ø E2 2F Ø8 AE F6 49
334Ø:3C 28 FØ 43 C9 3A FØ 3F 79
3348:C9 3B DØ ØC 2Ø 11 31 AE 93
335Ø:Ø2 3D 8E Ø9 3D 4C 87 33 C6
3358:8D AE 3B AD F4 3C DØ ØD BA
336Ø:AD AE 3B C9 2Ø DØ CB 2Ø 49
3368:38 35 4C 32 33 AD AE 3B CD
337Ø:99 85 3B C8 C9 2Ø FØ 18 C1
3378:C9 ØØ FØ 14 C9 3A FØ 1Ø 4C
338Ø:9D E7 3B E8 4C 32 33 EE 26
3388:FB 3C 8D AF 3B 4C 58 33 97
339Ø:A9 E7 85 87 A9 3B 85 88 BC
3398:8C F7 3C 2Ø FB 2F AE E2 A9
33AØ:3C 2Ø 23 35 AC F7 3C A9 4C
33A8:ØØ A2 Ø5 9D E7 3B CA DØ C4
33BØ:FA 4C 32 33 AD F4 3C DØ AB
33B8:Ø3 2Ø 38 35 AD AF 3B C9 6F
33CØ:3A FØ Ø3 2Ø D8 31 8D Ø4 8D
33C8:3D EE Ø8 3D 68 68 AD F4 93
33DØ:3C FØ Ø8 AD Ø6 3D FØ Ø3 77
33D8:4C 75 2A 4C 91 27 48 A9 3Ø
33EØ:ØØ 8D 5B 34 A9 Ø2 8D 5C 26
33E8:34 68 2Ø Ø8 34 48 A9 85 A3
33FØ:8D 5B 34 A9 3B 8D 5C 34 13
33F8:68 6Ø A9 BF 85 87 A9 3C B6
34ØØ:85 88 2Ø 4Ø 35 4C C6 2A E7
34Ø8:8C F5 3C 38 E9 7F AØ 17 E4
341Ø:84 8E AØ 44 84 8F C9 4F FB
3418:DØ 11 AØ C9 84 8E AØ 46 C3
342Ø:84 8F 2Ø E2 2F A8 88 98 A6
3428:4C 3D 34 C9 7F DØ ØE AØ 25
343Ø:Ø9 84 8E AØ 46 84 8F 2Ø 9D
3438:E2 2F A8 88 98 AA AØ ØØ 2C
344Ø:CA FØ ØE B1 8E 48 E6 8E 19
3448:DØ Ø2 E6 8F 68 1Ø F4 3Ø ØD
345Ø:EF AE F5 3C AØ ØØ B1 8E D5
3458:3Ø Ø7 9D 85 3B C8 E8 DØ 46
346Ø:F5 29 7F 8E F7 3C AC F7 E8
3468:3C 6Ø ØØ AØ ØØ A2 ØØ B9 55
347Ø:85 3B C9 2B FØ Ø4 C8 4C CB
3478:6F 34 C8 B9 85 3B 2Ø 8A 3E
```

```
3480:34 BØ 12 9D C2 3B E8 4C 6C
3488:7A 34 C9 3A BØ Ø6 38 E9 1Ø
3490:3Ø 38 E9 DØ 6Ø A9 ØØ 9D BØ
3498:C2 3B A9 C2 85 87 A9 3B 6B
34AØ:85 88 2Ø FB 2F AD E2 3C E3
34A8:8D FD 3C AD E3 3C 8D FE E3
34BØ:3C 6Ø AD F4 3C DØ Ø4 2Ø A1
34B8:38 35 6Ø AD Ø6 3D FØ ØC 84
34CØ:2Ø CC FF AE D9 3C 2Ø 5A B1
34C8:35 2Ø 51 35 AE D9 3C 2Ø C6
34DØ:23 35 6Ø AD F4 3C DØ Ø4 3D
34D8:2Ø 38 35 6Ø AD Ø6 3D FØ FC
34EØ:Ø6 AE E2 3C 2Ø 5A 35 AE 9B
34E8:E2 3C 4C 23 35 AD F4 3C 14
34FØ:DØ Ø7 2Ø 38 35 2Ø 38 35 DA
34F8:6Ø AD Ø6 3D FØ Ø6 AE E2 71
35ØØ:3C 2Ø 5A 35 AE E2 3C 2Ø C8
35Ø8:23 35 AD Ø6 3D FØ ØE AD DE
351Ø:Ø7 3D FØ Ø3 2Ø 51 35 AE FA
3518:E3 3C 2Ø 5A 35 AE E3 3C 95
352Ø:4C 23 35 8E E1 3C AD Ø3 67
3528:3D FØ ØD EA EA EA EA EA 81
353Ø:AØ ØØ 8A 91 FA EA EA EA 99
3538:18 E6 FA DØ Ø2 E6 FB 6Ø D8
354Ø:AØ ØØ B1 87 FØ ØA 2Ø 2D C6
3548:C7 2Ø D5 35 C8 4C 42 35 DD
355Ø:6Ø A9 2Ø 2Ø 2D C7 2Ø D5 F9
3558:35 6Ø 8E F6 3C AD Ø7 3D 9A
356Ø:FØ ØB 8A 2Ø A6 36 2Ø FF A7
3568:35 AE F6 3C 6Ø A9 ØØ 2Ø 85
357Ø:32 8E 2Ø FF 35 AE F6 3C 2A
3578:6Ø AD Ø7 3D FØ ØE A5 FB 3A
358Ø:2Ø A6 36 A5 FA 2Ø A6 36 A1
3588:2Ø 3C 36 6Ø A6 FA A5 FB 47
359Ø:2Ø 32 8E 2Ø 3C 36 6Ø A9 9Ø
3598:ØD 2Ø 2D C7 2Ø D5 35 6Ø D6
35AØ:AE DD 3C AD DE 3C 2Ø 32 96
35A8:8E 2Ø 79 36 6Ø A9 85 85 2F
35BØ:87 A9 3B 85 88 2Ø 4Ø 35 83
35B8:6Ø A9 Ø7 2Ø D2 FF 2Ø D2 4A
35CØ:FF 2Ø D2 FF A9 12 2Ø D2 36
35C8:FF 2Ø AD 35 A9 ØD 2Ø D2 D8
35DØ:FF EE 1F 3D 6Ø 2Ø BF 36 E7
35D8:AE F4 3C DØ Ø4 AE F6 3C 71
35EØ:6Ø AE Ø2 3D DØ Ø4 AE F6 26
35E8:3C 6Ø 2Ø CC FF A2 Ø4 2Ø ØD
35FØ:C9 FF AD F5 3C 2Ø D2 FF 5D
35F8:2Ø CC FF 2Ø C6 36 6Ø 2Ø 98
36ØØ:BF 36 AE F4 3C DØ Ø4 AE DA
36Ø8:F6 3C 6Ø AE Ø2 3D DØ Ø4 AØ
```

```
3610:AE F6 3C 60 20 BF 36 20 AB
3618:CC FF A2 04 20 C9 FF AD 55
3620:07 3D F0 09 AD F6 3C 20 EF
3628:A6 36 4C 35 36 A9 00 AE 59
3630:F6 3C 20 32 8E 20 CC FF DC
3638:20 C6 36 60 20 BF 36 AE 4E
3640:F4 3C D0 04 AE F6 3C 60 BA
3648:AE 02 3D D0 04 AE F6 3C 46
3650:60 20 CC FF A2 04 20 C9 BD
3658:FF AE 07 3D F0 0D A5 FB 28
3660:20 A6 36 A5 FA 20 A6 36 83
3668:4C 72 36 A5 FB A6 FA 20 49
3670:32 8E 20 CC FF 20 C6 36 AE
3678:60 20 BF 36 AE F4 3C D0 0B
3680:04 AE F6 3C 60 AE 02 3D 3C
3688:D0 04 AE F6 3C 60 20 CC 14
3690:FF A2 04 20 C9 FF AD DE B0
3698:3C AE DD 3C 20 32 8E 20 55
36A0:CC FF 20 C6 36 60 48 29 D0
36A8:0F A8 B9 75 3B AA 68 4A F4
36B0:4A 4A 4A A8 B9 75 3B 20 E2
36B8:D2 FF 8A 20 D2 FF 60 8D C6
36C0:F5 3C 8C F7 3C 60 AD F5 FC
36C8:3C AC F7 3C 60 C9 46 D0 C8
36D0:08 20 30 37 68 68 4C 91 D1
36D8:27 C9 80 D0 06 20 7A 37 45
36E0:4C D4 36 C9 44 D0 03 4C C3
36E8:C4 37 C9 50 D0 03 4C 24 13
36F0:39 C9 4E D0 03 4C 58 39 76
36F8:C9 4F D0 03 4C 50 39 C9 48
3700:53 D0 03 4C 10 3A C9 48 B6
3708:D0 03 4C 2A 3A 99 85 3B 4A
3710:20 A0 35 20 51 35 20 79 78
3718:35 20 B9 35 20 AD 35 A9 7F
3720:A5 85 87 A9 3C 85 88 20 77
3728:40 35 20 97 35 4C 37 39 04
3730:20 E2 2F C9 20 F0 03 4C 01
3738:30 37 A0 00 20 E2 2F C9 55
3740:00 F0 0E C9 7F 90 03 20 AD
3748:08 34 99 85 3B C8 4C 3C 25
3750:37 8C EA 3C A0 00 B9 85 9C
3758:3B F0 07 99 D7 3B C8 4C A4
3760:56 37 20 79 35 20 51 35 65
3768:20 AD 35 20 97 35 20 4B 18
3770:2E 20 E2 2F A2 00 8E DF 5F
3778:3C 60 AD F4 3C F0 03 4C 1A
3780:A9 37 A9 2E 20 D2 FF A9 9F
3788:45 20 D2 FF A9 4E 20 D2 95
3790:FF A9 44 20 D2 FF A9 20 FD
3798:20 D2 FF 20 E2 2F 20 3A 1C
```

```
37A0:37 AD F4 3C F0 03 EE DF C9
37A8:3C EE F4 3C AD F4 3C C9 D6
37B0:02 D0 03 4C 3F 3A AD DB 93
37B8:3C 85 FA AD DC 3C 85 FB BF
37C0:20 88 30 60 EE 03 3D EE 5A
37C8:1E 3D EE 01 3D 20 E2 2F E2
37D0:C9 20 F0 F9 A0 00 C9 7F 02
37D8:90 1C 4C E8 37 20 E2 2F DD
37E0:C9 20 F0 1C C9 7F 90 0E 97
37E8:8C 6A 34 48 20 08 34 68 35
37F0:AC 6A 34 20 4A 3A 99 85 CC
37F8:3B 99 D7 3B C8 4C DD 37 84
3800:8C EA 3C 99 85 3B A0 00 EC
3808:A9 40 99 EE 3B C8 A9 30 FF
3810:99 EE 3B C8 A9 3A 99 EE 55
3818:3B C8 20 E2 2F F0 2D C9 EB
3820:7F 90 18 48 A9 EE 8D 5B 7B
3828:34 A9 3B 8D 5C 34 68 8C 6E
3830:F7 3C 20 08 34 20 ED 33 61
3838:AC F7 3C C9 20 F0 DB 99 37
3840:85 3B 99 EE 3B C8 4C 1A 14
3848:38 20 37 39 8C EB 3C 20 04
3850:D8 31 A2 00 8E DF 3C A0 DA
3858:00 B9 0A 3D 99 37 27 C8 0D
3860:B9 0A 3D 99 37 27 C8 B9 13
3868:0A 3D 99 37 27 C8 A9 80 04
3870:8D BD 2F A9 EA 8D C0 2F D5
3878:8D C1 2F 8D C2 2F B9 0A 2F
3880:3D C8 8D ED 2F B9 0A 3D 04
3888:C8 8D EE 2F B9 0A 3D C8 CA
3890:8D EF 2F B9 0A 3D C8 8D A9
3898:F0 2F B9 0A 3D C8 8D F1 3F
38A0:2F B9 0A 3D C8 8D F2 2F BD
38A8:B9 0A 3D C8 8D F3 2F B9 01
38B0:0A 3D C8 8D 2B 35 B9 0A 13
38B8:3D C8 8D 2C 35 B9 0A 3D 50
38C0:C8 8D 2D 35 B9 0A 3D C8 2B
38C8:8D 2E 35 B9 0A 3D C8 8D 32
38D0:2F 35 B9 0A 3D C8 8D 33 59
38D8:35 B9 0A 3D C8 8D 34 35 81
38E0:B9 0A 3D C8 8D 35 35 B9 4A
38E8:0A 3D C8 8D 36 35 B9 0A A3
38F0:3D 8D 37 35 A9 EA A2 00 DB
38F8:9D 99 27 E8 E0 08 D0 F8 D3
3900:A9 FF 8D 8B 2E 68 68 AD 43
3908:1E 3D C9 01 F0 03 4C 91 DF
3910:27 A9 91 20 D2 FF 20 D2 5E
3918:FF A9 44 20 1E C0 20 4B FE
3920:2E 4C 3A 27 AD F4 3C F0 21
3928:0E 20 05 2F EE 02 3D 20 57
```

```
3930:CC FF A9 01 8D 06 3D 20 6D
3938:E2 2F F0 07 C9 3A F0 06 95
3940:4C 37 39 20 D8 31 68 68 94
3948:A2 00 8E DF 3C 4C 91 27 39
3950:A9 01 8D 03 3D 4C 37 39 7C
3958:AD F4 3C F0 DA 20 E2 2F C1
3960:C9 50 F0 0C C9 4F F0 3A 52
3968:C9 53 F0 6A C9 48 F0 4C F6
3970:A9 2E 20 D2 FF A9 4E 20 D7
3978:D2 FF A9 50 20 D2 FF 20 FA
3980:97 35 CE 02 3D 20 CC FF 0A
3988:A2 04 20 C9 FF A9 0D 20 CE
3990:D2 FF A9 04 20 C3 FF 20 12
3998:CC FF A2 01 20 FA 2F 4C 6D
39A0:37 39 A9 2E 20 D2 FF A9 0B
39A8:4E 20 D2 FF A9 4F 20 D2 42
39B0:FF 20 97 35 A9 00 8D 03 DC
39B8:3D 4C 37 39 A9 2E 20 D2 70
39C0:FF A9 4E 20 D2 FF A9 48 9B
39C8:20 D2 FF 20 97 35 A9 00 E6
39D0:8D 07 3D 4C 37 39 A9 2E 58
39D8:20 D2 FF A9 4E 20 D2 FF 43
39E0:A9 53 20 D2 FF 20 97 35 13
39E8:A9 00 8D 06 3D 4C 37 39 05
39F0:A6 90 D0 01 60 A9 00 20 CE
39F8:5A 35 20 51 35 A9 63 85 9B
3A00:87 A9 3C 85 88 20 B9 35 EF
3A08:20 40 35 68 68 4C C6 2A F5
3A10:AD F4 3C F0 12 A9 2E 20 E2
3A18:D2 FF A9 53 20 D2 FF 20 CC
3A20:97 35 A9 01 8D 06 3D 4C 3E
3A28:37 39 A9 2E 20 D2 FF A9 94
3A30:48 20 D2 FF 20 97 35 A9 9E
3A38:01 8D 07 3D 4C 37 39 AD A4
3A40:01 3D F0 03 20 B4 2E 4C 4F
3A48:B1 2A 48 A9 D7 8D 5B 34 A3
3A50:A9 3B 8D 5C 34 68 20 08 6B
3A58:34 20 ED 33 60 4C 44 41 DD
3A60:4C 44 59 4A 53 52 52 54 B8
3A68:53 42 43 53 42 45 51 42 C0
3A70:43 43 43 4D 50 42 4E 45 02
3A78:4C 44 58 4A 4D 50 53 54 7A
3A80:41 53 54 59 53 54 58 49 70
3A88:4E 59 44 45 59 44 45 58 16
3A90:44 45 43 49 4E 58 49 4E 2A
3A98:43 43 50 59 43 50 58 53 7E
3AA0:42 43 53 45 43 41 44 43 B0
3AA8:43 4C 43 54 41 58 54 41 D4
3AB0:59 54 58 41 54 59 41 50 E0
3AB8:48 41 50 4C 41 42 52 4B 73
```

```
3ACØ:42 4D 49 42 5Ø 4C 41 4E 7B
3AC8:44 4F 52 41 45 4F 52 42 DF
3ADØ:49 54 42 56 43 42 56 53 CF
3AD8:52 4F 4C 52 4F 52 4C 53 A8
3AEØ:52 43 4C 44 43 4C 49 41 3C
3AE8:53 4C 5Ø 48 5Ø 5Ø 4C 5Ø 55
3AFØ:52 54 49 53 45 44 53 45 29
3AF8:49 54 53 58 54 58 53 43 Ø5
3BØØ:4C 56 4E 4F 5Ø Ø1 Ø5 Ø9 8A
3BØ8:ØØ Ø8 Ø8 Ø8 Ø1 Ø8 Ø5 Ø6 3A
3B1Ø:Ø1 Ø2 Ø2 ØØ ØØ ØØ Ø2 ØØ CB
3B18:Ø2 Ø4 Ø4 Ø1 ØØ Ø1 ØØ ØØ 25
3B2Ø:ØØ ØØ ØØ ØØ ØØ ØØ Ø8 Ø8 AE
3B28:Ø1 Ø1 Ø1 Ø7 Ø8 Ø8 Ø3 Ø3 59
3B3Ø:Ø3 ØØ ØØ Ø3 ØØ ØØ ØØ ØØ 58
3B38:ØØ ØØ ØØ ØØ ØØ A1 AØ 2Ø 96
3B4Ø:6Ø BØ FØ 9Ø C1 DØ A2 4C 1D
3B48:81 84 86 C8 88 CA C6 E8 E3
3B5Ø:E6 CØ EØ E1 38 61 18 AA C6
3B58:A8 8A 98 48 68 ØØ 3Ø 1Ø 11
3B6Ø:21 Ø1 41 24 5Ø 7Ø 22 62 FC
3B68:42 D8 58 Ø2 Ø8 28 4Ø F8 BB
3B7Ø:78 BA 9A B8 EA 3Ø 31 32 5D
3B78:33 34 35 36 37 38 39 41 ED
3B8Ø:42 43 44 45 46 ØØ ØØ ØØ F7
3B88:ØØ ØØ ØØ ØØ ØØ ØØ ØØ ØØ FE
3B9Ø:ØØ ØØ ØØ ØØ ØØ ØØ ØØ ØØ Ø7
3B98:ØØ ØØ ØØ ØØ ØØ ØØ ØØ ØØ ØF
3BAØ:ØØ ØØ ØØ ØØ ØØ ØØ ØØ ØØ 17
3BA8:ØØ ØØ ØØ ØØ ØØ ØØ ØØ ØØ 1F
3BBØ:ØØ ØØ ØØ ØØ ØØ ØØ ØØ ØØ 27
3BB8:ØØ ØØ ØØ ØØ ØØ ØØ ØØ ØØ 2F
3BCØ:ØØ ØØ ØØ ØØ ØØ ØØ ØØ ØØ 37
3BC8:ØØ ØØ ØØ ØØ ØØ ØØ ØØ ØØ 3F
3BDØ:ØØ ØØ ØØ ØØ ØØ ØØ ØØ ØØ 47
3BD8:ØØ ØØ ØØ ØØ ØØ ØØ ØØ ØØ 4F
3BEØ:ØØ ØØ ØØ ØØ ØØ ØØ ØØ ØØ 57
3BE8:ØØ ØØ ØØ ØØ ØØ ØØ ØØ ØØ 5F
3BFØ:ØØ ØØ ØØ ØØ ØØ ØØ ØØ ØØ 67
3BF8:ØØ ØØ ØØ ØØ ØØ ØØ ØØ ØØ 6F
3CØØ:ØØ ØØ ØØ 4E 4F 2Ø 53 54 53
3CØ8:41 52 54 2Ø 41 44 44 52 38
3C1Ø:45 53 53 ØØ 2D 2D 2D 2D 1Ø
3C18:2D 2D 2D 2D 2D 2D 2D 2D 9Ø
3C2Ø:2D 2D 2D 2D 2D 2D 2D 2D 98
3C28:2Ø 42 52 41 4E 43 48 2Ø CF
3C3Ø:4F 55 54 2Ø 4F 46 2Ø 52 58
3C38:41 4E 47 45 ØØ 55 4E 44 58
3C4Ø:45 46 49 4E 45 44 2Ø 4C C2
3C48:41 42 45 4C ØØ 2Ø 2Ø 2Ø 4Ø
```

```
3C50:20 20 20 20 20 20 20 4E F6
3C58:41 4B 45 44 20 4C 41 42 28
3C60:45 4C 00 20 20 20 20 20 72
3C68:20 3C 3C 3C 3C 3C 3C 3C D2
3C70:3C 20 44 49 53 4B 20 45 79
3C78:52 52 4F 52 20 3E 3E 3E 72
3C80:3E 3E 3E 3E 3E 20 00 20 E5
3C88:20 20 20 20 20 2D 2D 20 4F
3C90:44 55 50 4C 49 43 41 54 7D
3C98:45 44 20 4C 41 42 45 4C 77
3CA0:20 2D 2D 20 00 20 20 20 FC
3CA8:20 20 20 2D 2D 20 53 59 F9
3CB0:4E 54 41 58 20 45 52 52 20
3CB8:4F 52 20 2D 2D 20 00 20 4E
3CC0:20 2E 46 49 4C 45 20 4F 39
3CC8:52 20 2E 45 4E 44 20 52 A2
3CD0:45 51 55 49 52 45 44 20 CF
3CD8:00 00 00 00 00 00 00 00 51
3CE0:00 00 00 00 00 00 00 00 59
3CE8:00 00 00 00 00 00 00 00 61
3CF0:00 00 00 00 00 00 00 00 69
3CF8:00 00 00 00 00 00 00 00 71
3D00:00 00 00 00 00 00 00 00 7A
3D08:00 00 20 4B 2E A9 41 A2 78
3D10:00 20 74 FF A9 FA 8D B9 2F
3D18:02 A2 01 20 77 FF 00 00 1A
3D20:20 45 52 52 4F 52 53 00 D5
```

### Program F-4. Loader

```
MH 1 REM 1571 DISK DRIVE USERS SUBSTITUTE 'BOOT' F
     OR 'BLOAD' IN LINES 30 AND 100
FK 10 PRINT"{CLR}
GD 20 KEY 1,""+CHR$(17)+CHR$(27)+CHR$(74)+CHR$(27)
      +CHR$(64)+"SYS 10000"+CHR$(13)
BQ 30 KEY 3,""+CHR$(17)+CHR$(27)+CHR$(74)+CHR$(27)
      +CHR$(64)+"BLOAD"+CHR$(34)+"LADS"+CHR$(13)
KA 40 KEY 5,""+CHR$(17)+CHR$(27)+CHR$(74)+CHR$(27)
      +CHR$(64)+"SYS 2816"+CHR$(13)
FR 45 KEY 2,""+CHR$(17)+CHR$(27)+CHR$(74)+CHR$(27)
      +CHR$(64)+"AUTO 10"+CHR$(13)
BJ 50 FOR I = 7169 TO 7224:READA:POKEI,A:NEXT
GP 60 DATA 13,28,10,0,172,178,32,36,66,48,48,0,20,
      28,20,0,46,83,0,27,28,30,0,46,79,0,49
PP 70 DATA 28,40,0,59,32,32,32,32,80,82,79,71,82,6
      5,77,32,78,65,77,69,0,55,28,50,0,59,0,0,0
SG 100 PRINT"{CLR}";:BLOAD "LADS
```

Appendix G

# Commodore ASCII Codes

<table>
<tr><th>Dec</th><th>Hex</th><th>Uppercase/Graphics Set</th><th>Lowercase/Uppercase Set</th></tr>
<tr><td>2</td><td>02</td><td colspan="2">underline on[1]</td></tr>
<tr><td>5</td><td>05</td><td colspan="2">white</td></tr>
<tr><td>7</td><td>07</td><td colspan="2">bell tone[2]</td></tr>
<tr><td>8</td><td>08</td><td colspan="2">disable SHIFT-Commodore[3]</td></tr>
<tr><td>9</td><td>09</td><td colspan="2">tab[2]</td></tr>
<tr><td></td><td></td><td colspan="2">enable SHIFT-Commodore[3]</td></tr>
<tr><td>10</td><td>0A</td><td colspan="2">linefeed[2]</td></tr>
<tr><td>11</td><td>0B</td><td colspan="2">disable SHIFT-Commodore[2]</td></tr>
<tr><td>12</td><td>0C</td><td colspan="2">enable SHIFT-Commodore[2]</td></tr>
<tr><td>13</td><td>0D</td><td colspan="2">RETURN</td></tr>
<tr><td>14</td><td>0E</td><td colspan="2">switch to lowercase</td></tr>
<tr><td>15</td><td>0F</td><td colspan="2">flash on[1]</td></tr>
<tr><td>17</td><td>11</td><td colspan="2">cursor down</td></tr>
<tr><td>18</td><td>12</td><td colspan="2">reverse on</td></tr>
<tr><td>19</td><td>13</td><td colspan="2">home</td></tr>
<tr><td>20</td><td>14</td><td colspan="2">delete</td></tr>
<tr><td>24</td><td>18</td><td colspan="2">tab set/clear[2]</td></tr>
<tr><td>27</td><td>1B</td><td colspan="2">ESCape</td></tr>
<tr><td>28</td><td>1C</td><td colspan="2">red</td></tr>
<tr><td>29</td><td>1D</td><td colspan="2">cursor right</td></tr>
<tr><td>30</td><td>1E</td><td colspan="2">green</td></tr>
<tr><td>31</td><td>1F</td><td colspan="2">blue</td></tr>
<tr><td>32</td><td>20</td><td colspan="2">space</td></tr>
<tr><td>33</td><td>21</td><td>!</td><td>!</td></tr>
<tr><td>34</td><td>22</td><td>"</td><td>"</td></tr>
<tr><td>35</td><td>23</td><td>#</td><td>#</td></tr>
<tr><td>36</td><td>24</td><td>$</td><td>$</td></tr>
<tr><td>37</td><td>25</td><td>%</td><td>%</td></tr>
<tr><td>38</td><td>26</td><td>&</td><td>&</td></tr>
</table>

| Dec | Hex | Uppercase/Graphics Set | Lowercase/Uppercase Set |
|---|---|---|---|
| 39 | 27 | ' | ' |
| 40 | 28 | ( | ( |
| 41 | 29 | ) | ) |
| 42 | 2A | * | * |
| 43 | 2B | + | + |
| 44 | 2C | , | , |
| 45 | 2D | − | − |
| 46 | 2E | . | . |
| 47 | 2F | / | / |
| 48 | 30 | 0 | 0 |
| 49 | 31 | 1 | 1 |
| 50 | 32 | 2 | 2 |
| 51 | 33 | 3 | 3 |
| 52 | 34 | 4 | 4 |
| 53 | 35 | 5 | 5 |
| 54 | 36 | 6 | 6 |
| 55 | 37 | 7 | 7 |
| 56 | 38 | 8 | 8 |
| 57 | 39 | 9 | 9 |
| 58 | 3A | : | : |
| 59 | 3B | ; | ; |
| 60 | 3C | < | < |
| 61 | 3D | = | = |
| 62 | 3E | > | > |
| 63 | 3F | ? | ? |
| 64 | 40 | @ | @ |
| 65 | 41 | A | a |
| 66 | 42 | B | b |
| 67 | 43 | C | c |
| 68 | 44 | D | d |
| 69 | 45 | E | e |
| 70 | 46 | F | f |

| Dec | Hex | Uppercase/Graphics Set | Lowercase/Uppercase Set |
|---|---|---|---|
| 71 | 47 | G | g |
| 72 | 48 | H | h |
| 73 | 49 | I | i |
| 74 | 4A | J | j |
| 75 | 4B | K | k |
| 76 | 4C | L | l |
| 77 | 4D | M | m |
| 78 | 4E | N | n |
| 79 | 4F | O | o |
| 80 | 50 | P | p |
| 81 | 51 | Q | q |
| 82 | 52 | R | r |
| 83 | 53 | S | s |
| 84 | 54 | T | t |
| 85 | 55 | U | u |
| 86 | 56 | V | v |
| 87 | 57 | W | w |
| 88 | 58 | X | x |
| 89 | 59 | Y | y |
| 90 | 5A | Z | z |
| 91 | 5B | [ | [ |
| 92 | 5C | £ | £ |
| 93 | 5D | ] | ] |
| 94 | 5E | ↑ | ↑ |
| 95 | 5F | ← | ← |
| 96 | 60 |  |  |
| 97 | 61 |  | A |
| 98 | 62 |  | B |
| 99 | 63 |  | C |
| 100 | 64 |  | D |
| 101 | 65 |  | E |
| 102 | 66 |  | F |

| Dec | Hex | Uppercase/Graphics Set | Lowercase/Uppercase Set |
|---|---|---|---|
| 103 | 67 |  | G |
| 104 | 68 |  | H |
| 105 | 69 |  | I |
| 106 | 6A |  | J |
| 107 | 6B |  | K |
| 108 | 6C |  | L |
| 109 | 6D |  | M |
| 110 | 6E |  | N |
| 111 | 6F |  | O |
| 112 | 70 |  | P |
| 113 | 71 |  | Q |
| 114 | 72 |  | R |
| 115 | 73 |  | S |
| 116 | 74 |  | T |
| 117 | 75 |  | U |
| 118 | 76 |  | V |
| 119 | 77 |  | W |
| 120 | 78 |  | X |
| 121 | 79 |  | Y |
| 122 | 7A |  | Z |
| 123 | 7B |  |  |
| 124 | 7C |  |  |
| 125 | 7D |  |  |
| 126 | 7E |  |  |
| 127 | 7F |  |  |
| 129 | 81 | orange[4] | |
| | | dark purple[1] | |
| 130 | 82 | underline off[1] | |
| 133 | 85 | F1 | |
| 134 | 86 | F3 | |
| 135 | 87 | F5 | |
| 136 | 88 | F7 | |

| Dec | Hex | Uppercase/Graphics Set | Lowercase/Uppercase Set |
|---|---|---|---|
| 137 | 89 | F2 | |
| 138 | 8A | F4 | |
| 139 | 8B | F6 | |
| 140 | 8C | F8 | |
| 141 | 8D | SHIFT–RETURN | |
| 142 | 8E | switch to uppercase | |
| 143 | 8F | flash off[1] | |
| 144 | 90 | black | |
| 145 | 91 | cursor up | |
| 146 | 92 | reverse off | |
| 147 | 93 | clear screen | |
| 148 | 94 | insert | |
| 149 | 95 | brown[4] | |
| | | dark yellow[1] | |
| 150 | 96 | light red | |
| 151 | 97 | dark gray[4] | |
| | | dark cyan[1] | |
| 152 | 98 | medium gray | |
| 153 | 99 | light green | |
| 154 | 9A | light blue | |
| 155 | 9B | light gray | |
| 156 | 9C | purple | |
| 157 | 9D | cursor left | |
| 158 | 9E | yellow | |
| 159 | 9F | cyan | |
| 160 | A0 | SHIFT-space | |
| 161 | A1 | ▌ | ▌ |
| 162 | A2 | ▄ | ▄ |
| 163 | A3 | ▔ | ▔ |
| 164 | A4 | ▁ | ▁ |
| 165 | A5 | ▏ | ▏ |
| 166 | A6 | ▒ | ▒ |

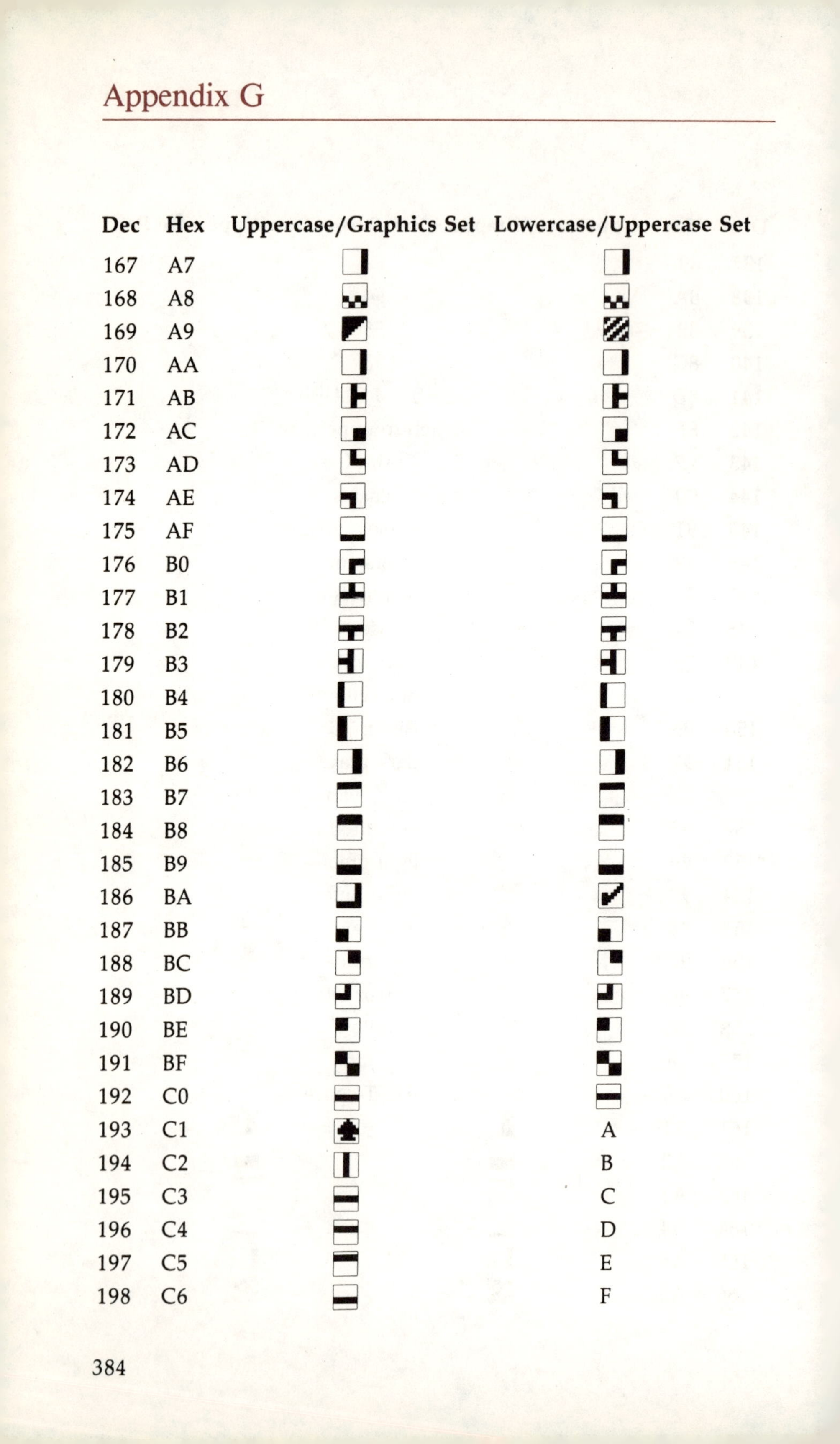

| Dec | Hex | Uppercase/Graphics Set | Lowercase/Uppercase Set |
|---|---|---|---|
| 167 | A7 | | |
| 168 | A8 | | |
| 169 | A9 | | |
| 170 | AA | | |
| 171 | AB | | |
| 172 | AC | | |
| 173 | AD | | |
| 174 | AE | | |
| 175 | AF | | |
| 176 | B0 | | |
| 177 | B1 | | |
| 178 | B2 | | |
| 179 | B3 | | |
| 180 | B4 | | |
| 181 | B5 | | |
| 182 | B6 | | |
| 183 | B7 | | |
| 184 | B8 | | |
| 185 | B9 | | |
| 186 | BA | | |
| 187 | BB | | |
| 188 | BC | | |
| 189 | BD | | |
| 190 | BE | | |
| 191 | BF | | |
| 192 | C0 | | |
| 193 | C1 | | A |
| 194 | C2 | | B |
| 195 | C3 | | C |
| 196 | C4 | | D |
| 197 | C5 | | E |
| 198 | C6 | | F |

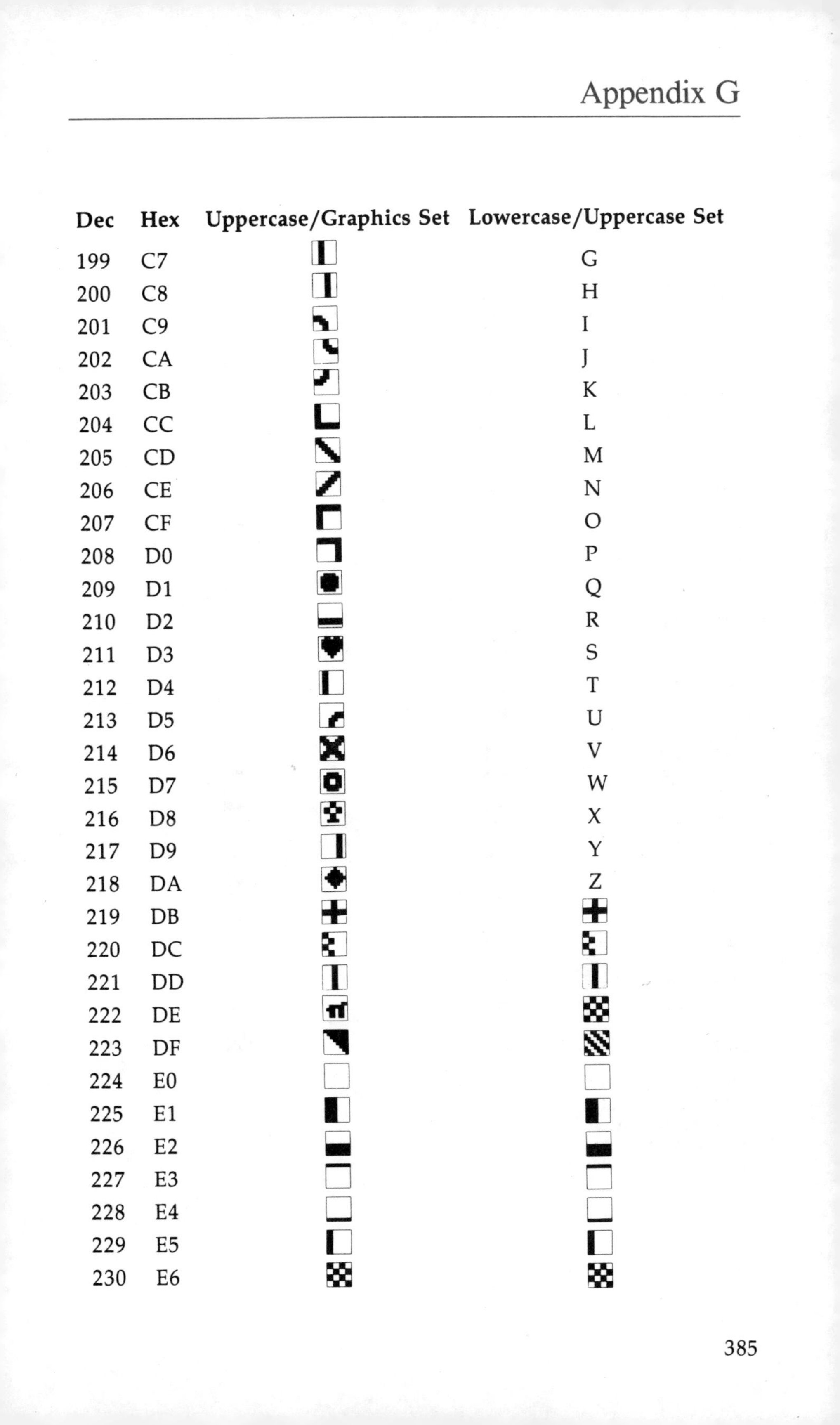

| Dec | Hex | Uppercase/Graphics Set | Lowercase/Uppercase Set |
|---|---|---|---|
| 199 | C7 | | G |
| 200 | C8 | | H |
| 201 | C9 | | I |
| 202 | CA | | J |
| 203 | CB | | K |
| 204 | CC | | L |
| 205 | CD | | M |
| 206 | CE | | N |
| 207 | CF | | O |
| 208 | D0 | | P |
| 209 | D1 | | Q |
| 210 | D2 | | R |
| 211 | D3 | | S |
| 212 | D4 | | T |
| 213 | D5 | | U |
| 214 | D6 | | V |
| 215 | D7 | | W |
| 216 | D8 | | X |
| 217 | D9 | | Y |
| 218 | DA | | Z |
| 219 | DB | | |
| 220 | DC | | |
| 221 | DD | | |
| 222 | DE | | |
| 223 | DF | | |
| 224 | E0 | | |
| 225 | E1 | | |
| 226 | E2 | | |
| 227 | E3 | | |
| 228 | E4 | | |
| 229 | E5 | | |
| 230 | E6 | | |

| Dec | Hex | Uppercase/Graphics Set | Lowercase/Uppercase Set |
|---|---|---|---|
| 231 | E7 | | |
| 232 | E8 | | |
| 233 | E9 | | |
| 234 | EA | | |
| 235 | EB | | |
| 236 | EC | | |
| 237 | ED | | |
| 238 | EE | | |
| 239 | EF | | |
| 240 | F0 | | |
| 241 | F1 | | |
| 242 | F2 | | |
| 243 | F3 | | |
| 244 | F4 | | |
| 245 | F5 | | |
| 246 | F6 | | |
| 247 | F7 | | |
| 248 | F8 | | |
| 249 | F9 | | |
| 250 | FA | | |
| 251 | FB | | |
| 252 | FC | | |
| 253 | FD | | |
| 254 | FE | | |
| 255 | FF | | |

**Notes**
**1. 80-column display only**
**2. 128 mode only**
**3. 64 mode only**
**4. 40-column display only**

## True ASCII

| ASCII Code | Character | ASCII Code | Character | ASCII Code | Character |
|---|---|---|---|---|---|
| 0 | NUL | 44 | , | 86 | V |
| 1 | SOH | 45 | — | 87 | W |
| 2 | STX | 46 | . | 88 | X |
| 3 | ETX | 47 | / | 89 | Y |
| 4 | EOT | 48 | 0 | 90 | Z |
| 5 | ENQ | 49 | 1 | 91 | [ |
| 6 | ACK | 50 | 2 | 92 | \ |
| 7 | BEL | 51 | 3 | 93 | ] |
| 8 | BS | 52 | 4 | 94 | ^ |
| 9 | HT | 53 | 5 | 95 | _ |
| 10 | LF | 54 | 6 | 96 | ` |
| 11 | VT | 55 | 7 | 97 | a |
| 12 | FF | 56 | 8 | 98 | b |
| 13 | CR | 57 | 9 | 99 | c |
| 14 | SO | 58 | : | 100 | d |
| 15 | SI | 59 | ; | 101 | e |
| 16 | DLE | 60 | < | 102 | f |
| 17 | DC1 | 61 | = | 103 | g |
| 18 | DC2 | 62 | > | 104 | h |
| 19 | DC3 | 63 | ? | 105 | i |
| 20 | DC4 | 64 | @ | 106 | j |
| 21 | NAK | 65 | A | 107 | k |
| 22 | SYN | 66 | B | 108 | l |
| 23 | ETB | 67 | C | 109 | m |
| 24 | CAN | 68 | D | 110 | n |
| 25 | EM | 69 | E | 111 | o |
| 26 | SUB | 70 | F | 112 | p |
| 27 | ESC | 71 | G | 113 | q |
| 28 | FS | 72 | H | 114 | r |
| 29 | GS | 73 | I | 115 | s |
| 30 | RS | 74 | J | 116 | t |
| 31 | US | 75 | K | 117 | u |
| 32 | (space) | 76 | L | 118 | v |
| 33 | ! | 77 | M | 119 | w |
| 34 | " | 78 | N | 120 | x |
| 35 | # | 79 | O | 121 | y |
| 36 | $ | 80 | P | 122 | z |
| 37 | % | 81 | Q | 123 | { |
| 38 | & | 82 | R | 124 | \| |
| 39 | ' | 83 | S | 125 | } |
| 40 | ( | 84 | T | 126 | ~ |
| 41 | ) | 85 | U | 127 | DEL |
| 42 | * | | | | |
| 43 | + | | | | |

# Index

To order your copy of *128 LADS Disk*, call our toll-free US order line: 1-800-346-6767 (in NY 212-887-8525) or send your prepaid order to:

*128 LADS Disk*
**COMPUTE!** Publications
P.O. Box 5038
F.D.R. Station
New York, NY 10150

All orders must be prepaid (check, charge, or money order). NC residents add 4.5% sales tax.

Send ____ copies of *128 LADS Disk* at $12.95 per copy. (033BDSK)

Subtotal $__________

Shipping and Handling: $2.00/disk $__________

Sales tax (if applicable) $__________

Total payment enclosed $__________

□ Payment enclosed
□ Charge □ Visa □ MasterCard □ American Express

Acct. No. ______________________________ Exp. Date ______ (Required)

Name ______________________________________________

Address ____________________________________________

City ________________________ State _______ Zip _______

Please allow 4-5 weeks for delivery.

46203323

# COMPUTE! Books

Ask your retailer for these COMPUTE! Books or order directly from COMPUTE!

[illegible]

If you've enjoyed the articles in this book, you'll find the same style and quality in every monthly issue of **COMPUTE!** Magazine. Use this form to order your subscription to **COMPUTE!**.

For Fastest Service
Call Our **Toll-Free** US Order Line
**1-800-247-5470**
**In IA call 1-800-532-1272**

# COMPUTE!

P.O. Box 10954
Des Moines, IA 50340

My computer is:
☐ Commodore 64 or 128 ☐ TI-99/4A ☐ IBM PC or PCjr ☐ VIC-20
☐ Apple ☐ Atari ☐ Amiga ☐ Other ____________
☐ Don't yet have one...

☐ $24 One Year US Subscription
☐ $45 Two Year US Subscription
☐ $65 Three Year US Subscription

Subscription rates outside the US:

☐ $30 Canada and Foreign Surface Mail
☐ $65 Foreign Air Delivery

Name ____________

Address ____________

City ____________ State ____________ Zip ____________

Country ____________

Payment must be in US funds drawn on a US bank, international money order, or charge card.
☐ Payment Enclosed ☐ Visa
☐ MasterCard ☐ American Express

Acct. No. ____________ Expires ____/____
(Required)

Your subscription will begin with the next available issue. Please allow 4–6 weeks for delivery of first issue. Subscription prices subject to change at any time.

46219333